D1536360

THE ROUSING DRUM

The ROUSING DRUM

Ritual Practice in a Japanese Community

Scott Schnell

 University of Hawai'i Press
Honolulu

04 03 02 01 00 99   5 4 3 2 1

Library of Congress Cataloging-in-Publication Data

Schnell, Scott, 1954–
    The rousing drum : ritual practice in a Japanese
community / Scott Schnell.
        p.   cm.
    Includes bibliographical references and index.
    ISBN 0–8248–2064–9 (alk. paper). —
    ISBN 0–8248–2141–6 (pbk. : alk. paper)
        1. Japan—Social life and customs. 2. Festivals—Japan.
I. Title.
    DS821.S3256   1999
952—dc21   98–46950
                                                        CIP

Design by Josie Herr

Printed by The Maple-Vail Book Manufacturing Group

To the people of Furukawa—
past, present, and future

CONTENTS

Acknowledgments

The research upon which this work is based began in 1989, and has continued off and on to the present day. Initial fieldwork during the period 1989–1991 was generously funded by the Japanese Ministry of Education (Monbushō). Follow-up research was made possible by an Ohio State University Graduate Student Alumni Research Award in 1991, a Research Travel Grant from the Northeast Asia Council (NEAC) of the Association for Asian Studies (AAS) in 1994, and small research grants from the University of Iowa Center for Asian and Pacific Studies (CAPS) in 1994 and 1995. The University of Iowa graciously allowed me a developmental leave of absence during the autumn of 1996, and a visiting research fellowship offered by the Japanese National Museum of Ethnology (Kokuritsu Minzokugaku Hakubutsukan) in Osaka enabled me to extend this leave into a full year. Thus from June 1996 to June 1997 I spent my days at the museum (or "Minpaku," an abbreviated version of its official name), happily availing myself of its excellent library facilities, interacting with the other researchers and staff, and making occasional forays into the field. This book could not have been written without the cooperation of the people at Minpaku. I earnestly thank them for their assistance and support.

A great many people have advised and informed me along the way. During my graduate school years, Richard H. Moore, my mentor, shared freely of his time and considerable expertise in the anthropology of Japan. Gary L. Ebersole first encouraged me to consider ritual as a medium for political maneuvering. James R. Bartholomew helped me incorporate a historical perspective, so vital to understanding social processes. Nagashima Nobuhiro kindly agreed to serve as my academic sponsor in Japan during the initial field research, and has been a valuable source of information and ideas ever since. Sonoda Minoru, who combines the roles of anthropology professor and Shinto priest, has also been a major influence and inspiration for my own work.

My sponsor at Minpaku was Nakamaki Hirochika. I have known Nakamaki-*sensei* since the time of my initial fieldwork, and he has provided continual guidance and support. I must have been a great burden to him during my stay at Minpaku, yet he always treated me with great kindness and hospitality.

As for my field site of Furukawa, the people to whom I am indebted are too numerous to mention individually. I thank them for welcoming me into their lives and tolerating my rather intrusive activities. Most of them had absolutely nothing to gain from facilitating my research, yet gave freely of their time and energies in doing so. There are a few individuals to whom I would like to offer some special words of thanks. Amaki Makoto, head priest of Ketawakamiya Shrine, was very gracious in permitting me to observe the Shinto rituals he performs there and explaining their background and significance. Tajika Bunzaburō, Kaba Shigetarō, Komura Katsue, and the other shrine officers were kind enough to allow me to attend their planning sessions as well as the fellowship meetings that invariably followed. Hashimoto Tomokazu, former head of the Furukawa Educational Committee, was always very supportive of my research and provided me with a great deal of help and advice in locating important source materials.

Tsuzuku Jun'ya, who had studied the social sciences at a national university and returned to the Hida region after graduation, assisted me in deciphering documents and provided valuable feedback on some of my theoretical ideas. In fact the entire Tsuzuku household has been very kind and supportive over the years.

I would like to express my gratitude to two households in particular—those of Kamamiya Yoshikatsu and Suzuki Yukihiro. Both have welcomed me into their homes as a member of the family and have consistently gone out of their way to ensure my general well-being—all with no other motivation than their own good will.

I would also like to thank the young men of the Sōgakubu in my home neighborhood of Mukaimachi for allowing me to join their group and participate in their practice sessions and performances.

The camaraderie I found among them was one of the most rewarding aspects of the field experience.

Koya Masanobu and Shirakawa Shūhei, two promising young officials at the Furukawa Town Hall, were very generous in providing introductions, securing photographs and other materials, and otherwise facilitating my efforts. If they are any indication of the quality of the new leadership, Furukawa's future looks very bright indeed.

With regard to the production phase, Patricia Crosby and Masako Ikeda, both of the University of Hawai'i Press, were patient and kind in guiding me through the editing process. Two anonymous reviewers provided me with many excellent suggestions on improving the text; I admire their depth of knowledge and sincerely appreciate the time and care they devoted to reading the manuscript. The text, whatever its original merit, was greatly enhanced by the skillful copyediting of Susan E. Schmidt. I would also like to thank Karen L. Myers for lending a sensitive ear and providing me with valuable feedback on matters of style and clarity.

Finally, I would like to express my deepest appreciation to Ōno Masao, an eminent teacher and historian who has devoted several decades to the study of the Hida region. I have always been in awe of Ōno-*sensei*'s meticulous scholarship and relentless pursuit of knowledge, which show no signs of abating even now in his late-eighties. Once, during a chance meeting on the train to Takayama, I confided to Ōno-*sensei* my concern that he might not approve of my ethnological interpretations. To this he replied, "You and I are from different backgrounds, different disciplines; it is to be expected that we should see things differently. You needn't be so reserved!" I thank him for all the knowledge he shared with me, and also for those reassuring words.

All translations appearing in this book are my own. Sources for the illustrations used in this book are acknowledged in the captions; those without acknowledgment are my own. I briefly presented some of the ideas contained in this book in an earlier article entitled "Ritual as an Instrument of Political Resistance in Rural Japan," which appeared in the *Journal of Anthropological Research* (1995). Portions of Chapter 2 appeared as "Sanctity and Sanction in Communal Ritual: A Reconsideration of Shinto Festival Processions" in *Ethnology* (1997).

Chapter 1

ETHNOLOGICAL
AND HISTORICAL
PERSPECTIVES

Deep within the mountainous interior of central Honshu, the main island in the Japanese archipelago, lies a small agricultural and commercial town called Furukawa. It is located in the center of a narrow basin, surrounded by rice paddies, and further enveloped by steep mountain slopes. The core community, which has for centuries been defined by its territorial affiliation with a local guardian deity, presently numbers about 7000 people.

This is not the idyllic farm village so frequently chosen as the focus of past anthropological studies (see for example Embree 1939; Beardsley, Hall, and Ward 1959; Dore 1978); nor is it the kind of populous urban environment that has served as the context for more recent analyses of Japanese social interaction (e.g. Bestor 1989; Kondo 1990; Robertson 1991). As a small provincial town, Furukawa lies somewhere in between, maintaining the close-knit insularity associated with smaller communities but exhibiting the kind of organizational complexity characteristic of larger demographic units.

Yet to see Furukawa merely as occupying some transitional point along a continuum of increasing population density would be to deny its special character. Unlike a farm village, it brings households of various occupational and economic categories into close association; unlike a metropolitan neighborhood engulfed by urban growth, it has managed to maintain an independent communal identity over a period of several hundred years. In addition, the distance separating Furukawa from major urban areas, combined with the ruggedness of the surrounding topography and heavy winter snowfall, has historically encouraged among its people a distinct sense of economic and administrative autonomy. This should not be taken to imply, however, that Furukawa has been immune to larger historical forces emanating from beyond its mountain perimeter; indeed, this book is largely concerned with how the local people have articulated these forces, specifically through the medium of communal ritual.

The pace of life in Furukawa is slower than in the congested urban lowlands, and its residents generally exhibit the kind of relaxed congeniality so often attributed to country people the world over. Even so, at certain critical moments, particularly when their own interests are threatened by outside forces, they are said to reveal another side of themselves—an unruly and aggressive attitude rather infamously known as "Furukawa *yancha.*"

The word *"yancha,"* meaning "mischief" or "unruliness," is generally reserved for disobedient or rambunctious children. In Furukawa, however, it is most commonly associated with adult proclivities; in fact, "Furukawa *yancha"* has assumed special significance as a defining element of the local character. The term elicits both positive and negative connotations, depending on one's point of view: it is invoked with pride by the townspeople in describing themselves, but is often used derisively by residents of neighboring towns and villages in denouncing what they consider a rough, uncivilized quality. Furukawa *yancha* is variously described as "a rebellious or unruly attitude," "making one's intentions clear and insisting that others comply with them," or simply "defying authority" (Kuwatani 1969: 23–25; Sugata 1975:8; Sonoda 1975:71, 1988:53; Sonoda and Uno 1979:176; Kaba 1984:24–44; Mabuchi 1990:57; Morishita 1991:6).

The quintessential expression of this rebellious attitude is a ritualized performance known as the *"okoshi daiko,"* or "rousing drum." The name refers to a large, barrel-shaped drum fixed atop a huge rectangular framework made of overlapping wooden beams. Every year on the night of April 19, the eve of the festival dedicated to the local guardian deity, the entire structure is borne through the narrow streets in a raucous procession by a mass of half-naked, inebriated men. Prominent members of the community are obliged to ride upon the structure, while teams of younger men, representing the various component neighborhoods, charge out at it from behind as it passes through their respective territories. Each team is armed with a drum of its own—a smaller version lashed tightly to a stout pole. This is called a *"tsuke daiko,"* or "attaching drum," since the basic objective is for team members to "attach" it to the rear of the main drum structure as it proceeds along its course.

The position directly behind the main drum is highly esteemed, and reaching it is a formidable task. The successful team must not only vie with several other neighborhood groups having similar intentions; it must also drive through the defenses of a gang of burly guardians positioned directly behind the main drum structure to keep the challengers at bay. All the action takes place within the confines of a narrow street, and the crush of bodies at the rear of the structure is intense. The participants can become very aggressive in performing their roles, and injuries are stoically accepted as inevitable consequences of the ritual experience.

In recent decades this rather unusual event has developed into a popular spectacle promoted by town planners as a means of drawing tourists to the area, thereby bolstering the local economy. Prior to Japan's period of rapid economic growth after the Second World War, however, there was no tourist industry to speak of, and the *okoshi daiko* was staged primarily by and for the local residents themselves.

Indeed, the ritual appears to have been considerably more boisterous in the prewar era. Anyone having a score to settle would wait for the night of the *okoshi daiko,* when seemingly random acts of violence would likely go unnoticed in the general confusion (Kaba 1984:35–36; Furukawa-chō Kankō Kyōkai 1984:80–81). The neighborhood teams were not always content simply to make contact with the main drum structure: they sometimes tried to cause its collapse, thereby bringing down its elite retinue (Ōno 1973b, 1976a:3). The massive drum itself was known to swerve on occasion, "inadvertently" crashing into the homes of greedy landlords, usurious merchants, or meddlesome administrative officials. Likewise, the *tsuke daiko* teams, in charging recklessly toward their goal, sometimes ran wide of the mark and ended up ramming their poles through an adjacent wall or storefront. Often the same establishments were victimized year after year. One of the more notable targets for such assaults was the local police headquarters.

Curiously, however, an examination of the written record reveals no evidence of such behavior prior to the late 1800s when Japan's period of rapid modernization began. The *okoshi daiko* of that time, when mentioned at all, is described simply as a single drum that passed through town at dawn to alert the townspeople that the main event, a Shinto-based religious observance, was about to begin (Tomita 1968 [1874]:399–400; Ōno 1973b; Furukawa-chō 1984: 655–656). Nowhere is there any indication of the raucous, unruly behavior it later came to embody. What caused the transformation? Indigenous accounts offer no satisfactory explanation, attributing the ritual to a seemingly spontaneous manifestation of Furukawa *yancha* (Kaba 1984:36; Furukawa-chō Kankō Kyōkai 1984:79–80; Furukawa-chō Kyōiku Iinkai 1990:207).

In fact the festival as a whole is widely assumed to embody a time-honored tradition, which has been faithfully handed down to the present from several centuries ago. This reflects a more general tendency to associate the term "ritual" with unvarying and repetitive behavior. There is of course a parallel inclination within the social sciences, where ritual tends to be viewed as merely a means of reproducing the social system, and religion in general as a basically conservative device for maintaining the sociopolitical status quo. The instrumental value of religious ritual as a means of adapting to—or perhaps even introducing—changes in the sociopolitical order remains largely unexplored.

The present study is guided by the assumption that ritual, as the active and physical expression of ideology through a symbolic medium, does not simply constitute the mechanical execution of preestablished patterns. Rather, it is an ongoing performative discourse whose contents are continually amended, reinterpreted, or transformed according to the needs of its practitioners—needs that clearly change over time in response to changing sociopolitical and economic conditions. Indeed, it is this adaptable quality that explains why rituals like the *okoshi daiko* have demonstrated such remarkable longevity, for without it they would inevitably be abandoned as wastes of time.

In the following chapters I will demonstrate that the *okoshi daiko* as it exists in the present day is only the most recent manifestation in a long series of developmental changes. I maintain that this, or any other, ritual must be considered within the context of larger historical patterns in order to grasp its deeper underlying significance. A historical perspective is thus vital to any analysis of ritual as a form of social practice.

Structure, Agency, and Practice Theory

Social scientists have long debated the capacity of individuals to shape the course of their own destinies as measured against the deterministic influence of the social system that encompasses and constrains them. Functionalists in the mold of Radcliffe-Brown tended to represent society as a coercive, inhibiting structure, equipped with institutions and ideologies for perpetuating itself through time. Individuals existing within this structure were seen as being wholly conditioned by its relationships and values, mechanically reproducing the structure through daily interaction. In accordance with this basic paradigm, ritual was explained as a means of reinforcing certain collectively held values and attitudes in the minds of its participants, thereby promoting social integration (Durkheim 1915; Radcliffe–Brown 1945; Turner 1957; Bellah 1968; Douglas 1973).

A major criticism of this approach has been its seeming denial of human agency—the propensity for individuals to manipulate the structure to their own advantage, or even to comprehend the forces that dominate and constrain them (Lukes 1975:293–297; Giddens 1979, 1984; Ortner 1984:144–145). The alternative viewpoint, more recently in vogue, insists that while individual members are undoubtedly influenced by their sociocultural milieu, they nevertheless have the ability to introduce or negotiate change in pursuit of their own interests. Individuals, in other words, are agents, not only in the sense of reproducing the social structure, but in transforming it as well. Structure may thus be considered enabling as well as constraining, insofar as it furnishes the actor with the means and opportunities to act:

> Every process of action is a production of something new, a fresh act; but at the same time all action exists in continuity with the past, which supplies the means of its initiation. *Structure thus is not to be conceptualised as a barrier to action, but as essentially involved in its production* (Giddens 1979:70, emphasis in the original).

This enabling aspect is implicit in Ortner's (1984, 1989) delineation of "practice theory," which, while conceding that the social system exerts a powerful and pervasive influence, nevertheless acknowledges the importance of human agency in shaping the development of social institutions and historical events. The practice approach articulates with efforts to incorporate a historical dimension into the structural analysis of social systems by viewing structure and agency as interacting or recursive entities, each continually redefining the other over time (Sahlins 1985; Comaroff 1985; Ortner 1989; Comaroff and Comaroff 1992). Ortner, in fact, envisions an eventual synthesis of anthropological and historical studies, guided by the recognition that "[h]istory is not simply something that happens to people, but something they make—within, of course, the very powerful constraints of the system within which they are operating" (1984:159).

The two disciplines would appear to be most clearly distinguishable in terms of methodology: historians rely primarily on written documents in attempting to comprehend the past; anthropologists combine direct observation and experience with informant interviews in their efforts to understand existing relationships and conditions. But such a hasty distinction masks large areas of overlap wherein each of these disciplines is influenced and informed by the other. One of the most obvious examples of a methodological crossover is the ethnohistorical approach, which Wood (1990:81) defines simply as "the use of historical documents and historical method in anthropological research." Ethnohistorical studies, he continues, "are based on historical documents, but they are written with anthropological insight."

This, however, raises a further discrepancy—one relating to representational concerns. From an anthropologist's perspective, focusing so extensively on the written record risks an undue bias toward the attitudes and opinions of the literary elite. Historians themselves have long debated the issue of where their proper focus should lie— on the major political, military, and intellectual figures who come to define an era, or on the so-called "common people" who constitute the vast majority of the population in the polities concerned. Anthropologists, for their part, have traditionally confined themselves to the study of small, seemingly insular communities, devoting scant attention to the larger economic and political forces that impinge upon and transform the lives of the people within them.[1]

The practice approach aims at a reconciliation of these two opposing viewpoints by relating local sociopolitical and economic conditions to larger historical processes and investigating how new developments are received, resisted, appropriated, and/or exploited by local actors in addressing their immediate needs. Ortner (1984: 143) asserts that anthropology is particularly amenable to a practice-oriented approach due to its traditional focus on the micro-societal level: "The attempt to view other systems from ground level is the basis, perhaps the only basis, of anthropology's distinctive contribution to the human sciences." Furthermore, "it is our location 'on the ground' that puts us in a position to see people not simply as passive reactors to and enactors of some 'system,' but as active agents and subjects in their own history."

Even so, a historical perspective requires the kind of extended time depth generally missing from ethnographic fieldwork, with its emphasis on the documentation of currently existing relationships and conditions. In fact this lack of a time dimension may partly explain the tendency to view religion and ritual as conservative forces, in that the ethnographer has not remained in the field long enough to directly observe their transformative potential. Any consideration of ritual as an instrument of sociopolitical change must therefore combine fieldwork with an analysis of the available historical data (see Bloch 1986:10–11). Sahlins (1985), Cohn (1987:73), and Comaroff and Comaroff (1992:31) have called for a historical anthropology capable of dealing with structural transformations induced by outside contact and the cultural responses they engender among indigenous populations.

This is the perspective Ortner (1989) adopts in her analysis of the strategies behind the first Sherpa temple foundings. Ortner suggests that incorporation into the Nepalese state and ultimately into the sphere of influence of the British Raj held certain advantages for Sherpa "small people":

[T]he "imposition" of state power from the outside was also an active appropriation of such power from the inside. Thus I will show how the Sherpas used both the British in India and the Nepal state in Kathmandu to bring in outside wealth and to achieve certain kinds of success, which in turn were celebrated in the foundings of the monasteries. (Ortner 1989:99–100)

In fact, Ortner goes so far as an attempt to "de-victimize the Sherpas (or any other group at the receiving end of world capitalist expansion) as much as possible" (1989:100). In line with Giddens' contention as noted earlier, she suggests that the imposition of authority from the outside represented a form of constraint, but also an opportunity. Thus, she maintains, "it is important for anthropologists . . . to recognize the ways in which people are *always* reinterpreting their situation, acting on it in their own terms, and making the most they can—materially, morally, and in every other way—out of it" (1989:100).

Bell (1992) adopts a similar position in her treatment of ritual as a form of social practice. She argues that participation in ritual is not simply the passive acceptance of a dominant ideology; it is a matter of self-interested appropriation which affords its participants some flexibility in negotiating the terms of their involvement.[2] Furthermore, a shared symbolic pattern does not necessarily suggest a shared understanding of its meaning, as participants in the same ritual may interpret its symbols differently. "People reproduce relationships of power and domination, but not in a direct, automatic, or mechanistic way; rather, they reproduce them through their particular construal of those relations, a construal that affords the actor the sense of a sphere of action, however minimal" (Bell 1992:84).

This is encouraging from a humanitarian point of view because it affords the disadvantaged or disenfranchised some leverage in dealing with the more powerful forces that seek to constrain them. The "small people" are no longer to be seen as hapless victims of historical precedent, but as actors who are fully conscious, and routinely avail themselves, of the opportunities which structure affords them. In fact Giddens (1979:72) suggests that failing to recognize such inherent potential constitutes a "derogation of the lay actor"; he objects to the tendency among social scientists to regard actors "as cultural dopes or mere 'bearers of a mode of production,' with no worthwhile understanding of their surroundings or the circumstances of their action."

Individual actors *are* credited with a more sophisticated understanding of their situation in Scott's (1976, 1985) analysis of peasant resistance in Southeast Asia. Through the anthropological methods of fieldwork and participant observation, Scott is led to conclude that focusing only on instances of organized rebellion is highly misleading. Resistance, he argues, is most commonly manifested in the form of individual, unorganized acts such as pilfering, false compliance, slander, and vandalism, as these may be the only means of opposition available to peasants living under a repressive regime. "To understand these commonplace forms of resistance is to understand what much of the peasantry does 'between revolts' to defend its interests as best it can" (1985:29).

Such tendencies are not always easy to recognize, especially when dealing with societies of the past. As previously noted, written accounts are typically biased toward the literary elite, ignoring the attitudes and perceptions of subordinate members. To complicate matters, Scott (1990:87) alludes to "the more profound difficulty presented by earnest efforts of subordinate groups to conceal their activities and opinions, which might expose them to harm." He employs the term "hidden transcript" in referring to the more antagonistic or subversive sentiments which the adherents generally keep to themselves, and which for this reason seldom find their way into the official record. This coincides with Wood's (1990:83) assertion that "only a small part of what takes place is observed; much less is recorded; and what has survived is surely not always the most important."

Thus the methodological problem that presents itself is how to achieve an accurate understanding of conditions and attitudes as they actually existed—how to recover the "hidden transcript." Scott himself hints at a solution; he notes that glimpses of the hidden transcript may be revealed during public events that confer some form of disguise or anonymity, thereby shielding the identity of the actors. "Rumor, gossip, folktales, jokes, songs, *rituals,* codes, and euphemisms—a good part of the folk culture of subordinate groups—fit this description" (Scott 1990:19, emphasis added).

The present analysis will focus on communal ritual as an opportunity for expressing discontent or negotiating more favorable conditions. As will be described more completely in the next chapter, the mass assemblages and atmosphere of temporary license associated with Shinto shrine festivals afford the very type of anonymity to which Scott was alluding, particularly when combined with the cover of darkness. It is vital, therefore, to consider such contexts in attempting to grasp the processes of sociopolitical change, especially as they invoke the forces of authority and resistance.

Ritual and Resistance

The ritual expression of rebellious tendencies is well documented in the anthropological literature, but the effort to link such tendencies with genuine sociopolitical change has been far less evident. Gluckman (1954) originally coined the term "rituals of rebellion" in referring to ceremonial occasions in which customary deference toward authority was temporarily abandoned, allowing participants to openly express their hostilities toward the dominant elite. Following the standard functionalist perspective, he argued that these seemingly subversive rituals actually helped maintain the existing social order through the cathartic release of divisive tensions. This has been labeled the "safety-valve theory" (Coser 1956:39–48); it explains ritual rebellion as an opportunity for the politically subordinate to vent their aggressive tendencies, thereby staving off the emergence of more serious forms of opposition. In other words, "ritual controls by forestalling overt rebellion or other threats to social unity" (Bell 1992:172).

Scott (1990:178) objects to such assertions, arguing that they risk confusing intentionality with result. Taking the carnival as an example, he notes that such a complex social event "cannot be said to be simply this or that as if it had a given, genetically programmed, function. It makes far greater sense to see carnival as the ritual site of various forms of social conflict and symbolic manipulation, none of which can be said, prima facie, to prevail." Furthermore, he wonders, if such rituals actually stave off the possibility of outright rebellion, as the safety-valve theory suggests, why are there so many instances of the authorities trying to control or suppress their performance (Scott 1985:331, 1990:178–179)?[3]

In fact several recent theorists have addressed the use of ritual by subordinated peoples in demonstrating their opposition to a dominant ideology (Comaroff 1985; Ortner 1989; Kelly and Kaplan 1990; Comaroff and Comaroff 1992). The recognized effects of such "rituals of resistance," however, still tend to be restricted to political consciousness-raising, as the following excerpt implies:

> If a system of domination controls the representation of what is possible and what is natural, then a ritual of resistance breaks the hegemony over the subjective consciousness of the ritual participants. It makes them conscious of the oppression and allows them to envision new communities and possibilities. (Kelly and Kaplan 1990:135)

Any attempt to act upon this new awareness would presumably be manifested in other forms; ritual *per se* is denied a direct, instrumental significance.

Bell (1992:71) attributes such tendencies to the way "ritual" has been constructed as an analytic category. She notes that Western scholarship consistently associates ritual with purely symbolic, as opposed to instrumental, activity. This fosters the impression that rituals of resistance serve merely as forms of catharsis which yield no practical result. But if such rituals *are* attributed with instrumental efficacy, what then distinguishes them from other activities? Is ritual an exclusive category or a dimension of all social behavior?

Bell offers a solution to this impasse by suggesting an alternative conceptual framework, focusing not on "ritual" as a discrete analytical category, but on "ritualization" as "a culturally strategic way of acting" (1992:8). She describes ritualization as the privileging of certain activities by ascribing to them a special sanctity or importance, thereby distinguishing them from other, more mundane forms of behavior. "As such, ritualization is a matter of various culturally specific strategies for setting some activities off from others, for creating and privileging a qualitative distinction between the 'sacred' and the 'profane,' and for ascribing such distinctions to realities thought to transcend the powers of human actors" (1992:74). The actors may then attempt to appropriate these privileged activities for their own purposes. The act of ritualization itself, in other words, has instrumental value.

This also solves the question of whether ritual should be regarded as a means of maintaining the status quo or of effecting sociopolitical change; it could just as readily serve in either capacity, depending on the actors' inclinations. Of course, different actors will undoubtedly harbor competing interests. Ritual, then, becomes not just the mechanical expression of previously existing patterns, but a forum for expressing opinions, airing grievances, and promoting one's own agenda.

Gerholm (1988) presages many of these sentiments in delineating a postmodernist approach to the study of ritual. He defines ritual as *"formal, rigidly prescribed action"*; its effectiveness derives from *"the focussing and intensifying of attention,* public and/or individual" (1988:198, emphasis in the original). Rituals, Gerholm insists,

are not usually the work of one "author" but the result of many individual contributions. Those contributions are made on the basis of individual interpretations of the "point" of the ritual and/or on the basis of the external, non-ritual uses of the ritual that a certain individual may see: an opportunity to enhance one's prestige etc. (1988:200)

These ideas are accompanied by a strong assertion that the study of the way individuals use ritual requires a historical perspective.

In keeping with this line of reasoning, the present analysis will assign an instrumental role to the ritual performance itself. It will adopt a historical perspective in examining how the residents of Furukawa have employed their local shrine festival as an effective means of negotiating sociopolitical and economic change. More specifically, it will focus on how a ritual component of the festival— the *okoshi daiko*—emerged as a vehicle of popular protest, which occasionally transcended the bounds of the "purely symbolic" by escalating into genuine acts of politically motivated violence.

Thus, while this study focuses on a Shinto shrine festival, my primary interest lies in symbolic forms of unity and opposition, as well as the larger issue of the role of ritual in adapting to changing sociopolitical and economic conditions. Before proceeding with my specific case example, however, it is necessary to ask an important question: why should such sentiments be expressed through ritual rather than some other medium? I shall address this question through a consideration of the Japanese concept of *matsuri* as communal ritual.

CHAPTER 2

MATSURI AS
COMMUNAL RITUAL

 Adherents of a practice-oriented approach insist that by serving as the agents of structural reproduction, individual actors can introduce changes in the social structure itself. The manner in which this is achieved, however, is far less explicitly described. I suggest that one way of introducing change is through the medium of communal ritual, and that such events mark crucial opportunities for sociopolitical maneuvering.

Ritual has been of major importance in the analysis of social patterns, largely because of its propensity for encapsulating central norms and values. Rappaport (1979:174) refers to ritual as "*the* basic social act," and Wilson (1954:240) sees in ritual "the key to an understanding of the essential constitution of human societies." Ritual is often cited as the primary medium for assigning meaning to experience, or transforming event into structure. According to Geertz (1973:112), "[i]n a ritual, the world as lived and the world as imagined, fused under the agency of a single set of symbolic forms, turn out to be the same world."

Another reason for the focus on ritual is that it renders cultural concepts into visible patterns, making them more accessible to ethnographic analysis. This is particularly evident in large ceremonial events that are performed publicly and at regular intervals. Following Singer (1955:23–26), Geertz refers to such major public ceremonies as "cultural performances," noting that "they represent not only the point at which the dispositional and conceptual aspects of religious life converge for the believer, but also the point at which the interaction between them can be most readily examined by the detached observer" (1973:113). As a succinct and highly visible expression of communal ethos, the Japanese *matsuri,* or Shinto shrine festival, fits nicely into this concept of "cultural performance." It is little wonder then that *matsuri* have figured so prominently in much of the recent literature on the anthropology of Japan (see, for example, Bestor 1989; Robertson 1991; Ashkenazi 1993; Nelson 1996).[1]

The word *"matsuri"* is roughly equivalent to the English "festival," though the Japanese term once held a more deeply religious connotation. Havens (1988:148) suggests that "the theological sense given to *matsuri* is probably closest to the English terms 'to worship' or 'to show reverence,'" and Shinto priests commonly refer to the religious rituals they perform for their parishioners as *"matsuri."* Recently the word has been used in referring to various secular celebrations, exhibitions—even promotional sales events. It is most commonly associated, however, with the Shinto shrine festival—a communal celebration performed annually by the residents of a delimited geographical area in tribute to their local guardian deity. It is in this sense that the term *"matsuri"* is employed in the present study.

Matsuri assume a variety of forms, and attempts to place them within a single category meet with some difficulty. However, all standard definitions describe the *matsuri* as an opportunity for humans to interact directly with the supernatural (Yanagawa 1987: 81–87). Another commonly mentioned feature is that the deity, after being summoned into the society of humans, is treated in the manner of an honored guest. This includes the offering of food and drink as well as lively entertainment. *Matsuri,* therefore, almost invariably contain a conspicuous "play" element, in which the deity, too, is thought to take pleasure. This aspect is perhaps better represented by the term "festivity" than by "ritual," and the event as a whole encompasses both categories.

Contemporary *matsuri* are considered by some to be largely secular affairs, having lost their former religious significance with the transition to an urban-industrial society (Bestor 1989:234). Yet I would argue that *matsuri* remain fundamentally religious, in that their sociopolitical messages are conveyed through the idiom of a supernatural referent. Havens (1988:148) argues that "the very assertion of secularity depends on its contrast to a specialized sense of the 'religious' which may not always be appropriate in discussions of Japanese life." He further suggests that the "secular" nature of *matsuri* derives from a long tradition of combining religion and government in Japan. This is exemplified by the use of the term *"matsuri-goto"* (literally "the activity of worship"), which is virtually synonymous with "politics" or "administration." The political aspect was readily apparent in the ritual performance itself:

> [T]he administration of *matsuri* was in ancient times the province of the leader of the community, whether the patriarch in the case of a single family or lineage group, or the emperor in the case of the nation. As intimated by the term *matsuri-goto,* the socio-political ruler legitimated his rule over everyday life by his simultaneous "rule" over the non-everyday activity of worship. (1988:149)

The postwar democratization of Japan supposedly mandated the strict separation of religion and government. Yet there continues to be a strong link between the performance of *matsuri* and the configuration of the sociopolitical order, as I hope to demonstrate in the following pages.

This raises the question of what seems a rather arbitrary distinction between religious ritual and its "secular" counterpart. Moore and Myerhoff (1977) have attempted to clearly differentiate the two, arguing first that, unlike religious ritual, the secular variety need not be attached to an established ideology and that its explanatory range is thus more limited: "Secular ceremony seems connected with specialized parts of the social/cultural background, rather than with the all-embracing ultimate universals to which religious rituals are attached" (1977:14). I disagree. Even so-called secular rituals appeal to some higher purpose, set of values, or guiding principles. As mentioned in the previous chapter, "ritual" as it is used in this study refers to the performative expression of ideology through a symbolic medium—regardless of whether the ideology is associated with any conception of a supernatural entity. It is the ideological element that distinguishes ritual from mere custom or habit.[2]

Second, Moore and Myerhoff maintain that secular ritual implies no influence beyond the mundane sociopolitical realm—no supernatural consequences, in other words. "The religious ritual moves the other world to affect this one. The secular ceremony moves this world and this world only. Hence two quite different explanations of causality underlie the two performances" (1977:14). Again I disagree. As is apparent in contemporary examples of fundamentalist religious movements, religion and politics are inseparably mixed—one world merges into the other. "Religious ritual" has sociopolitical and psychological ramifications; "secular ritual" appeals as well to spiritual and moral principles. In fact the two are distinguishable only by virtue of what is perhaps a rather trivial criterion: whether or not they are associated with some sort of obscure supernatural presence.

Certainly, all categorical distinctions are somewhat arbitrary; they may nevertheless serve a useful analytical purpose provided they are recognized as purely heuristic devices and applied with caution. The distinction between religious and secular ritual is misleading because it implies that the two are characterized by different properties and directed toward separate realms of human endeavor. The Japanese *matsuri* is an excellent example of the way ritual combines the secular with the religious. Through the performance of *matsuri,* social relationships and ideals are imbedded in a religious idiom, lending them greater legitimacy and wider acceptance.

Following a standard functionalist approach, most analysts describe *matsuri* as a self-fulfilling expression of local values, being performed through and thereby perpetuating a social hierarchy that could not endure without periodic exercise. The *matsuri* is thus seen as a kind of social template, imprinting its coded messages on succeeding generations of participants. This is an example of what Lukes (1975) calls a "Neo-Durkheimian" analysis—referring to attempts at applying Durkheim's ideas to the interpretation of political rituals in advanced industrial societies. The basic premise is that ritual promotes social integration by reinforcing shared values and building consensus opinion. I do not wish to deny such integrative potential, but rather call attention to another important aspect—the use of large communal rituals like the *matsuri* to air alternative opinions. I will argue that the *matsuri* creates opportunities for expressing social discontent or opposition, and should therefore be considered not simply a passive acknowledgment of the existing sociopolitical order but a continuing interplay of competing interests whereby the various participants become actively engaged in pursuit of their own agendas.

Liminality and Conflict

The suggestion of competing interests runs counter to the standard image of Japan as a cooperative, harmonious society. Krauss, Rohlen, and Steinhoff (1984) refer to this image as the "harmony model," asserting that it has misled researchers into ignoring the importance of conflict as a stimulus for change. The harmony model thus promotes a static image of Japanese society, in much the same manner as the old structural-functionalism. In contrast, the authors' own approach is based on "the assumption that conflict is ubiquitous, normal, and integral to the workings of every society. More explicitly, conflict is viewed as arising from the very structure of society itself, not as something alien which occasionally emerges to disrupt the normal order" (1984:5).

Most significantly in terms of the present study, the authors also address the institutionalization of conflict. This includes "conflict behavior that has become ritualized—that is, performed in a predictable manner (often implicitly expected and accepted by the adversary) primarily for the purpose of symbolically affirming the separate interests, identities, and goals of the participants" (1984:9). The authors mention farmers' rice-price demonstrations and organized labor's annual "May struggle" for better wages and benefits as examples of regularly scheduled protest. It is noteworthy that both are staged as annual events, and are in this sense similar to the communal rituals known as *matsuri*. There are, however, more compelling affinities, relating to an ambiguous and ephemeral condition that Turner (1967, 1969, 1974) referred to as "liminality."

The core of the *matsuri* as a religious observance generally consists of a visit by the local guardian deity to the community under its protection. During a ceremony conducted by a Shinto priest, the deity is ritually summoned to the main shrine building and its spirit "bound" to a talisman.[3] It is then transferred to a palanquin-like vehicle called a *"mikoshi."* The *mikoshi,* which resembles a small, portable shrine, rests on a set of parallel beams so that it can be shouldered by a mass of bearers. Secured in this manner, the deity is taken out from the shrine precincts and directly into the community.

In large metropolitan areas, this often assumes the form of a raucous procession, the *mikoshi* being rhythmically jostled up and down by the bearers as it advances through the streets. The attitude here is that the deity is not only being welcomed by its constituents but entertained as well. The bearers, who must "purify" themselves by ingesting liberal amounts of *sake,* are frequently described as achieving a trance-like state of ecstasy or altered consciousness. This condition is induced by the consumption of alcohol, rhythmic movement combined with the chanted utterance *"wasshoi, wasshoi!,"* and the physical exertion of bearing a heavy object (Yanagawa 1988: 17–18; Sadler 1972:98).[4] In their intoxicated condition, the bearers are easily swayed by the force of momentum. This makes the *mikoshi*'s movement rather uncertain, lending it an eerie sense of being self-animated. As Bestor observes:

> Once the priest sanctifies a mikoshi and installs the deity in it, the mikoshi is said to be under the deity's control, not the bearers'. And indeed the mikoshi appears to take on a life of its own and becomes a bucking, pitching, careening force beyond the control or influence of any single bearer (who may be more than a little influenced by *sake*). (1989:239)

The *mikoshi* eventually completes a circuit of its entire territory, the avowed purpose being to dispel evil and revitalize the community through its sanctifying presence. It is then returned to the shrine and the deity ritually "unbound," following the steps of the opening ceremony in reverse order.

The *matsuri,* therefore, represents an opportunity for humans to interact directly with a supernatural entity, drawing it into their own purposes and agendas. Whether the participants believe in the literal existence of this entity has little bearing, for it is as a *symbol* that its presence is being employed.

From a social-sciences perspective, *mikoshi* processions are customarily explained as means of marking territorial affiliations. Since the path of the *mikoshi* traces the boundaries of the neighborhood, it may be seen as symbolically identifying the inscribed population as a cohesive social unit. Indeed, Western characterizations of *mikoshi* processions have focused almost exclusively on their role in reaffirming the social order and instilling a sense of communal solidarity (Bestor 1985, 1989:240–241, 1992:35; Littleton 1986; Ashkenazi 1988, 1993:53, 145; Ben-Ari 1991; Reader 1991:66–69; Kalland 1995a:174–175; Nelson 1996:260). Reader (1991:67), for example, asserts that "[t]o carry or draw the *mikoshi* along requires that the men pull together and in harmony, and is thus also a symbolic reminder to all in the community of the necessity to co-operate and work together for the communal good."

Yet ritual affirmation of the social order is only one aspect of the total *matsuri* experience; equally significant is a breakdown of order and the relaxation of social restraints (Dore 1978:220; Sonoda 1975, 1988; Ashkenazi 1993:67–69). In fact, for many Japanese, the first impression that comes to mind upon hearing the word *"matsuri"* is "chaos." This is clearly evident in the widely used phrase *"matsuri sawagi"* ("festival uproar"). Sonoda (1988:34–35) recalls that the local *matsuri* was for him, as a child growing up in Japan, a cause of considerable anxiety due to the rowdy behavior of drunks wandering freely about the neighborhood. It was not drunkenness *per se,* however, that he found so distressing, but rather the transformation it effected in seemingly ordinary individuals: "What I could not comprehend was the fact that at the time of *matsuri,* some men, and on occasion even some women—people who normally were among the most upright and proper of those known to me—could pull out all the stops and engage in unrestrained uproar."

Building on this tendency toward the momentary abandonment of restraint, Sonoda (1988:36) proceeds to identify two contrasting aspects of the *matsuri* experience: "On the one hand are highly dignified rites of seclusion and purification, [characterized by] bodily actions and behavior of the most restrained and solemn kind. But on the other hand, there is also generally an expectation of a thorough liberation of mind and body, a destruction of the existing order. Festival days involve a kind of public license for the casting away of everyday restraints and for the kind of behavior which in normal common sense would be disdainfully dismissed as vulgar."

Sonoda further notes that the licentious behavior is far more likely to emerge at night than during the day. This he relates to ancient religious beliefs in which night was perceived as the realm of the mysterious and supernatural. "The very act of humans awakening from that night and becoming active was a kind of offense against order, and such activities were thus permitted only during sacred festivals which were aimed at concourse with the divine spirits" (1988:59).

This experiential dichotomy is clearly evident in the *matsuri* at Furukawa, the small town that serves as the subject of this study. In Furukawa the *mikoshi* procession is a stately, dignified affair performed in broad daylight. It is accompanied by formal ceremonies in which the shrine officers and other representatives assemble to pay their respects to the local guardian deity. "[H]ere is presented the world of order set out in its perfection, with the deity before all. With the deity occupying the central place of honor, those men greeting the deity express their own relative rankings by sitting in a strict order on the left and right sides" (Sonoda 1988:61). At night, however, a quite different kind of procession takes place—the wild and boisterous *okoshi daiko.* "Here, the minority of formally attired, 'named' powers lose their central role to the majority in the stark naked, 'unnamed' mass, and it would appear that the direct clash of nakedness against nakedness makes possible not only the communion of fellow human beings, but that between human and divinity as well" (1988:64).[5] Sonoda applies the term "sacred transgression" to this second tendency, which he suggests holds an important key to understanding the religious vitality of the Japanese *matsuri* (1988:69).

There is an obvious parallel here with Turner's (1967, 1969, 1974) distinction between social structure and "communitas." The latter refers to the temporary abandonment of role and status through joining in an ecstatic union with other human beings. To place Sonoda's argument in Turner's idiom, "ritual" may be described as a manifestation of social structure, while "festival" is an expression of communitas.

Turner, of course, based his thinking on the concept of ritual liminality, a transitional interlude in which hierarchical social relationships are temporarily abandoned or even reversed, offering subordinates a kind of momentary license for engaging in subversive behavior. The liminal phase is significant in terms of social process, as it represents an opportunity for introducing new ideas. "Without liminality," Turner suggests, "program might indeed determine performance. But, given liminality, prestigious programs can be undermined and multiple alternative programs may be generated" (1974: 14). The liminal moment, therefore, creates a situation "in which all previous standards and models are subjected to criticism, and fresh new ways of describing and interpreting sociocultural experience are formulated" (1974:15). Such an opportunity may be especially useful to the politically subordinate, for whom any expression of opposition might under ordinary circumstances result in punitive action by the authorities.

In Japan, the risks of expressing disapproval are compounded by a social ethic that places great emphasis on harmony and self-restraint as guiding principles of daily interaction. Under such conditions, alcohol is often considered a necessary catalyst in promoting the open expression of personal opinions. It is customary in Japan that an individual is not held responsible for abusive words or actions while under the influence of alcohol (Nakane 1970:125, Moeran 1984:84–85, Pharr 1990:126). As Allison (1994:46) notes, "[t]he Western praise for those who 'can hold their liquor well' misses the point in Japan, where many drink to achieve the freedom and the chance to act irresponsibly that come with drunkenness." Drinking thus confers a kind of temporary immunity for engaging in unusual behavior. This includes the public airing of concerns or grievances.

Bailey (1991:36, 68, 99), for example, tells of a rural community whose residents opposed a government proposal to amalgamate them with a neighboring village, but who felt such strong pressure from higher government officials to accede to the plan that they could not bring themselves to openly voice their objections. At a formal gathering intended to celebrate the successful conclusion of the merger negotiations, however, the local mayor got roaring drunk, and, acting as a mouthpiece for the collective sentiments of his fellow villagers, issued forth with a tirade of insults directed at the government officials, the neighboring village, and the merger plan itself. The plan was abruptly halted at that point. Bailey describes such use of alcohol as "an ultimate form of resistance to pressure from higher authority." The mayor had conveyed his message "in a context that provided a socially effective outlet for complaint and resistance when more formal structures had proven inadequate" (1991:99).

Such examples demonstrate that the expression of alternative viewpoints is acceptable in certain culturally prescribed contexts, typically involving the consumption of alcohol. The *matsuri* represents one of these contexts. It might be said that drinking offers those who indulge in it a form of anonymity or disguise, which they can use to their own advantage.

In this sense, the *matsuri* is highly reminiscent of the Latin carnival, as widely reported in both the social sciences and humanities (Turner 1974; Gilmore 1975, 1987; Abrahams and Bauman 1978; Le Roy Ladurie 1979; Bakhtin 1984; Scott 1990).[6] Gilmore's (1975) example is particularly relevant to the present discussion; it includes a public procession of masqueraders, armed with stout poles which they use in chastising their fellow townspeople. "All masqueraders speak in a squeaky falsetto voice when accosting bystanders and are also careful to alter their manner of walking and other personal mannerisms in order to remain anonymous." Significantly, Gilmore notes that the majority of the celebrants are of the landless agrarian working class, and that the masqueraders are mostly "young unmarried people under the age of thirty" (1975:335–337). He refers to the carnival as a "festival of gossip," suggesting that it "is a time when all townsmen are brought before the people's informal court of justice, and when any moral transgression may be mercilessly ridiculed" (1975:340).

Scott (1990:173) offers a similar observation on the political opportunities inherent in carnival:

[W]hat is most interesting about carnival is the way it allows certain things to be said, certain forms of social power to be exercised that are muted or suppressed outside this ritual sphere. The anonymity of the setting, for example, allows the social sanctions of the small community normally exercised through gossip to assume a more full-throated voice. . . . Disapproval that would be dangerous or socially costly to vent at other times is sanctioned during carnival. It is the time and place to settle, verbally at least, personal and social scores.

Relating this condition to his "hidden transcript" theory, Scott adds that "[m]uch of the social aggression within carnival is directed at dominant power figures, if for no other reason than the fact that such figures are, by virtue of their power, virtually immune from open criticism at other times" (1990:174).

Such political ramifications are clearly evident in the Japanese *matsuri*. Yamamoto Yoshiko's (1978) description of the Namahage festival in northeastern Japan is a case in point. The young men of the village dress up as demons (the *namahage*) who break into people's homes and admonish those who have been bad. This allows the young men to express feelings and opinions that would otherwise remain suppressed. "One middle-aged man recalled a time in his youth when he wished to marry, but his father did not recognize his wish. So when he visited his own house disguised as a Namahage, he said to his father, 'Your son is ready to marry. Do you intend to choose a girl for him or not?'" (1978:118). These young men are normally obliged to bow to the wishes of their parents and other elders, with little say in determining their own futures. The *namahage* persona allows them to confront the uncertainties of their situation, again assisted by drinking *sake*. "With the help of the *sake* and the disguises, which in a sense separate them from the real world and provide a different identity, the young men are able to discuss openly the question of their future. *Even when the drunkenness is pretended,* the same principles motivate the masqueraders' behavior" (1978:124, emphasis added). This last sentence is particularly significant; it implies the participants view the event as an *opportunity* —one that is not merely induced by the consumption of alcohol, but freely chosen as an outlet for suppressed feelings. The threatening remarks and antagonistic behavior are *intentional.* This does not suggest a simple safety-valve mechanism for relieving divisive pressures, but rather a premeditated exercise of human agency. Again, the villagers *know* that there are young men inside the costumes, and can perhaps guess at their identities, but the costume itself confers a kind of temporary immunity for voicing discontents.

Moeran (1984) describes a similar situation involving social drinking in Sarayama, a community of potters in central Kyushu. He begins by challenging the conventional explanation for drinking behavior in Japan, which is highly reminiscent of the safety-valve explanation for rebellious ritual:

> It has often been suggested that, in Japan, what is said during the course of a drinking session is soon forgiven and forgotten. Drinking acts as an outlet for repressed feelings, seen to be brought on by the way in which the individual is expected to subordinate his own interests to those of the group in Japanese society. I soon discovered that this was *not* exactly the case. . . . In fact, local residents not only remembered what was said during drinking sessions; they stored this information away, to use for their own political ends. (1984:84)

Moeran proceeds to describe these drinking sessions as a form of covert discourse, foreshadowing Scott's distinction between publicly acknowledged attitudes and opinions on the one hand and the so-called "hidden transcript" on the other.[7]

> There were, in other words, two discourses in action in Sara-yama. One was the overt daytime discourse, conducted mainly by the elders and in fairly formal situations. The other was a covert night-time discourse entered into by the middle-aged group of men, mainly under the informal influences of *sake*. It was vital for any man who wished to gain access to authority and power to be aware of the night-time discourse and to make use of it as and when appropriate. (1984:98–99)

But, again, it is not merely the alcohol which motivates the actors to assert themselves. Moeran notes that one's presence and partici-pation, rather than simple inebriation, is the critical factor. To illus-trate his point, he includes an example of a man with kidney prob-lems who was advised by his doctor to drink tomato juice, but was nevertheless able to stay with the drinkers and even adopt a pseudo-inebriated demeanor. Moeran (1984:98) concludes that "drinking is thus the idiom in which decisions are made, and not necessarily their cause."

Communal drinking presents an opportunity for the open expres-sion of conflicting viewpoints, owing to the tolerant attitude with which drunkenness is viewed. People are obliged not so much to *ignore* what one says and does under the influence of alcohol as to *tolerate and accept* it. As with numerous cases of spirit possession reported in other societies, the medium or "mouthpiece" of such utterances remains entirely identifiable, but by achieving an altered state of consciousness it assumes a persona that can express itself with impunity. Individual actors—the so-called "victims" of the pos-sessing spirit—may use this persona to their own advantage (Kakar 1982:68–88; I. M. Lewis 1989:67–71).

The air of permissiveness that surrounds the Japanese *matsuri* provides a similar kind of opportunity, especially for the politically subordinate. Ordinary restraints are temporarily abandoned, and personal animosities freely expressed. Anyone with a grudge or score to settle may wait for the occasion of the local *matsuri,* when acts of vengeance will generally be overlooked or forgiven. It is understandable, then, why quarreling and even physical violence are accepted as inevitable correlates of the *matsuri* experience.

Sanctity and Social Sanction

The procession of the deity which forms the core of the *matsuri* may now be seen from a perspective quite different from the standard interpretation. What is significant is not so much that the *mikoshi* traces the territorial boundaries of the community, but that it *passes in front of every constituent home or workplace.* As previously mentioned, the intoxicated condition of the bearers, combined with the sheer bulk of the object itself, adds an ominous uncertainty to its movement. At times it may "mysteriously" lurch to one side, crashing into the home of a greedy merchant, acrimonious neighbor, or exacting public official.

Sadler (1972:90) alludes to the following account of a *mikoshi* procession, quoting Maraini (1962:85): "The palanquin advanced, now slowly, now quickly, lunging and swerving to right or left, or turning completely in its tracks, or sometimes spinning like a top. 'It goes where the gods want it to,' an old man explained to me." Sadler notes that the bearers take periodic rest breaks during which they drink more *sake,* then rejoin their comrades with renewed vigor. "By the time evening comes, every member of the team has benefitted by these periodic pauses to refresh, and . . . the *mikoshi* goes more and more 'where the gods want it to'" (Sadler 1972:100).

It is important to note in this regard that the deity is attributed with a dual personality. Its ordinary condition is referred to as *"nigimitama"*—a calm or gentle spirit. At times, however, it reveals its vengeful nature in the form of *"aramitama"*—a rough or violent spirit (Blacker 1975:45; Nelson 1996:27, 154). The latter is key to understanding the social significance of the festival procession. Consumption of alcohol is important in inducing a trance-like condition. It is through the consumption of alcohol and subsequent intoxication that the spirit of the deity enters the bodies of the *mikoshi* bearers: it is "embodied" so as to express either its benevolence or displeasure. The *mikoshi* becomes a kind of surrogate through which the people air their true opinions. Takie Lebra (personal communication) has referred to this device as a form of "ventriloquy," noting that its employment is widespread in Japanese society and history. Perhaps the most obvious example lies in the treatment of the emperor, who, as Reischauer (1988:240) observes, has long been the object of both "awed respect" and "callous manipulation." Even under ordinary circumstances it is customary to express one's objections through some form of intermediary, thereby avoiding direct confrontation.

Writing around the turn of the century, Lafcadio Hearn (1904: 116) provides the following explanation for the *mikoshi*'s erratic movements:

[A]ll this pushing and pulling and swaying signifies only the deity's inspection of the dwellings on either hand. He is looking about to see whether the hearts of his worshippers are pure, and is deciding whether it will be necessary to give a warning, or to inflict a penalty. His bearers will carry him whithersoever he chooses to go—through solid walls if necessary. If the shrine strike against any house,—even against an awning only,—that is a sign that the god is not pleased with the dwellers in that house. If the shrine breaks part of the house, that is a serious warning. But it may happen that the god wills to enter a house,—breaking his way. Then woe to the inmates, unless they flee at once through the back-door; and the wild procession, thundering in, will wreck and rend and smash and splinter everything on the premises before the god consents to proceed upon his round.

However, further investigation reveals more to the story than mere supernatural impulse.

Upon enquiring into the reasons of two wreckings of which I witnessed the results, I learned enough to assure me that from the communal point of view, both aggressions were morally justifiable. In one case a fraud had been practised; in the other, help had been refused to the family of a drowned resident. Thus one offence had been legal; the other only moral. (1904: 116).

Note that in the latter instance the *mikoshi* was used to punish an offense not covered by formal law but nevertheless considered a violation of local mores. This distinction between local tradition and an official codified law imposed by an outside, centralized authority is typical of small neighborhood and village studies in Japan. Smith (1961), in a classic article on the use of social ostracism in a Japanese hamlet, describes a distinct reluctance by hamlet members to take internal matters to the authorities, preferring to administer their own form of justice by severing ties with the offending household.

Smith himself has observed the use of a local festival procession as a form of social sanction. This is evident in the following excerpt from his field notes made in a Shikoku village, dated 1951.

In former years the procession went from the main Hachiman Shrine building down the long steps to the entrance of the shrine grounds, from where the god surveys the rice crop, and then returned. Recently, however, it has been the practice of the *mikoshi* to enter the shopkeepers' [hamlet] of Chūtoku, where it is set down before the houses of five or six wealthy merchants in turn. This is said to insure the best possible fortune for the house during the coming year, and also earn for the bearers a *shō* [roughly 1.8 liters] of *sake,* for that is the appropriate gift. The *sake* is usually drunk on the spot, and by the time the god is carried back to the shrine, his progress is boisterous and somewhat unsteady.

This year, I was told, all the target houses provided the *sake,* lest the *aramitama* nature of the god be roused and the *mikoshi* "accidentally" crash into the store-front. No one is sure when the practice of entering Chūtoku began, but it seems to have been the practice long enough for the shopkeepers to take precautions. (Robert J. Smith, personal communication, April 5, 1994)

In this instance the *mikoshi* bearers were looking for a donation, the implication being that they would damage a merchant's house if no gift of *sake* was forthcoming. This implies an expectation that the affluent play the role of benefactors, redistributing some of their surplus wealth back to the community, whose patronage had ensured their success. Any display of stinginess could invite social sanction. This was particularly significant during the immediate postwar period, when merchants began to enjoy the benefits of economic prosperity well before other households. It is important to note that those enlisted to bear the *mikoshi* generally belonged to the lower socioeconomic categories, suggesting a certain class-consciousness in their actions.

Folklorist Yanagita Kunio reports a similar incident decades earlier in a town "not too far from Tokyo." The local branch of the Bank of Japan had been asked for a contribution to the *matsuri* festivities, but since there was no provision in the budget for such expenditures, the bank managers declined. Subsequently, during the *mikoshi* procession that year the bank was attacked, the *mikoshi* smashing its iron fence and most of its windows. The following year the bank's budget contained a new entry labeled "*matsuri* payment" (Yanagita 1962b:400).

Mikoshi processions reveal an important generational distinction as well. This relates to the fact that the bearers consist mostly of younger men—those with the stamina to shoulder a heavy object for extended periods. Younger residents, having yet to assume positions of real authority, generally have less vested interest in maintaining the sociopolitical status quo, and are thus more inclined toward disharmonious or subversive behavior. Sadler (1972:99), provides the following example from an urban setting—the Asakusa district in Tokyo:

I saw one immense *mikoshi* round a corner, careen down the street, and then bash into a seven-foot high wooden garden fence. The owner peeped out of his second floor window just in time to see one well-intentioned elder prop up a shattered fence post as best he could, shrug his shoulders and amble off to catch up with the *mikoshi*. (The [owner], I was told, was a bit of a grouch, and therefore not too popular with the youth of the neighborhood.)

Both attributes—economic and generational—place the bearers lower down in the hierarchy of authority, with little or no political voice. The *matsuri* may in fact represent one of the few opportunities available to them to openly express their dissatisfactions.

It may thus be seen that, in addition to their widely acknowledged role of marking territorial boundaries and reaffirming the social order, festival processions that involve the bearing of *mikoshi* or similarly bulky objects constitute an effective means of punishing deviations from accepted norms or seeking retribution for perceived injustices. In other words, such processions represent a latent form of social sanction, applied not through the exercise of formal legal institutions but rather through the informal practice of communal ritual. Intentionally moving the palanquin-like vehicle in any particular direction represents a collective social act, due largely to the sheer weight and bulk of the object itself. As Bestor (1992:35) recalls being told by informants, "a *mikoshi* should be so heavy that no single person's actions could affect or even be noticeable in its movements." Any attempt to crash the structure into a targeted building would thus require a concerted effort; the sanctioning action must of necessity derive from widely shared opinion.

This aspect of the *matsuri* is not well publicized, perhaps due to the pervasiveness of the "harmony model." It remains, however, an ever-present possibility, even in the densely populated urban environment of contemporary Japan. This is clear from Bestor's (1992: 42–43) own account of the following incident, which took place during the shrine festival in his Tokyo neighborhood field site. A crew of rowdy day laborers had been recruited to build a new *mikoshi,* despite the objections of "respectable" citizens who opposed their involvement. During the festival itself, these same laborers assumed the role of bearing the *mikoshi*—a role they intended to fulfill in the raucous manner they felt appropriate to the occasion. When the neighborhood leaders decided to postpone the procession due to rain, however, the laborers became very upset, and demanded the *mikoshi* be brought out in spite of the weather.

> Suddenly, an argument broke out between a neighborhood leader, a merchant, and the local labor boss. Within seconds the merchant was jumped by half a dozen laborers who stomped him as he lay in the gutter, his festival garb covered with mud. . . . Eventually the rain broke, and the *mikoshi* made its rounds. The workmen were allowed to carry it, but they were surrounded by the burliest men the respectable leadership could muster; and when the procession passed the shopfront of the festival leader who had been beaten to the ground, a phalanx of "respectable" leaders formed a conspicuous but passive human shield in front of the shop's plate glass windows to guard against a sudden lurch of the heavy *mikoshi.*

In this instance no property damages were actually incurred. Even so, the immediate reaction of neighborhood officials in rushing to guard the storefront reveals an obvious familiarity with *mikoshi* bashing episodes.

Several features make *matsuri* particularly conducive to the public airing of animosities. Participants can rely on the anonymity conferred by a mass assembly of people and the impunity associated with both the liberal consumption of alcohol and the atmosphere of permissiveness surrounding the event. They can also cite intervention by the supernatural as a way of excusing their actions and avoiding the blame. A *matsuri* is at its core a sacred performance ostensibly controlled by the will of the deity. Whatever happens during a *matsuri* is thus considered an "act of god" which could not have been foreseen or prevented (Moriya and Nakamaki 1991:54).

This sense of impunity is enhanced by a reluctance on the part of the targeted households to draw attention to their having been victimized. Here again, since the *mikoshi*'s movement is supposedly being controlled by the will of the deity, crashing into adjacent buildings would be interpreted as a sign of the deity's displeasure with those dwelling therein. But the power of the social sanction depends not so much on genuine fear of supernatural disfavor as on the more immediate concern with public opinion. On a more worldly level, being injured or having one's property damaged could be taken as evidence of ill feelings or resentment against oneself; the community at large would automatically assume the victims had done something to deserve it. This helps ensure the matter will not be taken before the formal authorities; the sanction remains an internal affair.

There is an interesting parallel between the religious symbolism being employed and the force of social sentiment. The idea that the deity is angered reflects the hostility of public opinion, enacted through the movement of the sacred object. Again, it is highly significant that any purposeful action by the bearers must take the form of a cooperative effort, as this in turn implies general agreement on the seriousness of the targeted household's misdeeds.

Undoubtedly, the heavy object will occasionally hit a building by pure accident, applying the sanction unjustifiably. But this element of uncertainty merely adds to the effectiveness of the social control mechanism: it causes the victims to ponder whether they have alienated anyone and to be vigilant against doing so in the future. It also serves as an example to others, demonstrating that the "deity's anger" is indeed periodically aroused.

This use of the *mikoshi* as an instrument of social sanction in no way negates the status of the *matsuri* as a "cultural performance"— it merely assigns the *matsuri* a more instrumental role in promoting communal-mindedness. The deity's annual visit enforces an attitude of humility and mutual concern, even as it traces territorial boundaries and reaffirms the solidarity of the neighborhood. Those who feel themselves superior to others or fail to demonstrate the proper communal attitude may be singled out and punished. It is in this sense that the community as a social construction is truly "revitalized."

Matsuri as a Political Instrument

As previously mentioned, in Furukawa the *mikoshi* procession is a solemn, dignified affair conducted during the daylight hours and devoid of the kind of boisterous activity alluded to above. The *okoshi daiko*, on the other hand, is performed at night and characterized by the wild, unruly attitude known as "Furukawa *yancha*." Like the *mikoshi*, the massive drum structure is considered a sacred object. Prior to the ritual, a Shinto priest performs a ceremony in front of the structure, ascribing it with a special purifying or expiatory quality.[8] Again like the *mikoshi*, the movements of the structure are uncertain, and it has been known to crash into buildings at opportune moments. In this particular instance, however, there is an added threat posed by the numerous small neighborhood drums, or *tsuke daiko*, running wide of the mark in their rush toward the main structure. The stout poles to which these drums are attached could easily become battering rams, as on occasion they have done.

Yet the political ramifications go well beyond this simple sanctioning mechanism. Previously I alluded to similarities between *matsuri* and certain predetermined, regularly scheduled political demonstrations. Like *matsuri,* such demonstrations constitute a socially acceptable or appropriate time for airing grievances. Considering the political aspects inherent in *matsuri* ritual on the one hand, and the ritualized nature of political demonstrations on the other, it becomes apparent that there is considerable overlap between these two phenomena. Robertson (1991:70) notes that "[a]s early as the eighth century, palanquin shrine bearing has been associated with protest riots, and in recent history 'wasshoi, wasshoi' has been adopted as the chant of student and labor demonstrators." Yanagawa (1972:66–67, 1988:4), too, draws intriguing parallels between *matsuri* and the Japanese student demonstrations of the late 1960s in terms of transcending the profane world of everyday existence and momentarily challenging the accepted social order.

I would like, therefore, to expand upon the notion of "cultural performance," raising it from a seemingly static expression of communally held values to an active public forum for expressing competing opinions and airing discontents. This makes the annual *matsuri* a critical time period—in terms not only of the ritual order, but of the political one as well. If the *matsuri* does indeed function as a "cultural performance," expressing social norms and values in a succinct and readily visible manner, then it is reasonable to assume that as those norms and values change, the changes will be reflected in the ritual symbolism employed in the *matsuri*. Therefore, examining the way the *matsuri* has developed over time should inform our understanding of sociopolitical and economic change by giving us another source of data in addition to standard documentary evidence. The evolutionary development of the *matsuri* becomes a historical narrative of social process.

In later chapters I will demonstrate how the people of Furukawa have employed their local *matsuri* as a forum for responding to the dramatic changes they have been subjected to in recent decades. First, however, I would like to provide some relevant background information on the town, its people, and the sociopolitical and economic relations that order their existence.

Chapter 3

TERRITORIAL
AND COLLECTIVE
IDENTITIES

Gifu Prefecture in central Japan is shaped a bit like a three-leaf clover, with one lobe extending north and the other two east and west. The northern lobe comprises a predominantly forested mountain region known since antiquity as "Hida." This region is spatially defined by the three counties of Mashita-*gun,* Ōno-*gun,* and Yoshiki-*gun,*[1] as well as the city of Takayama which lies in their midst. The name "Hida" itself, however, refers to a province that no longer officially exists. It ceased to function as a distinct political unit shortly after the Meiji Restoration in 1868, when new prefectural boundaries were instituted to replace the old feudal domains. In the intricate array of Japanese territorial categories, Hida is merely a *"chihō"*—a vicinity or region. Even so, a strong sense of cultural identity remains firmly entrenched among the local people, who persist in associating themselves with the Hida region first and Gifu Prefecture second. In major cities like Tokyo and Osaka there are regular meetings of *Hida-kai*—associations of former Hida residents who have been obliged to move away to the cities in search of employment or other opportunities, but who nevertheless retain a strong emotional attachment to their homeland.[2]

What explains this continuing association with a local region, even in the absence of any formal integrative framework and despite continual efforts by more encompassing political entities to direct allegiance toward themselves? Is it simple nostalgia, the force of tradition, or a conservative mentality resistant to change? Are there perhaps benefits to remaining affiliated at some more immediate territorial level? Does affiliation imply exclusive loyalty, or can individuals shift their allegiance between levels as the need arises? These are the questions this chapter will address, while at the same time providing some contextual background for the remainder of the study.

Environmental Context

Hida lies near the center of the Japanese archipelago. It is bounded on the east by a range of lofty peaks popularly known as the "Japan Alps," which divide the island of Honshu longitudinally into two halves. Scholars in various disciplines have used this mountain divide in distinguishing two broad cultural areas: the northeast, dominated by Tokyo (formerly Edo), the center of power held by the warrior establishment during Japan's late medieval period; and the southwest, centering around Kyoto, the former capital and locus of an older, more refined aristocratic court tradition. The geographic distribution of cultural traits is often perceived in terms of these two broad areal categories. In analyses of patterns of rural social organization, for example, the northeast is supposedly characterized by a rigid hierarchy based on the genealogical relationship between a main household *(honke)* and its derivative branches *(bunke),* while the southwest is thought to exhibit a more egalitarian community structure based on neighborhood affiliation and reciprocal exchange relationships (Fukutake 1949; Izumi and Gamo 1952; Befu 1963; Izumi et al. 1984; Ueno 1987:S77–S78). In cartographic representations of this division, Hida usually appears along the boundary separating the two areas, or in some nebulous intermediate zone (see Nagashima 1984, for example).

Hida is ambivalent in another sense as well: it straddles the divide between two major drainage systems. The southern portion of the region is drained by the Hida River, which flows south to join the Kiso and eventually empties into the Pacific Ocean at Ise Bay near Nagoya. The northern portion, however, is drained by the Miya, Takahara, and Shō Rivers, all of which run north. The Miya and Takahara join to form the Jintsu River, which flows into the Sea of Japan at Toyama Bay. The Shō follows a parallel course, entering the same bay a little further west. Settlements lying in Hida's northern portion were thus historically linked by the drainage pattern to the Sea of Japan—the side that faces the Asian mainland. This places them in what is prejudicially referred to as *"ura-Nihon,"* or

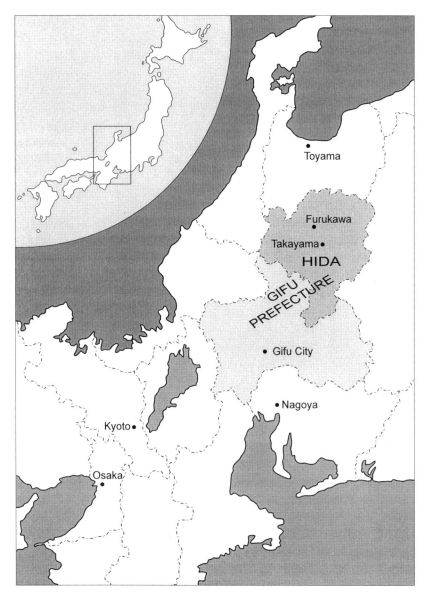

Map 1. Central Japan, showing the position of Gifu Prefecture and the Hida region in relation to major urban areas, as well as the locations of Takayama and Furukawa. Map by Patricia J. Conrad.

Japan's "backside," as opposed to the far more densely populated and heavily industrialized Pacific coastal region.

The Hida landscape is characterized by rugged slopes and swiftly flowing rivers, with villages and rice paddies squeezed into the narrow valleys. The Miya River flows north from the heart of the region and for most of its length is confined to a narrow valley. Not far from the river's headlands, however, the valley expands to form a broad basin. Therein lies the city of Takayama, Hida's largest municipality, which has for centuries served as the region's cultural, economic, and administrative center.

Several kilometers beyond Takayama the river makes a sharp bend to the northwest and the mountains open up to reveal a second, more elongated basin. A tributary river, the Araki, flows in from the east and assumes a parallel course, finally merging with the Miya at the center of the basin. The town of Furukawa, whose name literally means "old river," is located just at the point where the two rivers converge. It is surrounded by rice paddies, and beyond them a number of small hamlets lining the basin's perimeter. The town itself consists of only about seven thousand residents. However, the administrative unit known as Furukawa Township (Furukawa-chō) encompasses not only the town, but most of the basin and peripheral hamlets, as well as a large portion of the surrounding forested mountain land. The entire area of 97.49 square kilometers contained a total population of 16,035 in 1995 (Sōmuchō Tōkeikyoku 1996).

The Furukawa basin is approximately ten kilometers long but only about fifteen hundred meters wide. Nevertheless, this narrow strip of land, along with the slightly smaller Takayama basin located just upstream, together constitute the only substantial areas of level ground in the entire Hida region. In a society whose economy was traditionally based on rice production, acquisition and control of this limited amount of arable land represented one of the major avenues to greater wealth and political influence. It is understandable, then, why much of Hida's history revolves around these two basin areas and the populations they sustain.

In addition to placing limits on the amount of arable land, the mountains pose formidable barriers to communication by virtue of both their physical presence and their influence on the local climate. Weather systems generally move in from the Sea of Japan, dumping moisture in the form of precipitation as they continue eastward over

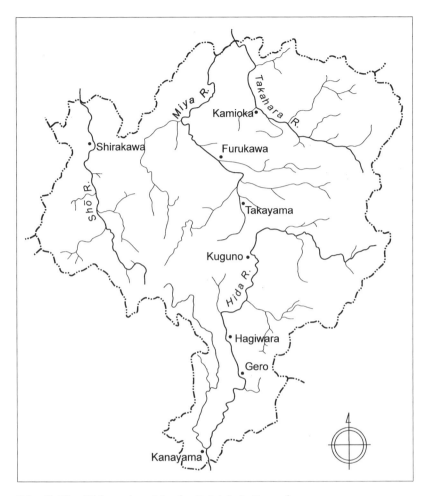

Map 2. The Hida region. Map by Patricia J. Conrad.

the Japan Alps. The Hida region lies on the western slope of this range and thus receives considerable accumulations of snow during the winter. Until as recently as the mid-1960s some of the villages higher up in the mountains were completely snowed in for months at a time—cut off from virtually all contact with the outside until the spring thaw.[3]

These various impediments, combined with distance from major population centers, kept Hida in the periphery of national development planning until well into the twentieth century. There were of course roads linking the region to other areas, but these were rough and narrow, most of them suitable only for foot traffic. With transportation limited to this extent, the people of Hida subsisted largely on the fruits of their own labors. Millet could be grown at higher altitudes without irrigation and was therefore used to supplement the meager rice harvest. Beyond this, townspeople and villagers alike relied heavily on resources available in the forested mountains.[4] Koyama (1981:93) notes that even after the introduction of agriculture "the Hida subsistence system was varied and complex, retaining many elements of foraging." Survival required a diversified subsistence strategy utilizing both the sparse lowland basin areas and the more abundant upland mountain resources.

The mountains yielded various species of wild vegetable *(sansai)*, most notably *warabi* (brackenroot), *zenmai* (royal fern), and *yomogi* (mugwort), all of which sprouted into edible form only in early to mid-May. The stem-like vegetables were heated in water with ash to leach out the acid, then dried in the sun and pressed into clumps for later use. Soaking the dried vegetables in water returned them to something like their original form. The object, then, was to gather as many of the stems as possible while they were in season so they could be preserved and eaten all year round. Nuts were an important source of vegetable protein. Chestnut, buckeye, and acorn were all available in the forested mountains. Again, these could be gathered in season, then dried and processed for later use (Matsuyama 1981).

The Miya River system was abundant in freshwater fish, including dace, trout, *ayu (Plecoglossus altivelis)*, and eel (Akimichi 1981: 148–149). The killing of game animals—particularly the four-legged variety—was discouraged by Buddhist tradition. Nevertheless, deer and wild boar were hunted and consumed, perhaps because they provided an important source of protein in an area so far removed from the sea. Bear meat was also consumed to a limited extent, as were certain species of birds, particularly pheasant (Koyama 1981: 100–102).

The mountains provided several other important resources in addition to the directly edible variety. The lowland villagers regularly went into the mountains to cut grass and carry it back to scatter over their rice paddies as a form of green manure. They also employed what is termed *"kyakudo"* (literally "visitor soil")—nutrient rich soil hauled down from the mountains and added to the rice paddies—again in an effort to raise yields. Perhaps the most important source of nutrients, however, was the water used for flooding

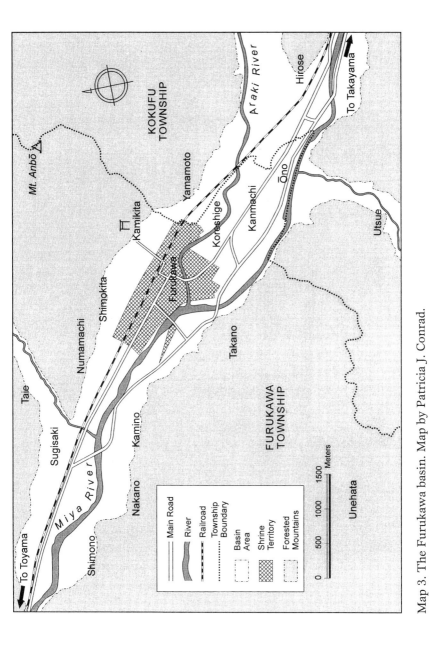

Map 3. The Furukawa basin. Map by Patricia J. Conrad.

the rice paddies prior to spring transplanting and throughout the growing season.[5] This too was channeled down from mountain streams through an intricate series of ditches and weirs. As in other parts of Japan, water rights were communally held and regulated, and disputes sometimes broke out between neighboring villages, or even fellow residents of the same village, over access to water during critical periods in the growing season.

Horses and cattle were kept as traction animals, and the forested mountains offered them forage. Trees were cut to provide lumber for housing materials. The smaller pieces of timber were processed into charcoal and used as fuel for heating and cooking. In fact the mountains provided so many of the basic resources necessary for subsistence that they were collectively referred to by the people of Hida as the "great mother" *(ōinaru haha).*[6]

While paddy land was privately owned by individual households, rights to the mountains were held communally.[7] The land was parceled out and each community assigned a particular area for its own use. Residents were thereby ensured access to the forest resources so necessary to their survival. As might be expected, rights of access were jealously guarded, and boundary disputes among neighboring communities were not infrequent.

Houses in this area were of the mud-and-wattle variety, consisting of a wooden frame interlaced with bamboo latticework for the walls, to which clay mud was affixed. The clay was mixed with rice straw for greater cohesiveness. Walls facing the outside were then covered with wooden siding to protect them from the elements. The roofs were originally made of thatch, but wooden shingles became increasingly prevalent during the Meiji (1868–1912) and Taishō (1912–1926) periods. The shingles were generally made of chestnut *(kuri)* wood because it was strong, resistant to water, and readily available in the forests nearby.

Traditional carpenters preferred not to use nails, as these tended to make the house rigid and less resistant to earthquake tremors. Instead they relied on joinery and rope bindings, leaving the house flexible enough to expand and contract with the shifting earth. Likewise, the wooden shingles on the roofs were not nailed down. Boards were laid laterally across the shingles, and stones placed on the boards to help hold the shingles in place against strong winds.

The wooden shingle roofs have now become extremely rare; they have to be replaced every twenty years or so, and rising timber prices make the cost prohibitive. Most home owners have switched to metal roofing. The clay tile roofs common in other parts of Japan are not practical in Hida due to heavy snowfall: on sunny winter days the snow would melt and moisture seep into the cracks between the tiles; then at night the water would freeze and separate one tile from the next. Metal roofs are not susceptible to this kind of damage, and the snow slides off them more easily.

Even so, one of the major winter chores for local inhabitants is to periodically shovel snow from the tops of their buildings to prevent the roofs from caving in under the extra weight. In Furukawa, the snow is pitched into gutters lining the streets, where a flow of water channeled in from the river carries it away. Before this municipal irrigation system was installed, however, the snow was simply thrown into the street to be packed down by foot traffic. The resulting accumulation sometimes reached as high as the eaves of the houses facing the street, forcing the occupants to exit from their second-story windows. The huge mass of packed snow took a considerable time to melt away, and some of the townspeople recall random patches of ice lingering in the streets until just before the *matsuri* in mid-April. It is not difficult to understand, then, why spring *matsuri* in this region were such joyous occasions, as they marked an end to the isolation imposed by the harsh winter and an opportunity to reestablish contact with relatives and friends in other communities.

The Local Economy

The people of Furukawa routinely characterize themselves as being *"hannō-hanshō"*—half-agricultural, half-commercial. This is meant to imply two things: (1) the town's economy is based on a combination of the two sectors; and (2) there is no clear distinction between farmers and merchants, as many households engage in both activities. This is not simply a function of recent government-sponsored development initiatives, but a condition with deep historical roots. Furukawa traditionally supplied tools and provisions to surrounding villages; it was thus home to a number of prosperous manufacturing and retailer households. Many of these also engaged in moneylending activities, assuming ownership of forest or paddy land that errant borrowers had offered as means of settling their debts.

Likewise, agricultural households commonly engaged in some form of cottage industry to supplement their incomes. One of the most widespread of such industries was the production of raw silk. Farmhouses in this region were generally built with low-ceilinged second stories for raising silkworms. Marginal paddy land was converted to growing mulberry trees, as their leaves were used to feed the worms. Other sources of supplementary income included the provision of horses or oxen as traction animals, hauling firewood down from the mountains, and short-term labor service.

The strategy of diversified subsistence activity thus has a long history in this region, and has continued into the present day. Japanese farming households rarely gain access to enough land to support themselves solely through the sale of their commodities, and while most continue to identify themselves as "agricultural households" (nōka), farm income must be supplemented with some type of wage labor or salaried employment. As a result, farming has become largely a part-time activity conducted on weekends or delegated to the older members of the household.

The seasonal round of labor has remained basically the same over the past several hundred years, though technological innovations have allowed the work to be completed with increasingly less expenditure of time and physical energy. Also, irrigation systems in which the water flowed through adjacent plots, thereby linking the community into a cohesive unit, have been replaced by an arrangement of rectangular paddies with irrigation ditches running between them in parallel lines so that every individual paddy can tap directly into one of the ditches. The result is that rice cultivation has become less dependent on the coordinated efforts of neighboring cultivators and more an independent family or household endeavor. Each household retains enough grain for its own consumption, and perhaps to supply kin-related households. The remainder is sold on the open market.

The pattern of land ownership is one of scattered, non-contiguous plots. Thus a single household may own paddies in several different locations in and around the central basin area, separated by considerable distances. Most of the work is now done using machinery, which has to be hauled from paddy to paddy on small, snub-nosed pick-up trucks with dropping side panels. Narrow access roads have been built along the main irrigation ditches running between the paddies to accommodate these trucks. The township is currently engaged in a government-subsidized project to pave all the access roads.

Rice is also important as the main ingredient in brewing *sake,* and about fifteen percent of the rice grown in Furukawa is destined for this purpose. A successful manufacturing enterprise requires not only a readily available supply of raw materials but also an accessible market for its product. It is not surprising, then, that most of the major *sake*-brewing households in Hida have been located in either Takayama or Furukawa, as the flat basin area surrounding these two municipalities contains the highest concentrations of both people and paddy land. Two major *sake*-brewers remain in Furukawa, the Kaba and Watanabe households. Though rivals in a single enterprise, their houses ironically stand in close proximity along the same street. Both have been prominent and highly respected members of the community for many generations.

Another major survival is the timber industry, and Furukawa is home to a number of small lumber yards. Most of the surrounding mountain land is now privately owned, though many of the less accessible areas are held by the government. A small portion is still communally owned and utilized. The lumber companies acquire rights to the timber only, clear-cutting small sections of forest and then replanting them before moving on, much in the manner of slash-and-burn agriculture. Most of the timber contracted in this fashion is pine, particularly *hinoki* (Japanese cypress), which combines great strength with flexibility and is therefore highly valued as a building material. The large, virgin stands of *hinoki* have, of course, long since disappeared, and new stands require a considerable length of time to reach maturity. As a result, demand has greatly exceeded supply, and the price for *hinoki* has sky-rocketed. Most new home-builders have had to settle for less expensive grades of timber imported from overseas, restricting use of the native *hinoki* to the house's main weight-bearing pillar *(chūbashira)* and perhaps some of the long horizontal crossbeams.

Though the traditional industries are still much in evidence, they have long been eclipsed by the small manufacturing and service sectors. The most dramatic shift from agrarian to commercial/industrial employment occurred during the early postwar period, but the trend has continued in recent decades. In 1975 about fifteen percent of the working population in Furukawa Township was directly involved in agriculture. By 1995 the proportion had slipped to just under nine percent. The service industry, on the other hand, expanded from sixteen to twenty-two percent during the same period, driven largely by the increase in tourism (to be discussed in Chapter 9). Construction held steady at around thirteen percent. Manufacturing did likewise at around thirty percent, one of the largest manufacturers in Furukawa being a pharmaceuticals company. The wholesale and retail industries have also stayed largely unchanged at around seventeen percent, though the number of small retail shops has declined considerably. The remainder of the population are involved in areas such as insurance and finance (two percent), transportation and communications (four percent), and civil administration (three percent) (Furukawa-chō Kikaku Shōkō Kankōka 1990:19, 1998:19).

State versus Region

The resources available in Hida are not solely of the material variety. Cultural tradition exists as a source of symbolic resources, and these too can be exploited by self-interested agents in pursuit of their own objectives. In the politics of collective identity, one such objective is generating a sense of shared tradition:

> Almost everywhere, it seems, the sense of belonging together is nourished by being cultivated in the fertile soil of the past. Even newly established collectivities quickly compose histories for themselves that enhance their members' sense of shared identity, while solidarity is fortified by a people's knowledge that their communal relations enjoy an historical provenance. (Brow 1990:2–3)

This is particularly applicable in a society like Japan, which places great emphasis on genealogical primacy and has such a long and venerable history to exploit (Nakane 1970:91; Robertson 1991).

The earliest mention of Hida in the historical record is the story of Ryōmen Sukuna, which appears in the *Nihon shoki* (*Chronicles of Japan,* the written version of which was completed in the year 720 C.E.). According to this account, there lived in Hida Province an unusual personage named Ryōmen Sukuna (*"ryōmen"* means "double-faced;" *"sukuna"* refers to an evil being or demon), who had two faces aligned in opposite directions and joined at the crown. Each face was served by its own set of appendages, resulting all together in four arms and four legs attached to a single trunk. The *sukuna* displayed great strength and agility, and is supposed to have taken pleasure in harassing the local people. He carried swords on both sides of his body and could shoot arrows using all four arms at once.

Confident in his physical prowess, the *sukuna* refused to acknowledge the authority of the imperial Yamato government, which was based in the Kansai area near present-day Osaka. Thereupon Emperor Nintoku, during the 65th year of his reign (purportedly 377 C.E.), dispatched a military general named Naniwanoneko Takefurukuma to vanquish the creature (see Aston 1886:298). This passage is thought to represent the subjugation of Hida by the imperial Yamato government, and may derive from an actual clash with a local Hida chieftain. The date, however, fails to mesh with the archaeological evidence, which shows no indication of Yamato influence until the latter half of the fifth century (Ōno 1983:108). Hida appears to have been formally established as a province under the imperial government sometime during the 660s (Tokoro 1989:864).

The *Nihon shoki* was of course written from the perspective of the imperial court as an effort to legitimize its authority over other territories. It therefore describes Ryōmen Sukuna as an unjust and rebellious ruler who deserved to be eliminated.[8] The entire episode is thus presented in terms of a civilizing mission, whereby the benefits of just government are bestowed upon a remote and backward region.

Indigenous folk legends, however, suggest an alternative point of view. They describe Ryōmen Sukuna as a benevolent ruler who perished trying to defend his people against the imperial forces (Taga 1988:4–5). According to these accounts, the two faces represent the strong and compassionate sides to his personality. In fact local depictions of the *sukuna* figure evoke images of the Bodhisattva Kannon (a personification of mercy), who was similarly equipped with multiple sets of appendages. The *sukuna* is customarily represented bearing a woodsman's ax; this is an obvious allusion to the local forested mountain environment, contrasting with the lowland rice plains which sustained the central government. Such depictions reveal autonomous—one might even suggest nativist—sentiments, and an underlying opposition to outside authority.

As part of the Taika Reforms instituted in 646 C.E., the imperial government had initiated a new tax system requiring all provinces under its jurisdiction to provide annual tribute either in the form of rice, other agricultural products, or labor service to the capital. In the ancient imperial ranking of provinces into four levels—"great" *(dai)*, "high" *(jō)*, "middle" *(chū)*, and "low" *(ge)*—Hida was jokingly referred to as a *"ge ge no gekoku"*—"low, low, low province" (Kuwatani 1971:12; Haga 1991:4). With their rugged terrain and harsh climate, the people of Hida could scarcely cultivate enough grain to satisfy their own demands, let alone send any surplus to the capital. They could, however, boast an abundance of high-quality timber and a number of woodworkers skilled in its utilization. The Taihō Code issued in 701 C.E. thus exempted Hida from the rice tribute, requiring instead the corvée labor of carpenters and sawyers. For every fifty households, ten such individuals were to be sent each year to the capital, where they were put to work building temples, shrines, and administrative facilities.

The Hida carpenters became so highly renowned for their skill that people in the capital began referring to them as the "Hida *takumi*" (artisans of Hida). A poem from the *Man'yōshū*[9] compares their unwavering devotion to their craft to the straightness of a carpenter's chalkline:

Kanikaku ni	In any case,
mono wa omowazu	with thoughts of nothing else,
Hidabito no	like the Hida people's
utsu-suminawa no	chalkline struck,
tada hito michi ni.	(I yearn) toward a single path.[10]

Their devotion to the imperial government, however, was apparently somewhat less certain. It seems that many of the *takumi* objected to the heavy labor required of them and tried to run away. A directive issued by the government in 796 C.E. requests their apprehension and return. It notes that Hida people are easily recognizable by their distinctive language and facial features, suggesting they were considered a separate ethnic category (Kuwatani 1971:30; Ōno 1983:108; Taga 1988:3–4). A ninth-century manuscript referred to as *Tōdaiji Fuju Monkō* mentions that the languages of Hida, the *emishi*,[11] and the eastern part of Japan are impossible to comprehend (Ōno 1983:108).

Most of the *takumi* eventually returned to their native Hida, bringing with them the skills they had acquired during their sojourn in the capital. The corvée labor requirement thus established a channel for introducing the refined court culture to the home province, and many of the important shrine and temple buildings located throughout the Hida region are attributable to the influence of the *takumi*. The system of obligatory labor service ended sometime during the latter part of the Heian (794–1185) period, but the tradition of fine wood crafting has survived in Hida to the present day, complementing the prolific timber industry.

The Heian period was followed by several centuries of feudal rule, which together constitute Japan's medieval era. Centralized authority was loosely maintained through the agency of a military dictator, referred to by the title *"shōgun,"* who was supposedly ruling in the name of the imperial family. The provinces were administered by local warlords linked to the *shōgun* through feudal ties of loyalty.

The feudal economy was based on rice production. Warlord governors extracted wealth from their peasant constituency by means of an annual land tax, which was levied in kind as a proportion of the harvest. This was known as *"nengu,"* or "annual tribute." The tax could range as high as sixty percent and placed a heavy financial burden on the actual cultivators, but as a proportion rather than a fixed amount it at least ensured that something would be left over for their own subsistence.

The emperor was briefly restored to power in 1333. By this time, however, the mechanisms of centralized authority had largely broken down, and control of Hida and other outlying regions was being contested by local warlords. The imperial house had split into two rival branches, each claiming to represent the legitimate line of descent. One of these branches moved out of Kyoto and founded a new government in the mountains of Yoshino to the south. This became known as the "southern court." The other branch remained in Kyoto under the tutelage of military general Ashikaga Takauji, who had assumed the title of *shōgun* along with the authority it implied.

In 1334, the southern court assigned one of its own generals, Anegakōji Ietsuna, to establish control over Hida Province. Ietsuna located his headquarters in what is now the Furukawa basin, and built a castle there to help defend it. The castle, known as Kojima-*jō* (-*jō* being a suffix denoting "castle"), is believed to have been located on a hill overlooking the area presently occupied by Sugisaki hamlet, just downstream from Furukawa.

In 1371, Ietsuna took some of his troops and headed north

toward the Toyama plain to help counter the Ashikaga forces, leaving younger brother Masatsuna to rule in his absence. Masatsuna was later killed in battle while defending the territory from some of Ashikaga's troops who were trying to invade from the northeast. The Anegakōji line subsequently split into three branches. One of them remained headquartered in Kojima-*jō*, another occupied a second castle located atop a hill on the other side of the Miya River in what is now Takano hamlet, and the third built yet another castle further downstream at the northern end of the basin. In this divided condition the Anegakōji clan grew increasingly weak and their territory began to collapse inward toward the center.

By the mid-fifteenth century, Hida Province was occupied by three separate warrior lineages. The Anegakōji retained control of the Furukawa basin. The Ema clan had moved in from the northwest to occupy the Kamioka area. The southern half of Hida (consisting of present-day Mashita and Ōno counties) was held by the Mitsuki clan—former allies of the Ashikaga. During the next several decades the Mitsuki became increasingly powerful and began to extend their control to the north. With the backing of powerful warlord Oda Nobunaga, they were eventually able to displace both the Anegakōji and Ema clans. In 1582 Mitsuki Yoritsuna took over the whole of Hida Province. He established his headquarters in the Takayama basin, located in Hida's very center. From this time forward, administrative control of the province would issue from the Takayama basin, positioned near the headwaters of the Miya River —not the Furukawa basin located further downstream.

Yoritsuna refused to align with the great general Toyotomi Hideyoshi following Oda Nobunaga's death. In 1586, Hideyoshi sent one of his own retainers, Kanamori Nagachika, to eliminate the Mitsuki resistance. Kanamori defeated the Mitsuki forces in 1586 and in return was granted Hida province as his own personal domain.

The Kanamori clan went on to fight at the Battle of Sekigahara on the side of Tokugawa Ieyasu, and were allowed to retain control of their Hida domain after Ieyasu established his new unifying government at Edo (now Tokyo). In 1692, however, the Kanamori were transferred to another province, and Hida was placed under the direct authority of the Tokugawa military regime, or *bakufu* (literally "tent government").

Throughout the Tokugawa period (1603–1867), the territory directly administered by the *bakufu* never exceeded more than about a quarter of the entire Japanese land mass, this portion containing most of the major cities and other strategically important areas. The rest of Japan was broken up into as many as 250 semi-autonomous domains, each governed by a warlord with the *bakufu*'s consent. Hida was thus rather unusual in being located far from the center of power, yet nevertheless included as part of *bakufu*-controlled territory. Most historians believe the principal motivation for assuming direct control was access to Hida's rich timber and mineral resources (Kuwatani 1971:81; Ōno 1983:108; Tokoro 1989:867).

As previously mentioned, Hida was predominantly mountainous and not well suited for growing rice. Most of the arable land was concentrated in the Takayama and Furukawa basins. Villagers living higher up in the mountains were unable to meet the designated rice quota, so the *bakufu* allowed them an alternative: they were to cut timber from surrounding forests, then transport it for sale to major cities like Edo and Osaka. In this way they were able to pay the land tax in the monetary equivalent of rice.

The *bakufu* administered the province through the services of a local magistrate (referred to as *"daikan"*). This position was generally not hereditary, but occasionally remained in the same line of descent for two or three generations. Ōhara Hikoshirō, for example, was appointed magistrate in 1765, and following his death was succeeded by his son Ōhara Kamegorō in 1781. The Ōhara were thus responsible for enforcing a number of unpopular economic policies that touched off a wave of rebellions during the years 1771–1789. These are collectively known as the Ōhara rebellions, and are often cited as classic examples of peasant resistance during the Tokugawa period (Ōno 1983:109–110; Tokoro 1989:868).

The main point of contention was the payment of an annual land tax, or "tribute." Again, many people in Hida had to engage in some form of wage labor—most commonly the cutting of timber—then credit their wages toward the rice tribute. The exchange rate for converting between rice and money was based on an average of the market price in five regional rice markets, one in Takayama and the others in neighboring provinces. This kept the rate within reasonable limits. In 1771, however, Ōhara Hikoshirō, the appointed magistrate, ordered the institution of a fixed exchange rate—one which made the monetary equivalent of rice much higher than before. At about the same time, the *bakufu* decreed that cutting timber in Hida would be temporarily suspended to avoid overexploiting the forests.

This left mountain dwellers with no means of generating the income necessary to substitute for the rice tribute, and many were forced to borrow from wealthy merchants. Late that same year, peasants from all over Hida gathered at Kokubun Temple just outside Takayama to demonstrate their opposition to these policies. The mob grew increasingly hostile and proceeded to wreck the homes of four local rice merchants who were seen as profiting from the new exchange rate.[12] Ōhara ordered the rebel leaders arrested; one of them was sentenced to death and three others banished.

In 1773, the *bakufu* initiated a new land survey for all territories under its immediate jurisdiction. The peasants opposed such surveys, which invariably revealed greater cultivated surface area than previously recorded. Since the land tax was based on annual yield estimates, greater surface area automatically translated into higher tax payments. Ōhara assured the Hida peasantry that the survey was aimed only at newly reclaimed land; old established arable would not be included. When the actual work began, however, the peasants noted with horror that the magistrate had lied—the surveyors were measuring both old and new arable and being very meticulous in their assessments. Peasant leaders appealed to Ōhara to discontinue the survey, but to no avail. They even went to the extent of petitioning senior officials of the *bakufu* in Edo, a breach of feudal protocol that was punishable by death; again they were denied. This touched off another wave of rebellion far more widespread than the first.

The peasant leaders needed a central location at which to gather and coordinate their efforts. The head priests at Suimu Shrine,[13] located at the drainage divide just south of Takayama, offered the use of their shrine compound. As sacred space, the compound was supposedly off-limits to violent intrusion, and was thus seen as a place of refuge. The priests at Suimu at that time espoused a form of Shinto–Buddhist syncretism, and they began to pray for the peasants' success.

With autumn approaching, the peasants adopted a new tactic: they would stop the supply of basic necessities such as grain, vegetables, and firewood to the townspeople of Takayama, thereby crippling the region's economy and forcing concessions. Peasants refused to sell their commodities in Takayama, and blockades were set up on roads leading into town to waylay supplies from the outside.

The supply stoppage began to exert its effect; the townspeople were running out of the basic necessities with cold weather approaching. Ōhara was outraged. Having no troops of his own, he called in warriors from neighboring domains to crush the rebellion. The soldiers of Gujō domain (bordering Hida to the southwest) were particularly ruthless. In a notorious incident, they ambushed a mob of peasants fleeing for Suimu Shrine and opened fire with muskets. Several of the peasants were killed or injured. Those already within the shrine compound began chanting to Amida Buddha, but the soldiers stormed in regardless and captured them. Twenty-one peasants were executed for their role in the rebellion, including the two priests of Suimu Shrine who had offered their compound as sanctuary. Many of the other participants were banished, imprisoned, or fined.

The new land survey resulted in a twenty-five percent increase in the official yield estimate. This translated into an additional eleven thousand bales of rice (one bale weighing approximately sixty kilograms) required annually from the Hida peasantry in meeting their tax quota. Ironically, the additional revenue moved Ōhara into a higher administrative category (from *"daikan"* to *"gundai"*). His good fortune was short-lived, however. On the day of his promotion, Ōhara's wife committed suicide, apparently out of remorse for all the peasants who had suffered under her husband's iron hand. Shortly thereafter the magistrate himself went blind; he fell ill and passed away in 1779. His son, Ōhara Kamegorō, was assigned to succeed him.

The son proved equally disagreeable, embezzling public funds meant to assist the destitute, then bribing officials of the *bakufu* to cover his indiscretions. Finally the peasants were able to register their complaints with one of the *shōgun*'s senior advisors in Edo, who promptly ordered an investigation. The young Ōhara was found guilty of corrupt government and sent into exile, while several of his top officials were sentenced to death. By appealing repeatedly to the Tokugawa government (as well as sacrificing a few of their own members), the peasants of Hida had prevailed. The entire episode is often used as an example of the importance of unity, persistence, and selfless devotion to a just cause.[14]

On the whole, however, peasant disturbances in Hida were relatively few, especially compared with Shinano Province (now Nagano Prefecture) immediately to the east. In fact, throughout the

Tokugawa period, while the population of Japan as a whole stayed more or less the same or even declined slightly, the population of Hida steadily increased. Rising population, together with the relative absence of peasant uprisings, suggest that subsistence needs were being adequately met. This is largely attributable to reduced numbers of parasitic samurai and the lower land tax requirement, both characteristic of areas directly controlled by the Tokugawa *bakufu* (Akagi 1935; Tsubouchi 1981). In the aftermath of the Ōhara rebellions, the land tax payment for villages in and around the Takayama and Furukawa basins was cut by one-third. Some of the villages located further up in the mountains were assigned to pay the tax in soybeans instead of rice; the remainder were once again allowed to pay in currency based on the lower market-indexed exchange rate.

In addition, the *bakufu* established two rice distribution policies aimed at ensuring inexpensive rice for people who were unable to produce sufficient quantities themselves. The first of these policies was known as *"ninbetsumai"* (census rice) and was directed at residents of the larger towns such as Takayama and Furukawa who had no access to paddy land of their own. The second policy, *"yamagatamai"* ("mountain region rice"), was to assist the inhabitants of remote mountain villages where arable land was scarce, who made their living primarily by cutting timber. Both policies offered its target populations rice that was considerably cheaper than that available on the open market.

In 1853, Commodore Matthew Perry sailed into Edo Bay with his infamous "black ships,"[15] demanding that Japan end its self-imposed isolation and open its ports to foreign trade. Faced with the military might of the industrializing West, the Tokugawa regime was left with little alternative but to comply. To the rest of the country, however, the *bakufu* had shown itself weak in failing to deal forcefully with the threat from abroad. In 1868, the old regime was overthrown by a coalition of rebellious domains. This event is known as the "Meiji Restoration," as its purported aim was to restore the emperor Meiji to direct rule. In reality, however, power was retained by the group of leaders who had engineered the revolution.

The new leadership effected the appearance of a constitutional monarchy, patterned after European models. By transforming purportedly indigenous religious traditions into a nationalist ideology known as State Shinto, they attempted to direct the Japanese people's allegiance toward the central authority of the state, as symbolized by the emperor. Government rhetoric emphasized what all Japanese shared, ignoring obvious linguistic, cultural, and socioeconomic distinctions. Efforts to rid Japan of competing allegiances included the persecution of Buddhism as a "foreign religion." At the same time, reference to Japan's supposedly divine origins served to mark the country as a sacred place distinct from the rest of the world. The encroachment of the West, conspicuously symbolized by Perry's arrival, provided a unifying threat from the outside.

To the people of Hida and other provincial areas, however, the threat lay not so much abroad as within the newly established nation-state itself. Shortly after taking power, the Meiji leadership assigned twenty-seven-year-old Umemura Hayami as the first governor of Hida, which was temporarily designated a self-constituting prefecture. The young governor, inspired by idealistic fervor, immediately initiated a number of dramatic reforms intended to "rationalize" the economy and enforce compliance with the administrative policies of the new central government. This included canceling the two popular rice distribution programs, *ninbetsumai* and *yamagatamai,* and returning the annual land tax payment to a fixed rate in hard currency. Such efforts were poorly received by the local population. The following year while Umemura was away in Kyoto the peasants of Hida rebelled, smashing and burning various administrative facilities as well as homes belonging to Umemura's leading supporters. Upon hearing news of the uprising, Umemura rushed back to Hida in an attempt to reassert his control. Soon after crossing the border into Hida, however, he and his soldiers were intercepted by a mob of angry peasants. During the fracas that ensued Umemura was shot, and later died in prison pending an official inquiry into his administrative policies.

The events outlined above occurred well in the past, and perhaps have little bearing in themselves on the present day. They are, however, incidents with which any Hida schoolchild is readily familiar (Takayama-shi Kyōiku Iinkai 1987; Furukawa-chō Kyōiku Iinkai 1990), and thus stand as symbolic qualifiers of a deeply rooted regional identity. Each of them sets the local area in opposition to centralized authority, providing a counterpoint to the rhetoric of unified nationalism. The subjugation of Ryōmen Sukuna, for example, represents the imposition of authority from the outside, an event which was contested in the local folk tradition. This pattern is repeated in relation to both the Hida *takumi* and the Ōhara rebellions, but is perhaps most poignantly represented by the Umemura incident. It is interesting to note that Umemura's return to Hida upon hearing news of the uprising retraces the path of Naniwano-neko Takefurukuma, the general sent to vanquish Ryōmen Sukuna. From the local perspective, the menace approached in both cases from the Kyoto area, the traditional locus of imperial authority.

Regional Center versus Auxiliary Town

In spite of the image I have portrayed of a provincial region united in opposition to the policies of the central government, Hida itself can hardly be said to represent a unified and homogeneous entity. Again, as a function of the drainage pattern, the northern portion of the Hida region (referred to as *"Oku-Hida"*) is associated with *"ura-Nihon,"* the so-called "backside" of Japan, as opposed to the *"omote,"* or "front," side of the country facing the Pacific Ocean. As might be expected, local people object to their home territory being referred to as the "backside." In fact, they insist, the coastline along the Sea of Japan was the original *"omote"* because it was oriented toward the Asian mainland, the locus of the outside world prior to Perry's arrival.

In the past, cultural influences from the coast followed the rivers upstream into the interior, as these represented the paths of least resistance in a mountainous terrain. Hida's geographical position, therefore, suggests a cultural ambivalence as well. Especially for the northern half, the drainage system links Hida with Toyama, the Noto Peninsula, and ultimately the Asian continent, in contrast to political authority issuing from the other direction.

In addition to the obvious geographical distinction formed by the drainage divide, there are socioeconomic, political, and cultural differences within the Hida region as well. In particular, there has been a long standing rivalry between the city of Takayama—located in the very heart of Hida and considered the region's economic and administrative center—and the somewhat smaller town of Furu-kawa located just downstream.

The two communities are similar in many ways: they occupy adjacent basins along the Miya River; both originated as castle towns laid out in parallel streets emulating Kyoto; both boast picturesque rows of old houses and a tradition of skilled wood crafting allegedly handed down from the Hida *takumi*. Furthermore, social structure in both communities was formerly dominated by a privileged stratum of wealthy landowners and merchants collectively known as *danna shū* (the "patron people").[16] Theirs is a story of shifting fortunes in which one household might rise dramatically to prominence only to tumble into obscurity one or two generations later. The landlord class as a whole was effectively dissolved through democratic reforms instituted after the Second World War (to be described in Chapter 9). A few, however, have managed to regain some of their former stature and continue to exert considerable influence in community affairs.

These patron households were a major factor in the political, economic, and cultural development of the Hida region. With their substantial wealth and taste for gracious living, they were able to import the accoutrements of cultural refinement from the urban centers of Kyoto and Edo. This is one of the main reasons provincial towns like Takayama attained such a high level of sophistication.

Furukawa, too, contained a number of prominent landowner and merchant households. In former times, in fact, the two towns were more nearly the same size, and rivaled each other in terms of economic stature. During the modern era, however, Takayama developed into a substantial city, expanding to fill most of its encompassing basin. It presently has around 65,000 inhabitants—nearly four times the population of Furukawa Township. Its economy is based largely on commercial activity, tourism being the major stimulus. Through the advertising media, Takayama has become virtually synonymous with Hida tradition, and tourists flock there in droves to bask in its nostalgic ambience.

Furukawa, on the other hand, remains a small town, its economy heavily based on agriculture and forestry. Though not lacking its own charm, it offers fewer of the amenities Japanese tourists have come to expect on excursions to the countryside to "rediscover their past."[17] Most visitors from major cities along the Pacific coast stop off at Takayama and return home from there, without venturing on to Furukawa.

Much of Takayama's appeal derives from its historical prominence. When Kanamori Nagachika assumed control of Hida Province in the late sixteenth century, he established his administrative headquarters at Takayama and erected a castle there. The location was strategically important in that it lay very close to the drainage divide separating Hida into its northern and southern watersheds. Takayama, whose name literally means "high mountain," was thus situated upstream from practically every other settlement in the province. In this sense geographical position reflected the administrative hierarchy, as all the other towns and villages in Hida were politically subordinate to Takayama.

In order to cover his northern flank, Nagachika stationed his adopted son Arishige about fifteen kilometers downstream in the neighboring basin. Arishige erected a castle of his own in the center of the basin, and the town of Furukawa developed adjacent to it. Furukawa was thus politically subordinate to Takayama, and from that time to the present day it has maintained a somewhat tributary relationship to the larger municipality.

Furukawa people are quick to point out, however, that their own basin was actually the first in Hida to be settled. As proof they point to its higher concentration of burial mounds and other archaeological remains dating from the Kofun period (roughly 300–710 C.E.). Since it is slightly larger and more productive than the Takayama basin, it has always been more important in terms of irrigated rice cultivation. When Anegakōji came to the province in the mid-fourteenth century, he located his headquarters there—not in the Takayama area.

But, with few exceptions, the historical prominence of provincial Japanese towns is measured by their status during the early modern period. Takayama is where the Kanamori based themselves, and Takayama is where the Tokugawa administration located its *jin'ya,* or regional administrative headquarters. As a result, Furukawa was doomed to remain politically subordinate to its upstream neighbor.

The Kanamori were aficionados of the refined Kyoto court tradition, and strove to introduce aspects of its art and architecture into their provincial domain. Takayama thus developed as one of the so-called "little Kyotos" scattered throughout central Japan. This is reflected in its grid-like street pattern and residential districts laid out in parallel bands.

Furukawa was arranged in similar fashion but on a smaller scale. It, too, could once boast an impressive castle with a number of samurai posted there to maintain it. In 1619, however, the Tokugawa *bakufu* issued a policy limiting each province to one castle. Thus while Takayama's castle was left intact (for the time being),[18] Furukawa's castle had its fortifications dismantled. For several decades the main building was kept as temporary housing (referred to as *"ryokan"*) for the Kanamori and other visiting dignitaries. But following takeover by the *bakufu* in 1692 the building itself was demolished and the site converted to a government rice distribution facility. Furukawa continued to prosper as a relay station along the western branch of the old Etchū Highway running north to Toyama, but had forever lost its claim to castle town status.

Both the Ōhara magistrates, provincial administrators for the *bakufu,* and Umemura Hayami, the idealistic young governor appointed by the Meiji leadership, were headquartered in Takayama. Thus, from the perspective of Furukawa, Takayama was the direction from which their hated edicts were issued. As one of Hida's major rice producers, Furukawa was naturally drawn into the center of both disturbances. During the final phase of the Ōhara rebellions, two residents of the Furukawa area were convicted for their role as instigators; both died in prison. Memorial services are held in their honor to this day.[19] It is also a matter of local pride that the Furukawa fire brigade led the attack on Umemura when he attempted to return from Kyoto. The Takayama fire brigade, on the other hand, continually lagged behind, appearing reluctant to join in the fray (see Ōno 1971c). This episode is fondly remembered by Furukawa residents, as it represents one of the few instances in which they managed to best their Takayama rivals.

Indeed, the people of Furukawa have a reputation throughout the Hida region for exhibiting aggressive, unruly behavior, especially when their own interests are at stake. This is implicit in their use of the term "Furukawa *yancha.*" As previously mentioned, the term is often used derisively by residents of surrounding towns and villages in denouncing what they consider a rough, uncivilized quality. In Furukawa, however, it is invoked with pride, and even celebrated in the name of a local brand of *sake.* It also stands as an important symbol of collective identity, especially in opposition to other communities like Takayama. Kaba (1984:36) describes "Furukawa *yancha*" as a combination of "gallantry and reckless violence, mixed with reproach—a term which appropriately expresses the spirit of the people of Furukawa."

Opinions vary as to the origin of the term. Some trace it back to the time of the Ōhara rebellions, when a contingent of about 200 peasants from Furukawa broke into the magistrate's headquarters in Takayama demanding a decrease in the land tax. Others attribute it to Furukawa's leading role in rising against the young governor Umemura, and more specifically the fact that the Furukawa fire brigade led the mob that intercepted him. A few mention an incident in which Furukawa had to steal its *mikoshi* back from Sugisaki, or the time a man from a neighboring village was found murdered in the riverbed the day after the *matsuri* (to be described more fully in Chapter 6; see Kuwatani 1969:23–25; Sugata 1975). Most, however, simply ascribe the *yancha* spirit to the behavior displayed during the performance of the *okoshi daiko*. On that night, it is said, people became barbaric *(yaban ni natta)*. Members of rival neighborhoods engaged in open fighting, and the police were afraid to go out in uniform for fear of being accosted by local rowdies (Kuwatani 1965:9; 1969:25; Kaba 1984:36).

In any case, such perceptions have engendered a kind of self-fulfilling prophecy, as the townspeople will invoke the *yancha* spirit in insisting on having their way. This has been a particular problem in disputes with neighboring villages over such issues as rights to irrigation water.

In the area of cultural achievements, however, Furukawa has consistently had to settle for second place. Indeed, much of its own cultural development has come by way of imitating Takayama. Furukawa is often described as the "younger sibling," seeking to emulate Takayama's grandeur but at the same time being resentful of always having to remain in its shadow (Mabuchi 1990:56–57).

The resentment is clearly noticeable in local attitudes. Furukawa people consider Takayama a rather cold, impersonal place where social interaction is governed by strict hierarchical principles, status consciousness is stronger, and boundaries between social strata are more rigidly defined. Their own town, they insist, is more egalitarian, its people hospitable and warm. Owing to its smaller size, neighbors in Furukawa interact with greater ease and frequency. Even the more prominent households remain readily accessible to their fellow townspeople, displaying little of the pompous arrogance attributed to their Takayama counterparts.

As might be expected, Takayama residents see things differently. They often refer to Furukawa using the rather disparaging epithet *"inaka"* (meaning "the country" or "countryside," but having connotations similar to "the boondocks"), relegating its people to the status of country bumpkins. This, they say, is revealed in Furukawa speech patterns, clothing style, and overall demeanor—particularly the unruly *yancha* attitude. To the people of Takayama, this attitude betrays a lack of sophistication and civility—a failure to comply with the proper order.

In sum, as Hida's second major town Furukawa constituted a substantial population of independently minded people, who occupied a principal rice-producing area but also benefitted from a fairly well-developed commercial economy. These factors are important because they developed *outside* the region's major locus of political authority. Furukawa thus posed a potentially subversive element—a rival town, resentful of having to bow to Takayama's wishes while at the same time possessing both the wealth and critical mass of people to aspire to greater influence itself. In a sense, Takayama has become the outside referent against which Furukawa's own collective identity is asserted. The people of Furukawa use their traditional rivalry with Takayama, the *yancha* attitude, and its ritualized expression via the *okoshi daiko* as symbolic qualifiers in perpetuating this identity.

One other unifying threat should perhaps be considered—that posed by natural forces. The Japanese are often said to be characterized by a "typhoon mentality," meaning that since their archipelago is prone to various destructive forces such as typhoons, earthquakes, tsunami, and flooding they have become highly mindful that humans are at the mercy of nature's vagaries and must take adequate precautions. Natural conditions, demographics, and the economic policies of the central government at times resulted in famine. This became a major concern in Hida during the late eighteenth century, and was partly what touched off the Ōhara rebellions. The larger communities were sometimes afflicted by disease epidemics, particularly cholera (Jannetta 1987). Furukawa experienced a serious cholera epidemic in 1886, which claimed the lives of many residents (Furukawa-chō 1986:235–237). In fact the epidemic led to the annual *matsuri* being moved from autumn to spring, as will be described later.

Fire, too, was an ever-present threat in communities like Furukawa, where the houses were made of flammable materials and placed in close proximity to one another. Furukawa was devastated by fire on two occasions, one in 1865 and the other in 1904. The latter incident is one of the most memorable tragedies in Furukawa's history. The fire broke out around noon on August 25, and within two hours had destroyed almost the entire town (Kuwatani 1970: 194–195; Furukawa-chō Kyōiku Iinkai 1987:513–519). It is said to have started at a tofu shop when some water fell into a vat of hot oil.

The following day, the owner is reported to have walked barefoot from site to site, apologizing to every member household (Kuwatani 1970:194–195). In response to the fire, shrines dedicated to Akiba, the fire deity, were erected all over town, one in every component neighborhood. To this day rituals are performed before these shrines on March 23–24 to request the deity's protection.

The great fire of 1904 evokes yet another strand of local tradition —this relating to the young women who went to work in the silk factories of neighboring Nagano Prefecture during the mid-Meiji (1868–1912) period. At that time the Japanese government was promoting silk as a marketable commodity overseas. Huge factories were established in Nagano and other areas to convert raw silk into thread. Girls about 12–14 years of age—that is, after they had completed the compulsory six years of education but before being married—were often sent by their parents to work in the factories to provide an additional source of cash income. Daughters, at times considered a liability, now became a major asset: wage-labor opportunities were rare, and women working in the silk factories could generate greater income than men. According to some sources, working conditions for these women were less than ideal (Yamamoto 1977; Hane 1982:173–204; Tsurumi 1990), but the additional income allowed their families to build new houses and perhaps purchase land. This was the basis for Yamamoto's (1977) somewhat melodramatic portrayal of the factory women of Hida in his book *Aa, Nomugi Tōge (Ah! Nomugi Pass)*, which was later made into a popular film. One of the episodes deals with the young women of Furukawa who went to work in the silk factories so their families could rebuild their houses after the great fire (Yamamoto 1977: 58–72). Similarly, Nakamura et al. (1972:1–2), in an analysis of rapid concentration of land holdings around the turn of the century, suggest that Furukawa farm households sent their daughters to work in the factories in an effort to buy back land lost through foreclosure (to be described later in Chapter 7).

Religious Milieu

Communal identity is perhaps most conspicuously demonstrated through ritual behavior. As noted in the previous chapter, the Durkheimian approach to ritual has been criticized for placing undo emphasis on social solidarity, neglecting the individual experience, and ignoring the potential for introducing change (Goldenweiser 1917; Malinowski 1948:38; Lukes 1975; Morris 1987:121). Nevertheless, Durkheim's assertion that the object of religious reverence functions as a symbolic representation of the social group itself is appropriate in certain sociopolitical contexts. The attempt to justify the existing order by ritually investing it with supernatural legitimacy is a fairly common pattern.

One of the frequently cited features of Japanese society is that different religious traditions are able to coexist in relative harmony. Indeed, most of the people of Furukawa maintain a Buddhist as well as a Shinto affiliation. The reason commonly given to explain this peaceful coexistence is that the two religious traditions have achieved a kind of metaphysical division of labor, addressing themselves to different aspects of human concern (see, for example, Beardsley, Hall, and Ward 1959:453–454). Shinto deals with life and the living. It focuses on worship of supernatural entities called *kami*. These can be conceptualized as pervasive forces which animate nature, or personified in the form of spirits or deities. The practice of Shinto is highly ritualistic, relying on direct experience rather than the propagation of moral or ethical principles. Its rituals aim at maintaining harmony with nature, purification through the exorcism of evil spirits, and regeneration of nature's vital forces. Buddhism, on the other hand (as practiced in Japan), concerns itself largely with death and the afterlife. Its teachings are ethical or philosophical in nature, and its rituals are primarily designed to care for the souls of the deceased. This often translates into expressions of reverence for ancestral spirits, which are conceptually linked with the household or family line. Buddhism, in other words, emphasizes familial ties while Shinto emphasizes ecological and communal associations.

This strict division of labor, however, is largely a product of the Meiji Restoration, and has more to do with nationalist political ideology than any inherent qualities of the two religions themselves. Prior to the Meiji period, Shinto and Buddhism in Japan had been closely intertwined, the majority of the peasantry making no clear distinction between them. This was particularly true in the Hida region, where Buddhist temples and Shinto shrines were often found in close proximity, if not occupying the same compound, with the resident Buddhist priest commonly in charge of both. Buddhism, particularly Jōdo Shinshū, the True Pure Land sect of Mahayana

Buddhism, has historically been very strong throughout the Hida region and remains so to this day (Iwamizu 1985).

Hida's isolation during the winter led to the development of a Buddhist custom called *shōtai* (literally "invitation"). People were invited to gather at a local temple to listen to teachings delivered by a visiting member of the Buddhist clergy. These sessions were held during the winter months when other opportunities for entertainment were lacking, and thus served both religious and social functions.

In Furukawa the custom developed into a major annual event known as *"sandera mairi,"* or "three-temple pilgrimage." There are three main temples in Furukawa: Honkō-ji (Original Light Temple), Enkō-ji (Circle Light Temple), and Shinshū-ji (True Teaching Temple). All are exponents of the Hongan branch of the True Pure Land sect. They are located so as to form a triangle, roughly encompassing the central part of town.[20] On the evening of January 15, the traditionally accepted date of the Buddhist saint Shinran's death, these temples are illuminated and the townspeople walk from one to another, pausing briefly to worship at each. This also gives them an opportunity to greet their fellow residents and exchange best wishes for the coming year.

In contrast with Buddhism, Shinto establishes a distinct territorial identity through symbolic association with the local guardian deity. The generic term for such a deity is *ujigami,* which literally means "clan god." As the name implies, it originally referred to the god worshiped or revered by a particular lineage group. Typically this would be the ancestral founder of the group, who was later elevated to the status of a deity and revered by group members as their supernatural patron. Over time the concept came to be associated with a specific territorial region, with the god extending its protection over the people residing therein (Kitagawa 1987:140–141; Weinstein 1983; Robertson 1991:113).[21] These people are referred to as *ujiko* (literally "children of the clan"). The term is usually translated as "parishioner," but the original meaning implied the notion of having descended from the founding ancestor.

The physical structure dedicated to this deity is called a *jinja* (written with two characters meaning "deity" and "association"). The English gloss "shrine" is perhaps a bit misleading, as it suggests a place where the deity habitually resides. According to Shinto belief, a *jinja* is a place to which the spirit of the deity is invoked or summoned to interact with its parishioners. While the deity is ethereal, however, the shrine building is not; it occupies a particular space and extends its protection over a distinct territory. In fact the shrine building is often referred to as if it were the deity itself, and thus becomes yet another symbolic qualifier of collective identity.

In Furukawa, the territory under the deity's protection roughly conforms to the town boundaries.[22] The shrine for invoking the deity is called Ketawakamiya Jinja. It is located to the northeast of town in the foothills leading to Mt. Anbō. The mountains are considered sacred space, the realm of the *kami*. The shrine thus serves as a kind of intermediary between the sacred and profane worlds, situated at a point where the two intersect.

Furukawa's Buddhist temples, on the other hand, are located directly within the realm of the profane—the central town area itself. In the case of the temples, however, geographic location has little significance other than convenience of access. This has not always been the case. During the Tokugawa period, the government required all its subjects to register as members of a Buddhist temple. Groups of households were organized into *danka,* or temple support associations, responsible for the upkeep of the temple building and grounds as well as revering the souls of their ancestors who were memorialized therein. The *danka* system was originally conceived as a means of countering the influence of Christian missionaries, but later served to ensure compliance with official administrative policies and keep tabs on local populations. All births, deaths, marriages, and adoptions were recorded in a register for each household, kept by the temple to which it belonged. The *danka* system was abolished by the new government at the beginning of the Meiji period, and the household registries (now referred to as *koseki*) were taken over by local administrative offices. Though many households continued their association with the ancestral temple, membership was no longer defined by place of residence. Due to increasing demographic mobility, one's temple may now be located a considerable distance away. Reader (1991:89) notes that "[t]he bonds that link household, ancestors and temple are far more dependent on tradition and empathy than anything else."

Thus, compared with Shinto, Buddhism is less relevant to a sense of communal identity. It does, however, provide an alternative focus of religious veneration, free of the nationalist political ideology with which Shinto has at times been associated—particularly following

Figure 1. Ketawakamiya Shrine.

the Meiji Restoration. During that period, Shinto received official favor because its rituals could be used to acknowledge the legitimacy of imperial rule and uphold the authority of those in power. Anyone seeking to resist the government's hegemony would have found a natural support in Buddhism. This is particularly relevant in the case of True Pure Land Buddhism, which had a long history of defending the peasants against oppressive authorities. In Furukawa during the 1770s, for example, the head priest of Enkō-ji espoused a doctrine of defying government coercion, and this became a leading cause of the Ōhara rebellions (Ōno 1974c:1, Gotō 1983:74).

The most important event in both the religious and social calendars of Furukawa is undoubtedly the annual *matsuri,* a Shinto festival performed in honor of the local guardian deity.[23] The basic elements of the *matsuri* were outlined in Chapter 2. Again, the central feature is the *mikoshi* procession, whereby the deity's revitalizing presence is brought into direct association with its human constituents. In other parts of Japan the *mikoshi* is led on a raucous joyride —bounced and jostled through the streets on the shoulders of a mass of high-spirited celebrants. But in Hida the vehicle is borne along in a stately procession, escorted by a retinue of local dignitaries. The procession is led by a simple drum and bamboo flute ensemble. During the spring and autumn festival seasons it is common to hear drums echoing through the mountains as the deity of some nearby village makes its rounds.

Another characteristic feature of *matsuri* in this area is the *shishimai,* a dance depicting an imaginary animal called a *shishi.* (This animal is thought by some to resemble a lion, and *"shishimai"* is generally rendered into English as "lion dance.") Each *shishi* consists of two performers—one assuming the role of the head and forelegs and the other the back and hind legs. Together they are covered with a large piece of cloth to lend the appearance of a single body. The lead performer holds in his hands a lacquered wooden mask with a moveable chin. This he maneuvers in time with the rhythm of the dance, making the *shishi* appear to be raising, lowering, and rolling its head. The dancers, too, are accompanied by flute and drum musicians.

At festival time, teams of *shishi* roam the streets, performing a brief dance at the entrance to every home in return for a voluntary contribution. The alleged purpose of the dance is to drive away evil influences, though there is undeniable entertainment value as well.

The *shishi* are a special attraction for young children, who giggle with delight as the imaginary animal chases after them clacking its wooden jaws.

Shishi dancing and the music it entails together belong to a category of sacred folk performance known as *kagura*. The term is written with the characters for "deity" and "pleasure" and, as the resulting image suggests, refers to the act of entertaining the supernatural entities known as *kami* and thereby gaining their favor.

Intra-Communal Categories

As will be evident in the following chapters, planning and participating in the *matsuri* are intimately linked with the organizational structure of the town itself. Furukawa is laid out in a series of parallel streets numbered consecutively in order of their distance from the old castle site. Each street constitutes a distinct residential district known as a *machi*. The word *machi* is employed in a variety of contexts: it is a generic term for small towns like Furukawa, but it is also used in referring to a particular section within a town or city, in this case corresponding to the aggregation of houses lining both sides of a major street. Tonomachi, located adjacent to the old castle site, was originally inhabited by warrior retainers employed by the Kanamori; it is followed in order by Ichinomachi, Ninomachi, and Sannomachi.[24] A small stream called Setogawa runs between Tonomachi and the other sections; during the Kanamori era, this stream physically separated the warrior class from the commoner population. As the population expanded, a fifth residential district called Mukaimachi developed on the other side of the Araki River. *Mukai* means "across" or "beyond," referring to the location of the more recent settlement in relation to the rest of the town.

Within each district, the houses sit side by side, with little if any space between them. Such close proximity lends itself to frequent interaction, mutual attention and concern, and a distinct lack of privacy. Within such a context, common place of residence becomes the primary basis for establishing a sense of group identity—perhaps stronger than actual kinship ties (Leach 1961:7, 304–305; Nakane 1967:168, 1970:148; Kondo 1990:121–124). People who live near one another share their everyday experiences; their well-being is largely dependent on mutual assistance in times of need, and their security on maintaining harmonious social relations with neighbor-

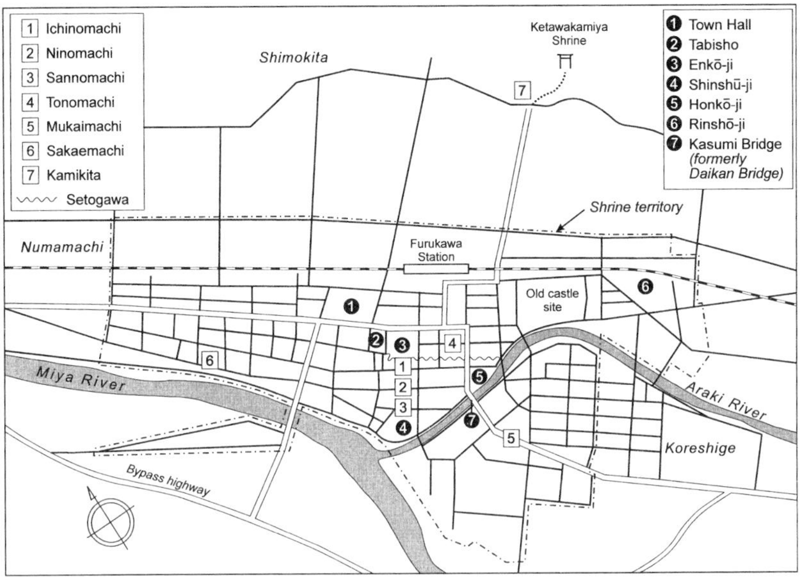

Map legend:

1	Ichinomachi
2	Ninomachi
3	Sannomachi
4	Tonomachi
5	Mukaimachi
6	Sakaemachi
7	Kamikita
〜〜〜	Setogawa

❶	Town Hall
❷	Tabisho
❸	Enkō-ji
❹	Shinshū-ji
❺	Honkō-ji
❻	Rinshō-ji
❼	Kasumi Bridge (formerly Daikan Bridge)

Shimokita · Ketawakamiya Shrine · Shrine territory · Numamachi · Furukawa Station · Old castle site · Miya River · Araki River · Koreshige · Bypass highway

Map 4. Street layout and major locations in Furukawa. Map by Patricia J. Conrad.

ing households. One of the basic principles of social organization in Furukawa is summed up by the phrase *"mukō sangen, ryō donari"* ("the three houses opposite, and the ones next door on either side"). This indicates that the closest bonds of reciprocity are with the three households immediately across the street from, as well as the two on either side of, one's own. These are the people one would turn to first and depend on most heavily in the event of a crisis such as fire or death in the household.[25] During the Edo period, one's own household could be held accountable for misdeeds committed by an errant neighbor, so the relationship also came to imply a certain degree of mutual surveillance.

Beyond the level of immediate neighbors, households residing in the same area are united into egalitarian clusters called *tonarigumi* (literally "neighbor groups"). Such groups were first organized by the government during the Second World War for the purposes of disseminating information, mobilizing defense efforts, and responding to emergencies such as the outbreak of fire. In Furukawa, the average size of these *tonarigumi* is ten to twelve households, with some containing as many as fifteen. These too provide mutual assistance in times of need, but more commonly serve the purpose of distributing information.

Tonarigumi are in turn united into residential blocks called *ku,* each with its own internally elected leader. These blocks are officially designated political units, and are generally mobilized for community cleanup and other projects. The informal, and for the purposes of the *matsuri* more important, unit is the *chōnai* (literally "within the town"),[26] which in this analysis will be glossed as "neighborhood." The town of Furukawa is divided into eleven such neighborhoods. In most cases their borders coincide with one of the official block designations. Some of the larger neighborhoods, however, encompass as many as four blocks.

As Bestor (1989) has asserted, such neighborhoods are not officially designated political units; they are informal associations, constituted and maintained through the collective efforts of their member households. In Furukawa, the most important function for which these neighborhood units are mobilized is the planning and execution of the *matsuri.* In fact it is questionable whether the *chōnai* could continue to exist as meaningful social groups without the *matsuri* to engage them.

As mentioned in the previous chapter, the annual *matsuri* was a time when normal social constraints were temporarily abandoned; it was therefore conducive to the expression of inter-neighborhood rivalries. During the *matsuri,* the various neighborhoods were inclined to compete with one another for pride of place. At times this took the form of actual fighting. More typically it was expressed through competitive displays of spirited involvement, each neighborhood attempting to outdo the others.

One very visible product of this competition are the elaborate wooden festival wagons locally referred to as *"yatai"* (literally "roofed vehicle"). Such vehicles were originally intended as ways of attracting the deity and enticing its presence directly into the community of humans. Given the expensive materials required to build and embellish them, however, they soon became objects of great symbolic value. Each vehicle has its own history of alterations and repairs, often involving complete reconstruction at considerable expense to neighborhood residents. Rival neighborhoods have gone to great lengths trying to sponsor the most impressive vehicle.[27]

Competition is more overtly expressed, however, during the rousing drum ritual. Those same neighborhood associations that build and maintain *yatai* also field their own respective *tsuke daiko* teams, which clash with one another in advancing upon the main drum. The *matsuri* thus provides a context for asserting a sense of discrete neighborhood identity, and *yatai* and *tsuke daiko* become symbols of—indeed, one might say monuments to—such an identity.

The obvious criterion for establishing these neighborhood associations is spatial contiguity of member households. But residential affiliation alone is an insufficient basis for defining common interests. Neighborhood boundaries are embedded in other socioeconomic and political categories and the tensions they engender. This too is to some extent a legacy of the past. Most of Furukawa's residents were farmers engaged in irrigated rice cultivation. However, owing to its role as a secondary commercial center serving the northern portion of Hida Province, a substantial number of merchant households had been established there as well. As a result, Furukawa combined the characteristics of both farm village and commercial town, as the term *hannō–hanshō* ("half agricultural–half commercial") implies. The most prominent townspeople were located in the two interior sectors, Ichinomachi and Ninomachi. Ichinomachi was occupied mostly by artisans and manufacturers, including the large *sake*-brewing households alluded to earlier. Ninomachi lined the main thoroughfare running through the center of town, linking Furukawa with other towns and villages; not surprisingly, most of the merchants were congregated there. Many of the large landowner households were also located in Ninomachi. Tonomachi, near the old castle site, enjoys the distinction of having once been home to the Kanamori warlords and their retainers. Following the transfer of the Kanamori, however, Tonomachi came to be overwhelmingly occupied by farming families. Sannomachi, on the other side of town, was also primarily agricultural, but contained a fair number of carpenters and other artisans. Mukaimachi originally consisted of only a few households clustered on the opposite side of the Araki River, most of them belonging to poor tenant farmers. Later it developed a sizable population, and contained a number of eating and drinking establishments.

Thus residential affiliation reflected occupation and social status. The majority of residents in Tonomachi, Sannomachi, and Mukaimachi were small landowner and tenant farmers. They undoubtedly harbored some resentment toward the prosperous landlords, merchants, and artisans of the interior sectors. Rivalry among the various neighborhoods, therefore, automatically invokes socioeconomic distinctions based on differential wealth and prominence. As a "cultural performance," the *matsuri* has been the most explicit manifestation of these various social and territorial distinctions.

This chapter has introduced a bewildering array of social configurations, from informal groupings such as household cluster *(tonarigumi)*, neighborhood association *(chōnai)*, residential district *(machi)*, and region *(chihō)* to official political units such as block *(ku)*, township *(chō)*, county *(gun)*, prefecture *(ken)*, and state *(kokka)*. The boundaries of these various social entities interweave and overlap, regardless of whether they are officially constituted. Which level is activated at any given time depends on the needs and aspirations of the individuals concerned. The sense of collective identity can either expand to include larger numbers of people or contract into a more exclusive membership. The resulting pattern may be envisioned as a series of concentric circles, progressively moving away from the center, where the self resides, to encompass ever-increasing numbers of people at higher levels of organizational complexity. Ultimately the boundaries can be expanded to include the entire nation, resulting in assertions of a homogeneous race and culture, distinct from the rest of the world.

As a major event that brings together masses of people under the pretext of a sacred observance, the local *matsuri* provides a forum for negotiating these various identities, as well as the self-interested motives they engender. It is to a detailed examination of this event that I now turn.

Chapter 4

FURUKAWA *MATSURI:* PERFORMANCE

The Furukawa *matsuri* is performed every April 19–21. It is scheduled to coincide with the emerging cherry blossoms and the long-awaited arrival of warmer weather. It is also seen as a prelude to the spring planting season, as local farmers begin tilling their rice paddies shortly thereafter. Spring *matsuri* in general derive from the tradition of petitioning the deities for a successful harvest. Such a petition had to be presented every year, and was considered an important rite of renewal.

The *matsuri* continues to be regarded as the most significant event of the year in the lives of the townspeople, far outweighing both the New Year festivities and mid-summer *Bon*[1] observances. Its agrarian origins, however, have long since been overshadowed by more socially oriented ideals. As a large-scale communal ritual, the *matsuri* is an event which mobilizes the entire town, drawing virtually every member household into its performative agenda.

Mobilization is achieved through an elaborate chain of command that mirrors the hierarchical structure of society in general. At the pinnacle is Ketawakamiya Shrine, which is dedicated to the local tutelary deity and sits in the hills overlooking the town.[2] The shrine is where the deity's presence is normally invoked. Once a year, however, the spirit of the deity is summoned forth and escorted down into the community to interact with its human constituents. This forms the core of the *matsuri* as a religious performance.

At the center of the performance is the shrine's leading exponent—the resident Shinto priest. Like his counterparts in shrines all over Japan, the priest's job consists mainly of ministering to the *kami* and conducting rituals on behalf of his parishioners. In communities the size of Furukawa this is a full-time occupation, and is often passed from father to son in a single line of succession. The current priest claims to represent the twentieth generation in his household to occupy the position—a lineage extending back over 250 years.

Next to the priest, the most influential figures connected with the shrine are the seven *ujiko sōdai,* or parish elders.[3] These are not professional clergymen; rather, they are prominent members of the lay population who donate their time to help manage the affairs of the shrine. Their duties consist mostly of attending to mundane logistical and budgetary concerns and participating in important events in the ritual calendar of the shrine.

The parish elders serve not as advocates of their own neighborhoods but as general representatives of all the people residing within the shrine's territory. One of them is chosen on a rotating basis to serve as their head *(ujiko sōdaichō).* In terms of the *matsuri,* this individual is recognized as holding ultimate authority for orchestrating the event, and is often referred to as *shinji torishimari* (supervisor of sacred rites). There is one additional individual on roughly the same level as the parish elders. He is referred to as a *sōdanyaku,* or consultant, and assumes the role of impartial observer.

As described in the previous chapter, the town of Furukawa is divided into eleven neighborhood associations, called *chōnai.* For the purposes of the *matsuri,* however, these associations are referred to as *taigumi,* or "*yatai* groups."[4] To the outsider this seems rather confusing and unnecessary, as the terms *chōnai* and *taigumi* are virtually synonymous. In fact the use of *taigumi* represents a clever way to bypass the legal separation of politics and religion, as specified by the postwar Japanese constitution. The *matsuri* is, after all, a Shinto observance, while *chōnai* are supposed to be purely secular groupings.

In addition to these eleven *taigumi,* there is one other neighborhood association that plays an important role in the *matsuri.* This is the Miyamoto-*gumi.* It is composed of residents from Kamikita, a cluster of houses at the base of the shrine grounds and separated from the town proper by a stretch of rectangular rice paddies.[5] The Miyamoto-*gumi* members consider it their duty to look after and protect the shrine *(jinja o mamoru).* They are thus in a sense elevated above the rest of the town, both geographically and in terms of their special status as shrine caretakers. In fact, Kamikita once comprised a community distinct from the rest of Furukawa. Though its residents play an active role in the *matsuri*, the nature of their participation is significantly different from that of the other neighborhoods. Miyamoto-*gumi* was traditionally the only neighborhood group that did not field a *tsuke daiko* team. In fact, until a few years ago it had never participated in the Rousing Drum ritual in any capacity. The reasons for this will become clear in the following chapters.

Each of the eleven *taigumi* selects one individual to serve as its official representative. These representatives hold the title *taigumi sōdai* (hereinafter referred to as "*taigumi* leaders"), and are immediately subordinate in authority to the parish elders. Miyamoto-*gumi*, too, provides a representative of its own at this same level, for a total of twelve individuals.

The *taigumi* leaders are assisted by the *jinja iin,* or shrine commissioners. One such representative is selected from each of the twenty municipal blocks *(ku)* which constitute the shrine's territory. However, since the *taigumi* themselves are divided according to block boundaries, each of the shrine commissioners is in turn linked to a particular *taigumi.* The number of commissioners to which each *taigumi* is entitled, therefore, depends on the number of blocks its neighborhood comprises. This is justified by the fact that the larger neighborhoods contain more people and thus require additional administrative attention.

It is apparent at this level that a hierarchy of authority deriving from the shrine has co-opted the institutions of local political administration—namely the official block designations employed by the town government. Even more to the point, the blocks are made directly subordinate to the neighborhood *taigumi.* The next higher institution within the civil administration above block level—the town council—is bypassed altogether.

The seven parish elders, one consultant, twelve *taigumi* leaders, and twenty shrine commissioners are collectively referred to as the "shrine officers" *("jinja yakuin"),* totalling forty individuals.

The parish elders at the top of the hierarchy are elected by the other shrine officers from among their own numbers, similar to the manner in which a prime minister is chosen by members of the Diet. The elders serve for an undetermined period and retire only when they choose to do so. The qualifications mentioned most often for becoming a parish elder are good character and special leadership abilities. The elders are without exception influential members of the community.[6] It is not surprising then that these positions tend to run in the same family lines and that many of the elders belong to prominent prewar landlord households.

Unlike the parish elders, *taigumi* leaders and shrine commissioners serve for a fixed period of three years. Some of them move on to the higher levels, eventually becoming parish elders themselves. In return for the prestige that accompanies their positions, shrine officers are obliged to contribute a considerable amount of their own time and energy with no financial compensation. This tends to limit membership to established households who own and operate their own businesses. The heads of such households can afford to take time away from work, and often leave their eldest sons in charge of the business while they attend to important community affairs.

Yatai and Neighborhood

Other ethnographers have identified Japanese communities defined by guild membership (Moeran 1984; Kelly 1990), descent group affiliation (Brown 1968), occupational category (Bestor 1989; Kalland 1995b), religious practice (Davis 1980; Guthrie 1988), and spiritualistic power (Namihira 1978; Yoshida 1984). In Furukawa, *chōnai* neighborhoods are defined by ownership of *yatai*. The original purpose of these vehicles was to welcome the deity on its descent from the shrine and serve as a kind of honor guard on its procession through town. Though their religious significance is all but forgotten, *yatai* continue to be highly valued as cultural artifacts. With their elaborate carvings and joinery, they stand as fine examples of wood craftsmanship in the tradition of the Hida *takumi*. As totem-like icons they are inextricably associated with communal pride and identity.

This is reflected in the fact that *yatai* and *taigumi* share the same name. The suffix *"tai"* from the word *"yatai"* is added to the name when referring to the vehicle itself. Tonomachi, for example, is represented by the Seiryūtai, and the group that maintains it is known as the Seiryū *taigumi*. The name "Seiryū" refers to a mythical blue dragon which, according to the ancient Chinese directional system, signified the east. This is appropriate since Tonomachi occupies the eastern part of town.

The current Seiryūtai was obtained secondhand from a neighborhood in Takayama in 1835. It required extensive repairs during the early Shōwa (1926–1989) period and had to be completely refurbished in 1940. The vehicle features *karakuri ningyō*—mechanical wooden puppets manipulated through an intricate series of wires and pulleys. The performance is staged on a narrow runway extending out from the upper level. The central character in this case is Fukurokuju, one of the seven Chinese gods of good fortune, who is depicted as having an elongated shaved head. His head extends so high, in fact, that he cannot reach the top with his own hands and must have an assistant stand upon a ladder to help him shave it. During the performance the Fukurokuju puppet ambles out to the end of the runway and waits while a diminutive assistant carries a ladder toward him from behind. The assistant then leans the ladder against Fukurokuju's back and proceeds to climb to the top. The ladder is pulled away and the assistant is left suspended over Fukurokuju's head. The assistant then begins to spin back and forth in the air. The spinning motion causes a pouch on his back to open up, spewing confetti over the crowd of onlookers below. These intricate movements are performed through the manipulations of as many as five people simultaneously. During the performance they are partially hidden within a recessed enclosure on the top level of the vehicle. The insignia of the Seiryū *taigumi* is the so-called "plum blossom" *(umebachi)* pattern (see Figure 2). This was the crest of the Kanamori clan—former lords of the Hida domain—who once lived in Tonomachi adjacent to their castle.

Tonomachi constitutes a single *chōnai* neighborhood. Ichinomachi, Ninomachi, and Sannomachi, however, are all divided into smaller units. These units are designated according to their topographical position. For example, Ichinomachi and Ninomachi are both divided into upper *(kami),* middle *(naka),* and lower *(shimo)* sections. Sannomachi is somewhat shorter than the others and is only divided into upper and lower sections. Thus while the difference in elevation is barely perceptible at ground level, the "upper" neighborhoods are oriented in the upstream (southeastern) direction. The boundaries between sections, too, are indistinguishable to the outsider, sometimes passing between two houses without so much as an alley between them.

Middle Ichinomachi owns the Hō-ōtai, whose name refers to the Chinese phoenix, or *"hō-ō."* An earlier vehicle dated from the early

Table 1. *Chōnai* (neighborhoods) and associated *taigumi* (*yatai* groups) juxtaposed against political divisions and residential designations. Adapted from Kuwahara et al. 1991:197–198.

Chōnai	Associated Taigumi	Constitu-ent block (ku)	No. of House-holds	Residential Designation
Tonomachi	Seiryū	19, 20, 21, 22	492	Tonomachi; Kanamori-chō; Higashi-chō; Kataharama-chi; Wakamiya Itchōme
Upper Ichinomachi	Sanbasō	15	31	Ichinomachi 1, 2, 3, 5
Middle Ichinomachi	Hō-ō	16	32	Ichinomachi 3, 5, 6, 7, 8
Lower Ichinomachi	Kirin	17	171	Ichinomachi 8, 11, 12, 13, 14, 15; Honmachi; Wakamiya-chō Nichōme, Sanchōme
Upper Ninomachi	Sankō	10	28	Ninomachi 1, 2, 3
Middle Ninomachi	Kinki	11	45	Ninomachi 3, 5, 6, 7, 8
Lower Ninomachi	Ryūteki	12, 18	289	Ninomachi 8, 10, 11, 12, 13; Matsuhiro-chō; Miyagi-chō
Upper Sannomachi	Seiyō	8	46	Sannomachi 1, 2, 3
Lower Sannomachi	Byakko	9	68	Sannomachi 3, 5, 6, 7, 8, 10
Mukaimachi	Kagura	4, 5, 6, 7	465	Mukaimachi Itchōme, Nichōme, Sanchōme; Masushima-chō; Kōei-chō
Sakaemachi	Tōkeiraku	13, 14	255	Sakaemachi Itchōme, Nichōme, Shinsakaemachi
Keta	Miyamoto	23	173	Kamikita

Seiryū (Tonomachi)	Sanbasō (Upper Ichinomachi)	Hō-ō (Middle Ichinomachi)
Kirin (Lower Ichinomachi)	Sankō (Upper Ninomachi)	Kinki (Middle Ninomachi)
Ryūteki (Lower Ninomachi)	Seiyō (Upper Sannomachi)	Byakko (Lower Sannomachi)
Kagura (Mukaimachi)	Tōkeiraku (Sakaemachi)	

Figure 2. Neighborhood *taigumi* symbols.

Figure 3. The Seiryūtai of Tonomachi. A mechanical puppet (*karakuri ningyō*) representing the god Fukurokuju appears on a runway extending from the upper level. Photograph courtesy of Furukawa Town Hall.

1800s, but was discarded in 1891 due to its dilapidated condition. The present version was completed in 1922. It is said that a children's kabuki play was once performed in front of the vehicle, but this was discontinued several decades ago. The group's insignia is an image of the *hō-ō* bird itself.

Lower Ichinomachi's Kirintai takes its name from the *kirin*, a mythical four-legged animal with a dragon-like head. An earlier version was built around 1846 but later burned in a fire. Another was obtained to replace it in 1881. It was last used in 1924 and eventually discarded. The current version dates from 1933. Kirintai, too, features *karakuri ningyō,* in this case employing a single puppet figure dressed in the manner of a *shishi* dancer. The figure walks out to the end of the runway carrying a large basket. He sets the basket down before him, then mumbles a few incantations. Suddenly he leans backward with his hands in the air as a flowering plant shoots up out of the basket. Here again, the puppet's body opens up as it spins back and forth, releasing a mass of confetti to rain out over the crowd. The symbol of the Kirin *taigumi* is a stylized image of the head of a *kirin.*

The Sankōtai belongs to Upper Ninomachi. The present vehicle was completed in 1862, with extensive alterations and additions thereafter. The name "Sankō" refers to the three lights—sun, moon, and stars—and its insignia is a stylistic representation showing the character *hikari,* meaning "light" (the Chinese-derived pronunciation is *"kō"*), radiating out in three directions from a central point. The name also alludes to Honkō-ji, the major temple which stands at the upper end of Ninomachi. The temple donated funds to help support the vehicle's construction, and the name is partially an acknowledgement of this assistance. It also demonstrates how closely Shinto and Buddhism were associated prior to the Meiji Restoration in 1868 (Morishita 1991:6).

Middle Ninomachi is represented by the Kinkitai, the word *"kinki"* meaning "golden turtle." This vehicle is said by some to date from as long ago as the 1680s, but there is no reliable documentation for this. Records do show that a new vehicle was built in 1776, and underwent extensive restoration in 1820 (Furukawa-chō 1986: 407–411). In 1840 this same vehicle was given to Mukaimachi and another one built to replace it. The most recent version underwent major repairs in 1897 and 1926, and is still in use today. Its symbol consists of segments of three interlocking hexagonal shapes which represent the pattern found on a turtle shell.

The Ryūtekitai of Lower Ninomachi allegedly dates from the 1770s, but the original was worn so badly that a new one had to be built to replace it in 1886. At present it is the largest *yatai* in Furukawa and is thought to have the most elaborate decorations. The name "Ryūteki" refers to the "dragon flute," which the boys of the neighborhood learn to play. The flute is made of bamboo with seven finger holes and makes a sound said to resemble the screech of a dragon. The insignia of the Ryūteki *taigumi* shows three dragon claws enclosing a sphere.

The Seiyōtai now belongs to Upper Sannomachi. An earlier version dated from 1818. All of Sannomachi once constituted a single neighborhood, but in 1839 it was split into upper and lower divisions. At that time lots were drawn to determine which division would be allowed to keep the Seiyōtai, and Upper Sannomachi won. The vehicle was heavily damaged when it overturned in 1893. It underwent major repairs and was used for several more years, but was eventually discarded. The present version was completed in 1941. The name "Seiyō" means "to shine purely." The insignia consists of three sword blades emerging from a central point with large dots filling the spaces between them, resulting in what is described as a three-pointed star. The swords are said to represent purity.

After the partitioning, Lower Sannomachi had its own *yatai* built. It was completed in 1842 and named "Byakkodai."[7] The term *"byakko"* means "white tiger," which by the old Chinese directional system indicated "west." The current vehicle is a reconstruction dating from 1986. It features a small stage jutting out from the second level for performing an abbreviated kabuki drama. The actors are children who dress in costumes of Japan's early feudal period to portray the story of the warrior Benkei's famous encounter with Ushiwakamaru (also known as Minamoto Yoshitsune) on the bridge. Byakkodai is the only remaining example anywhere in the Hida region of an older style of *yatai* characterized by a more vertically extended lower level and the relative lack of embellishments. Its symbol is the *sasarindō,* or paulownia flower.

The *taigumi* of Upper Ichinomachi is called "Sanbasō," though its *yatai* no longer exists. "Sanbasō" refers to a dance included in the *nō* performance "Okina." The old vehicle was equipped with a female *karakuri* puppet designed to reproduce the dance movements on a narrow wooden runway. With thirteen pulleys operated by five individuals working at the same time, it was the most intricate *karakuri* in Furukawa. The play "Okina" was customarily performed on auspicious occasions such as the New Year holiday. For this reason, it is said, Sanbasō always occupied the lead position in front of the other *yatai* whenever they appeared together in procession. In 1894, damages forced the vehicle to be retired. Most of it was later destroyed in the great fire of 1904, and all that now remains are the puppet (a reconstruction), its original runway, and a single decorative tapestry. The vehicle has not been replaced, as the cost of such a project would place a tremendous financial burden on the relatively few households now comprising Upper Ichinomachi. Even so, Sanbasōtai is currently described as undergoing a "rest" period, leaving open the possibility of its eventual return. In the meantime it is represented during the *matsuri* by a banner bearing its name. The *taigumi*'s symbol is the image of a folded paper crane.

So far I have described nine *chōnai* and their related *taigumi.* These nine constitute what is sometimes referred to as *"honmachi"* (literally "original" or "main town"), the original castle town as it existed during the Tokugawa period. The boundaries of some of these neighborhoods, however, have since expanded outward into the surrounding territory. Sakaemachi, located on the downstream end of town, and Mukaimachi, which lies on the other side of the Araki River, are of more recent origin and play somewhat different roles in the *matsuri.*

Sakaemachi developed as an extension of Ninomachi, and was once referred to as *"yon-chōme"* ("block four," referring to its position as the fourth block in Ninomachi Street). As in many Japanese communities, the downstream end was considered less desirable, and, indeed, *yon-chōme* was populated mostly by poor tenant farmers. The very name, in fact, came to be used pejoratively, so the town council decided to rename the area "Sakaemachi" ("Prosperity Street"). Despite this rather hopeful appellation, the residents of Sakaemachi never amassed the resources necessary to build their own *yatai.* Instead they assumed the role of performing the *tōkei-raku,* or "fighting cock music," in 1924. The young boys of the neighborhood play a small hammer and gong instrument that produces a distinctive clanging rhythm. Their role is to lead the way before the deity on its procession through town, and their symbol is the character *"sakigake,"* meaning "forerunner." [8]

Mukaimachi is responsible for performing the sacred *kagura,* and its vehicle is known as the "Kaguradai." Though it is of similar size, the Kaguradai is structurally and functionally distinguishable from the other vehicles. It has only three wheels and no roof. A large drum is suspended inside a circular frame on the upper level, and is beat in unison by two men seated one on either side. In addition,

Figure 4. A member of Mukaimachi's Sōgakubu sits atop the Kaguradai. The *gohei*, holding a portion of the deity's spirit, is visible to his left.

two flute players sit in front of the drum, facing forward. During the *matsuri* the Kaguradai carries a portion of the spirit of the deity *(bunrei)* wrapped in a talisman and bound to a stick erected at the front of the vehicle. For this reason it always takes the lead in the procession of *yatai,* with the Sanbasō banner following immediately after.

Mukaimachi did not always play this special role. In fact it originally developed as a separate village outside the precincts of Ketawakamiya shrine. Even so, in 1840 its residents obtained a *yatai* secondhand from Middle Ninomachi, restored the vehicle, and began participating in Furukawa's *matsuri.* Their *yatai* was given the name "Suzakudai," referring to the red sparrow which, according to the Chinese directional system, indicated "south." Again, this reflected the neighborhood's geographical position, as Mukaimachi lay south of Furukawa.

In 1883 Mukaimachi obtained an old Kaguradai from a shrine in Takayama. The young men of the neighborhood then formed a group called the "Sōgakubu" ("musicians' league") and assumed the role of performing *kagura* and the *shishi* dancing it entails. Due to heavy damages the Kaguradai had to be completely refurbished in 1889, but the same vehicle is still in current use. The identifying mark of the Sōgakubu is a circle inscribed with a cross. This is known as the *"kutsuwa"* (an ornament on a horse's bridle), but is more commonly referred to as *"maru ni jūji"* (the character for "ten" inside a circle). The mark is thought to be associated with Kogaidaijin, the patron deity of sericulture (Kuwahara et al. 1991:186).

Entertaining the Sacred Presence

The *matsuri* constitutes a sacred interlude in that the presence of the deity is brought directly into the community itself. During its brief sojourn, the deity is treated as an honored guest, with offerings of food, alcohol, and entertainment. Every year one of Furukawa's component neighborhoods assumes the role of hosting the event on behalf of the entire community. This role is referred to as *"shuji,"* or "director," [9] and is accepted with great seriousness. While the title is generally applied to the host neighborhood as a whole, it is often used more specifically in reference to that neighborhood's designated leader.

Up until the end of the Second World War, a single director held responsibility for all events. Now, however, two *shuji* are chosen each year—one to direct the *okoshi daiko* and the other to orchestrate the *yatai* procession. In fact the former role has become such a cumbersome task that several individuals have to be enlisted from the chosen territory to plan and direct it. These are collectively referred to as *"tōban"* (or "special duty officers"). Their designated leader is given the title *"sōtsukasa"* ("commander"). Later during the actual performance this individual will ride atop the drum structure in the forward-most position.

The *yatai* procession originated under the pretext of entertaining the deity. As its name implies, the position of Mukaimachi's Kaguradai as the lead vehicle means that its residents must assume the special role of performing *kagura*. Part of their responsibility in this role is to accept the *bunrei*[10]—a portion of the deity's spirit—and place it atop their vehicle. This involves a special ceremony conducted early on the morning of April 19, prior to the other events. Members of the Sōgakubu, along with some of the older residents, assemble themselves in front of Mukaimachi's public meeting hall, and two pairs of dancers perform a *shishimai*. At about 6:30 a.m. they set out for the shrine in a slow procession to the accompaniment of flutes and drums. A man positioned near the rear holds a large *gohei*, a ceremonial stick to which folded paper streamers have been attached at the top. It is this man who will carry the spirit portion back to the home neighborhood.

The procession climbs the long flight of stone steps leading up to the shrine and comes to a halt in front of the main shrine building. The members disassemble and take their positions inside, kneeling on the *tatami* matted floor. The *gohei*-bearer sits front and center. The ceremony is led by the head priest alone, who begins by asking the musicians to play a brief *kagura* tune. He then waves a *sakaki* branch over the assembled group as a means of removing impurities and/or dispelling evil influences. The members bow forward with their eyes toward the floor to receive this treatment. Next the priest opens the curtains leading up to the main altar and ascends the stairs. From somewhere inside the inner shrine emerges an elongated moan (uttered by one of the priest's assistants), rising both in pitch and volume then falling back again. This is called *"keihitsu,"* and marks the arrival of the deity's spirit. The priest then comes back down the staircase and, after delivering a brief prayer, hands the representative from Mukaimachi a leafy twig from the *sakaki* tree to place upon a wooden stand in front of the altar. The twig is called a *tamagushi* (literally "spirit skewer"), and is used as an offering of goodwill to the deity.

Again the priest ascends the stairs. This time he returns with a talisman wrapped in an embroidered cloth, allegedly containing the spirit portion. He attaches the talisman to the *gohei,* while the other participants avert their gaze.[11] All the participants then proceed back outside. The talisman is held aloft while a *shishi* dance is performed before it on the grounds directly in front of the shrine building. The Mukaimachi contingent reassembles into its processional order and heads back into town much as it had come. When they arrive at the meeting hall in their home neighborhood, a *shishi* dance is performed again in front of the building and the talisman taken inside. Later the Kaguradai will be brought round and the talisman installed atop it.

At 9:00 a.m. a group of about 150 men gathers at the shrine to perform the *hōheisai,* a ceremonial offering to the deity. The group includes the parish elders, other lay officers of the shrine, and an assembly of representatives from major institutions within the community. The parish elders and lower ranking shrine officers are dressed in *montsuki,*[12] a formal black kimono reserved for special occasions. The other representatives wear black suits and white neckties—customary attire for auspicious occasions. They are joined by a group of *miko* (shrine maidens), girls about 10–12 years old dressed in white *kimono* and red *hakama* (a long, divided skirt). Also present are a group of young men who play *gagaku*—an ancient court music used to accompany Shinto rites. They are dressed in the costume worn by court nobles during the Heian period (794–1185).

The ceremony begins at 10:00 a.m. It is conducted by the head priest, assisted by a number of additional priests from nearby shrines. The parish elders assemble in front of an auxiliary building while the lower-ranking shrine officers and *miko* line up on the grounds directly in front of the shrine. The priests emerge from the auxiliary building. They are easily recognizable in their ceremonial garments, which, again, recreate the court costume of ancient Japan. One by one they rinse their hands and mouths with water at a basin located just outside the building's entrance. Then they proceed in single file toward the main shrine building with the parish elders in tow.

As the priests and elders head up the stairs into the building's interior, the others fall in behind, starting with the *miko,* then the *gagaku* musicians, and finally the lower-ranking shrine officers. Once inside, they all solemnly take their positions kneeling on the floor. As in the earlier rite, the head priest begins by waving a *sakaki* branch over the assembled group, who bow forward with their eyes toward the floor. Then the priest opens the curtains to the inner shrine, and he and an assisting priest ascend the stairs to the main altar. Again the elongated moan issues from the inner shrine. The spirit of the deity is present.

The musicians begin playing their sacred music and the *miko* position themselves at intervals upon the stairs before the main altar. An assistant hands them a series of food offerings carefully arranged on special trays.[13] Each tray is passed from *miko* to *miko* until it reaches the top of the stairs, where the priest places it on the altar. The *kami* is essentially being treated as an honored guest at a banquet, with all the offerings arranged in the form of a table setting oriented toward the altar.

When the offerings have been presented the priest delivers a *norito*—a humble appeal for the welfare and prosperity of the towns-people. Next the *miko* rise to perform a ritualistic dance before the altar for the entertainment of the deity. The dance consists of a series of slow, graceful movements oriented toward the four cardinal directions, and is accompanied by the mystical *gagaku* music.

When the *miko* have finished their dance, the representatives from various community and regional organizations are called forward in turn to present their *tamagushi* offerings. The representatives are summoned in pairs, using positional titles relating the individual to the group he (or she, in the case of the *miko*) represents. The order proceeds as follows:

1. Parish elders (*ujiko sōdai*—in four pairs[14])

2. Head of the Yoshiki County branch of the shrine association (*jinjachō Yoshiki-gun shibuchō*) and head of the Furukawa section of the shrine association (*jinjachō Furukawa bukaichō*)

3. Representative of the *taigumi* leaders (*taigumi sōdai daihyō*) and representative of the shrine commissioners (*jinja iin daihyō*)

4. Representative/delegate from the town at large (*shichū sōdai*

daihyō) and representative of Miyamoto-*gumi (Miyamoto-gumi daihyō)*

5. Mayor of Furukawa *(Furukawa chōchō)* and chairperson[15] of the Furukawa town council *(Furukawa chōgikai gichō)*

6. Chief of Furukawa police department *(Furukawa keisatsu shō-chō)* and Furukawa middle school principal *(Furukawa chūgak-kōchō)*

7. Furukawa primary school principal *(Furukawa shōgakkōchō)* and chief of Furukawa fire department *(Furukawa shōbōdanchō)*

8. Chief of the Yoshiki County branch of the agricultural cooperative *(Yoshiki nogyō kyōdō kumiai kaichō)* and chief of Furukawa tourist association *(Furukawa kankō kaichō)*

9. Chief of the chamber of commerce and industry *(Furukawa-chō shōkō kaichō)* and chairperson of the cultural assets council *(bun-kazai shingi iinchō)*

10. Local representative to the Gifu prefectural assembly *(Gifu-ken gikai giin)* and representative of the *yatai* director *(yatai shuji daihyō)*

11. Representative of the rousing drum director *(okoshi daiko shuji daihyō)* and representative of the special duty officers *(tōban daihyō)*

12. Representative of the *kagura* musicians and *miko (kagura miko daihyō)* and representative of the *gagaku* musicians *(gagaku daihyō)*

Each pair of representatives approaches a low stand set up at the bottom of the steps leading to the altar. Together they kneel and place their branches upon the stand with the cut end of the stem oriented toward the deity. Then in unison they bow twice, clap twice, bow once more, and return to their former positions.

After all have made their presentations, the *miko* rise to perform another rendition of their ritualistic dance. This brings the offertory to a close. The procedure used to open the ceremony is now followed in reverse order: the offerings are handed back down the stairs, the long moan is uttered—this time indicating the deity's departure, and the curtains are closed. The entire ceremony lasts a little over an hour and maintains an air of strict formality throughout.

At 1:00 p.m. a mass of townspeople assembles at the shrine to escort the *mikoshi* on its procession into town. First, however, the deity's spirit must be transferred to the *mikoshi* in a ceremony known as *"kamiutsushi"* ("moving the deity").[16] The transferral itself is a rather secretive process. The *kami*'s spirit consents to enter a small talisman wrapped in embroidered cloth. To handle the talisman, the head priest dons white gloves and a white mask over his mouth and nose.[17] *Kagura* performers from Miyamoto-*gumi* provide a musical accompaniment. At the actual moment when the transfer is made the drums grow considerably louder and assume a regular one–two, one–two cadence, while the flutes settle into a prolonged trill. At this point all onlookers bow their heads, keeping their eyes to the ground. The head priest emerges rather dramatically from the shrine with the talisman in hand. He hurries down the steps and deftly places the talisman inside the *mikoshi*. When he has finished, the musicians return to their original melody.

The *mikoshi* was originally borne shoulder-high in the manner of a palanquin, using a pair of parallel wooden beams extending from the front and back. Ten men would be stationed on each beam, yielding a total of forty bearers. Following the deity's installation, they would carry the *mikoshi* down the long flight of steps leading away from the shrine and proceed along a narrow road through the rice paddies and on into town.

As the town expanded, the deity had more territory to cover and the heavy *mikoshi* became a considerable burden. About twenty years ago, for the sake of convenience, the *mikoshi* was placed on a small automobile chassis complete with inflatable tires. Over the chassis sits a heavy wooden box frame. The *mikoshi* is positioned atop the chassis and frame such that it remains at approximately shoulder height; now, however, it is pulled along its route using two large ropes, with ten men to a rope, so that the total number of "bearers" has been reduced to twenty. There is a steering mechanism and hand operated brake lever located in front of the vehicle to aid in negotiating turns and gradients.

The number of participants in the *mikoshi* procession varies slightly from year to year, but totals well over three hundred individuals. The components of the procession are arranged in the following order:

1. A drum on a wheeled cart guided by two men and beat by a third

2. A banner indicating that the procession has been designated an intangible folkloristic cultural property *(mukei minzoku bunka-zai)* by the Japanese government

3. A *sakaki* tree in a wheeled cart pulled by two men

4. Two "forerunners" *(senku)*

5. Six "procession monitors" *(gyōretsu shinkōkei)*

6. A banner bearing the name of Ketawakamiya Shrine

7. *Kagura* musicians and *shishi* dancers from Miyamoto-*gumi*

8. Banners representing each of the neighborhood *yatai* (led by the Kaguradai, with Sanbasō in second position)

9. The *yatai* director banner

10. The Tōkeiraku banner

11. Sixty Tōkeiraku performers

12. Six adult Tōkeiraku escorts

13. The Tōkeiraku leader

14. Representatives from each of the eleven *chōnai* as well as Miyamoto-*gumi*, with the number each provides commensurate with the size of its population, as follows:

Miyamoto-*gumi:*	4
Sakaemachi:	8
Mukaimachi:	14
Tonomachi:	16
Upper Ichninomachi:	1
Middle Ichinomachi:	1
Lower Ichinomachi:	6
Upper Ninomachi:	1
Middle Ninomachi:	2
Lower Ninomachi:	10
Upper Sannomachi:	2
Lower Sannomachi:	3
Total:	68

All the representatives dress in the manner of the elite samurai class during the Tokugawa period, with *kamishimo* overmantles and *hakama* worn over their formal kimono *(montsuki)*. In the present day, however, this particular role has become more egalitarian. The quotas are allotted each neighborhood based on the size of its population, rather than the status of its residents, and the role itself rotates from household to household. These men are referred to as *keigo* ("guard" or "escort") and are seen as a kind of advanced guard

15. Thirteen shrine maidens *(miko)*

16. Four female shrine dancers *(maihime)*

17. Seventeen *gagaku* musicians

18. Banners representing sun and moon

19. Fourteen *kagura* musicians

20. Banners representing the Suzaku and Byakko *okoshi daiko* territories (to be described in Chapter 5)

21. Two standard bearers

22. Three offering collectors

23. Another shrine banner

24. The *mikoshi,* pulled by twenty men dressed in white livery (called *"hanten"*) of the type worn by religious pilgrims[18]

25. Yet another shrine banner

26. A halberd bearer

27. Two standard bearers

28. Banners representing the Seiryū and Genbu *okoshi daiko* territories (to be described in Chapter 5)

29. The head priest of Ketawakamiya Shrine

30. The priest's attendants, one holding a large red umbrella over the priest as a symbol of the priest's authority, the other carrying a folding stool for the priest to sit on when the procession is at rest

31. The parish elders (wearing *montsuki, kamishimo,* and *hakama)*

32. The banner of the supervisor of sacred rites *(shinji torishi-mari)*

33. Sixteen *taigumi* leaders and shrine commissioners (wearing *montsuki, kamishimo,* and *hakama*)

34. An offering box on a wheeled cart pulled by two men

35. A cart containing folding stools pulled by two men. The stools are for the shrine officers and neighborhood representatives to sit on while the procession is at rest

Upon entering town, the *mikoshi* is met by a Shinto priest who recites a prayer and offers rice and *sake* to the deity inside. Then the procession sets off on a grand tour, eventually passing through each of the eleven *chōnai.* This formerly began the next day—April 20. Over the years the town has expanded to such an extent that the tour now has to begin on the afternoon of April 19 and continue through the morning of April 21 in order to cover all of the shrine's territory.

As the procession approaches, the townspeople emerge from their homes to sprinkle a line of salt along the path it is to follow. Branch segments of salt are then drawn from the main line to the entrances of houses and shops lining the way. This is intended both to purify the path before the deity and entice its sacred presence into their homes.

The *mikoshi* stops at predetermined locations in every neighborhood. At each stop the priest comes forward to perform an abbreviated version of the shrine ceremony. The procession is so long that a man with a radio must walk beside the *mikoshi* to inform the head of the procession when to stop. Folding stools are taken out of a cart and set up in the street; these are for the shrine officers to use while they wait for the ceremony to be concluded. A small crowd of local residents emerges from their homes bearing offerings to the deity. Some of them bring rice piled high on a tray. Others offer money in the customary white envelopes bound with the red-and-white ribbon used on auspicious occasions. Many employ a combination of both rice and money, sticking the envelope into the pile of rice.

The wooden box frame supporting the *mikoshi* now becomes a makeshift altar, and an assisting priest places the offerings upon it. A second priest waves a *sakaki* branch before the altar, then over the bowed heads of the assembled crowd, who stand quietly to the side

Figure 5. The *mikoshi,* a portable shrine bearing the spirit of the local guardian deity, is pulled through town by the *yakudoshi hoshiin,* or "dangerous year attendants."

Figure 6. The *mikoshi* stops at prearranged intervals where an abbreviated religious ceremony is performed. Here a priest presents the *sakaki* branch before the deity.

near the entrances of their homes. The head priest steps forward and prays to the deity for the protection of the people. The second priest invites the people to clap their hands twice in unison, then bow their heads as they present their own invocations to the deity *("Dōji ni awasete, ichidō hairei!")*. At a sign from the head priest the *kagura* music strikes up anew and the procession moves on to the next stop.

The offerings of rice and money are poured together into a large bag pulled along behind in a cart and the trays are handed back to their owners. Young men walk ahead of the *mikoshi* with collection baskets to accept contributions along the way. The whole event thus becomes a combination sacred rite and collection drive for the shrine. Some of the people offer *sake* as well—usually two bottles wrapped together in white paper.[19]

At about 4:30 that afternoon the deity is escorted to the *tabisho*[20] —its temporary resting place within the town for the remainder of the festival. The *miko* perform a dance, and then the *mikoshi* is placed inside the *tabisho* building with the front facing toward the open door. The banners and other equipment are put inside as well. The priest conducts a brief rite, Miyamoto-*gumi* performs a spirited *shishi* dance on the grounds outside, and the participants disperse. Three guards dressed in formal kimono are posted at the door to keep watch. This vigil will continue through the night and as long as the deity resides in the *tabisho,* with the guard being changed every two hours.

At 6:00 that evening a special ceremony is held at the *tabisho* as a means of officially welcoming the deity's presence. It follows a pattern similar to that observed at the shrine earlier in the afternoon, but in abbreviated form. Again the group leaders come forward to offer a *sakaki* branch, but this time the groups represented are limited to the parish elders, *taigumi* leaders, shrine commissioners, *yatai* director, rousing drum director, special duty officers, and *tabisho* guards.

Though the *yatai* no longer take part in the *mikoshi* procession, they still make a cursory pass through town on the evening of April 19. At about 5:30 they line up at the lower end of Ichinomachi with Kaguradai in the lead, the banner representing Sanbasō second, and the others following along in a prescribed order. Again, the *yatai* director brings up the rear. Each *yatai* is adorned with tiers of paper lanterns hanging from its upper levels. At a signal from the director the lanterns are lit and the *yatai* begin making their way slowly up through Ichinomachi in the twilight.[21] The lanterns sway gently with the rocking motion of the vehicles as they move along the darkening streets, and young flute and drum players riding inside provide a musical accompaniment. When the procession reaches the upper end of Ichinomachi the *yatai* disperse, each returning to its home neighborhood. This is known as the *"hikiwakare,"* or "pulling away." Formerly this illuminated procession was conducted on the evening of April 20 and officially marked the end of the *matsuri* festivities. Since it is currently held on the 19th and the *yatai* reappear on the following day, the event has lost some of its original significance, and is now considered a prelude to the major attraction of the evening—the *okoshi daiko.*

The Rousing Drum

The solemn rituals which attend the local guardian deity by day stand in dramatic contrast to the drunken revelry and atmosphere of general unruliness which pervade the *okoshi daiko* at night. Though the official starting time for the *okoshi daiko* is 10:00 p.m., an expectant crowd of onlookers starts to gather at around 7:00 p.m., shortly after the evening parade of *yatai* has ended. Some of the more enthusiastic *tsuke daiko* teams can already be seen at this time parading through the streets, shouldering their drums and chanting the names of their respective neighborhoods. Most of the participants in the *okoshi daiko* dress in white cotton shorts (generally called *"han-momohiki"* but known locally as *"yancha pantsu"*), *sarashi*—a long white cotton cloth wound tightly around the midsection, and *jikatabi*—the black ankle-length canvas footwear with split toe worn by manual laborers. Despite the chill air of early spring in the mountains, their upper bodies and legs remain exposed, which is why the Furukawa *matsuri* is referred to as a "naked festival" *(hadaka matsuri).*

Most of the participants emerge from their homes at around 9:00 p.m. to meet with their teammates and head for the official starting point. The ritual will be launched from an open plaza near the center of town, and an excited crowd of spectators has gathered there already. The participants huddle around bonfires placed sporadically throughout the plaza, drinking *sake* and engaging in some good-natured jostling. They are easily recognizable in their distinctive white costumes and exposed flesh, as well as the self-assured swagger many of them assume as the *sake* begins to take hold. The crowd of spectators parts for them as they make their way through the plaza, lending them a distinct air of celebrity.

The *sake* is referred to as *"omiki,"* the same term applied to the sanctified *sake* used in the shrine rituals. It is passed around in big bottles from one participant to another, and sometimes foisted upon an unsuspecting tourist. It is customary for the participants to take big mouthfuls and spit it out in a fine spray over the chest and back of a waiting comrade. This is ostensibly done as a form of purification but is also believed to help keep the body warm.

Here and there throughout the crowd the *tsuke daiko* poles are stood on end. Team members then take turns climbing to the top, balancing themselves spread-eagled with the end of the pole positioned in the center of their abdomens. Random exclamations of *"sugoi!"* ("amazing!"—a standard expression of awe) are heard through the crowd of awestruck spectators.

In the midst of it all, illuminated by floodlights, sits the massive drum structure. The drum itself is positioned atop a turret made of short overlapping beams, raising it well above the level of the supporting framework. A *sakaki* branch has been placed at each of the rectangular framework's corners and another on either of its lengthwise sides. Boards have been laid over the front of the framework to form a makeshift altar, and traditional Shinto offerings representing the fruits of the harvest have been placed upon it. Votive lanterns have been hung from long poles on each side of the altar. The entire structure has thus been transformed into a huge religious object, and the activity surrounding it assumes the nature of a sacred rite. Indeed, some of the spectators squeeze in close to touch the beams of the platform for good luck, just as the *tsuke daiko* teams will later press forward in an effort to attach themselves to the structure when the event is underway.

Prominently displayed upon the altar and looming over the other offerings are two large kegs of *sake*. One bears the name "Hōrai," the Watanabe household's leading brand; the other bears the name "Shiramayumi," the Kaba household's major product. It is impossible, therefore, to view the structure without drawing an immediate association with two of Furukawa's most distinguished patrons.

At around 9:30 a loudspeaker crackles into life. A loud voice welcomes the crowd on behalf of the directing territory and announces that the *okoshi daiko* is about to get underway. This is met with a great cheer and round of applause from the assembled masses. The head priest steps forward to conduct a brief rite of purification, waving a *sakaki* branch over the drum structure, then in turn over the bowed heads of the "commander" *(sōtsukasa)* and special duty officers, the fire brigade who will patrol the event, and a group of visiting dignitaries. Through the loudspeaker the priest delivers a prayer, asking the *kami*'s favor in ensuring that the event be completed without incident. He then sprinkles some salt on the drum structure, again for purification.

Next the various representatives are summoned forward in turn to place a *tamagushi* on the altar in honor of the deity. The first to be called is the "commander," who is met with cheering and applause. He too is dressed in short pants and belly wrapping, and despite his advanced age will ride at the helm of the drum structure when the ritual gets underway.

Next comes the head of the parish elders *(ujiko sōdaichō)*, who is also met with enthusiastic cheering. He, however, is dressed in formal *montsuki* kimono, befitting a special occasion. Following him in order are the leader of the Furukawa Festival Preservation Association *(Furukawa matsuri hozonkaichō)*, the mayor, the town council

Figure 7. The head priest conducts a rite of purification over the front of the drum structure just prior to its launch. The drum beaters stand in the background. Photograph by Naoi Ryūji.

chairperson, the vice governor of Gifu prefecture, the local representative to the prefectural assembly, a representative of the local construction company which helped set up the facilities, the chief of police, the head of the engineering office, the chief of the fire department, the fire brigade leader, the chairperson of the local chamber of commerce, and the leader of the tourist association. Finally come representatives of the various groups of participating young men: the drum bearers, the drum beaters, the *tsuke daiko* team members, and one additional individual referred to simply as a "general representative" *(ippan daihyō).*

The applause has been steadily waning with the introduction of each representative, and the crowd is growing impatient. The priest opens a bottle of *sake,* places it upon the altar, and offers another brief prayer. The formal religious service *(saiji)* is drawn to a close.

The religious paraphernalia are cleared away from the drum structure, and the mass of bearers begins to squeeze in underneath it. The commander climbs by himself up onto the structure with a microphone to offer his official greeting. He thanks fellow residents of his home territory for all their hard work, the priest for his purifying rituals, and the visiting dignitaries for their esteemed presence. He requests the cooperation of police and fire brigade in preventing mishaps. He invites the spectators to allow themselves to become intoxicated by the drum. Finally he mentions that his home territory is delighted to sponsor this year's event, and adds his wishes that it be concluded without serious injury.

The commander will soon be joined upon the structure by several other men. By far the most conspicuous role is assumed by two young men who sit back-to-back atop the drum itself, dramatically poised to strike it with long sticks held vertically above their heads. These young men are called *"ueuchi"*—literally "top strikers." They grasp their sticks by the handle with both palms facing forward. At regular intervals one of them swings his stick downward in an arc, striking the head of the drum positioned squarely between his legs. He then raises the stick slowly and dramatically back into place, making ready for the next strike. Several seconds later his partner behind follows suit by performing the same action. The two men alternate back and forth, maintaining a steady cadence of one beat every 10–12 seconds. With all their energies focused on the appointed task, they stare intently into space, seemingly oblivious to the action below.[22]

Two auxiliary drum beaters stand down upon the beams of the platform at either end of the drum. They are called *"yokouchi,"* or "side strikers," because they are positioned off to one side, striking the drum in a horizontal arc rather like swinging a baseball bat. Each is careful to coordinate his own strikes with those of the drum beater sitting atop the drum at the opposite end. This allows both drum heads to be employed simultaneously, thereby amplifying the sound.

In addition to the side strikers, eight somewhat older men position themselves on the platform in front and back of the drum. One is the commander, who, as mentioned previously, stands in lead position at the head of the platform. The others are evenly spaced behind him, facing forward and aft, with their backs toward the drum as if to guard it from attack. Indeed, these men are collectively referred to as the *"hon'ei,"* or "main guard." They generally range from 45 to 65 years of age and occupy special leadership positions within the community. All eight main guard members hold lanterns in their right hands as symbols of their authority. The commander's lantern bears his title, *"sōtsukasa."* The others simply read *"shuji,"* in reference to the directing territory.

All those who ride upon the drum structure—the main guard and drum beaters alike—are dressed in the same costume as the mass of participants on the ground, with the exception of two distinguishing features. Instead of the black canvas laborer's boot, the riders wear white *tabi*—a sock-like garment with a split toe and thin rubber sole. They also wear *hachimaki*—a white strip of cloth tied around the head like a headband. In this instance, however, the *hachimaki* is worn with the knot neatly tied at the center of the forehead and the ends sticking out to the sides in the manner of a bow tie. This is opposite the usual fashion in which the knot is tied behind the head just at the base of the skull.

Precisely at 10:00 p.m., the two lucky young men chosen to serve as "top strikers" climb up the turret and position themselves back-to-back astride the drum. To keep from falling off, they bind themselves together by wrapping a long piece of white cloth around both their waists. Next the two auxiliary "side strikers" take their places on the beams of the platform at either end of the drum. They hand the wooden sticks to their comrades above, then take up sticks of their own.

The other members of the main guard now climb aboard to join the commander, who takes his position at the front of the platform, still holding his microphone. A hush falls over the crowd of onlookers as he begins to sing the opening lines of the "Furukawa Medeta." The song is solemn and the words prolonged and chant-like:

Wakamatsu-sama.	Young pine tree.
Eda mo sakayuru	Its branches flourish
ha mo shigeru.	and its needles grow thick.

Then abruptly the song breaks into the familiar *"medeta, medeta"* verse,[23] at which point the rhythm picks up considerably and all the local people—participants and onlookers alike—join in.

When the song has ended, the bearers, numbering over 170, slide their shoulders under the beams of the massive framework and lift it from its supports. The crowd roars its approval as the two young men atop the drum raise their sticks high into the air, poised for the first strike. Suddenly the forward-facing member of the pair swings his stick down, hitting the drumhead with a resounding "boom." He is followed a moment later by his counterpart behind, and the two begin to alternate strikes. The mass of bearers below them now begins to rock the drum structure back and forth like a seesaw. The drum beaters coordinate their strikes with the rocking motion, which rapidly gathers speed. The undulations cause the other riders to crouch down toward the beams of the platform to avoid being pitched off. Soon, however, the rocking slows to a halt and the top drum beaters settle into their somber cadence. At this point the auxiliary drum beaters join in below, adding force to the percussion. A gang of about eighty or ninety rather burly men gathers together behind the drum platform. These men are referred to as the *"kōei,"* or "rear guard," their duty being to repel the charges of the *tsuke daiko.* The platform itself appears for a moment to float above the masses like a magic carpet as it swivels around and heads out into the streets. The rousing drum ritual has begun.

The drum produces a thunderous booming sound that reverberates through the night air. Added to the drum are the voices of the main guard, who in unison lower themselves into a crouch by bending at the knees, then rise together with an upward sweeping motion of their arms while shouting *"wasshoi!"* as if to rally the masses below them.

The drum itself, however, is only the climactic feature in a long procession of townspeople extending for perhaps two hundred meters. At the head of the procession is a banner identifying the *okoshi daiko* as an intangible folkloristic cultural property *(mukei minzoku bunkazai)*, officially designated by the Japanese government. Next comes a banner inscribed with the name of the director's territory. After this is a group of large paper lanterns held high above on long poles which, by means of their inscriptions, represent the commander and his assistants. They are followed by a similar lantern for every component block within the director's territory.

But the bulk of the procession consists of over a thousand townspeople, most of them women, children, and senior citizens. Each

Figure 8. The *okoshi daiko* (rousing drum) ritual. Photograph by Naoi Ryūji.

holds a round red-and-white paper lantern on a short stick, illuminated by a candle. Together they form a river of flowing lights, adding to the mystical atmosphere. Along the outside edges of this massive column are more of the large, elevated lanterns, each bearing the name of a neighborhood *taigumi*. They are arranged in a prescribed order, with Kaguradai in the lead, followed by Sanbasō, then all the others trailing along behind. The lanterns of the *yatai* director, Tōkeiraku, and Miyamoto-*gumi* bring up the rear. As they move along, the participants sing the "Furukawa Medeta."

This mass of townspeople is followed by the director's banner, more of the large, elevated paper lanterns bearing the name of Ketawakamiya Shrine, and finally the drum structure itself. The drum is immediately preceded by a small group of men referred to as the *zen'ei,* or "lead guard." Their function is mostly symbolic, however, as the *tsuke daiko,* the only major threat to the drum's progress, advance exclusively from the rear.

A *tsuke daiko* consists of a small keg-shaped drum attached to the middle of a stout wooden pole. During the ensuing melee, this drum will serve as an identifying symbol, rallying flag, and makeshift jousting instrument suitable for engaging other neighborhoods in ritualized confrontation. Each drum bears on its leather heads the insignia of the *taigumi* to which it belongs, so its team remains easily identifiable even within the mass of participants. *Tsuke daiko* and *yatai* should thus be seen as alternative expressions of a single neighborhood identity. Unlike the *yatai* in their stately procession, however, the competition among *tsuke daiko* will be quite overt.

As the main drum moves through town, the neighborhood teams lie waiting at strategic intersections to rush out and attack it as it passes by. Team members hold the pole jointly overhead as they charge forward, the drum aligned upward so that the neighborhood symbol is clearly visible. Each group tries to fight its way past—or, more correctly, through—any competing teams as well as the gang of drum guardians posted by the director at ground level immediately behind the drum structure to repel the attackers. The object for each team is to advance all the way to the fore and hold its *tsuke daiko* pole crosswise over the trailing end of the drum structure with the neighborhood insignia proudly displayed for all to see. The verb used to describe this action is *"tsukeru"* ("attach"), referring to the fact that the neighborhood team is attaching itself to the lead drum. Indeed, until fairly recently the aim was to make direct contact with the drum structure, which often entailed setting the *tsuke daiko* onto the back end of the framework. This has been outlawed out of consideration for the safety of the riders. Generally the team that has succeeded in attaching itself to the drum structure tries to remain there in the lead position for as long as possible, glorying in their achievement as the moving melee continues down the street. Eventually they will be forced to yield to the pressure of other teams pressing in from behind, and will veer off to the outside at a convenient intersection.

Participating in the attack induces a curious mixture of fear and exhilaration. The teams gather at a designated intersection, waiting for the arrival of the main drum. A bonfire has been lit in the middle of the intersection, enveloping the area in an eerie glow and the smell of burning wood. The half-naked men huddle around the fire, passing bottles of *sake* and singing the "Medeta" song. Some of them engage again in the spread-eagled pole-balancing act, largely for the entertainment of the assembled spectators. Team members gather in a tight circle with the pole of their *tsuke daiko* stood on end in the center. Each member puts one foot at the base of the pole to anchor it in place. One of the members is then hoisted up onto the attached drum, where he stands clinging to the pole while his teammates swing it back and forth as if trying to shake him off. Finally the pole is steadied and he is allowed to climb on up to the top, positioning the end of the pole directly at his mid-section and extending his arms and legs. Though it places considerable pressure on the man's stomach,[24] he is obliged to remain in this position until his comrades below have completed one chorus of the "Medeta." He then gets down accompanied by a round of applause, and another member takes his place. This custom allows the participants to demonstrate not only their personal fortitude but also an unwavering faith in their comrades to support the pole from below. Occasionally a man will fall off the top, but this is due more to the alcohol and his own lack of caution than failure of his teammates to provide the necessary support.

Soon the peal of the great drum can be heard in the distance, growing closer with each repetition. Water is poured over the burning timbers, generating clouds of smoke and steam. The remains of the bonfire are quickly cleared away. Each team assembles in the cross street with one end of its pole pointing out toward the main thoroughfare. Team members place the trailing end of their pole on the ground, then alternately raise and lower the lead end accompanied by the rhythmic chant of *"wasshoi, wasshoi."* The peal of the great drum grows louder. Spectators back away from the street and squeeze in against buildings. Others lean out from second-floor windows in the houses lining the street, all eyes toward the drum. The mass of lanterns begins to file past, adding to the other-worldly atmosphere. The singing of the "Medeta," cheers from the crowd, and chanting of *"wasshoi"* by the *tsuke daiko* all build to a climax.

Finally the drum arrives in a dramatic burst of sound and spectacle. As it passes by, the *tsuke daiko* rush out from the side to begin their attack. The men shout to rally themselves as they advance toward their goal, charging into the rear guard with reckless abandon. The chaotic melee which develops is called the *"sentō arasoi,"* or "battle at the fore," referring to the *tsuke daiko* teams struggling against the rear guard—and one another—in trying to reach the drum structure. The crush of hundreds of bodies is intense. In their zeal to make contact with the drum structure the other teams shove their way in from behind, their momentum sometimes carrying them over or through anyone who stands in their way. Various tactics are employed in reaching the goal. The pole may be used as a combination wedge and lever for cutting in front of another team. Two or three teams may temporarily band together in squeezing out a rival neighborhood. It is not unusual to get knocked in the back of the head by another team's *tsuke daiko,* or have one's hands pinched between two of the poles. Participants must also be careful not to stumble and fall, as this would almost certainly result in being trampled by the masses advancing from the rear.[25] The novice is advised always to cling to the pole with both hands. If he falls or the pressure becomes excessive he should scramble toward the outside as quickly as possible to avoid being run over.

Members of the local fire brigade run along both sides of the column, blowing their whistles to warn spectators out of the way. They are easily identifiable in their traditional jackets and caps. The struggle at the rear of the drum is by its very nature largely uncontrollable. Participants often are thrown to either side, crashing into houses, utility poles, and unwary bystanders. The fire brigade tries to keep onlookers in against the buildings where there is more protection, though many like to stay as close as possible to the action, drawn by the excitement it engenders.

In advancing toward the goal, it is important for a *tsuke daiko* team to keep its pole perpendicular to the direction of movement, with all the members working together. If the pole gets turned it can easily be deflected by the rear guard or muscled out of the way by another team. Teams that cannot succeed in pushing through to the fore are broken up and dispersed, at which point the members attempt to veer off to the side and out of harm's way. Once beyond the crush of bodies they quickly regroup and circle around via the narrow side streets to the next point of ambush, where they try again.

A successful strike is said to entail good fortune throughout the coming year, but for the most part the teams compete against one another to bring honor upon their respective neighborhoods. Competition between the teams is very lively, but much of the friction develops from the *tsuke daiko* clashing with the rear guard, whose duty is to defend the drum structure. The *okoshi daiko* is thus characterized by two dimensions of struggle: (1) neighborhood versus neighborhood in vying for position, and (2) neighborhood versus director in attacking the drum.

Figure 9. The "battle at the fore" *(sentō arasoi)*. Teams of young men bearing *tsuke daiko* (attaching drums) charge toward the drum structure from behind. Photograph by Kinoshita Kunitarō.

Based on direct experience of both aspects I am convinced that the more aggressive confrontation is definitely the latter. Members of the rear guard do what they can to repel the attacking waves, meeting them head on and attempting to hold them back while the drum structure recedes, or reaching up to grab a *tsuke daiko* and pull it down to the ground. It is common for fights to break out between the *tsuke daiko* teams and rear guard, and participants on either side are not above kicking the legs of their opponents. In addition, the drum structure itself can suddenly reverse direction and come careening back toward its challengers, a menacing prospect considering its great bulk and the combined strength of the mass of bearers underneath. The whole event essentially constitutes a running battle between the director and *tsuke daiko*.

The battle is not without rules, however. There is an unwritten code of etiquette that when the drum passes through a particular neighborhood the *tsuke daiko* team from that neighborhood has preference over the others in advancing upon the target. Indeed, the home team is often permitted to push through with little resistance from either the other teams or the rear guard, allowing it to succeed in its own territory—in front of the home crowd, as it were. This arrangement is especially important for the smaller neighborhoods, which suffer a serious numerical disadvantage. In actuality, however, these preferential rights are often ignored. One of the larger neighborhoods in particular has a nasty reputation for refusing to give way. This is a source of continuing resentment among the other neighborhoods.

The big drum makes prearranged stops at intervals of about 45 minutes to give the men underneath it a rest. When it starts up again an entirely new group of drum beaters and main guardsmen climb up onto the structure to relieve the previous shift. The commander's role is taken by one of the directing territory's special duty officers, who now assumes the title of "assistant commander" *(fuku-sōtsukasa)*. The men who ride the drum structure are changed four times through the course of the evening. Those who labor underneath, however, carry on all the way through to the end.

The *okoshi daiko* continues for about four hours, eventually passing through every neighborhood in Furukawa. The route varies from year to year, but must always begin and end at the same point. The highlight of the event is when the drum structure passes through Ichinomachi. This particular street contains the largest concentration of traditional old buildings and is considered the most picturesque. Photographers, amateurs and professionals alike, try to capitalize upon this opportunity to capture the essence of the ritual on film. It is here that all of the *tsuke daiko* in Furukawa come together to rush upon the big drum at one time.

Independent attacks do occur from time to time as the night wears on. In general, however, it is through the combined pressure of several teams advancing that the rear guard is most likely to cave in.

The drum finally arrives back at its starting point at around 2:00 a.m. The "assistant commander," still atop the drum structure from the final shift of riders, takes up a microphone to thank the participants and offer a few closing remarks. He then urges everyone to return home safely. Many of the participants appear reluctant to leave; they continue to mill through the crowd, hugging and congratulating one another. A few of the team captains are tossed in the air by their comrades. The overall mood is one of joyous exhaustion. Eventually everyone returns home for a hot bath and perhaps a late-night bowl of noodles, finally getting to bed a little before dawn.

Yatai Maneuvers

The *mikoshi* procession traditionally began later the same morning of April 20. As mentioned earlier, it now begins on the afternoon of April 19 and continues on through the morning of April 21. Nevertheless, April 20 is still officially designated the *"hongakusai,"* or "main festival." This includes not only the *mikoshi* procession, but also a display of neighborhood *yatai* and the various forms of entertainment they purvey.

The *yatai* are cumbersome and difficult to maneuver. They are pulled by hand using a pair of heavy ropes attached to the front of the vehicle. The solid wooden wheels are fixed on their axes—they do not swivel to either side when the vehicles are turned. Instead, each *yatai* is equipped with a fifth, somewhat smaller side-facing wheel positioned at the front of the vehicle. A crank is employed to lower this wheel into position and jack the front of the vehicle slightly off the ground. This allows the entire vehicle to be swivelled about. A long pole is inserted into the front and used as a lever.

Provided the weather is favorable, the *yatai* emerge from their garages at around 7:00 a.m. After an initial pass through their home neighborhoods, they head in the direction of the *tabisho,* arriving there at around 8:00 a.m. Initially all the vehicles line up along

Lower Ichinomachi with Kaguradai at the head, facing out toward the side street where the *mikoshi* will pass. As mentioned earlier, the *yatai* formerly led the procession, but now banners bearing their names have been substituted for the *yatai* themselves. The narrow and lengthy course through town had become increasingly difficult to maneuver. It was also seen as causing excessive wear to the precious old vehicles. The actual *yatai* continue to assemble before the *tabisho* to honor the deity. Now, however, they merely stand in attention as the *mikoshi* passes by, then at a command from the director set out on a brief pass of their own through the town's center. For the remainder of the day they are involved in separate activities for the benefit of the spectators, while the *mikoshi* makes its way through other parts of town.

When the *mikoshi* has passed, the procession of *yatai* turns the corner onto Ōyokochō (the major cross street in the old part of town) then makes another turn a short distance away onto Ninomachi (the major commercial street). At this main intersection formed by Ōyokochō and Ninomachi the whole column comes to a halt. The vehicles position themselves so that Byakkodai, Kirintai, and Seiryūtai all point into the middle of the intersection from different directions. This is to allow space for a crowd to gather to witness the performances of the three vehicles. As previously described, both Kirintai and Seiryūtai feature mechanical puppetry, and the Byakkodai sponsors the children's kabuki. These are performed at the intersection once in the morning and once again in the early afternoon. There are also several performances by each of these vehicles in its home territory.

Returning the Sacred Presence

Though most of the events are performed on April 19 and 20, the *matsuri* does not officially conclude until April 21, when the deity is returned to Ketawakamiya shrine. Before this can happen, however, the two divided portions of the deity's spirit must be reunited so that both can be returned together. At around 7:30 a.m. the Sōgakubu members line up outside their public meeting hall to escort their portion of the spirit back across the river to the *tabisho,* where it will be combined with the other portion inside the *mikoshi.* A man emerges from the meeting hall holding the *gohei* (to which the spirit is attached), and a *shishi* dance is performed before it. The other members then assemble into the same processional order as two days before when the spirit was brought down from the shrine—again accompanied by drums and flutes playing the sacred *kagura* music. Along the way some of the residents come out to watch from their doorways and respectfully bow as it passes.

When the procession arrives at the *tabisho,* the Mukaimachi contingent performs a *shishi* dance before the *mikoshi,* now visible through the building's open doors. Then with the drums settling into a regular one–two, one–two cadence and the flutes going into a prolonged trill, as is customary when the deity is being transferred, the head priest removes the talisman from the *gohei* and places it inside the *mikoshi.* The musicians return to the original melody and bring their performance to a close.

From this point the dancers and musicians of Miyamoto-*gumi* take over, for it is their duty to escort the *mikoshi* back up to the shrine. They too begin by performing a *shishi* dance in front of the *mikoshi.* Then the vehicle is rolled out of the *tabisho* and the procession assembles around it, setting out on the final leg of its circuit into parts of town not covered during the previous two days. Again the procession stops at certain predetermined points along the way for the performance of an on-site religious ceremony. The *mikoshi* typically makes a total of over sixty such stops during the entire three-day event.

When the course has been completed the procession heads back to the shrine, arriving at around 11:00 a.m. The deity is taken back inside the shrine building following a ritual procedure similar to that used when it was installed in the *mikoshi,* but in reverse order. Representatives of each group of shrine officers again present a *sakaki* branch before the altar. This time, however, the political administrative officials (mayor, chiefs of police and fire departments, school principals, etc.) are not in attendance. The Sakaemachi contingent performs its circular *tōkeiraku* dance movements on the grounds directly in front of the shrine. Miyamoto-*gumi* does yet another *shishi* dance, and the *matsuri* is officially concluded.

Gendered Participation

It is obvious from the foregoing account that participation in the public rituals contained in the *matsuri* is dominated by males. With the exception of the *miko* who dance before the altar at the ceremonial offering to the deity and who then accompany the *mikoshi* on its visit to town, females are generally relegated to assisting the male members of their households. When their home territory is chosen as rousing drum director, women may walk along with their children and elderly neighbors as part of the procession of paper lanterns which leads the way before the drum structure. Otherwise their involvement in the *okoshi daiko* is restricted to passive observation.

The *okoshi daiko* itself is pervaded by phallic symbolism—not surprising in a performance involving hundreds of young men inclined toward demonstrations of their virility. Perhaps the most visible manifestation involves the two young men positioned atop the drum. They are chosen partly based on their physiques, and the semi-naked condition accentuates their bodies. Both hold long sticks in vertical position, striking the drum with a swift downward motion, then raising their sticks slowly back into place in preparation for the next strike. They are seated with the great drum positioned squarely between their legs, its thunderous peal emanating from the same locus.[26]

Phallic symbolism is also inherent in the large *tsuke daiko* poles wielded by the teams of young men who charge upon the main drum from behind. Again, in rallying themselves prior to the drum's arrival, the young men raise and lower their poles as they chant *"wasshoi."* The rhythm of both chant and movement gradually builds in tempo until the moment when the men rush out at the drum.

It is this aggressive action between the drum and its challengers that defines the ritual in the popular imagination. There is another side to the *matsuri,* however, which takes place within the home and is largely beyond the range of public view. It relates to the custom of *yobihiki*—inviting relatives, friends, and business associates at *matsuri* time to partake of a lavish feast. This behind-the-scenes aspect places the women in charge.

The custom is said to have originated as a celebration of the coming of spring and an opportunity to reestablish contact with friends and relatives after a long period of winter isolation. As the term *"yobihiki"* (literally "calling/pulling") suggests, prosperous households tried to draw as many guests as possible, the number of guests serving as a rough measure of the host's social prominence. Many of the less affluent, too, would sponsor some kind of feast, relying upon the wild mountain vegetables *(sansai)* they had gathered and preserved the year before to round out the fare.

Feasting at *matsuri* time is common for communities all over the

Hida region. A reciprocal relationship exists whereby the host household is expected to attend similar feasts sponsored by its guests when their own community festivals are being performed. Each household keeps a schedule of local festivals and the people whose feasts they are obliged to attend. The spring and autumn festival seasons are thus times of concentrated social activity, and heads of well-connected households are kept very busy moving from place to place, perhaps staying only long enough to offer a few words of appreciation and exchange a cup of *sake* with the host before moving on to the next destination.

In Furukawa, most households now schedule their feasts for the night of April 19 to coincide with the *okoshi daiko*. The guests are generally entertained on the upstairs level. Two or more adjacent, *tatami*-matted rooms are opened up by removing the sliding doors which divide them, thereby forming one large room. Low tables are laid end-to-end through the center of the room, and the guests seated around them on floor cushions. The tables are laden with all manner of delicacies, as well as numerous bottles of *sake* and beer. It is still customary to serve the wild mountain vegetables, which are symbolic of traditional Hida cuisine. In recent times, however, these have been eclipsed by huge plates of *sushi,* fried chicken, and other specialty foods ordered from local catering establishments.

Houses lining the streets in Furukawa are invariably equipped with large second-floor windows. These can be slid open to afford a grandstand overview of the *okoshi daiko,* placing the viewer at roughly the same level as the young men who ride atop the drum. Due to the narrowness of the streets, the drum itself passes by only three or four meters away, so the effect is quite dramatic. When the drum approaches everyone runs to the window to watch it go by. This is widely acknowledged as the best way to view the *okoshi daiko.*

The type of guests invited varies from one household to another. In some they are mostly friends and relatives; in others they are work-related acquaintances. With improvements in transportation and communications facilities, the local people have been able to extend their network of interpersonal relations over much broader areas, and guests may now be invited from considerably farther away. It is also common for households whose heads are engaged in the commercial sector to invite some of their business associates—perhaps a senior executive from the main office in a major city. Such special guests are given the place of honor at the head of the table.

The women are very busy cleaning the house and preparing food, then acting as hostesses when their guests arrive. They have little time to enjoy the festivities going on out in the streets. In fact some of the women look forward to the approach of the *matsuri* with something less than eager anticipation due to all the extra work it entails. A common greeting among Furukawa women as the *matsuri* approaches is "Isn't this *matsuri* dreadful?" (*matsuri ga kowai, naa*).

One of my informants, a woman born in 1923 who has lived all her life in Ninomachi, had this to say about the participation of women in the outside events:

There's not the slightest chance [for women] to enter in, you see, what with sponsoring the feast. All we do is entertain. Then after that [the men] go out to join the rousing drum, and some of them come back with injuries. Washing all their dirty clothing is a chore. Then the next day they all have to go back out in formal attire, so we have to get [them] ready for that. The women really have their hands full!

Figure 10. A typical household feast given on the night of the *okoshi daiko.* Some guests remain throughout the evening, while others stop only briefly before moving on to other households.

There is little in the way of compensation for their efforts, though most of the women say they enjoy the opportunity to entertain their friends and relatives. They often add that when their guests are happy, they themselves feel happy too.

Before the advent of household refrigerators there was a problem of what to do with all the leftover food, so people used to gather it up and take it out to the mountains for a leisurely picnic under the cherry blossoms. This was known as *"atofuki,"* or "mopping up after-wards," and was seen partly as an expression of gratitude to the women for all their hard work. The custom has declined in recent decades, as many of the townspeople are employed outside the home and cannot afford to take the extra time away from their jobs.

The gender-based division of labor is thus reinforced through participation in the *matsuri.* Men dominate the public rituals as representatives of their households or neighborhood groups, while women are largely confined to managing the domestic sphere.[27] Women native to the Hida region say they have resigned themselves to this condition, having grown accustomed to it from the time they were children. Women who marry into the area from outside, on the other hand, especially if they come from the more Westernized urban areas, report having trouble making the adjustment.

There is one aspect of the *matsuri* to which females have gained entrance. Girls were at one time prohibited from riding in their neighborhood *yatai.* However, in recent years some of the small interior neighborhoods have been obliged to allow girls to participate. This does not necessarily reflect a growing recognition of gender inequality so much as simple demographics: the smaller neighborhoods no longer contain the requisite number of boys to carry on the tradition. The girls now learn to play the flute and drum—once a strictly male activity—and ride on the upper level of their *yatai* to help provide the musical accompaniment.

As Bestor (1989:240–241), Reader (1991:66–69), and Ashkenazi (1993:53, 145) have noted, *matsuri* performances lend symbolic support for existing social relationships and values. In this sense, the *matsuri* conforms nicely to Paden's (1988:102–103) characterization of the annual "great" festival:

Major festivals always reconstitute social relations and roles. They create a flow of communal energy. The festival provides for the group an experience of itself in its ideal social form, thus setting up paradigms of social existence that contrast with the imperfections of society during the ordinary time of the year.

Yet focusing only on the performance itself would be missing an important aspect of how sociopolitical structures are created and reproduced. This has less to do with symbolism than with the actual exercise of authority, and begins well before the public performance of April 19–21.

Chapter 5

FURUKAWA *MATSURI:*
MOBILIZATION

The Lottery Ceremony

Preparations for the *matsuri* officially begin on the first Sunday in March, when the *taigumi* leaders gather at the shrine to participate in the so-called "lottery ceremony" *(chūsen sai)*. The purpose of the ceremony is to select a director for both the rousing drum and *yatai* procession, as well as determine the order the *yatai* will follow. As the name "lottery ceremony" implies, the matter is decided by drawing lots. Since the ritual is conducted at the shrine under the auspices of the head priest, it may actually be considered a form of divination, as the outcome is being left to the will of the deity.[1] The selection process is not entirely random, however. Serving as director involves considerable effort and expense. In order to ensure that the burden is equally shared, those neighborhoods that have recently been selected are not required to participate in the lottery again until all the other groups have served as well, at which point a new round begins. Furthermore, even at the start of a new round the group that served the previous year is obliged to sit out the current year's lottery. This ensures that the responsibility will not fall on the same neighborhood two years in a row.

In the case of the *okoshi daiko,* for example, the town is divided into four territorial groups, so the directorship alternates among them in four-year intervals. The lottery is employed during the first three years but is unnecessary during the fourth, as the responsibility that year automatically passes to the only group left unchosen in that particular round.

Selection of the *yatai* director follows a similar procedure, but utilizes a different set of geographical divisions. These correspond to the eleven traditional *chōnai* neighborhoods that make up Furukawa. Technically, it is the neighborhood association, or *taigumi,* which is chosen during the lottery, though, as mentioned in the previous chapter, the terms *"taigumi"* and *"chōnai"* are largely synonymous.

Of these eleven *taigumi,* no more than seven are ever involved in the drawing during any given year. In the first instance, only those who sponsor genuine *yatai* are eligible to serve as *yatai* director, which immediately eliminates both Mukaimachi and Sakaemachi. Upper Ichinomachi is exempt from participating in the lottery as well. This is not because its *yatai*—Sanbasō—was destroyed by fire, as might perhaps be suspected; it is rather due to the fact that the group's position was traditionally fixed as the lead vehicle, as will be described in Chapter 6. The field of eligible groups is thereby narrowed to eight. As with the *okoshi daiko* director, those groups that have already served are ineligible until all the other groups have taken their turns as well. Again, at the end of each cycle the group that served last is obliged to sit out the following year, so the lottery never involves more than seven participants. A new rotation begins every eight years.

It was mentioned previously that the term "director" *("shuji")* is applied in general to the chosen neighborhood group, but more

Table 2. Composition of the four *okoshi daiko* territorial groups.

Okoshi Daiko Gumi	Component Taigumi	Associated Neighborhood (Chōnai)	Number of Households
Seiryū	Seiryū	Tonomachi	492
Suzaku	Kagura	Mukaimachi	465
Byakko	Sanbasō	Upper Ichinomachi	505
	Hō-ō	Middle Ichinomachi	
	Sankō	Upper Ninomachi	
	Kinki	Middle Ninomachi	
	Seiyō	Upper Sannomachi	
	Byakko	Lower Sannomachi	
	Tōkeiraku	Sakaemachi	
Genbu	Kirin	Lower Ichinomachi	460
	Ryūteki	Lower Ninomachi	

specifically to the individual leader within that group. In the case of the *yatai* director it is the resident *taigumi* leader who assumes the responsibility, and it is he who comes forward to draw lots during the lottery ceremony. In the case of the *okoshi daiko* director, however, the matter is somewhat more complicated.

Referring to Table 2, it is evident that two of the neighborhoods, Mukaimachi and Tonomachi, are both large enough to comprise an entire *okoshi daiko* territory in themselves. Thus in each of these two cases the *taigumi* and *okoshi daiko gumi* represent a single geographical area. Another of the *okoshi daiko* territories—Genbu—consists of only two *taigumi:* "Kirin" of Lower Ichinomachi and "Ryūteki" of Lower Ninomachi. However, the remaining territory—Byakko—contains seven separate *taigumi,* each with its own resident leader. This means that there are seven individual *taigumi* leaders—all of them on roughly the same level in the hierarchy of authority—within this single group. The result is that problems are more likely to occur when the Byakko-*gumi* is chosen to serve as director due to a lack of unified leadership. In a sense there are too many heads vying for control of a single body. Each time Byakko-*gumi* is chosen, one of the component *taigumi* leaders is customarily appointed commander *(sōtsukasa)* for the *okoshi daiko*—the office passing from one leader to the next in a fixed rotation. Since Byakko-*gumi* is selected as director only an average of once every four years and there are seven *taigumi* within it, to work through the entire order would take about twenty-eight years. Consequently many of the *taigumi* leaders never receive the honor of serving as commander. Such problems occur far less frequently in the Genbu-*gumi,* which contains only two leaders, and are nonexistent for Suzaku-*gumi* and Seiryū-*gumi,* which have only one leader each.

A third drawing is conducted during the same ceremony to decide the order in which the *yatai* will line up whenever they assemble together. Again, Mukaimachi's Kaguradai always occupies the lead position. The Sanbasō, too, though now represented only by a banner bearing its name, occupies a fixed position as the next in line. The directing neighborhood, on the other hand, is automatically obliged to bring up the rear. This leaves seven remaining *taigumi,* and their leaders draw lots to determine which position their respective neighborhoods will occupy. Thus with the exception of the first, second, and final positions, the order is established by random selection.

The three lottery drawings are conducted in succession by the head priest: first the *yatai* director is chosen; next the order of *yatai* is established; finally the *okoshi daiko* director is determined. The two new directors are each presented with banners bearing the characters *"shu-ji,"* which they carry with them to designate their roles. The same banners are used every year and passed from one neighborhood to the next in the order determined by the lottery.

After the ceremony, the representatives return to their respective neighborhoods to inform their fellow residents of the results. The role of director carries with it additional responsibilities which the entire neighborhood must share, so the news is received with great interest.

An officers' meeting *(yakuin kai)* is held on March 30 with all the shrine officers, as well as an additional representative from both the *yatai* and *okoshi daiko* directors, assembling at the shrine to discuss any problems that might interfere with the smooth functioning of the event. A representative of the "dangerous year" attendants *(yakudoshi hōshiin)* is also invited.[2]

Chain of Command

From this point forward the *matsuri* is directed through the hierarchical chain of command illustrated in Figure 11, with orders passing from the parish elders to each of the two directors and on down through several intermediate ranks to the level of the individual household. The director holds authority over all the other *taigumi* leaders. Likewise, each of the *taigumi* leaders holds authority over all the component blocks *(ku)* within his neighborhood; the block chief in turn controls each *tonarigumi*—or group of contiguous households—within his block; and finally the *tonarigumi* leader (referred to as *"kumichō"*) presides over each of the ten to fifteen member households that constitute his or her group.[3]

For the purpose of directing the *okoshi daiko,* the chain of command is somewhat simplified when either Mukaimachi or Tonomachi is chosen. Since each consists of only one large *taigumi,* the second and third levels are combined, with the block chiefs being immediately subordinate to the director.[4]

A few days after the lottery ceremony the new director meets with his *taigumi* leaders to decide how many people each of their constituent blocks should provide for the various activities. The figure is adjusted to the population, with the more populous blocks furnishing a larger number of participants. Next the director gathers together the block chiefs *(kuchō)* of all the blocks in his territory to deliver their assigned personnel quotas. Each block chief then holds a similar meeting with the heads *(kumichō)* of his component neighborhood groups *(tonarigumi)* to pass out their assigned quotas, again based on population. Finally, at the neighborhood group level, representatives from every member household meet on a designated evening to choose their assignments and preferred time slots from a prearranged schedule. If a household contains no able-bodied members, it may call upon relatives, friends, or acquaintances from outside the group to perform its allotted role. In this case the household commonly pays the enlistees for their services.

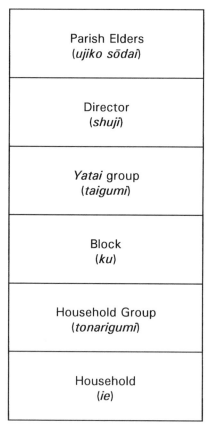

Parish Elders
(ujiko sōdai)

Director
(shuji)

Yatai group
(taigumi)

Block
(ku)

Household Group
(tonarigumi)

Household
(ie)

Figure 11. Chain of command for performing the *matsuri*.

Only the quotas are passed down from above. It then becomes an internal matter for the appropriate subunit to delegate responsibility among its constituents. The role designations are reported back up through the hierarchy and recorded by the director. The vast majority of households engage in some form of participation in the *matsuri*. The only exceptions are strict adherents to Christianity or those who are philosophically opposed to any form of religious activity.

Mobilization

In mobilizing the town for the festival two organizational principles are clearly evident. At the level of the entire town, great care is taken to ensure equality, with the role of director rotating among the various component neighborhoods. Within the neighborhoods themselves, however, mobilization is achieved through an established hierarchy, which is largely determined by gender and age.

After the individual responsibilities have been assigned, the residents begin preparing for the festival. This applies not just to the two directing territories but to the entire town, as each neighborhood *taigumi* has its own duties to perform. Much of the activity revolves around the *yatai* vehicles, which serve as highly visible symbols of their respective neighborhoods.

Again, one of the major reasons cited for performing the *matsuri* is the desire to maintain local traditions by passing them on to future generations. Thus vital to the preparations are the resident young people, who for the next few weeks meet every evening after returning home from school or work to practice their assigned roles. They gather together as neighborhood youth groups led by the senior members—or perhaps by recent graduates who have agreed to stay on as advisors. This leadership role is considered an important responsibility, as it helps instill communal values in the local youth (Furukawa-chō Kankō Kyōkai 1984:48).[5]

Most of the *chōnai* have a public meeting hall located central to their territories, and this is where the practice sessions are held. Children learn to play the drum, flute, and sometimes a pair of small cymbals called *surigane*. An age-graded hierarchy is observed, with elementary school students learning first to play the simpler instruments before advancing to the flute when they enter middle school. During the festival, these children will take turns riding in the neighborhood *yatai,* playing their music while the vehicle is pulled through the streets.[6]

As mentioned earlier, two neighborhoods, Tonomachi and Lower Ichinomachi, stage *karakuri ningyō* (mechanical puppet) performances from the upper levels of their *yatai*. In both cases this responsibility is assumed by young adult males, organized into *"deku hozonkai,"* or "puppet preservation associations." Each puppet is manipulated by several individuals using cables and pulleys and working together as a unit. This requires mutual awareness and coordination, and each member is expected to learn more than one role. The young men meet regularly in the evenings for practice sessions, followed by relaxed socializing. Later they will form the core of the *tsuke daiko* team representing their home neighborhood.

It has been mentioned that Sakaemachi never sponsored a *yatai;* instead it adopted the role of performing the *tōkeiraku*, a percussive rhythm produced by using a distinctive hammer and gong instrument together with a small drum. The *tōkeiraku* performers wear colorful costumes and lead the way before the long procession which accompanies the deity on its circuit through town. Their singular rhythm can be heard from a great distance and is the first indication to local residents that the deity is approaching. The members also perform a set of ritualistic dance movements in circular formation on the grounds directly in front of the shrine, both before the deity emerges and after it is returned. Membership in the group is restricted to elementary and middle school-aged boys. They begin practicing in the fourth grade but do not actually start performing until the fifth. The training sessions are led by the young men of the neighborhood.

The *matsuri* functions of two of the *chōnai* have yet to be discussed: Kamikita, the area located immediately adjacent to the shrine and distinguishable from the town proper, and Mukaimachi, which lies just across of the Araki River on the opposite side of town. These two neighborhoods are alike in that they both perform *kagura/shishi* dancing.

Kamikita is the home of the Miyamoto-*gumi,* which, as alluded to earlier, is considered the caretaker of the shrine. Its members are present to perform *kagura* when the deity is transferred to the *mikoshi,* and lead the way before the deity during its procession through town. Until about twenty years ago Miyamoto-*gumi* held its own independent *matsuri* on April 21—the day the deity was returned to the shrine. This underscores the fact that Kamikita has traditionally been considered distinct from the rest of the community.

The *kagura* music and *shishi* dance are performed by young men, who join the group upon entering middle school and are allowed to remain until the age of thirty. The older members train initiates and lead practice sessions. Practices begin on March 23 and are conducted at the neighborhood public meeting hall, located near the bottom of the stone steps leading up to the shrine.

Looking out across the basin from Kamikita, one can see Mukaimachi on the other side of town. This geographical opposition between the two neighborhoods is reinforced by the fact that both perform similar roles (*kagura* and *shishi* dance), and could thus be considered rivals in the same enterprise. The Mukaimachi group, called "Sōgakubu," is described as a "young men's association" (*seinendan*—not to be confused with the prewar version). Since Mukaimachi is the neighborhood where I lived during my fieldwork, I am most familiar with its efforts in preparing for the *matsuri*. I myself, in fact, was allowed to join the Sōgakubu and participate in the *matsuri* as one of its members. For this reason I will use Mukaimachi as a case example of how such groups conduct themselves.

Male residents of Mukaimachi join the Sōgakubu following graduation from high school and may remain active members through age 45, after which a few remain attached to the group as senior advisors. Most of the members are eldest sons who have been designated to take over their respective households and in some cases the family business. This is not so much a matter of policy as simple demographics—the designated heir often being the only offspring to remain at home upon reaching adulthood. In the past, membership was rather selective, and those seeking admittance had to demonstrate the proper character. In recent years, however, the number of young people has declined to such an extent that practically any resident male who desires to join may do so. The elder members continue the formality of meeting to decide whether to grant or refuse entrance. They also attempt to recruit young men who seem to be good candidates. Belonging to the Sōgakubu is still a source of pride for the young man's family, as it indicates that he is a responsible member of the community. The official membership roster now contains the names of around sixty members, though only about half of these regularly attend the practice sessions.

Three different instruments are employed in performing the *kagura* music: a bamboo flute (*yokobue*), a small drum (*shime daiko*) placed on a low stand with one side facing up, and a much larger drum *(shishi daiko)* of about 1.3 meters in diameter suspended from a wooden framework. These are employed on the upper level of the Kaguradai whenever it is in motion.

All members must begin by learning to play the flute, as it is considered the most difficult and therefore requires the longest time to master. Later, those inclined to do so can move on to the *shishi* dance, and perhaps to one of the two types of drum. Some eventually become proficient in all four roles.

Practice sessions serve to instill not only musical ability but important structural principles as well. The musicians sit in the formal *"seiza"* position, their lower legs tucked underneath them for continuous periods of up to an hour. There is no written score to follow. Rather, the junior members learn by eye and ear, sitting to the rear and imitating the fingering positions of the senior members. The seniors recognize their responsibility in passing on the tradition and try to set a good example. The whole structure of participation thus reinforces the vertical principle of an age-graded hierarchy.

Since the *shishi* dance requires special strength and stamina it is generally performed by younger men, though the older members remain active in teaching the correct postures. The dance uses the entire body and involves a considerable amount of low dynamic movements of the legs and hips. The dancers may become sore during the initial sessions, but as training progresses their bodies grow accustomed to the strenuous activity, and it is said that through practicing the *shishi* dance one develops the strength of a *shishi*.

Following every practice session the members gather in the back of the meeting hall to drink beer and *sake*. The atmosphere is generally relaxed, and the meetings become rather boisterous. Some of the members eventually head off in smaller groups to continue drinking at a local bar. Thus the Sōgakubu serves as a social organization for young men who either choose or are obliged to remain in Mukaimachi while their friends and siblings move away to the cities.

Final Preparations

In former times there were often problems and disputes during the *yatai* procession.[7] Certain *chōnai* would fail to observe the designated order or perhaps cut through a side street in an attempt to jump ahead of the others. This led to the institution of a formal stamp-affixing ceremony *(chōinshiki)* in which the leaders of all the *taigumi* were obliged to vow strict conformity to the prescribed order.

The stamp-affixing ceremony itself is held a few days before the *matsuri* begins, but the formal invitation to attend the ceremony *(chōin annaijō)* is delivered personally by the *yatai* director to each of the other *taigumi* leaders on April 9. At 9:00 a.m. the director sets out from his own home accompanied by an assistant. Both are dressed in *montsuki* kimono. They are accompanied by a banner bearer, carrying the flag of the director and leading the way before them as they proceed from door to door. The invitation must pass directly from the hands of the director to the *taigumi* leaders themselves. Each of the leaders has been notified beforehand when to expect the visit, and meets the visitors at his doorway dressed in a black suit and white tie. The director and *taigumi* leader briefly exchange greetings; then the former hands the latter the invitation wrapped neatly in a silk cloth and placed on a small lacquered tray. Clearly this is an important transaction, as attested by the formal dress, accoutrements, and demeanor that go with it. In addition to all the *taigumi* leaders, invitations are delivered in the same manner to two of the parish elders. The entire round of visits takes a little over two hours.

On the afternoon of April 10 the shrine officers gather with civil authorities at the town hall to hold the festival consultation meeting *(Furukawa matsuri uchiawasekai)*. The streets and alleys of Furukawa become the stage upon which much of the *matsuri* is performed, and the purpose of the meeting is to discuss logistical problems such as rerouting traffic, controlling damages, dealing with temporary disruptions of electric power and telephone service, and how best to ensure the safety of participants and visitors. Those invited to attend the meeting include the head priest of the shrine, parish elders, *okoshi daiko* director, *yatai* director, and police and fire department officials, as well as representatives from the Chūbu Electric Power Company (Chūbu Denryoku), Nippon Telephone and Telegraph (NTT), the Furukawa Tourist Association (Furukawa Kankō Kyōkai), and the street vendors' guild. Everyone's cooperation is requested in the effort to perform the *matsuri* without mishap.

That same evening a similar meeting is held at a prearranged location somewhere within the *okoshi daiko*'s directing territory. This meeting is attended by representatives from all the *tsuke daiko* teams, the purpose being to present the proposed route of the *okoshi daiko* and discuss any problems that might arise during the ritual's performance. Of particular concern is the clash between the rear guard, which protects the drum, and the *tsuke daiko,* who charge upon it from behind, as this is one of the areas where fighting is likely to occur. Again, everyone's cooperation is requested in helping to ensure that the event proceeds as safely as possible. The representatives then return to their home neighborhoods to pass the information on to the other members of their respective teams.

On April 13 the commander and other high ranking members of the *okoshi daiko*'s directing territory meet with police officers, NTT representatives, and an agent of the Planning, Commerce/Industry, and Tourism Department (Kikaku Shōkō Kankōka) of the town hall to inspect the entire route the *okoshi daiko* will follow. Trouble spots are identified and immediately repaired. These include potholes, low hanging wires, and gaps between the concrete slabs that cover the gutters.

On April 16 a work crew assembles at the shrine to clean the shrine grounds and prepare the equipment that will be used during the *mikoshi* procession. The crew is composed of representatives from every *chōnai,* the number each provides being determined by the size of its population. Small interior neighborhoods like Upper Ichinomachi or Upper Sannomachi send only two or three workers, while large neighborhoods like Mukaimachi may provide as many as thirty. Most of the workers are housewives or senior citizens—those who can take time away from their daily routines. Each contingent is assigned a particular area where it sets to work pulling weeds, raking leaves, and burning the refuse. Inside the shrine building the shrine officers busy themselves attaching the shrine's banners to long poles so that they can be borne aloft during the *mikoshi* procession.

The stamp-affixing ceremony was traditionally held on April 18, two days before the *mikoshi* procession. Recently, however, it has been set for the Sunday immediately preceding the *matsuri* so that participants do not have to take time away from their weekday work schedules. The ceremony is held in a large *tatami*-matted room attached to the rear of the newly renovated *tabisho* and begins promptly at 1:00 p.m. Each *taigumi* is represented by its leader, accompanied by two special duty officers. Also in attendance are two of the parish elders. The proceedings relate only to the *yatai* procession, so representatives from the four *okoshi daiko* territories are not involved. All those in attendance wear the *montsuki* kimono, appropriate for formal occasions such as this.

A brief document describing the order of *yatai* as well as the route they will follow is presented and scrutinized by all. A few minor points of concern are raised and discussed, but serious problems are likely to have been resolved through informal consultations beforehand,[8] and ordinarily no changes have to be made before the signing begins. Each representative signs the document with an ink brush and affixes his stamp. This indicates his neighborhood has agreed to abide by the prescribed order.

Everyone is required to sign three copies of the same document, with the head priest, supervisor of sacred rites *(shinji torishimari)*, and *yatai* director each receiving one copy. The ceremony ends with a ritual toast of *sake*—the customary way to conclude a formal agreement. Unlike the other events, however, the stamp-affixing ceremony does not degenerate afterwards into a lively drinking party; rather, it retains an air of dignified formality from beginning to end, with all the participants filing out in solemn silence much as they had arrived.

Various preparations are conducted independently within each individual neighborhood. These include raising the huge sets of banners (called *"nobori"*) which mark the neighborhood boundaries. The banners are long strips of heavy canvas attached lengthwise to a stout pole. Like the *yatai* vehicles, their original purpose was to welcome the deity, and they often bear inscriptions designed to gain the deity's favor. The banners are always set in pairs, one on either side of the street, forming a gateway into the home territory.[9] A *sakaki* branch is attached at the base of each pole.

Traditionally every neighborhood erected two pairs of banners—one at either end of its territory. A row of paper lanterns was suspended from a beam spanning the poles. The beam was hinged at one end; it was high enough to allow foot traffic to pass freely underneath, but had to be swung open so that the *okoshi daiko* and *yatai* could get through.

This custom is no longer so strictly observed. In the present day only three of the twelve neighborhoods continue to raise both pairs of banners. Seven of them raise only one pair. The remaining two neighborhoods suspend a row of paper lanterns over the street, but these are used in lieu of, rather than to complement, the banners.

The other neighborhoods have abandoned the row of lanterns altogether, as they interfere with the passage of the *okoshi daiko, yatai,* and ordinary traffic. Instead, huge lanterns are suspended near the base of the banner poles, one on either side of the street.

The day for raising the banners was originally fixed at April 17. Now, however, the individual neighborhoods are allowed to choose for themselves any day falling between April 12 and 18. Some of the neighborhoods choose Sunday, as the task can then be accomplished without interfering with people's everyday work schedules. The majority, however, remain with the traditional date of April 17.

Whichever date is chosen, each neighborhood on that same day establishes a *"tōban kaisho,"* or "temporary meeting place" somewhere within its territory. This will serve as its local headquarters for the duration of the *matsuri.* For neighborhoods that have a citizens' hall *(kōminkan),* the hall itself becomes the meeting place. Other neighborhoods will commandeer part of a building at some convenient location. In any case, the location will be open to the street so that passers-by can look inside and admire the items put there on display. Each meeting place contains a makeshift altar bearing trays of rice, flasks of *sake,* and other fruits of the harvest as offerings to the Shinto deities. The front of the altar is lined with scores of bottles of *sake* donated by resident households. Much of this *sake* is destined to be consumed by participants during the *okoshi daiko.* On the wall hangs a large list showing the names of individual residents and the duties they have been assigned to perform. A short divided curtain *(noren)* bearing the neighborhood insignia is draped over the entrance to the meeting place and a *sakaki* branch erected on either side. Several neighborhoods also build a small bridge leading into the entrance. The bridge is covered with an auspicious red soil, or *"akatsuchi"* (described later in Chapter 6), to entice the spirit of the deity to enter therein.

Also on April 17 the neighborhood *yatai* is rolled out of its garage to be cleaned and polished. The vital components are given a thorough inspection, and any necessary repairs immediately made so that the vehicle will be ready for the events of the next few days.

Most of the residents of Furukawa hang large white paper lanterns in front of their homes, with decorative bamboo and wax paper umbrellas over their tops. This is one of the characteristic features of *matsuri* in the Hida region. At night the lanterns are illuminated, lending a mystic beauty to the otherwise darkened streets.

Figure 12. The "temporary meeting place" *(tōban kaisho)* in Mukaimachi.

Figure 13. Inside the "temporary meeting place" in Mukaimachi. The neighborhood *tsuke daiko* and *shishi* masks are among the items on display.

The lanterns bear the name of the neighborhood *yatai* (or, in the case of Sakaemachi, the *Tōkeiraku*). On the other side is an inscription identifying the lantern as a *kagaribi,* or votive fire, being directed toward the *kami.* All of the lanterns employed in the Furukawa *matsuri* are handmade by a local artisan who lives in Lower Ichinomachi.

At around 8:00 a.m. on the morning of April 18, men from the directing neighborhood gather to assemble the massive drum structure (referred to as the *"yagura"*) which will be used during the performance of the *okoshi daiko* the following evening. The entire weight of the drum and its supporting framework was until recently shouldered by the mass of men underneath it. Unbeknown to most of the spectators, however, the structure now rides on a special undercarriage consisting of a single axle and two rubber-tired wheels positioned at the middle to support the bulk of the weight. During the actual performance of the ritual, the wheels remain hidden within the mass of bearers and thus go largely unrecognized.

The assembly work is performed at the place designated as the official starting point. This used to be located somewhere within the directing territory and thus changed from year to year. Recently, however, following the construction of a new museum complex adjacent to the *tabisho,* the starting point was permanently established in the accompanying plaza. This offers a considerably wider area to accommodate larger crowds of spectators.

Though the assembly is directed by a professional builder, the bulk of the workforce consists of neighborhood volunteers. These are predominantly retired men—those with free time to devote to such activities. Most of them have participated in this assembly process several times in the past and are already familiar with what needs to be done.

The term *"okoshi daiko"* alludes to a large, barrel-shaped drum with a leather head on either end. Each head bears the symbol of Ketawakamiya Shrine—a cluster of three hollyhock leaves radiating out from the center. The drum is normally housed in the main shrine building next to the stairs leading to the altar.

Pickup trucks bring the big drum and other equipment down from the shrine. The undercarriage and beams are stored in the *tabisho,* and these too are brought to the assembly area. All pieces of the drum structure have been numbered to ensure they will be placed in the same order every year. The timbers are made of *hinoki,* which is known for its strength and resilience.

The work force splits into teams, each devoted to a specific activity. One team begins to assemble the rectangular framework. Four rounded joists of about eight meters in length are placed parallel to one another upon the undercarriage at intervals of .7 meter. A wooden trestle the same height as the undercarriage supports the joists at either extremity, forming the rudiments of an elevated platform. Eight similarly rounded crossbeams measuring 2.8 meters in length are then laid atop and perpendicular to the joists to form a grid, and the crossbeams and joists bound tightly together with rope at each point of intersection.

The workers then begin constructing the wooden turret which supports the drum. The turret consists of a number of short overlapping beams joined at right angles with a long iron pin running through each corner. Unlike the crossbeams of the framework itself, these beams are angular to ensure greater stability. Initially two timbers the same length as the crossbeams of the framework are placed parallel to one another and the iron pins inserted vertically from the bottom. Then a number of short beams of .7 meter in length, each with a hole drilled in either end, is fitted down over the pins in layers, a single layer consisting of two parallel beams oriented perpendicular to those immediately below them. The four-sided turret is then fitted into the midsection of the rectangular framework. The parallel timbers which form the base of the turret thus become the framework's two central crossbeams and are attached to the joists with rope.

At the same time, another group engages itself in wrapping the drum in a sheath made of rice straw. First the sheath is laid flat on the ground. Then the drum is placed upon it and the ends of the sheath wrapped over the top, girding the body of the drum but leaving the leather heads exposed. The sheath is bound tightly to the drum by ropes passed several times around the middle and again at each end. The excess straw is trimmed away from the edges, so that the sheath is flush with the ends of the drum. Cylindrical bundles of straw are fitted over the rim of the drum, one at either end, providing a cushion to prevent the riders from sliding off the edge. Similar bundles are fastened lengthwise along either side of the drum, providing footrests to help the riders maintain their balance. Photographs taken during previous years are consulted periodically to avoid errors in detail.

The drum is then hoisted up onto the turret and temporarily secured with rope. The two uppermost beams of the turret are

Figure 14. Assembling the drum structure.

aligned crosswise to the length of the drum. A shallow concave space has been carved into each of these, and the drum's cylindrical body is fitted into them. The drum is equipped with two metal rings attached one on either side to the middle of its body. The rope is passed through both rings several times, wrapped around the beams of the framework below, and drawn very tight to prevent slippage. Finally *sake* is poured over all the rope joints holding the structure together. This is considered a rite of purification, but has the practical advantage of causing the ropes to become tighter as they dry.

When the drum structure has been completely assembled, cups of *sake* are handed around to all those involved. Casual passersby are invited to join in sharing a drink, and a relaxed atmosphere prevails. Red-and-white striped curtains will later be hung around the perimeter of the grounds, marking the event of the next evening as an auspicious occasion. The drum itself is adorned with blue-and-white striped curtains hung from the outside edges of the rectangular platform, thereby concealing the set of wheels and trestles upon which it rests.

Later that evening a practice session is held for all the people chosen to ride upon the drum structure—the young drum beaters as well as the more senior "main guard." As previously mentioned, the drum is equipped with foot rests and rim cushions to keep its riders from sliding off. There is also a metal loop attached to the upward-facing surface of the drum, and a long piece of white cloth is passed through it; when the riders take their positions they wrap the cloth around their waists, simultaneously binding themselves to each other and the drum itself. The drum beaters take a few practice swings to familiarize themselves with their assigned roles. Some of the old veterans look on from below, shouting advice and encouragement: "Hold the stick higher!" "The cadence is too fast; you'll never last at that rate!" "Now you're getting it—that looks fine!"

The members of the main guard are considerably older than the drum beaters. Many of them have ridden the drum structure before, and perhaps served as drum beaters in their younger years. Nevertheless, all are given advice on how to keep their balance while standing on the rounded beams. Riding the drum structure is described as like being on a small boat in a choppy sea, and it is necessary to keep the knees bent to absorb the bobbing motion and avoid being pitched off. The men briefly practice moving together in unison, first lowering themselves into a crouch by bending at the

Figure 15. The completed drum structure.

Figure 16. The front of the drum structure becomes a makeshift Shinto altar. The two large containers on the upper level are kegs of *sake*, each representing one of Furukawa's major brewing households.

knees, then rising with an upward sweep of the arms and a shout of *"wasshoi!"*

After this team of men has practiced sufficiently, another shift climbs aboard to take its place. The position of the commander at the front of the drum structure will be taken in turn by other prominent individuals, each referred to as "assistant-commander" *("fuku-sōtsukasa")*. The *okoshi daiko* will come to rest four times during the course of the next night. Each time the drum beaters and main guard will be changed, creating five separate shifts. Each shift consists of twelve men—four drum beaters and eight main guard members—for a total of sixty riders. The practice session continues until all have had an opportunity to briefly rehearse their assigned roles.

While the director's personnel are engaged in their practice session, young men in each neighborhood gather at their respective headquarters to bind their own drum—the *tsuke daiko*—to a stout wooden pole. The pole measures about 3.5 meters in length and about twelve centimeters in diameter, and like the beams of the main drum structure is made of *hinoki*. The drum attached to it is about .3 meter in diameter and shaped like a keg. Both heads of the drum bear the symbol of the *taigumi* to which it belongs.

Binding the drum to the pole so tightly that it will not slip during the action is no easy task. The rope has to be wound around the drum many times using an intricate series of loops and knots. Each neighborhood employs its own special procedure, registered only in the collective memory of the group. Though senior members are present to oversee the project and offer advice, the younger ones are generally left to try to figure things out for themselves. They stop periodically to scratch their heads and discuss the situation, and perhaps start again from the beginning several times before eventually rediscovering the correct way. This allows them to ingrain the procedure into their own minds through direct experience, ensuring that the tradition will be faithfully transmitted to succeeding generations.

When the drum has been attached, *sake* is applied to the ropes so that they tighten as they dry. The completed *tsuke daiko* is placed before the makeshift altar at the neighborhood headquarters with the insignia proudly exhibited for passers-by to see. In fact the entire display becomes a temporary shrine dedicated not only to the deity but also in a sense to the solidarity of the neighborhood. Other treasured objects may be exhibited there as well. Upper Ichinomachi, for example, displays its reconstructed mechanical puppet as well as the few remnants of its beloved old *yatai* that survived the fire in 1904. Likewise, Mukaimachi places its *shishi* masks in a row before the makeshift altar when they are not in use.

The Politics of Participation

At this juncture I would like to pause briefly to consider the qualifications for participation in the rousing drum ritual. While friends and visitors from other places are sometimes invited to join the *tsuke daiko* teams, riding upon the drum structure holds a special significance, and only a select number are eligible. As previously mentioned, the main guard *(hon'ei)* who stand to the front and rear of the drum are all prominent citizens. Each holds some special position of authority or responsibility, such as block leader *(kuchō)*, shrine officer *(jinja yakuin)*, or head of a public office. These individuals range in age from their mid-forties to their mid-sixties. They are without exception influential figures within their home neighborhoods, and usually within the town at large.

Standing at the head of them all is the commander, who traditionally occupies the very front of the drum framework during the first shift of riders. Again, this role is usually assumed by the leading member of the directing territory. During succeeding shifts his position is taken in turn by one of the four previously designated assistant-commanders, each of whom is either a *taigumi* leader or block chief within the directing territory.

The most envious position of all, of course, is riding atop the drum itself as one of the "top strikers." It is considered a great honor to perform this role—indeed the experience of a lifetime—and most young boys in Furukawa dream of growing up to one day ride the drum. If they were fortunate enough to be born into one of the *taigumi* neighborhoods there is a chance that they will be able to fulfill their dream, but the opportunity is open to only a select few.

When its turn comes to serve as director, each of the four *okoshi daiko* territories is allowed to select its own drum beaters, and the criteria vary somewhat from one territory to another. Holding a large stick over one's head, swinging it down to strike the drum several hundred times, and raising it slowly back into position after each strike require special strength and stamina, so the role is necessarily restricted to able-bodied young men. There is no standard age limit, but the upper range appears to be somewhere in the mid-thirties.

In the past, the aspiring candidate reportedly had to be a native of the town, unmarried, and the eldest son and designated heir of his household. In recent years, however, the qualifications have had to be relaxed due to the tendency for young men to move off to the cities, leaving a more restricted pool of suitable candidates. This has been a problem particularly for the smaller neighborhoods. Some informants claim that a candidate still must be the eldest son, but this does not seem to be so much a fixed rule as the corollary outcome of other social practices—eldest sons being the most likely to remain at home to succeed their fathers as heads of their households.

One criterion which continues to be strictly observed by all the neighborhoods is that the role be filled by their own native sons. This means those who were born and raised in the neighborhood and who have committed themselves to remaining there for the rest of their lives, or at least returning after a period of educational training or employment in some other area. It is not enough simply to have resided there, however; one must have been actively involved in neighborhood affairs. Young boys learn to play the flute and drum music which accompanies their *yatai*. Those who remain in the neighborhood after graduating from high school join with the other young men in the rousing drum ritual. They help wield the *tsuke daiko* in attacking the drum structure, and when their neighborhood is chosen to serve as director, the drum beaters are selected from among their ranks.

The drum beaters are also expected to exhibit good character—to maintain a reputation in the community for being fine, upstanding young citizens. Several informants mentioned that they should be of good family or lineage *(iegara)*. This is understandable in that, in Japan and other East Asian societies, the character of an individual is closely associated with the reputation of his or her household. It is not surprising that many of those chosen belong to prominent households, especially ones in which the current head is a shrine officer.

Since four drum beaters are employed at one time and there are five separate shifts, a total of twenty young men must be selected every year. Following the normal chain of command, each *taigumi* within the directing territory is assigned to provide a certain number of drum beaters. The number varies with the size of the *taigumi* neighborhood. Middle Ichinomachi, for example, is very small and is generally required to supply only a single individual. Even this has proven difficult, however, and in recent years the neighborhood has been obliged to drop the restriction against married men.

Again, each *taigumi* follows its own selection process, and the procedure varies from one to another. As previously mentioned, Genbu-*gumi* consists of two component *taigumi,* and responsibility for providing the drum personnel rotates back and forth between them. The young men's association within each *taigumi* selects the drum beaters from among its own members and informs the *taigumi* leader who they will be. In other groups the *taigumi* leader assumes a more active role, choosing the young men himself—after consulting, of course, with the other neighborhood leaders. Byakko-*gumi* contains seven different *taigumi,* all of them somewhat limited in size. In this case the responsibility is parcelled out among them, each being responsible for selecting a few suitable young men from among its member households.

There is also the matter of deciding which of the young men will serve as "top strikers" and which as "side strikers." The top position is much more visible and is by far the more desirable of the two roles. For most of the *taigumi* these specific roles are determined by drawing lots, and the participants must abide by the results of the drawing. This is unfortunate for those who aspire to the top position but have to settle for the auxiliary role, since serving as drum beater is generally considered a one-time opportunity and repeat performances are not allowed.

In Mukaimachi the drum beaters are drawn exclusively from the ranks of the Sōgakubu—the group responsible for providing the sacred dance and music *(kagura)* associated with the Kaguradai vehicle. They are chosen by the elder members of the group—veterans of many years' experience who have previously served atop the drum themselves. Selection is based on how faithfully the candidates have attended group practice sessions and performances, and may thus be seen as a reward for faithful service. The senior members also decide which of the young men will serve as top strikers and which as side strikers. In Mukaimachi, however, the restriction against a repeat performance is not observed. Any member who is chosen as side striker can expect to be assigned the top striker position when the neighborhood next becomes director. Twenty members (five separate shifts with four drum beaters in each) must be chosen each time, and the director responsibility comes round on an average of once every four years. Thus any member who remains actively involved in the group can expect to eventually ride atop the drum. Indeed, this is one of the main incentives for resident males to join the Sōgakubu and participate in its functions.

The role of drum beater is further differentiated in that, of the two top strikers, the one facing toward the rear (where all the action takes place) is considered to be in the better position. This derives in part from the fact that this position is most prominently featured in the photographs which appear in newspapers and promotional materials. Also, the first shift—the one that kicks off the event—is considered more important than the others, though the shift which serves during the pass through Ichinomachi is perhaps equally desirable. The front and back positions, as well as shift membership, are determined by drawing lots.

The wooden sticks used in striking the drum are specially made for that purpose alone. Willow wood *(yanagi no ki)* is used because it is strong yet lightweight and flexible. It also possesses a whiteness that shows up nicely in the dark of night. Willow trees grow wild alongside the Miya River, and each of the young men chosen as drum beater is required to go there himself in search of an appropriate branch to be made into his own personal stick. He cuts the branch from a living tree, then takes it to a local woodworker to be dried. He then has the woodworker pare it down to approximately the correct size and shape, then sands it smooth himself. The sticks are slightly curved in the manner of a traditional wooden training sword. The curvature makes for better contact with the leather drum head. The shaft is rounded and flares out slightly toward the striking end. The other end is wrapped with white adhesive tape to serve as a hand grip. The finished product is about one meter in length and about four centimeters in diameter.

While searching alone for the right branch and shaping it into a proper stick is hardly comparable to some sort of vision quest, it does resonate nicely with common folktale scenarios about confronting challenges or attaining one's manhood. The phallic symbolism inherent in the stick underscores this impression. When their service has ended, the young men will retain these sticks as cherished keepsakes.

A few days before the *matsuri* begins, the designated drum beaters all have their hair cut short in a close-cropped crewcut style. A short haircut is often recognized in Japan as a demonstration of serious intent. In a cross-cultural context, cutting the hair is commonly employed in rites of passage, marking the initiate's transition into a new social category.

Veterans of this special role almost without exception describe riding atop the drum as an unforgettable moment that cannot be truly understood or appreciated without directly experiencing it. Upon being invited into a Furukawa home it is quite common to find proudly displayed somewhere therein a large photograph of the *okoshi daiko*. On closer inspection one may notice that the individual riding atop the drum on the end facing the camera is none other than the host himself, appearing as a young man several years earlier. The photograph is a valued document of that brief moment of glory—a once-in-a-lifetime experience that belongs only to a true son of Furukawa.

Follow-up Activities

After the deity has been returned to the shrine on April 21, the residents of each neighborhood busy themselves with cleaning and putting away all the equipment used during the *matsuri*. The *yatai* are inspected for damages and made ready for storage. The territorial group in charge of the *okoshi daiko* disassembles the huge rectangular drum structure and returns the drum to Ketawakamiya Shrine. In the afternoon the parish elders visit the shrine, and a feast is held in gratitude for their services.

On the afternoon of April 22 some of the shrine officers meet in Kaba's *sake* brewery to "count the rice" *(kome o kazoeru)*. During the *mikoshi* procession all the rice, money, and bottles of *sake* collected from the townspeople were thrown together into bags; now they must be separated. The officers empty the contents of the bags into sorting boxes with wire mesh screens in the bottom, then shake the boxes back and forth over large steel vats. As the rice sifts through, the envelopes containing cash donations emerge from the pile, eventually settling in a heap on the wire mesh. The money is placed in boxes and taken to the office upstairs for counting. The rice is scooped up and poured into thirty-kilogram bags. Each bag is weighed to make sure it holds the right amount and then tied shut. The rice will later be sold and the money deposited in the shrine treasury. The *sake,* on the other hand, will be used during ceremonial occasions and meetings of the shrine officers throughout the coming year.

The leaders of the directing neighborhood generally hold a meeting about two weeks after the *matsuri* to assess their conduct of the event and make suggestions for improving it when their turn comes round again. This kind of reflective interlude is called *"hanseikai"* (introspection meeting), and has been employed as a common managerial tool in various Japanese organizational settings, from elementary schools to company offices (Rohlen 1974; Steinhoff 1989).

As might be expected, serving as director places a considerable financial burden on the chosen neighborhood. In 1991, the total cost for Mukaimachi was 1,110,145 yen. The shrine provides the directing neighborhood with 400,000 yen. The rest must come from contributions by individual households. During the *matsuri* the name of each household and the amount of its contribution are posted on a signboard at the neighborhood headquarters, making those who fail to contribute conspicuous by their absence.

Most of the residents are engaged in regular employment which does not cease during the *matsuri,* and all the additional planning and preparation required of them at that time creates a substantial burden. Even so, the extra work is accompanied by the excitement the event generates, the opportunity to interact with other members of the community, and the pride of participating in a fine old tradition. In the words of one of my informants: "When the *matsuri* is over I breathe a sigh of relief. Then I start looking forward to the next one."

Sociopolitical Significance

In keeping with the notion of a "cultural performance," the Furukawa *matsuri* may be seen as an annual expression of the values and ideals that define the local population as a cohesive social unit. Perhaps the most obvious element is a hierarchical principle based on several distinct levels of seniority and prestige. Elder members of prominent households occupy positions of special honor and authority, acting as leader-representatives of their respective neighborhood associations. By assuming the most prestigious roles—participating in the lottery and stamp-affixing ceremonies, leading the *mikoshi* procession, riding upon the drum structure during the *oko-*

shi daiko—men who occupy influential positions within their communities engage in a visible demonstration of their status.

Even more significantly, the *matsuri* is executed through the very structure of authority it symbolically affirms. Organizing and performing the various activities creates chains of command, group identities, and interpersonal relations which persist long after the *matsuri* itself has been concluded, and extend into other aspects of community life. Like a self-fulfilling prophecy, the *matsuri* simultaneously expresses a condition and helps bring that condition into being. In fact, since the *matsuri* is the most visible and explicit manifestation of these social phenomena, it is questionable whether they could persist for long in its absence.

This also applies to the maintenance of gender distinctions. Males dominate the leadership positions as well as the performance of public rituals. With the exception of the *miko* dancers, it is the males who participate in the shrine ceremonies and accompany the deity during the *mikoshi* procession. The *okoshi daiko* in particular is a predominantly male event, and the young men's association in each neighborhood assumes leadership at practice sessions as well as in forming a *tsuke daiko* team. Women are for the most part restricted to activities within the domestic sphere—preparing food and entertaining their guests during household feasts, for example. It has only been recently that girls were allowed to ride in the *yatai* of some neighborhoods, and, as mentioned in the preceding chapter, this was more a matter of necessity than an attempt to encourage gender equality.

Restrictions apply to the planning phase as well. As previously described, Furukawa neighborhoods are comprised of blocks *(ku)*, which are further divided into groups of contiguous households *(tonarigumi)*. Each of these groups elects a leader *(kumichō)* to serve for one year, the responsibility rotating from household to household. The position involves distributing information and collecting money for local projects. Women are more closely integrated into the neighborhood communications network, as the men are away at their jobs for much of the day. It is common, then, for women to be designated group leaders. Significantly, however, when the block chief calls his constituents together to distribute roles for the *matsuri,* it is not the group leaders themselves who attend but rather their husbands. The women explain, with no visible sign of resentment, that it is the men who tend to the "important matters" *(daiji na koto)*. After the planning meetings, they add, the men hang around and drink, and it would be considered unusual and improper for women to join in.

The gender distinction is further enhanced by an insider/outsider dichotomy. In a society where patrilocal residence is the norm,[10] females born into the neighborhood are destined to marry into other households. Most likely they will marry outside the neighborhood altogether—whereupon their residential affiliation with it will cease. They are therefore considered temporary residents and as such denied the symbols of territorial identity (participating in the shrine ceremonies, *mikoshi* procession, *okoshi daiko;* riding in or pulling the *yatai*) afforded the males. Again, one of the most important qualifications for young men chosen to serve as drum beater during the *okoshi daiko* is their commitment to residing permanently within their home neighborhoods. This tends to restrict the role to eldest sons, who customarily remain in their natal households to succeed their fathers. In fact the position of eldest son may hold little significance when taken at face value; it is important by virtue of its association with permanent membership in the community.

The *matsuri* provides a powerful symbolic association with native place. Typically a child born in Furukawa first experiences the *matsuri* in the arms of a parent, gazing in wonder from a second-floor window as the drum passes by at eye level. Later the children themselves participate in the event, carrying a lantern and singing the "Furukawa Medeta" as part of the long column preceding the drum. On the day of the main event, elementary school children are allowed to ride inside the *yatai* vehicles on the lower level. Middle schoolers learn to play the bamboo flute and drum, and later ride on the vehicle's upper level to provide the musical accompaniment.

At this point the gender roles become more distinct. Young unmarried women will likely be enlisted by their mothers to help with the household chores. Young men begin participating in the *tsuke daiko* activities. Those who serve faithfully and demonstrate the proper attributes may one day be chosen to ride upon the drum itself.

As the young men marry and begin raising children, their attentions will turn to other responsibilities. They may continue to participate in the *tsuke daiko* as long as they feel able, and when their neighborhood is chosen director they may serve as members of the rear guard or help shoulder the drum structure. As they grow older they may eventually become shrine officers or assume positions of civic responsibility such as block chief, entitling them to ride upon the drum framework as part of the main guard. They may even one day occupy the lead position in the role of commander.

The *matsuri* thus represents a sequential rite of passage. Participants graduate from one stage to the next, assuming roles appropriate to their ages. Participation in the annual event comes to be equated with the course of life itself. This leads Furukawa natives to associate their own identities with the home neighborhood and, by extension, with the town wherein it lies. In the words of a local publication: "[F]rom childhood they take part in the *matsuri* over and over again, and through the *matsuri* deepen their understanding of proper human relationships and affectionate attachment to their native place" (Furukawa-chō Kankō Kyōkai 1984:89).[11]

Hierarchy and Communalism

Anthropologists have often observed that group cohesiveness in Japan is maintained through a combination of two seemingly antithetical principles: (1) a hierarchy of authority consisting of clearly defined status distinctions and (2) a pervasive sense of communal egalitarianism based on shared attributes and experiences.[12] Such observations are accompanied by the recognition that without sufficient emphasis on the egalitarian ethos the hierarchical structure of authority will break down. In terms of maintaining the structure, therefore, it is important that group leaders create regular opportunities for promoting a sense of shared identity with and among their fellow constituents (Nakane 1970; Rohlen 1974:105–107; Atsumi 1979; Bestor 1989:164–165).

Both aspects are clearly evident in the performative context of the Furukawa *matsuri*. Despite the hierarchical distinctions within component neighborhoods, great emphasis is placed on egalitarianism at a level which encompasses the entire town. This is clearly indicated by the fact that the role of director is shared equally among the various neighborhood associations and that the order of *yatai* (excluding Sanbasō) rotates annually. Both are determined by lottery under the pretext of a rite of divination; thus no single neighborhood can be seen to predominate. Likewise, the *mikoshi* procession passes through every constituent neighborhood, symbolically drawing the residents into a single unity. It is significant here that the route has been extended over the years to incorporate new territory as the town expands.

Within this delineated area, however, the *okoshi daiko* and *yatai* activities break the town into smaller units, creating a context for inter-neighborhood competition. A rival neighborhood thus becomes the antithetical referent against which one's own group identity is defined. As Bestor (1989:3–4) perceptively observes, communities are created and maintained not in isolation, but through oppositional engagement with other entities.

This perhaps explains why the hierarchical structure of authority within a single neighborhood persists. The *matsuri* creates opportunities to cultivate a sense of collective identity through shared experience, thereby deemphasizing internal status distinctions that might otherwise prove divisive. Residents of a particular neighborhood are drawn together through shared responsibility and competition with rival groups. Focusing on a threat from the outside takes emphasis away from the inequities within; the hierarchy becomes more tolerable.

But the rousing drum adds an additional element, what Turner (1967, 1969, 1974) might recognize as a periodic descent into chaos and subsequent return to order in keeping with his emphasis on ritual liminality. Participation in the *okoshi daiko* is a singular sense experience—an altered state of consciousness that, for many, is worth pursuing in itself. The consumption of alcohol, the charged atmosphere, and the distinct element of danger are partly responsible for the transformation. But added to these is the effect on the emotions produced by the sound of the drum. One of my informants, a man in his mid-forties who has enthusiastically participated in the *okoshi daiko* every year since his late teens, confided that as he gets older he finds himself increasingly less enthusiastic about running around half naked in the cold night air, not to mention getting battered and mashed during the *tsuke daiko* charges. But when he hears the sound of the drum approaching, the old spirit returns. It is this sound reverberating through the night that stirs the soul, rousing the men of Furukawa to action as its name implies.[13] Since the *okoshi daiko* is an expression of virile youth, it is easy to understand why men approaching middle age insist on participating as long as they are able. The naked condition suggests the shedding of social responsibilities and a return to primal emotions. It also conveys an appealing sense of being reborn, "a return of the self to the state of cosmic chaos" (Sonoda 1988:74).

Gilmore (1975, 1987), Le Roy Ladurie (1979), and Scott (1990:

173), among others, have alluded to the use of carnival as an opportunity for expressing disapproval or settling old scores. In Furukawa too it is customary among local residents to wait for the night of the *okoshi daiko* to settle grievances and vent their hostilities (Furukawa-chō Kankō Kyōkai 1984:84, Furukawa-chō Kyōiku Iinkai 1987: 474). The rules and strictures that govern ordinary social interaction are temporarily abandoned, allowing the expression of animosities that would otherwise remain suppressed. "Fellow residents who for some reason oppose each other engage on this night in unrestrained fist fighting. But at daybreak they put on their *kamishimo* and join the *yatai* escort, wearing innocent faces as if nothing had happened. Revenge will have to wait until next year's *matsuri*" (Kaba 1984:35).

It is significant here (in terms of Turner's work) that the antistructural element *(okoshi daiko)* takes place *prior* to the "main event" (*yatai* and *mikoshi* processions). Dawn signals a rebirth, and along with it the restoration of order. In this case the actual venting of hostilities coincides nicely with the ritual symbolism being employed—that is, ridding the community of evil influences. The cathartic release of divisive tensions makes possible the tolerance and orderly comportment that life in a highly integrated society ordinarily demands.

This applies to the community as well as the individual. The *okoshi daiko* divides the town into competitive segments; the *mikoshi* procession draws it back together. Through the performative structure of the *matsuri,* social values and organizational structures are recreated even as they are being acted out—they are literally "enacted." The annual shrine festival is not simply a symbolic expression of renewal; it is the actual process of renewal itself.

But renewal does not necessarily imply exact replication. The *matsuri* is a communal effort—the product of various actors' contributions. Each actor assesses its meaning based on his or her individual needs and perceptions. As Gerholm (1988:200) notes, "[t]his has implications for how rituals are maintained and elaborated, how they evolve and change. . . . To study this process in detail one would need a deep historical perspective as well as the possibility to focus on the persons who have been responsible for modifications of the ritual."

This underscores the importance of a time dimension. The people of Furukawa imbue their festival with great antiquity. Most place its origins at around four hundred years ago, though some insist it dates from as early as the ninth century. Moreover, the festival is seen as a time-honored tradition that has been handed down faithfully through successive generations to the present day. But how can an event that originated several hundred years ago among a rather isolated community of subsistence farmer–foragers possibly retain any significance in the highly integrated postindustrial society to which Furukawa now belongs, and why would the townspeople continue performing an event that bears little relevance to their present situation?

The answer seems obvious: the festival *has* in fact changed over the years in response to changing conditions—otherwise it would have been abandoned long ago, as has happened with so many other institutions. The *matsuri* must thus be seen as the ritual expression of an ongoing sociopolitical process, continually adapting to the changing needs of the townspeople. The impression that ritual merely perpetuates the status quo is the result of focusing on an overly narrow time frame. That is why it is important not to stop with a description of the *matsuri* in the present day, but to investigate its historical development, relating changes in its performative structure to larger sociopolitical and economic patterns.

Chapter 6

ORIGINS AND EARLY DEVELOPMENT

Historical ethnography is seriously complicated by a lack of ample source materials, or doubts concerning their accuracy. As in archaeology, fragments can be pieced together using the available evidence, but a certain amount of informed conjecture is required to fill in the gaps. The fieldwork upon which this analysis is based was initiated in 1990. The memories of my most senior informants thus extend back only to around the mid-Taishō period (1912–1926). In attempting to reconstruct the *matsuri* prior to this time, I was obliged to resort to whatever written documents were available. These, however, had to be used with caution due to several limitations: (1) the written record being biased toward the interests and perceptions of the literary elite, and (2) potentially embarrassing or incriminating details being intentionally elided due to fear of public disapproval. Both are relevant in the case of the *okoshi daiko,* as it emerged from the ranks of the common people and was considered by many a gross perversion of the *matsuri*'s religio-political essence.

In the case of Furukawa, however, there is an additional problem: many of the written documents pertaining to the conduct of the *matsuri* were destroyed in the great fire of 1904. What records do remain were salvaged from family *kura*—the thick-walled structures made of fire-resistant clay, located adjacent to the main dwellings. *Kura* were used by old established households for storing important possessions, including the year's rice supply. Many of these structures were left intact after the fire, and some contained documents relating to Furukawa history. In the 1980s, local historians, assisted by the town administration, led a project to gather these scattered documents and publish them in more accessible form. The result was a hefty three-volume collection entitled *Furukawa-chōshi—Shiryō Hen* (History of Furukawa Township: Materials Compilation; see Furukawa-chō 1982, 1984, 1986). The data are presented in raw form as they appeared in the originals. They are organized into various topical categories, but are unaccompanied by commentary or analysis beyond a brief introductory section at the beginning of each volume. The glimpses they provide into the economic, sociopolitical, and religious institutions of the past are useful but highly fragmented, consisting of whatever happened to be documented initially and later to survive the fire.

I also made extensive use of previous work by local historians. Two individuals in particular stand out: Ōno Masao and Kuwatani Masamichi. Both are highly regarded scholars whose careers have been devoted to Hida history. Both researched the Furukawa *matsuri,* at times employing the recollections of their own elderly informants. These recollections were particularly useful in that they were obtained twenty to thirty years prior to my own fieldwork and thus represent a previous generation of participants which had since passed away. Another important source was Kaba Ikumi, a Furukawa native who has written many books and articles on Hida culture, though her works are aimed at a more general readership. A few early articles on the *matsuri* published in folklore studies journals were useful in reconstructing the hidden transcript, as they generally focused on participation by the common people. The earliest photographs of the *matsuri* date from the mid-Taishō (1912–26) period, and these were extensively employed. Observations contained in travelogues and private journals were utilized as well.

A less conventional source is the historical novel *Yama no Tami* (The Mountain Folk), a narrative account of the Umemura rebellion by proletarian writer Ema Shū (1985a, 1985b). Elsewhere (Schnell, n.d.) I have asserted the importance of this work as a source of ethnographic data. Ema, himself a Hida native, was using the novel to indirectly criticize the militarist Japanese government of the 1930s. The government began to monitor his activities, so to allay their suspicions he assumed the guise of an ethnographer, even founding and editing a journal on local folklore called *Hidabito* (The People of Hida). In gathering his data, Ema relied heavily on native informants, interviewing older residents about their experiences during the rebellion as well as carefully documenting the daily lives of the local peasantry. Essentially he was conducting ethnographic fieldwork, later incorporating his informants' accounts directly into the historical narrative. This information is useful in reconstructing the lives and culture of the people of Hida, and their reaction to the dramatic changes imposed upon them during Japan's modernization.

Despite a shortage of documents, one highly reliable account does exist in the form of a regional survey conducted shortly after the Meiji Restoration. This is an excellent place to begin an inquiry on ritual and change because the Restoration marks a major turning point in Japan's social, economic, and political development—one that had dramatic repercussions in the rural countryside. More specifically to the Hida region, the initial years of the Meiji period coincide with a major peasant uprising—the Umemura Rebellion—which occurred as a backlash against the new order.

The Furukawa *Matsuri* on the Eve of the Modern Era

In 1869, prefectural governor Miyahara Taisuke[1] commissioned Tomita Iyahiko to conduct a general inventory of the entire Hida region. The results were published in the *Hida Gofudoki* (Updated Geographical Description of Hida), issued in 1874. This document contains a detailed inventory of cultural as well as natural resources, including a lengthy description of the Furukawa *matsuri*. In compiling his inventory, Tomita relied upon information contributed by local residents. His description of the *matsuri* was taken almost verbatim from a previously existing document entitled *Fudo Kakiage Chō* (Written Geographical Register), which is attributed to Furukawa scholar and local historian Kaba Masamura (Furukawa-chō 1984:655–656).[2] Kaba's account is dated the Third Month[3] of 1870, and thus provides a glimpse of the Furukawa *matsuri* as it existed roughly at the time of the Meiji Restoration. The following is a direct translation of Tomita's (1968:399–400) account. Any deviation from Kaba's original will be noted therein.

Shrine of tutelary deity Sugimoto. Located in Kamikita Village. Enshrined deity. Shrine precinct, Furukawa: the town district, Ryokan, Naka no Tame, Machiura, and Shimomachi.[4] The deity's conveyance and festival are Eighth Month, Fifth, Sixth, and Seventh Days. Records in Kamikita. The sacred rites are every year Eighth Month, Sixth Day. Shrine precinct: Kamikita Village, its environs, and Wada in Yamamoto Village.[5] The Fifth Day is called the pre-festival *(shigaku)*, while the day of the sacred rites is called the main festival *(hongaku)*. There is a procession of *yatai* much the same as during the spring and autumn festivals in Takayama. A day or two before, the festival banners are raised at the entrances to streets and alleys. Below them a votive fire is lit and pine trees erected. On the day of the pre-festival, each man helps pull his *yatai* through town, then back to his own neighborhood for a display of artistic dancing. This is performed atop a stage extending out from the middle level of the *yatai.* The dances change every year and consist of famous excerpts from *kabuki* plays. The performers are children of about ten years old. Then at dawn on the day of the main festival the beating of a drum reverberates as it circles through town. This is called the *"okoshi daiko."*[6] With the first glimmer of day the *mikoshi* is shouldered, originating from Kamikita Village, circling the residence for visiting dignitaries (a custom remaining from when the Kanamori's castle stood there) then heading on into town.[7] Before the *mikoshi* enters the *tabisho,* the *yatai* are pulled from all over town and assembled there to meet it. Soon the dances performed the day before begin anew. Included among them are puppet performances [apparently in reference to the *karakuri ningyō*]. The order of *yatai* always begins with Sanbasō, the remaining sequence rotating annually. In final position is the *"nengyōji"* [that year's acting referee] who directs all aspects of the *matsuri.*[8] The day before, two officials arrive from the prefectural headquarters in Takayama to discourage disturbances from occurring. They are called *"bugyō"* ["magistrates"]. For the remainder of the day the *yatai* are pulled through the various neighborhoods in town. As evening approaches lanterns are hurriedly attached, then from the section of town where the procession ends they each depart for their home neighborhoods. This is known as the *"hikiwakare"* [which means "pulling away"]. The *mikoshi* is accompanied by town leaders, one on each of the four sides, wearing hemp overmantles and bearing standards. It is preceded by young men from Kamikita Village wearing *shishi* masks, who dance along to the rhythm of flutes, drums, and small cymbals. The shrine officials walk along behind as the procession makes its way around town, then returns back up to the shrine on Higashi Hill.[9] The *mikoshi* is both met and seen off by the town officials. The main thoroughfares are swept clean, then purified using piles of sand and strewn earth, and a bucket of water is placed at every home. Members of the fire brigade patrol the town day and night in shifts. The chief dons a soldier's helmet and *haori*[10] and walks bravely along carrying a ladle, fan, hook, bucket, standard, and other fire fighting equipment. On the evening of the Fifth and likewise on the Sixth every household lights a paper lantern, and to see them all lit up in a row is quite beautiful. In the evening the government officials visit Sugimoto Shrine and on the morning of the Seventh return to Takayama. That same day the men and women of Furukawa go together to visit the shrine. This is always a boisterous occasion.

Yatai names:[11]

Sanbasō:	Upper Ichinomachi—leads the procession every year
Byakkodai:	Lower Sannomachi
Seiryūtai:	Tonomachi
Hō-ōtai:	Ichinomachi, blocks two and three
Kirintai:	Ichinomachi, block four
Sankōtai:	Ninomachi, block one
Seiyōtai:	Upper Sannomachi
Ryūtekitai:	Ninomachi, block four
Suzakudai:	Mukaimachi
Kinkitai:	Ninomachi, blocks two and three

This was the order in Meiji 3 (1870). With the exception of Sanbasō, the *yatai* are arranged in the order they were acquired. Each year the one occupying the final position is designated acting referee and is responsible for directing all of the festival proceedings. The one immediately behind the *Sanbasō* becomes acting referee the following year.[12]

At first glance the general form of the *matsuri* in 1870 appears to have been much the same as in the present day. On closer inspection, however, a number of significant differences may be noted. One of the most obvious is that the *matsuri* was at that time held in early autumn. The East Asian "Eighth Month" is usually translated "August." However, depending on the year, the old lunar–solar calendar could begin anywhere from three to seven weeks later than the Western (Gregorian) calendar, so the date of the *matsuri* generally fell in early to mid-September. The Furukawa *matsuri,* in other words, used to take place just prior to the rice harvest rather than as a prelude to spring transplanting as it does today.[13]

The 1870 description notes that on the day of the main event the *yatai* assembled at the *tabisho* to greet the *mikoshi*. It then describes both *yatai* and *mikoshi* being hauled around town. In fact, the visit of the *mikoshi* and the *yatai* parade were at that time combined in a single grand procession; they were not conducted as separate events as they are in today's version. (Indeed, the unified procession was standard procedure until 1961.) It is also apparent that the lottery ceremony for determining the order of *yatai* had not yet been implemented. Instead, the vehicles followed an established rotation, with the exception of Sanbasō, whose position was fixed at the head of the procession. As can be seen from the list of vehicles included at the end of Tomita's description, Mukaimachi at that time sponsored an ordinary *yatai;* it had not yet assumed its special role of performing *kagura* and leading the way before the deity.

The mention of two administrative officials from Takayama in the 1870 version acknowledges that Furukawa was politically subordinate to the larger town. Use of the term *"bugyō"* (Kaba's account originally employed the highly honorific form *"obugyō-sama"*) in referring to these officials is a holdover from the Tokugawa period, but nevertheless implies considerable authority. Their purpose was to direct the proceedings, prevent deviations from the prescribed order, and discourage disputes. Furukawa is no longer under the administrative control of Takayama, so obviously there is no reason for such official representation in the present day.

Neither does the fire brigade join the procession as it did in 1870. Their presence among the village leaders and ritual specialists may seem a bit incongruous. At that time, however, the constant threat of conflagration made the local fire brigade a very powerful and important presence. When fire broke out there was no time for deliberation, and the orders of the fire chief were to be obeyed without delay. As a logical extension of their duties, brigade members assumed the role of protecting their neighborhoods against other dangers as well, and until the Meiji Restoration of 1868 they served as a combination of local militia and neighborhood police.

Such responsibilities required physical strength and agility; for this reason the fire brigade was largely staffed by younger men. In fact the fire brigade *(hikeshi)* and the young men's association *(wakamono gumi)* contained virtually the same membership. Several scholars have alluded to the fact that the young men of rural Japan traditionally comprised the village workforce. This gave them considerable leverage in village affairs, the threat being that they could withhold their labor services in obtaining what they wanted (Befu 1965:31, Furukawa 1986, Ueno 1987:S79).

The list of *yatai* near the end of the document shows a slightly different territorial arrangement than is presently recognized. Prior to around 1879, the town was divided into eleven neighborhoods, roughly corresponding to the *chōnai* divisions that exist in the present day. In both Ichinomachi and Ninomachi, blocks two and three were later combined to form the middle sectors, leaving block four to constitute the lower one. Mukaimachi existed as a separate com-

Table 3. Tokugawa period (1600–1868) neighborhood designations versus those of the present day.

Tokugawa Period Division	Current Division
Tonomachi	Tonomachi
Ichinomachi, block 1	Upper Ichinomachi
Ichinomachi, block 2 Ichinomachi, block 3	Middle Ichinomachi
Ichinomachi, block 4	Lower Ichinomachi
Ninomachi, block 1	Upper Ninomachi
Ninomachi, block 2 Ninomachi, block 3	Middle Ninomachi
Ninomachi, block 4	Lower Ninomachi
Sannomachi, block 1	Upper Sannomachi
Sannomachi, block 2	Lower Sannomachi

munity on the opposite bank of the Araki River. Sakaemachi had not yet been established as a distinct neighborhood on the northwest end of town.

Perhaps the most conspicuous discrepancy between today's *matsuri* and the 1870 account lies in the nature of the *okoshi daiko,* which receives only cursory mention: "at dawn on the day of the main festival the beating of a drum reverberates as it circles through town." Kaba's original adds that it "sets out from the neighborhood of that year's acting referee." Nothing else is written: there is no evidence of a huge wooden framework with several men riding atop, being hefted through the streets by a mass of bearers; no procession of townspeople leading the way before it; no *chōnai* teams vying with one another for position and advancing upon the great drum from behind as there are in the present version. The changes in the *okoshi daiko,* as well as the socioeconomic and political developments that accompanied them, will be taken up in the next chapter. For now I would like to address the nature of the *matsuri* as it existed prior to the Meiji Restoration.

Kami and Community

Though the specific origins of the Furukawa *matsuri* are unknown, it is commonly assumed to be as old as Ketawakamiya Jinja, the shrine from which it derives. While some form of ritual activity was undoubtedly directed toward the shrine from its inception, this by no means implies the type of communal celebration that presently exists. A 1934 publication issued by the Furukawa town hall (Honda 1934:29) alludes to indications that "modest rites" were performed at the shrine during the Seiwa period (858–876 CE). The author does not cite the specific source, but is probably referring to the *Nihon Sandai Jitsuroku* (Factual Record of Three Generations in Japan), one of the early imperial histories, completed in 901 CE. Its fifty volumes provide scrupulous details of a thirty-year period, covering the reigns of Emperors Seiwa (858–876), Yōzei (876–884), and Kōkō (884–887). The document states that during the sixteenth year of Seiwa's reign (873, referred to in the text using the era name Jōgan 15), the Ketawakamiya Shrine in Hida Province was raised to the rank of "lower fifth" (Tokoro 1989:1002). This has fostered the assumption that the roots of the Furukawa *matsuri* extend back over a thousand years.

As a religious observance, the *matsuri* bears structural affinities to widely held folk beliefs, suggesting a possible genetic link. As mentioned earlier, the mountains provided many of the basic necessities for human subsistence, and were thus vital to life in the communities below. This relationship was symbolically expressed through folk rituals designed to entice the mountain spirits *(yama no kami)* down into the rice paddies at spring planting time, where they remained for the duration of the growing season as "spirits of the paddies" *(ta no kami),* thereby ensuring a bountiful harvest. In the autumn the spirits were ritually sent back to the mountains to become *yama no kami* once again, and there they remained until the following spring (Yanagita 1962a:54, Hori 1968:150–151).

With the development of more highly integrated communities, the mountain spirits appear to have been reconceived as tutelary deities *(ubusunagami),* each represented by a shrine building overlooking the community under its protection. The shrine is customarily positioned to the northeast, as this is considered the direction from which evil approaches.[14] The structural equivalent of the spirits' descent into the rice paddies is the annual visit of the deity during the shrine festival. The fact that the deity is escorted down from the mountains, then back up again at the conclusion of the festival, enhances the parallel.

During the late fourteenth century, as mentioned in Chapter 3, a branch of the Anegakōji family built a castle on the opposite side of the Miya River in the proximity of what is now Takano hamlet. There were, of course, a number of small peasant settlements already located throughout the basin. Principle among them was a village called Furukawa, which had developed in conjunction with Anegakōji's castle. The village was located in the basin area lying between the Miya and Araki Rivers, just south of what is now Mukaimachi.[15] To protect the castle from evil influences, a shrine was established to its "dangerous" northeast. This put the shrine in the area now known as Koreshige. The guardian deity associated with the shrine was called "Sugimoto."[16]

When Kanamori Nagachika took over Hida during the latter half of the sixteenth century, he moved the region's administrative headquarters to Takayama, leaving his son Arishige in charge of the Furukawa area. Arishige had the old fortress once occupied by Anegakōji razed, and began construction of a new castle just north of the Araki River where it joins the Miya. The new castle was christened

Masushima-*jō,* and was the only one in Hida built on level ground. Its location was strategically important. Due to Hida's rugged topography, the Miya River valley was the only route an enemy force approaching Takayama from the north could have seriously considered. Positioned at the confluence of two rivers, the castle simultaneously controlled access to both. It was also located in the only major agricultural area outside the Takayama basin, placing most of the region's rice production potential under the immediate surveillance of the Kanamori.

Arishige needed merchants and artisans to supply his contingent of warrior retainers, and set about establishing a town adjacent to the castle site. The rudiments of such a town already existed in the village of Furukawa. Arishige kept the name, but moved the village to the other side of the Araki River, directly adjacent to his new castle. In 1589 he issued a proclamation guaranteeing a favorable economic environment for merchants willing to locate in "Furukawa *akinai machi*" ("Furukawa merchant town") (Taga 1982:84, Tanibana 1991:73).

The town was laid out in bands running parallel to the Miya River southwest of the castle. Directly adjacent to the castle walls were the spacious homes of Arishige's chief retainers. This area was accordingly referred to as Tonomachi ("lords' district"). Middle and lower-level retainers lived in a band of smaller houses further north. The merchant district was located to the south, between Tonomachi and the Miya River. Water was diverted from the Araki to form an irrigation canal called Setogawa, which ran northwest through town and out into the adjacent rice paddies. This canal formed a physical boundary between Tonomachi and the merchant district. The latter was further divided into Ichinomachi, Ninomachi, and Sannomachi, the streets being numbered consecutively with distance from the castle.

Arishige also dismantled three Buddhist temples at various locations on the other side of the river and had them repositioned in his new castle town, even donating the timber to facilitate their reconstruction. These temples were Enkō-ji (at that time called "Shōkaku-ji"), Honkō-ji, and Shinshū-ji. All belonged to the True Pure Land sect, which held a distinct majority in Hida. The three temples formed a triangle roughly encompassing the merchant district, thus being easily accessible to the residents therein. At the same time, Arishige had a Zen temple built just on the other (southeast) side of the castle and named it Rinshō-ji. This was intended as his own family temple.[17]

Establishing a guardian deity to the northeast was apparently deemed a necessary condition for defense of the town and castle, as Arishige immediately took steps to do so. Coincidentally, there already existed a small shrine on a hill directly to the northeast of the new castle. Arishige had Furukawa's deity Sugimoto moved there and merged with the existing deity. This second shrine had been called "Ketawakamiya," but Arishige changed the name to Sugimoto Myōjin ("Gracious Deity Sugimoto"), indicating that he was retaining the village's guardian deity *(ubusunagami)* as the clan god *(ujigami)* of his new castle town. Originally, therefore, the guardian deity of Furukawa was Sugimoto, not Ketawakamiya. In fact to this day some residents refer to their deity as "Sugimoto-sama" (employing the honorific name ending).

In 1608, Arishige was obliged to move to Takayama to assume control of the entire province following the death of his father. At this point, work on fortifications for Masushima-*jō* came to an abrupt halt. The main donjon had been fully constructed, and this continued to be used as an auxiliary headquarters. Arishige's own son took over the castle, and his warrior retainers remained in Furukawa to help administer the area.

In 1615 the Tokugawa regime, from its headquarters in Edo, issued a policy of one castle per administrative domain. In effect, this meant that all castles in Hida except the principle one in Takayama would have to be abandoned. The outer walls and other fortifications of Masushima-*jō* were taken down, but the main donjon was retained as a *ryokan*, or temporary lodging, to be used by the Kanamori while travelling in that part of their domain. Two of the castle's outer gates were salvaged: one was placed in front of Enkō-ji and the other in front of Rinshō-ji. They remain there to this day, each serving as the main entrance to the temple grounds.[18]

In 1692 the Kanamoris were transferred to Dewa Province in the northeast, and Hida was placed under the direct control of the Tokugawa *bakufu*. The main donjon of Masushima-*jō* was demolished, and a shrine to the deity Tenjin erected on the site. The central castle in Takayama was demolished at the same time.

Hida culture had long been linked with Kyoto, as both the Anegakōji and Kanamori lines had originated there. Now for the first time it experienced a heavy infusion of so-called "Edo *bunka*"—the

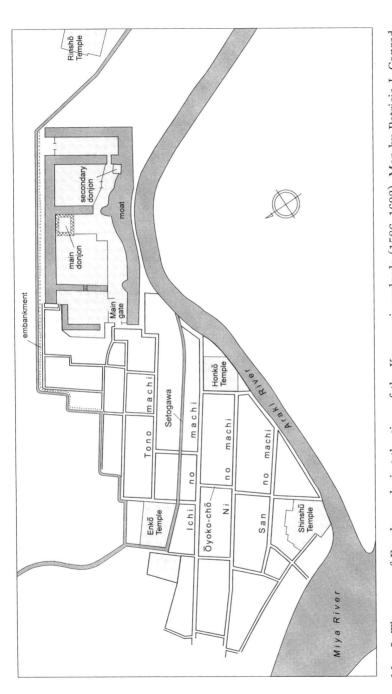

Map 5. The town of Furukawa during the time of the Kanamori warlords (1586–1692). Map by Patricia J. Conrad, adapted from Iwai et al. 1991:87–89.

culture developing around the military government at Edo. Again, religious institutions were coopted by the new regime, and Sugimoto was retained as the tutelary deity of Furukawa. A document dating from 1695 (cited verbatim in Kuwahara et al. 1991:5) certifies that permission had been granted by the *bakufu*'s magistrate for the observation of a yearly festival dedicated to Sugimoto Myōjin of Kamikita in the village of Furukawa. The festival is to be held during the Eighth Month, Sixteenth to Eighteenth Days. The document warns to take precautions with fire and not to engage in fighting or verbal disputes. It is witnessed by the Shinto priest, Furukawa's headman (referred to at the time as *"kimoiri"*) and a single village elder (presumably from Kamikita where the shrine itself was located).

Thus it was in honor of Sugimoto that the Furukawa *matsuri* was originally performed. Assertions that the *matsuri* dates from a thousand years ago are misinformed, as the shrine referred to in the *Nihon Sandai Jitsuroku* is Ketawakamiya, the one that had been there previously, not Sugimoto, the one that was moved there by the Kanamori. It was not until 1871 that Furukawa's tutelary shrine adopted the name Ketawakamiya (as will be described in Chapter 7).

The emergence of a larger, more diversified community was accompanied by a fundamental change in ritual treatment of the deity. Once a year the deity would be ceremoniously summoned forth, installed in a palanquin-like conveyance, and led in grand procession through the streets of Furukawa. The purported aim of this excursion was to dispel evil and revitalize the community. This marks the origin of the *mikoshi* procession, which still constitutes the essence of the *matsuri* as religious ritual. The supernatural visit came to be attended by feasting and revelry, with the *mikoshi* escorted by a retinue of local dignitaries. What had been a primarily religious observance now expanded into the kind of communal celebration more properly known as *"sairei"* (roughly synonymous with *matsuri,* but with less religious connotation).

Spring and autumn, of course, remained critical time periods in the agricultural calendar, and rites continued to be observed on both occasions. Each individual community, however, chose one or the other for performing its annual festival. Following the former tradition, spring *matsuri* were considered opportunities to request the deity's benevolence *(onegai suru tame)* while autumn *matsuri* were primarily intended as expressions of thanksgiving *(kansha suru tame*). Significantly, both occasions preceded busy periods in the agricultural calendar, holding open the possibility that reciprocal household feasting was being used to establish or maintain cooperative labor exchange relationships. The shrine ceremonies and annual visit of the deity, however, were oriented more toward promoting communal solidarity and reaffirming the social order.

Political Administration

Japan has a long tradition of combining religion with politics, as is apparent in terms like *matsuri-goto* ("political or governmental administration," but written using the term *"matsuri"*—"worship"; see Kitagawa 1987:117). Consequently, it is impossible to consider the historical development of the Furukawa *matsuri* without also addressing concurrent changes in the political administrative system.

According to standard historical accounts, the Tokugawa *bakufu* maintained a rigid four-tier social structure with the warrior class at the top, followed in order by the peasants, artisans, and merchants. The members of a particular class were restricted to its occupational category. Membership was determined by birth, and the boundaries between classes were rigidly enforced. This also implied a geographical separation. The peasants, who constituted the majority of the population, remained in their farm villages while the warriors who governed them were billeted in the castle towns. Merchants and artisans, too, were largely confined to the towns and cities and thus seldom came in contact with the peasantry.

Towns like Furukawa represent an exception to the standard model. The narrow but variegated confines of a small castle town brought merchants, artisans, and farmers into close proximity. Peasants from surrounding villages sometimes relinquished their occupational status and moved into town to engage in merchant or manufacturing activities. This was particularly common for younger sons in farm households, since the custom of male primogeniture denied them an inheritance. Likewise, while merchants were restricted from buying arable land, they could acquire it by foreclosing on loans for which the land had been offered as collateral. The original owner was then retained as a tenant cultivator. As a result, the boundaries between occupational categories became somewhat blurred.

Kanamori Arishige's attempts to attract merchants to Furukawa apparently met with great success. Local census figures show that a total of 290 merchant households had established themselves in Furukawa by 1695 (Furukawa-chō 1982:491–515).[19] Factoring in the previously existing peasants and a few religious specialists, Taga (1982:90) estimates a total of around five hundred households for the entire town at that time. This is supported by a 1746 document which lists Furukawa as containing around 560 households. Due to the concentration of merchants and higher overall population, the town came to exhibit characteristics of both farm village *(mura)* and town *(machi)*. The Tokugawa government used the term *machi-kata-mura* (town-type village) to distinguish diversified communities like Furukawa from agricultural-type *(murakata)*, mountain-type *(yamakata)*, and fishing-type *(urakata)* villages. In official documents Furukawa is thus referred to as "Furukawa *machikata-mura*," or simply "Furukawa-*machi*."

Following its takeover by the *bakufu*, Hida was no longer subjected to the billeting of large numbers of samurai retainers, which individual warlords deemed necessary for defending themselves and administering their personal domains. This was fortuitous for Hida in that the samurai, an elite warrior class that engaged in no productive economic activity, would have created a serious drain on local resources. Equally important is the fact that the *bakufu* customarily extracted a lower percentage of the annual rice harvest than did warlord domains—welcome relief in predominantly mountainous areas like Hida. As mentioned earlier, throughout the Tokugawa period the population of Hida province rose steadily, suggesting that subsistence requirements were being adequately met. Also, the absence of large numbers of samurai, combined with the distance separating Hida from *bakufu* headquarters in Edo, meant that the Hida peasantry enjoyed a relatively autonomous existence—as long as they continued to meet their annual land tax quota.

In a classic article on rural social organization during the Tokugawa period, Befu (1965) explains how the *bakufu* administered peasant villages through previously existing local institutions. Village officials were chosen from among the old established resident households—almost invariably members of the landholding peasantry. This proved reasonably effective. In addition to being insiders who were intimately familiar with local traditions, such households generally held the respect and trust of their fellow villagers, and already wielded considerable influence. In many cases their official positions were made hereditary, passing from father to son in the same household.

At the top of the village hierarchy was the *nanushi,* or headman. Though a member of the peasant class, he was often allowed a family name and the right to wear swords—privileges usually accorded the samurai alone. Under the headman came the *kumigashira,* or village elders, who were chosen to represent neighborhoods within the village. Below these were the so-called *"gonin-gumi,"* or "five-person groups." Despite the name, these groups were composed of contiguous households rather than separate individuals, and may be seen as forerunners of today's *tonarigumi.* They could range in size from only two or three to over fifteen households. Their leader was called a *"gonin-gashira."* Village officers were compensated with rice stipends, another privilege generally accruing only to the elite samurai.

In Furukawa the position of headman *("nanushi")* was hereditary. It was occupied by members of the Katō lineage, whose house was located in Upper Ichinomachi. The headman was assisted by eleven village elders *("kumigashira"),* one for each of Furukawa's component neighborhoods: Tonomachi; Ichinomachi, blocks one, two, three, and four; Ninomachi, blocks one, two, three, and four; and Sannomachi, blocks one and two. Following the removal of the Kanamori clan and their warrior retainers, Tonomachi came to be inhabited mostly by peasant farmers. The location afforded them ready access to the large rice paddy and dry field area to the north. It was also convenient in that many of the farmers kept a horse or an ox, which would not have been appropriate in the middle of town.[20] The rest of Furukawa maintained essentially the same structure as before, with the majority of the merchants clustered together in Ninomachi.

There was also an elder for each of the five outlying communities: Ōno, Kanmachi, Ryokan, Naka no Tame, and Machiura. These individuals were called *"jikata gashira."* Though under the administrative jurisdiction of the town government, they lay outside the territorial protection of Sugimoto Shrine, and thus played no active role in the performance of its annual festival.

Befu (1965:31) describes *bakufu* and village as having their own agendas, which often failed to coincide:

Village goals were to maintain internal peace and to defend itself against external threat. The goals of the military government, on the other hand, consisted of economic exploitation of the peasants and maintenance of a static society in which the peasantry was given a well defined place. To the village, the welfare of the larger society, of which it was a part, was irrelevant; to the village, too, the exploitative state, represented external threat as much as, or even more than, say a neighboring village trying to steal water.

This last comment underscores the fact that the villagers viewed centralized authority as an outside entity, distinct from themselves. The government's regulations were aimed at maximizing yields and minimizing expenses in order to ensure that the annual lump-sum tax payment would continue unabated. Tax assessment on individual households, on the other hand, was an internal village matter, and wealthier peasants were often obliged to pay more so as to assist their less fortunate neighbors. Befu notes that "villagers were more likely to connive with one another against the government rather than blackmail a fellow villager" (1965:24). This also illustrates a marked preference among villagers for handling their own affairs without appealing to the higher (outside) authority of the *bakufu*.

Rise of the Patron Landlords

Social and economic conditions during the period in which Hida was administered by the *bakufu* led to the emergence of a privileged stratum of wealthy landowners and merchants collectively known as *danna shū* (the "patron people," as introduced in Chapter 3).[21] These wealthy households constituted the upper level of the rural social hierarchy until the land reforms were instituted after the Second World War. Kuwatani (1971:53) notes that true *danna* households are characterized by the following three features: (1) they possess considerable wealth and property; (2) they are old families which first rose to prominence during the Tokugawa period; (3) they maintain a tradition of bestowing economic favors on the local community. This patron class has been a major factor in the political, economic, and cultural development of the Hida region, and no study of Hida's social history would be complete without considering their role.

Patron households can roughly be divided into two categories, the agricultural landlord patrons *(jinushi danna)* and the town-dwelling merchant patrons *(shōbai danna)*. The former prospered less through their own productive efforts than by extracting rent from their tenant cultivators. They were considered of higher status and maintained a rather superior attitude toward other members of the community. The merchant patrons, on the other hand, engaged in a variety of commercial activities. They recognized that their success depended largely on harmonious social relations and assumed a more humble demeanor in interacting with their fellow residents. There is no clear distinction between the two categories, however, as the agricultural landlord patrons sometimes invested in commercial enterprises—especially following the Meiji Restoration—and the merchant patrons were able to acquire vast tracts of land as their businesses prospered. The term *"danna shū,"* then, is roughly synonymous with the prewar landlord class.

The *danna* were assisted by a special category of economically dependent yet biologically unrelated subordinates known euphemistically as the *deiri shū* (going out/coming in people). As the name implies, these people did not belong to the main household, but came and went as the need for their services demanded. The *deiri* were essentially wage laborers, not full-time servants. Neither should they be equated with the landlord's tenant farmers; though there were tenants among them, the category included small owner–cultivators as well.

The bond between *danna* and *deiri* was characterized by the recognition of mutual loyalties and obligations. The *deiri* reportedly took pride in their association with a wealthy patron, and often participated in ceremonial events at the patron's household. In fact some of these households had special tombs for their *deiri* members placed next to their own.

Even though they had acquired considerable wealth and influence, the *danna* nevertheless had to maintain the appearance of conforming to Tokugawa-period social strictures, and assumed the position of lower-level retainers in the overall status hierarchy. It was necessary for them to present gifts as tribute to the local magistrates, and periodically they were called upon to make rather large contributions. In return they were sometimes granted surnames and honorary samurai status.

The largest agricultural landlords in the Furukawa area were the Sugishita, Okamura, and Satō households.[22] Though many of their tenants lived in Furukawa, each of these three were themselves located in separate villages a little further upstream in what is still considered the most fertile part of the Furukawa basin. The Sugishita were based in the village of Utsue, but maintained secondary residences in both Takayama and Furukawa. The Okamura were located a bit further downstream in the village of Hirose. The Satō lived in Ōno, which was under Furukawa's civil jurisdiction but fell within the precincts of another shrine. All three houses rose to prominence during the mid-Tokugawa period, and even though they belonged to the peasant class they were awarded surnames sometime prior to the Meiji Restoration. All held land not only in Furukawa but in several other villages as well. Indeed, the Sugishita were at one time the largest landowners in the Hida region, and third largest in all of Gifu Prefecture. The storehouse for their rice—most of it taken as rent from their tenant cultivators—was located in Middle Ninomachi.

As for the merchant *danna*, Kuwatani (1971:56–57) traces their origin to the custom of male primogeniture *(chōnan sōzoku)*. Established farm households generally designated the eldest son as heir and successor. The daughters were expected to marry into other families, but the younger sons were often left with no means of livelihood. Some remained in their natal villages as day laborers, but others were drawn to the newly emerging castle towns of Takayama and Furukawa in hopes of making a living as apprentices and merchants. A few managed to become quite successful and eventually established their own businesses.[23]

After two or three generations their households had acquired substantial wealth and began engaging in money lending activities. With interest rates as high as 30–40 percent, many borrowers found themselves unable to repay their loans and were obliged to relinquish whatever they had offered as security—most commonly land, livestock, or their own labor services. The merchant moneylenders were thus able to acquire land and other assets; a few transformed themselves into full-fledged landlords.

One of the most lucrative trades was *sake* production. However, establishing a *sake* brewery required a considerable up-front investment. For this reason, most of Furukawa's *sake* manufacturers began in other occupations, converting to the brewing business when they had acquired sufficient capital. Several of the newly emerging merchant landlords established breweries and began making *sake* with the rice they collected as rent from their tenants. This proved a very lucrative combination and raised their fortunes even higher. There were no retail outlets for *sake* during the Tokugawa period, so customers bought the product directly from the manufacturer.

In addition to being heavily engaged in commercial activities, the merchant patrons of Furukawa were distinguishable from the large agricultural landlords in that they lived within the town itself. Most of Furukawa's commercial establishments were clustered together in Ichinomachi, home to the local headman and his administrative facilities, or Ninomachi, the town's major thoroughfare.

Tradition holds that when Anegakōji assumed control of the Hida region in the mid-fourteenth century he was accompanied by four trusted warrior retainers, whose family names were Tajika, Kaba, Gotō, and Kusakabe. Following Anegakōji's decline, all four lineages chose to remain in Hida but converted to other occupations. The Kusakabe lineage eventually relocated to Takayama. Tajika, Kaba, and Gotō, on the other hand, remained in the Furukawa area and to this day are highly respected members of the community.

Two major lines of Tajika emerged, both claiming direct descent from Anegakōji's retainer. One was located in Middle Ninomachi at the intersection with Ōyokochō, and prospered as dry goods merchants. The other was located downstream in Lower Ninomachi and was engaged in the lumber business. Using the Miya and Jintsu Rivers, these latter Tajika floated timber from the surrounding area to the feudal lords of Etchū and Kaga Provinces to the north. Later they diversified into brewing *sake* and dying cloth.

The Gotō line originally settled about two kilometers downstream in Sugisaki. Later they moved to Furukawa and located in Ninomachi. There they split into three separate lines. The main household was referred to as "Sugisaki-Gotō," owing to the founder's origins. Their business was brewing *sake,* but later they diversified into paper making. One of the branches was located west (i.e., downstream) of the main household and came to be known as "Nishi-Gotō" ("West Gotō"). They started out in silk production but later dealt in salt and *miso.* The other branch was located between the main household and the first branch, but on the other side of the street. At some point members of this second branch began referring to their household as "Hon-Gotō" ("original/main Gotō") in an attempt to pass themselves off as the main line.[24] They were primarily engaged in *sake* brewing.

Like the Gotō, the Kaba household was originally located in Sugisaki, where they first gained wealth through silk production. During the late Tokugawa period they switched to *sake* brewing and relocated in Furukawa's Upper Ichinomachi, where Setogawa, the canal running between Ichinomachi and Tonomachi, provided them a convenient supply of fresh water. Their lineage included a number of accomplished scholars and literary figures, including the author of the 1870 description of the Furukawa *matsuri* alluded to earlier.[25]

The remaining large merchant households conform to Kuwatani's model of having moved to Furukawa from surrounding farm villages. Just downstream from Kaba and separated by only a narrow side street and one other building was the Watanabe household. The Watanabe moved to Furukawa in 1735, having originated in a more remote Hida village where they served as politicians and administrators. With the second generation they began to engage in money lending and silk production, and later (sometime during the early Meiji period) switched to brewing *sake*. Though relative newcomers, they nevertheless came to rival old established households such as Kaba, Tajika, and Gotō.

Most of the other major merchants were clustered together with Tajika and Gotō in Ninomachi. Most prominent among them was the Nakamura household, located immediately adjacent to Hon-Gotō in Middle Ninomachi. The Nakamura were *sake* brewers who became involved in moneylending activities, assuming control of the land offered as security when the borrowers found themselves unable to repay.

Other prominent merchant households included Hasegawa, Kumazaki, Fuse, Ushimaru, and Kiriyama, all of whom were located in Ninomachi. Though not on the same scale as the large agricultural landlords, they were nevertheless able to acquire substantial wealth and property. They were sometimes referred to as *"chōnin jinushi,"* or "town-dwelling landlords."

These prominent households were not concerned exclusively with amassing wealth. In the manner of true patrons, they were also aware of their responsibilities as members of the community and felt obliged to offer assistance to those less fortunate than themselves. Landlords provided funds and materials for repairing flood damages, building new roads and bridges, and maintaining fire-fighting equipment. In the event of a poor harvest or natural calamity, they often lowered the rent payment required of their tenant cultivators. Perhaps most significantly for the present analysis, they also helped underwrite the local *matsuri* with liberal contributions of *sake,* food, and other provisions.

The local landlord invariably assumed a position of leadership within the community, as wealth and property went hand-in-hand with political power.[26] In the days before the so-called "citizens' halls" *(kōminkan)* were established, a resident landlord's house was customarily used for public meetings because it was one of the few buildings spacious enough to accommodate large numbers of people. As host, the household was obliged to provide its guests with food and drink, which could result in considerable expense. Landlords also served as intermediaries between the townspeople and higher authorities, and their scholarly efforts were useful preparation for this role. In effect they became both legal and administrative representatives for the local people.

Relations within the landlord class itself were both cordial and competitive. Though they were rivals in the struggle for wealth and prestige, it was nevertheless important for fellow landlords to maintain their socioeconomic positions through alliances with one another. Marriage, of course, is commonly employed as a means of creating alliances and retaining control of land and other assets. As a rule, members of landlord households married within their class, the most obvious and accessible prospects being members of equally prominent households in the immediate vicinity. As widely reported in other areas, it was common for households without male heirs to have a young man marry in and become the nominal successor. Typically this involved a younger son from a household of comparable status. Such marriages resembled adoption—in fact the term used in referring to the incoming groom was "adopted son-in-law" *("muko yōshi")*. As a result of such strategies, most of the prominent households in and around Furukawa were allied through marriage and/or adoption, and subsequently became biologically related as well.

This did not rule out rivalry among them, however, as economic concerns and personal aspirations often overrode the bonds of kinship. Even within a single neighborhood, rival households competed with one another for greater prominence. This led to periodic bouts of competitive largesse, especially within the highly visible context of the annual *matsuri.* Less prosperous residents, of course, were the direct beneficiaries.

Indeed, performing the *matsuri* required considerable resources.

Though every household in the neighborhood—rich and poor alike —was obliged to provide its share of money, labor, and materials, the wealthier households were naturally expected to give more. The prescribed amount was based on the individual household's ability to pay, rather like a graduated income tax. The contribution of large sums of money and materials during the *matsuri* thus served as a form of redistribution: by giving back some of their accumulated wealth, prominent households were able to acknowledge their commitment to the welfare of the community, casting themselves in the role of patron or benefactor.

Such patronage was not motivated by charitable sentiments alone. The amount of each contribution was carefully tallied on a signboard for public inspection. In order to maintain their prestige, prominent households were obliged to contribute at least as much as their rivals. Even more ominously, those who failed to make contributions appropriate to their status were labeled stingy and subjected to malicious gossip or even vandalism. The signboard provided a means of attesting to one's own benevolence, thereby avoiding retribution. Wealthy landlord and merchant households were often the objects of envy and derision; after all, they had achieved their special prominence largely by exploiting their less fortunate neighbors. Their contributions to the *matsuri* were in part intended to relieve aggressive tensions among the peasantry generated by poverty and a heavy tax burden (Kuwatani 1971:75).[27]

Ritual and Social Order

The most visible displays of landlord patronage were the magnificent *yatai*. The original purpose of these vehicles was to welcome the deity on its descent from the shrine, then lead it through town in a stately procession. This derives from an even earlier practice of using tall objects to attract the attention of benevolent spirits. According to ancient religious belief, the *kami* were thought to move freely about the heavens, and had to be drawn into some stationary object to secure their proximity. They were particularly attracted to high places, such as mountains and trees. The early myth-histories relate that the god Ninigi, grandson of the sun goddess Amaterasu and entrusted by her with founding a worldly government, first descended to earth by alighting on a mountaintop. Folk tradition likewise held that the forested mountains were the dwelling place of the *kami*. In order to entice them down into the profane realm of human existence, some suitably high object was thought necessary to attract their attention. Originally mounds of earth were constructed as artificial mountains to draw the *kami* to level ground. Later, however, elevated platforms were created for the same purpose, and equipped with wheels so that they could be moved from place to place as the occasion demanded (Ōno 1974b, Yamamoto 1986:216). These were the forerunners of today's festival wagons. In fact, the wagons themselves are sometimes referred to as *"yama"* ("mountain"), alluding to their structural antecedents.[28]

With the development of substantial towns and villages, the supernatural was reconceptualized as a local guardian deity, and a sacred space (shrine) created where it could be more readily invoked. The deity continued to be invited down into the community on special occasions; now, however, its presence was actively conveyed by humans using a *mikoshi*, and temporarily housed in the *tabisho*. Moveable *"yama"* were no longer required to beckon the *kami*, and the vehicles came to be employed as forms of entertainment and display.

In the case of Hida, however, such vehicles appear to have been introduced fully formed. They are referred to as *"yatai,"* alluding to their sharply peaked roofs that resemble those found on Shinto shrines. In the towns of Takayama and Furukawa, the deity's visit developed into a stately procession, and the *yatai* were employed as a kind of honor guard leading the way before the *mikoshi* as it made its way through town. This custom is thought to have been borrowed from the famous Sannō *matsuri* in Edo. The vehicles themselves, however, combine Hida wood crafting with Kyoto lacquerwork, tapestries, and performative traditions; they thus represent a blend of Edo, Kyoto, and native Hida influences.

It is not known exactly when the practice of pulling *yatai* began in Furukawa. Hida historians typically assume that, from the time of the Kanamori, all new cultural developments began in Takayama, then spread from there to other parts of the region. *Yatai* were first employed in Takayama in 1718; Furukawa's *yatai,* therefore, are thought to have appeared well after this date (Ōno 1974a:7; Kuwahara, et al. 1991:21). Residents of Middle Ninomachi maintain that their Kinkitai was originally built during the Jōkyō period

(1684–1688), but there is no concrete evidence to support this contention. There is, however, reliable documentation for the building of a new Kinkitai in 1776. Whether this refers to the original vehicle or a replacement for an earlier version is unclear. In any case, an account roster lists every household in Middle Ninomachi and the amount they donated toward the construction effort. At the head of the list are Tajika, "Sugisaki" Gotō, and "Nishi" Gotō, who each contributed one gold coin (Furukawa-chō 1986:407–411).[29] As previously mentioned, these were some of the most prominent residents of Ninomachi, and therefore of the entire town as well.

Most of the other neighborhoods lacked the resources to build such fine structures; they were obliged instead to obtain old, worn-out *yatai* from Takayama and fix them up for use in their own *matsuri*.[30] A 1782 travel documentary entitled *Hida Miyage* (Souvenir of Hida), written by Buddhist priest and haiku poet Rinkō,[31] includes the following observation:

> The Furukawa *matsuri* takes place on the sixth day of the eighth month. There are nine *hikiyama*. These too [comparing them with the Takayama vehicles described earlier in the account] are called *"yatai."* The *matsuri* is in honor of Sugimoto Myōjin, who is said to derive from Amaterasu Daijin. On the day of the *matsuri*, the *hikiyama* provide artistic entertainment in front of the headman's home. Following this, offerings are made before the sacred palanquin [referred to here as *"okago"* rather than *"mikoshi"*]. Two Shinto priests arrive and perform various rites. (Furukawa-chō 1986:61)

The passage confirms that by this time the other neighborhoods had acquired *yatai* of their own. Though by today's reckoning there is one vehicle missing, this is easily explainable by the fact that Sannomachi constituted a unified neighborhood until 1839 and thus maintained a single *yatai*.

The *yatai* themselves became visible expressions of collective identity and (literally) vehicles for competing with other neighborhoods. At one time all of Furukawa's *yatai* offered some kind of theatrical performance. Byakkodai, Hō-ōtai, Sankōtai, Ryūtekitai, and Suzakudai all purveyed excerpts from famous kabuki dramas, performed on a stage extending out from the second level. Seiryūtai, Kirintai, Kinkitai, and Sanbasō featured the mechanical puppets known as *karakuri ningyō.* The performances were ostensibly designed for the deity's amusement, but in reality became a way of competing with other neighborhoods. Not surprisingly, wealthy households took the lead in the competition, supplying timber for new *yatai* construction and repair. They also contributed money for additional carvings and embellishments, often ordered from as far away as Kyoto.

Yatai building is an example of the strategy alluded to at the end of the preceding chapter. Engaging in some kind of collective effort reinforces the sense of a unified group, and simultaneously sharpens the distinction between insiders and outsiders. The townspeople were thus encouraged to identify upward toward the apex of the social hierarchy (i.e., the local *danna*) rather than horizontally toward fellow members of the same socioeconomic category.[32]

In the course of everyday life, the heads of prominent households were accustomed to issuing orders and managing important affairs, while their less influential neighbors were resigned to deferring to their authority. This naturally carried over into the planning and execution of the *matsuri,* with landlords assuming the principal leadership roles. This is clearly indicated in a document entitled *"Teishiki"* ("Established Form"), issued during the "Eighth Month" of 1831 (unpublished document, cited verbatim in Ōno 1973a), which prescribes the manner in which the *matsuri* is to be conducted.[33] A seal bearing the characters for *"shimariyaku"* ("controlling officer"—comparable to today's *shinji torishimari*) appears at the end. This presumably refers to Furukawa's headman, though his actual name does not appear. The document is addressed to Nakamura Zenbei, who is further identified as the village elder *(kumigashira)* of Ninomachi, block three. As previously mentioned, Nakamura was one of the large merchant/landholding households of that neighborhood. A similar directive was undoubtedly issued to each of the other village elders as well.

The 1831 document briefly establishes the schedule the *matsuri* is to follow, though it provides little in the way of descriptive details. The *mikoshi* procession is to begin at 2:00 p.m. on the Fifth Day (presumably of the Eighth Month), and is to continue beginning at 4:00 a.m. on the Sixth Day. The *yatai* are to make another pass through town that same evening, and are to follow the prescribed order. The Kinkitai is assigned the eighth, or penultimate, position (the directing neighborhood would have brought up the rear). There is a warning to be careful in handling fire. In the event of rain, the participants are given permission to don rain gear as they so desire. Similarly, as evening approaches they are directed to light their lanterns at their own discretion. A brief addendum states that the *okoshi daiko* is not to begin before 2:00 a.m. It also mentions that "pounding boards and mischievous acts are strictly prohibited." Finally, the document emphasizes that any directives issuing from the *yatai gyōji* (literally *"yatai* referee"), are to be followed immediately and without question. *"Gyōji"* thus appears to have been comparable to today's *"shuji"* ("director"), but in this case refers to a single individual—most likely the village elder from the directing neighborhood.

An 1846 document entitled *"Goshinji Yatai Gishiki"* (*"Yatai* Ritual for the Sacred Rites") provides a much more detailed description of the proceedings (Furukawa-chō 1986:398–401). It also suggests increasing connection with Mukaimachi, which was emerging as a rival neighborhood on the other side of the Araki river. A durable bridge had been erected across the river to facilitate travel along the Etchū Highway. The bridge was called "Daikanbashi" (Magistrate's Bridge), apparently in reference to its leading toward the magistrate's headquarters in Takayama.[34] Mukaimachi developed as a cluster of houses and shops lining both sides of the road, later spreading out along the riverbank between the bridge and the river's mouth.

The document begins by declaring that Mukaimachi's sacred rites *("shinji")* are held on the Fifth Day of the Sixth Month, and that all *yatai* from the Furukawa side will be pulled there to attend. Each *yatai* is to proceed up its own street toward Honkō Temple, then with Sanbasō in the lead they are to cross the bridge into Mukaimachi. Mukaimachi's *yatai,* however, is to wait on its own side in a designated open area. The other *yatai* will join it there and offer their respective performances before Mukaimachi's headman and village elders. Next they will proceed as far as the border with Koreshige, then return. Upon crossing back to the Furukawa side, they will wait for the referee's signal that they may disperse. The document warns that the prescribed order must be observed at all times. It also mentions that, after the signal to disperse, the *yatai* are to use side streets in returning to their home neighborhoods. This is specifically described as a precaution to avoid disputes.

The next day marks Furukawa's own sacred rites. The *yatai* will assemble before the magistrate *("obugyō-sama,"* presumably referring to a representative from the *bakufu's* regional administrative headquarters in Takayama) and again offer their various performances. This may be interpreted as a symbolic acknowledgment of the political power of the magistrate, much in the manner of a military parade or inspection of troops. Actual direction of the festivities, however, was at that time assumed by the local headman.

The document emphasizes that the *yatai* should be pulled "peaceably" so as not to create a disturbance in front of the magistrate. Throughout the festival, in fact, those in charge are advised to watch out for arguments and fighting. The "referee" *(gyōji)* is vested with the authority to arbitrate, and his decision must be accepted without complaint. In case of rain, all should attach their rain gear as they see fit. The referee is to guard against blunders, and is to see that the "pulling away" *("hikiwakare")* is performed by 4:00 p.m.

There follows a description of the course the *yatai* will follow after the performances before the magistrate. Basically they are to pass through every major street, stopping in front of the headman's dwelling as well as the home of every resident village elder (ten in all, excluding Lower Sannomachi, which was designated referee that year). Some time is allowed for lunch and a brief afternoon repast. After covering the entire town, the *yatai* are to disperse at the referee's direction. Again there is a warning to avoid confrontations, and the request to use side streets whenever possible. If one *yatai* group finds it necessary to pass another, they are to greet each other in good faith and return peaceably to their own neighborhoods. As in the earlier (1831) document, the *okoshi daiko* is not included in the official schedule of events; in fact it receives no mention whatsoever. The document is signed by the village elder and two additional representatives from every neighborhood. This in fact marks the initiation of the signing ceremony *(chōinshiki)* described in Chapter 4. A contractual agreement was apparently deemed necessary to prevent any deviation from the prescribed order.

In recognition of their prominent status, elite patrons were privileged to stroll along at the head of the deity's grand procession, while ordinary people were enlisted to pull the *yatai.* Wearing the formal *montsuki* kimono with *kamishimo* overmantle was a privilege granted by the authorities, and was generally reserved for those who owned their own land and homes (these were referred to as *"iemochi"*—"householders"). Offices such as headman and village elder were likewise restricted to this select group. Appearing in the procession thus became a ritual "who's who" enactment, visually acknowledging the participants' status as prominent members of the community.

This same demonstration of sociopolitical order was played out at a regional level through the periodic observance of the Hida *"taisai,"* or "grand festival." Once every four years the tutelary deities of all the towns and villages in Hida Province were brought together at a single location. The gathering rotated among five major Hida shrines, and Furukawa's Sugimoto was privileged in being one of the five. Furukawa thus played host to the *taisai* once every twenty years.

The origin of the *taisai* is attributed to Ōhara Hikoshirō, the unpopular magistrate whose policies ignited the Ōhara rebellions. As described in Chapter 3, during the second wave of the rebellions, soldiers from neighboring Gujō domain had opened fire on a crowd of peasants, then invaded their refuge at Suimu Shrine. Two of the shrine's priests were arrested for harboring the rebels and later sentenced to death. The main shrine building itself was heavily damaged and riddled with bullet holes. Ōhara decided to have the shrine refurbished and invited a Shinto priest from Shinano province (bordering Hida to the east) to conduct its affairs. The new priest was opposed to Shinto–Buddhist syncretism and converted the shrine to pure Shinto. At the official reopening, all the tutelary deities in Hida province were invited to attend, suitably ensconced in portable shrines. Each was of course accompanied by a contingent of its parishioners, thereby adding a sociopolitical, as well as religious, dimension to the proceedings. Ōhara's efforts are thought to have been motivated by a desire to dispel some of the deep-seated resentment the peasants held against him, and regain supernatural favor following the death of his wife and loss of his own eyesight (Hishimura 1965:2–3, Gotō 1983:96).

The gathering developed into a regular event—the *taisai*—held at intervals of several years. It was later appropriated by "National Learning" *(Kokugaku)* advocates such as Tanaka Ōhide in seeking to propagate the Confucian and Shinto-based values of the bureaucratic elite.

Airing Grievances

It is clear that the *matsuri* functioned in one sense as a means of legitimating political authority through the use of religious symbolism. But it also became a medium for airing grievances. The 1846 document summarized above implies that arguing and fighting during the Furukawa *matsuri* had become a serious problem, as well as an embarrassment to local officials in the presence of the magistrate's representatives from Takayama. This in turn suggests some discrepancy between the official and folk understandings of the *matsuri*. From the perspective of the common people, the sacred purview of the *matsuri* permitted activity that was normally prohibited or suppressed to be given free expression. It also allowed the peasants a brief respite from their everyday drudgery. For many it was one of their few opportunities to drink *sake,* largely at the expense of their more prosperous neighbors. The air of licentiousness surrounding the event allowed them to engage in a little innocent debauchery, and since whatever happened was attributed to the will of the deity, misbehavior tended to be overlooked or forgiven. Under circumstances such as these, even trivial matters could cause tempers to flare. Fighting was accepted as an ever-present aspect of the *matsuri* experience, and part of the reason people found it so gratifying.

Habitual resentments *(higoro no urami),* normally held in check by strict social mores, were most likely to emerge during the procession of *yatai,* which brought members of rival neighborhoods into close proximity. This is why the shrine regulations contain such explicit warnings against open conflict. A dispute between two neighborhoods could bring the entire procession to an abrupt halt, raising fears that the *mikoshi* would be prevented from completing its rounds. Participants capitalized upon the opportunity to express grievances and objections, referred to in Japanese as *"kujō."* This tactic was most commonly employed by the less prominent neighborhoods, allowing them to demonstrate that they were not to be taken for granted. The town leaders were often obliged to humble themselves, bowing in apology to the offended parties in order to get the procession moving again.

In a broader context, the *matsuri* as a whole was conducive to acts of retribution, particularly under the cover of darkness. One particularly famous incident involves a peasant named Zenkichi from the nearby village of Unehata. The day after the *matsuri* in 1868, he was found murdered and lying in the gravel of the Miya River bed. Zenkichi had been involved in a legal battle with Furukawa residents over rights of access to some common mountain land nearby. At that time, Furukawa held communal rights to about 2000 hectares (4900 acres) of such land, but since it lay adjacent to land assigned to other communities there were frequent boundary disputes.

Zenkichi was on his way home from the court hearing in Takayama, which had ruled in his favor. Instead of heading directly back to his own village, however, he decided to stop off in Furukawa to enjoy the festivities. Some angry residents learned of Zenkichi's presence and began to chase after him. For a time he took refuge in the home of his friend Ushimaru in Ninomachi. He reportedly hid himself inside the *butsudan* (a household Buddhist altar kept inside a closet-like enclosure), but was forced to flee when the mob threatened to burn down the house. He was eventually captured and beaten to death. His body was discovered near an old pontoon bridge leading back across the Miya River to his own village. The assailants were never identified, but are widely assumed to have been the losers in the court battle (Kuwatani 1969:23–24, Furukawa–chō Kyōiku Iinkai 1987:427–436, Ōno 1972b).

The presence of ill feelings stemming from limited access to material resources sheds some light on the frequent expression of hostilities during the *matsuri*. The number of merchants in Furukawa had been steadily increasing throughout the latter half of the Tokugawa period, and, again, most of them were located in Ninomachi along the main thoroughfare linking Furukawa with other towns and villages. Neighborhoods were somewhat segregated by household occupation, giving each of them a distinctive socioeconomic character. This is clearly indicated in a survey conducted in 1869, listing every household in Furukawa that carried on some form of merchant, small manufacturing, or service activity (Furukawa-chō 1982: 749–759, Tokoro 1989:1000). The following is a brief summary of that survey, indicating the neighborhood, the number of households listed for each, and the principle commercial activities that were reported among those households. Please note that, for each neighborhood, only the *principal* commercial activities are shown here. Most of the remaining households were engaged in some form of outside employment or peddling of goods.

Tonomachi:	31 households	12 horse or ox drivers 4 carpenters and sawyers 2 ditch diggers *(kurokuwa)*
Ichinomachi, block one:	33 households	12 carpenters, sawyers, and woodworkers 10 merchants
Ichinomachi, block two:	18 households	14 merchants 3 carpenters and woodworkers
Ichinomachi, block three:	21 households	9 merchants (including 1 *sake* brewer) 8 carpenters and woodworkers
Ichinomachi, block four:	30 households	7 merchants 3 carpenters and woodworkers 3 horse or ox drivers 3 ditch diggers
Ninomachi, block one:	24 households	15 merchants
Ninomachi, block two:	18 households	16 merchants (including 1 *sake* brewer)
Ninomachi, block three:	14 households	13 merchants (including 2 *sake* brewers)
Ninomachi, block four:	65 households	52 merchants (including 1 *sake* brewer)
Upper Sannomachi:	23 households	7 woodworkers
Lower Sannomachi:	42 households	9 carpenters, sawyers, and woodworkers 5 ditch diggers 4 horse or ox drivers

Clearly, most of the merchants were concentrated in the two interior sectors, particularly Ninomachi. Most notable is the profusion of *sake* brewers—an immediate indication of wealth. This stands in obvious contrast with Tonomachi, which, again, was populated mostly by small farmers; the most common form of non-farm employment was ox or pack-horse driver—hardly among the more lucrative trades. From the perspective of the interior merchant neighborhoods, Tonomachi was considered *inaka*—rustic or rural, with the implication of being somewhat backward.

The socioeconomic differences are enhanced by the fact that in each neighborhood all the houses faced inward toward the street and each other rather than outward toward the other neighborhoods. The area in back of a house was occupied by its *kura* (storehouse) and perhaps a small garden, but offered no right of access to the houses beyond them, even though the properties were contiguous. This gave each neighborhood a distinct sense of insularity. The point is most clearly illustrated by Tonomachi, which was separated from the rest of the town by an irrigation canal, and Mukaimachi, which was located on the opposite side of the Araki River.

Though quite distinctive individually, however, the various neighborhoods nevertheless belonged to the same town, were governed by the same administrative institutions, and were linked into the same local economy. This brought them into frequent interaction and occasional conflict. The *matsuri* served as a forum for enacting inter-neighborhood rivalries. It thus became an opportunity for political expression as well as a religious and social observance.

The interior neighborhoods held a distinct advantage in terms of wealth, and could more easily absorb the cost of maintaining the expensive *yatai*. This is why both Ichinomachi and Ninomachi split into three separate neighborhood associations, each sponsoring its own vehicle. Sannomachi remained unified for a longer period, but it also eventually split into two. The outer neighborhoods of Tonomachi and Mukaimachi could afford their own vehicles only by remaining unified. What they lacked in terms of wealth, however, they made up for in strength of numbers. This was later reflected in their participation in the *okoshi daiko,* as will become clear in the pages that follow.

Economic disparities grew even more pronounced during the early stages of the modern era, with the lifting of restrictions on commercial activity and transition to a market system based on the use of hard currency. These were accompanied by the erosion of traditional subsistence support mechanisms, rigid tax policies introduced by the central government, increasing land concentration and higher rates of tenancy, and the imposition of authority by outside agents—most conspicuously the police. In the following chapters I will describe the *matsuri* as a forum for responding to these dramatic sociopolitical and economic changes. More specifically I will demonstrate how a ritual component of the *matsuri*—the *okoshi daiko*—emerged as an institutionalized opportunity for negotiating power relationships and redressing perceived social injustices. My assertions will be supported by the symbolic structure of the ritual, continual efforts by the authorities to control its development, and several instances in which the ritual performance itself escalated into genuine acts of destructive violence.

Chapter 7

AUTHORITY, RESISTANCE, AND RITUALIZATION

Up to this point little has been said about the nature and conduct of the *okoshi daiko*. This reflects its relative lack of importance within the performative structure of the *matsuri* as a whole. The 1870 account (cited in the preceding chapter) describes the drum as a minor preliminary, having little or no bearing on the course of subsequent events. Likewise, a passage from the 1782 travelogue entitled *Hida Miyage* by haiku poet Rinkō (also alluded to in the preceding chapter) describes the procession of nine *yatai* during the main event on the Sixth Day of the Eighth Month, but makes no mention at all of an associated drum ritual (Furu-kawa-chō 1986: 3–4, 61). In fact the first reference to the *okoshi daiko* in the extant literature does not appear until 1831, when it is mentioned in an addendum to the *"Teishiki"* document. Again, the addendum states simply that the *okoshi daiko* is not to begin before 2:00 a.m.; there is also a hint that it is associated with rowdy behavior. But it is not included in the program of sacred rites and seems to have been performed independently by some of the townspeople.

References to other drums appear in so-called "ritual form" *(gishiki)* regulations beginning in 1855. At this time there was no special drum designated as the focal point of the ritual. Rather, each neighborhood *taigumi* had a drum of its own, and when its turn came to serve as "referee" it used this drum to perform the *okoshi daiko.* Judging by the regulations, however, it appears that the other *taigumi* had now started using their drums every year to compete with the referee. These may be seen as early precursors to the *tsuke daiko,* though the documentary evidence by no means suggests the kind of aggressive tactics they later employed. Regulations issued by the shrine authorities in 1858 state emphatically that only one drum —that of the directing *taigumi*—is authorized to make the rounds, and is to set out precisely at the break of dawn (Ōno 1973b). The bold *okoshi daiko* so visible today does not appear in any of these sources. This conspicuous absence is made even more curious in light of later accounts, which characterize the ritual as being far more aggressive than it is in the present. During the mid-Meiji period (around 1900) the neighborhood *tsuke daiko* teams used to charge toward the great drum intent on toppling it over. Several times the authorities attempted to ban such behavior, only to be defied by the townspeople. Fighting among the participants was commonplace and random acts of vandalism not infrequent. This so-called ritual, in other words, was more on the order of a genuine brawl (Matsui 1965:7; Kuwatani 1965:15, 1969:25; Ōno 1973b, 1975b:3, 1976a:3; Kaba 1984:35–36; Furukawa-chō Kankō Kyōkai 1984:80–81). By 1911, author Okamura Rihei (1911:313) could describe the *okoshi daiko* as a "strange custom" which had gained considerable notoriety. And while the 1870 account had stated that the drum *began* at dawn, Okamura now reports that it begins at "midnight" (*"yahan,"* more precisely "middle of the night") and *continues until* dawn.

Apparently, then, at some time during the late 1800s, this minor and seemingly innocuous feature called the *okoshi daiko* began to assume a dramatic new importance. Returning to the question posed in Chapter 1, what caused its transformation? What conditions led to its emergence as a forum for expressing wild, unruly behavior—the very epitome of the defiant attitude known as "Furukawa *yancha?*" And why did it develop here, specifically, and not in other places? After all, the Furukawa *matsuri* as a whole is largely patterned after its more famous counterpart in Takayama—the major distinguishing feature being the *okoshi daiko.*

In addressing such questions it is important to remember that while the shrine rituals and *mikoshi* procession served to acknowledge the ascendancy of the local elite, the *okoshi daiko* emerged from the ranks of the common people. In this chapter I will describe the *okoshi daiko* as a ritualized expression of opposition—a symbolic response to the exploitative tendencies of wealthy landlords and the imposition of authority by the central government over local affairs.

Origins

The origin of the *okoshi daiko* remains a topic of local conjecture. Uncertainty is compounded by an inclination to project the ritual far back into the past, thereby endowing it with the sense of awe and legitimacy associated with a time-honored tradition. Some residents insist that it dates from as many as a thousand years ago. Popular opinion on its origin is divided between two well-known explanations. Both relate to the fact that the *matsuri* formerly began during the early predawn hours.

The first explanation maintains that a single drum passed through the major thoroughfares just before dawn, its purpose being to serve notice that the *matsuri* was about to begin and that the townspeople should ready themselves to participate. Each individual neighborhood then used a drum of its own to awaken its constituent households. As dawn broke the main drum withdrew. The day's festivities then began with the *yatai* gathering to escort the *mikoshi*. In time, however, the passing of the drum itself became an important event, with the various neighborhood groups competing to be first to complete the circuit through their home territories. These individual neighborhood drums allegedly became what we now know as the *tsuke daiko* (Mizuma 1931:389, Yamada 1938:171, Kuwatani 1965:9, Ōno 1973b, Furukawa-chō Kankō Kyōkai 1984:77, Uno 1987:101).

This explanation is supported by the name of the event itself (recall that *"okoshi daiko"* means "rousing drum"—in other words, rousing people from their slumber to prepare for the day's events). It is also congruent with the written evidence, particularly the 1870 account of the *matsuri,* which, again, mentions that "at dawn on the day of the main festival the beating of a drum reverberates as it circles through town. This is called the *"okoshi daiko."* It sets out from the neighborhood of that year's acting referee" (Furukawa-chō 1984:655).

A competing theory begins with the premise that the shrine was once surrounded by dense forest, which served as a haven for fierce animals such as wild boar and wolf. On their way to the shrine to escort the deity back into their settlement, the townspeople used to beat a large drum to frighten the animals away so they could proceed unmolested. A variation of this story adds that every year one neighborhood was chosen to lead the procession while the others vied with one another to be next in line—again an obvious precursor to the *tsuke daiko* (Mizuma 1931:389; Honda 1934:29; Yamada 1938: 171; Inokuma 1958:55; Kuwatani 1965:13, 1969:9; Furukawa-chō Kankō Kyōkai 1984:77; Uno 1987:101).

Some local residents have attempted to combine the two explanations into a single story-like account, which proceeds as follows:

> Four hundred years ago the local *ujigami* was Sugimoto Myō-jin, located in what is now the Koreshige area of Mukaimachi. When Kanamori Arishige established himself here and built Masushima Castle, he moved the *ujigami* to the castle's northeast. This put the shrine in its present location in the foothills overlooking the basin. The annual *matsuri* began with a night-time procession up to the shrine to greet the *ujigami* Sugimoto. The path from town up to the shrine led through dense forest, and the *okoshi daiko* originated as a means of scaring away the wild animals during this procession. Later the drum began to circle through town before proceeding up to the shrine, thereby alerting the residents that the *matsuri* was about to begin.

This account has the dual advantage of reconciling the two competing theories *and* pushing the roots of the drum ritual several hundred years into the past.

Ōno (1973b:4, 1974a:7) dismisses the "wild animal" theory as pure folk legend which first emerged during the early Shōwa (1926–1989) period. At that time the following poem was included in a textbook for local school children (see Kawakami 1933:3):

Furui hibiki da.	The ancient rumbling.
Jōgan no mukashi,	From back in Jōgan times,
mureru yajū o	warding away packs
ikaku shisusumu,	of wild beasts, the echo of
wagasatobito no	our native people
kamimukae suru hibiki da.	going to greet their god.
Tsutae tsutaete issen-yo nen,	Passed down, passed down, over
masumasu takamaru	a thousand years, ever-swelling
aikyō no kokoro.	heart of love for our homeland.
Ima mo kawaranu, furui	Even now unchanged, the
hibiki da.	ancient rumbling.

The Jōgan period alluded to in the poem spanned the years 859–876 C.E. The assertion that the ritual has been passed down for a thousand years undoubtedly derives from Ketawakamiya Shrine being mentioned in the *Nihon Sandai Jitsuroku,* as described in the preceding chapter. Again, the assumption being made here is that the Furukawa *matsuri* and its *okoshi daiko* date from the same period, though neither is mentioned in the *Jitsuroku* itself. And, in any case, the Furukawa *matsuri* was originally directed toward Sugimoto, not Ketawakamiya.

Ōno (1973b) cites this poem as the first allusion to the "wild animal" story in the extant literature, implying that it was purely a product of the author's imagination. Mizuma (1931:389), however, mentions the story in an article appearing in 1931, so it had obviously been circulating for sometime prior to its appearance in the school textbook. Mizuma also dismisses its usefulness as valid explanation, attributing such stories to folk beliefs related to driving away evil spirits.[1] Kuwahara et al. (1991:16) note that "packs of wild beasts" are not likely to have prowled about the area even in the distant past.

But many children of the immediate prewar generation who read the poem in school undoubtedly accepted it at face value, including the thousand-year tradition it alleges. Later they passed it on to their own children, not to mention inquisitive outsiders (I was told the story myself on several occasions). In fact the wild animal theory has been accepted and reconveyed as plausible explanation by a number of prominent folk historians (see, for example, Yamada 1938:171, Inokuma 1958:55, Tsuchida 1962:422, Kuwatani 1965: 13). It has thus become entrenched in the local folklore and now enjoys fairly wide acceptance.

Other ideas have been advanced as well. Yamada (1938:211–212) suggests that although *"okoshi daiko"* is written using the character for "rousing" *(okoshi),* the term originally referred to the act of bringing the deity over into the society of humans, using *"koshi,"* the nominalized form of the verb "to cross over," preceded by the honorific *"o."* To support his claim, he notes that the drum is borne in the manner of a palanquin[2] and accompanied by other drums, neither of which is necessary for a simple wake-up signal. As will be explained in the following pages, however, these are later innovations which had nothing to do with the original form of the ritual.

On the whole, the theory describing the *okoshi daiko* as a kind of community wake-up call is the most plausible. The use of a drum circling through the community to announce the beginning of an important event was a fairly widespread practice. It can still be seen, in fact, prior to the opening of every sumo tournament. The drum itself is a small, keg-shaped object suspended from a wooden pole. The pole is shouldered by two men, while a third walks alongside and beats the drum with sticks. This is commonly referred to as a *"fure daiko,"* or "shaking drum"—the original purpose being to shake up or rouse the townspeople *("machi o fureru")* to turn out in support of the event.

Wake-up drums once appeared in *matsuri* throughout central Japan. Some were even called *"okoshi daiko,"* just as the one in Furukawa. Indeed, Takayama employed an *okoshi daiko* of its own until 1919. Nagakura (1988:18) explains that it functioned much like a weather bulletin, informing the people that it was safe to bring their splendid *yatai* out into the open air. It is likely, therefore, that Furukawa borrowed the *okoshi daiko* in its original form from Takayama along with the use of *yatai.*

In Takayama the *okoshi daiko* was eventually abandoned when it no longer served a useful purpose. In other areas, however, the custom has survived to the present in its original form. There are *okoshi*

Figure 17. *Fure daiko* (shaking drum) used to announce the beginning of the grand sumo tournament in Nagoya, 1991.

daiko at the spring *matsuri* of Yatsuo in Toyama Prefecture and Nagahama in Shiga Prefecture, as well as the remote mountain village of Kamitakara not far from Furukawa. All are performed in the early predawn hours as a preliminary to the main events, ostensibly for rousing the participants to action.

Judging from the available evidence, the *okoshi daiko* in Furukawa originated in the same manner. In fact the smaller *tsuke daiko* used by competing neighborhoods closely resembles the *fure daiko* described above, except that it is bound more tightly to its supporting pole. This does not explain, however, why the lead drum became so large, and why the other neighborhoods began attacking it with such obvious fervor. Nor does it explain why the ritual as a whole began to eclipse the other events, eventually coming to epitomize not just the *matsuri* but the very character of Furukawa itself.

In short, a similar custom was at one time being employed in several different locations in and around the Hida region. In some places it was eventually abandoned, while in others it has survived largely unaltered to the present day. But only in Furukawa has this rather innocuous custom evolved into a rebellious expression of open conflict. I will explain the transformation as a ritual response to concurrent social, economic, and political developments.

Restoration Politics and Religious Symbolism

From the mid-Tokugawa period, Japanese scholars belonging to an intellectual movement known as *"Kokugaku,"* or "National Learning," had been endeavoring to establish Shinto as an independent religion, free of the Buddhist influence with which it had become so intimately entwined. The Shinto tradition, they maintained, represented the true Japanese spirit as it existed prior to the influx of "foreign" religions from the Asian continent. "Implicit in their criticism was the idea that everything Japanese had been natural, spontaneous, and pure, but foreign influence had destroyed that naturalness and purity. The tone of the criticism was often irrational, even mystical, advocating a return to the original state of purity from which the Japanese had fallen" (Earhart 1982:145).

Adherents of the National Learning movement advanced their arguments largely through reinterpretation of the ancient myth-histories, which justified the authority of the imperial family by tracing its descent back to the sun goddess Amaterasu. The movement contributed to the rise of nationalist sentiments and constituted an important ideological element of Restoration politics after the Tokugawa regime was overthrown in 1868. By virtue of his supposedly divine origins, the Japanese emperor had always been a figure of religious as well as political significance, and "the restoration of monarchical rule was considered a return to the ancient polity of Japan with its ideal of the unity of religion and government *(saisei-itchi)*" (Kitagawa 1987:166).

The new government launched an ambitious effort to catch up with the West in terms of industrial and military capacity, thereby propelling Japan into the modern era. The old feudal domains were abolished and a new set of geo-political units (*ken,* referred to in English as "prefectures") established in their place. Many of these new units followed the old provincial boundaries, and for a brief period of about four years, Hida was designated a self-constituting prefecture with its capital at Takayama. Initially it was dubbed "Hida Prefecture" (Hida-*ken*), but a few weeks later the name was changed to "Takayama Prefecture" (Takayama-*ken*).

In the spring of 1868, twenty-seven year-old Umemura Hayami was appointed the region's first governor and arrived in Takayama to set up his administrative headquarters. Hida had belonged to the so-called *"tenryō"* ("heavenly domain")—that part of Japan directly administered by the Tokugawa *bakufu*.[3] The new government was wary of the former *tenryō* areas as potential zones of resistance and dealt with them much in the manner of conquered territory. Umemura himself was from Mito Province—a member of the Satsuma-Chōshū coalition that had engineered the Restoration. To the people of Hida he was considered an outsider—even an enemy—and his motives were viewed with suspicion from the very beginning.

The young governor was inexperienced but ambitious and immediately embarked on a bold new program of social and economic reforms. The local people, however, were accustomed to the administrative policies of the Tokugawa regime, which allowed them a fair degree of autonomy as long as their taxes were paid. They resisted the dramatic changes now being foisted upon them. Part of their opposition stemmed from Umemura's failure to honor a promise made by interim governor Takezawa Kanzaburō. To ensure the peasants' cooperation during the transition to the new government, Takezawa had promised to cut their annual land tax in half.[4] Upon assuming control of Hida, Umemura recognized that it would be virtually impossible to administer the territory on such drastically reduced revenue, and rescinded the order almost immediately. From the perspective of the Hida peasantry, the central government, as represented by Umemura, had broken its promise.

Other concerns included Umemura's cancellation of the two rice distribution arrangements—*ninbetsumai* and *yamagatamai*—in favor of a free market system. Likewise, communal rights to the forested mountains were replaced by a system of private ownership, thereby limiting access to those who could afford to purchase the land. In addition, Umemura had initiated an "agricultural promotion" *(kannō)* program, the major element being reclamation of more land for growing rice. The peasants opposed the program because it diminished their forest and pasture reserves, increased competition for irrigation water, and threatened to raise their land taxes yet again.

These policies were directly related to the murder of peasant Zenkichi (described near the end of Chapter 6). Umemura wanted to promote agriculture by bringing uncultivated mountain land into production, and appointed local leaders to administer the conversion of forest to field. Zenkichi was one of these leaders. Under the pre-Meiji *bakufu* administration, the people of Furukawa had been assigned communal use rights to certain mountain areas, where they went regularly to cut grass for green manure and gather wood for fuel. One of these areas was located near Zenkichi's village of Unehata. Zenkichi began converting this land to cultivation, which greatly angered the Furukawa people. They challenged Zenkichi's actions at a hearing in Takayama, but, not surprisingly, the officials ruled in Zenkichi's favor. This led to his murder in Furukawa on the night of the *okoshi daiko* in 1868 (see Hishimura 1994:166–167).

In the realm of commercial activity, a centralized department of commerce was established in Takayama to set prices and regulate the flow of goods. Tariffs were levied on the transportation of raw materials and finished products. Individual households were limited to one product or service activity. These policies angered many of the local merchants, who had been accustomed to greater autonomy under the Tokugawa regime.

In short, Umemura's economic reforms had alienated the common peasantry and townspeople alike. His only true support came from prominent households who viewed his policies as progressive or who stood to benefit from the new economic opportunities they engendered.

But dissatisfaction with Umemura's leadership went well beyond his economic policies. In seeking to institute his ambitious reforms, Umemura imposed his authority on even the most intimate aspects of the peasants' daily lives, including religious practices and sexual activity.

Umemura was an instrument of official policy emanating from the central government. In attempting to restore the nominal authority of the emperor, the Meiji leadership was trying to elevate Shinto into a nationalist cult, and began suppressing Buddhism to eliminate competing ideologies. Umemura's home province of Mito was a hotbed of loyalist sentiment, and had been suppressing Buddhism since well before the Restoration.[5] Umemura had thus been raised with a deep dislike for the Buddhist priesthood. The peasants, on the other hand, drew no clear distinction between the two religious traditions. Unlike the nationalistic State Shinto now being propagated by the government, their own brand of Shinto–Buddhist syncretism offered some relief from their suffering in this world by promising them salvation in the next. Their contributions to Buddhist priests and temples were a means of gaining favor for the souls of their ancestors as well as themselves, and they took great pride in the temples they supported. Umemura equated such beliefs with superstition. To him, support of Buddhist institutions was a waste of valuable resources—one that the poor peasantry could ill afford. He therefore prohibited such support in the interest of the public welfare.

As previously mentioned, the annual *matsuri* was an important respite in the harsh lives of the peasantry. It allowed them to escape the drudgery that governed their daily existence and engage for a brief moment in unrestrained revelry. Though they recognized the *matsuri* as a religious event, it had none of the moralist overtones of State Shinto. Umemura was unfamiliar with peasant attitudes; he failed to recognize their need for periodic diversion from their everyday labors. To him, the drinking and licentious behavior surrounding the *matsuri* were immoral. More importantly, while conducting routine inspections of local Shinto shrines, Umemura's officials would often find a shrine compound being maintained by a Buddhist priest, and a Buddhist statue kept inside the inner sanctuary to represent the local guardian deity. The statue would be summarily seized, and the celebration of the local *matsuri* prohibited on the grounds that the proper Shinto deity had not been enshrined there (Gifu-ken Shakai Undōshi Hensan Iinkai 1971:366–367; Ema 1985a:345, 1985b:32–35).[6]

Umemura also thought the people of Hida were lacking in discipline and public morality. He tried to instill in them what he believed were proper attitudes. These, of course, were based on the values of the elite samurai class, of which he was a product. His reforms included outlawing what he considered illicit sexual behavior. For example, peasant youth had long enjoyed the custom of *"yobai"* (literally "night-crawling") in which a young man would sneak into the home of a young woman late at night to have intimate relations with her in secret—provided, of course, that the young woman consented.[7] This was widely practiced in rural areas and was apparently considered a normal part of the courtship process (Koyama 1960:1545, Kuwatani 1971:143–145, Furukawa-chō Kyōiku Iinkai 1990:392–395). Umemura declared such activities illegal, and began punishing a few unfortunate offenders as examples to the rest. In one notorious incident he had a young sixteen-year-old girl bound to a bridge in Takayama and displayed there in public for three days. Her crime had been consorting with a married man (Ōno 1972b, Hachino 1979:95–96, Ema 1985b:80–95, Matsubara 1987:246).

There were other issues relating to autonomy and defense. The power traditionally held by young men in rural Japan has been alluded to already. The local fire brigade in particular represented a formidable and rather intimidating presence. In addition to their obvious role of fighting fires, these young men considered themselves defenders of their own communities, and thus functioned as a local militia. One of the basic features of state-level political organization, however, is a monopoly on the use of force; Umemura soon took steps to establish his own prefectural army. This alienated members of fire brigades all over Hida, as it essentially robbed them of one of their most important and prestigious duties. Moreover, service in the army was to be compulsory for young men of ages twenty-one and twenty-two, excluding eldest sons.[8] Umemura enlisted the aid of certain prominent households to organize the new recruits into local squads.

Buddhist temples were slated to be used as administrative facilities. Honkō Temple was commandeered as an army barrack, but

Enkō Temple resisted. In one famous episode, a group of soldiers forced their way into Enkō Temple to take control, whereupon they were confronted by the resident priest and one lone samurai. The priest is said to have scolded the intruders so severely for failing to show the proper respect that they all bowed in apology and meekly withdrew (Ōno 1972b; Hachino 1979:419–421).

Opposition to Umemura's governance became so widespread that talk of rebellion began to circulate. Early in the spring of 1869, representatives of an anti-Umemura movement travelled to Kyoto to meet secretly with government officials and apprise them of the situation. When Umemura heard of the meeting he immediately set out for Kyoto himself in an attempt to clear his name. While he was gone the rebellion broke out, first in Takayama and Furukawa, then spreading to other areas. Under cover of darkness, angry mobs took to the streets, attacking the homes of people seen as supporting Umemura. Seventeen buildings were wrecked within the boundaries of what is now Furukawa-chō. Among them were the homes of local notables such as Tajika, Watanabe, Hasegawa, and "Sugisaki" Gotō, all of whom resided in Ninomachi Street. According to one eyewitness, the mob passed through Ninomachi armed with spears and hoes, shouting "Come out! Come out! If you don't come out we'll smash you!" Wealthy patrons fled from their homes, some hiding out in the hills of Mt. Anbō, others seeking shelter with their *deiri* employees. In their absence the mob broke into their homes and storehouses, smashing furniture and throwing valuables into the street (Ōno 1972b; Furukawa-chō Kyōiku Iinkai 1987:136–137). Six other buildings were burned to the ground, including the home of Satō Hikozaemon, one of the area's major landlords (Ōno 1971b, Furukawa-chō 1986:327–331).[9]

These homes were targeted because they had agreed to help administer Umemura's programs. Many of the local elite had been followers of National Learning scholar Tanaka Ōhide, who espoused loyalist values similar to those of Umemura. Tajika Rokusaburō, Hasegawa Kanshichirō, Gotō Hikobei, and Sugishita Tarōyuemon had all been appointed squad leaders in Umemura's fledgling army (Ōno 1971b, Ema 1985b:38), and would undoubtedly have been rewarded for their services with influential (and lucrative) political positions. Satō Hikozaemon had been put in charge of agricultural improvement projects (Gotō 1983:115). Honkō Temple, too, was attacked, as it had been commandeered by Umemura to serve as an administrative facility. Enkō Temple, on the other hand, was left untouched due to its refusal to cooperate with the new regime (Ōno 1972b, Hachino 1979:421). This incident, therefore, was not simply a case of angry citizens attacking the local advocates of an unpopular reform policy; it contained elements of a class struggle pitting the common peasantry against the more prosperous landowning and merchant households.[10]

The violence spread to other parts of Hida and raged for several days. The central government, uncertain of Umemura's leadership abilities, had ordered him to remain in Kyoto. But Umemura defied the order and hurried back to Hida hoping to set things right. Fearing a repeat of the Ōhara situation of several decades earlier, the rebels were determined to prevent the young governor from regaining control. A large mob of peasants, led by the Furukawa fire brigade, set out to intercept him at Hagiwara shortly after he had crossed the border into Hida. When they surrounded Umemura's lodgings his guards opened fire. Three of the peasants were killed, including one man from Furukawa.[11] Umemura tried to escape but was wounded in the shoulder by a rifle bullet fired by a member of the rebel faction. He withdrew temporarily into neighboring Naegi province, but was later taken into custody by the Meiji government pending an official investigation to determine whether he had been guilty of abusing his authority. He died, purportedly of his shoulder wound, in a Tokyo prison at the age of twenty-nine, still awaiting his trial.[12]

There are two ways of looking at Umemura's brief but tragic sovereignty. One is that he was an inept and autocratic administrator whom the peasants had every right to resist. The other holds that he had good intentions but simply moved too quickly. It is interesting to note that Umemura's given name, "Hayami," is written with two characters meaning "rapid" and "water." Together they evoke the image of a swiftly flowing stream, an apt allusion to Umemura's ambitious character. Moreover, Umemura was from a distant region, a product of disciplined samurai ethics, and steeped in the ideology of Restoration politics; he did not understand the local peasantry. The people of Hida had grown accustomed to the comparative autonomy they enjoyed under the Tokugawa regime. They had developed their own sociopolitical, economic, and religious institutions and did not welcome the intervention of an outsider bent on rapid change. The entire episode, in other words, may be seen as a clash between two distinct value systems—that of the local mountain peasant versus that of the centralized administrative bureaucracy.

Umemura was succeeded by Miyahara Taisuke, a more experienced and conservative administrator. By that time the government had backed away from its suppression of Buddhism, and had settled on a policy of Shinto–Buddhist separatism. The peasants came to realize that change was inevitable; many, in fact, were won over by the promise of social and economic reforms. This was especially true of the more prominent households, who in turn used their own stature to influence others. The fact that Umemura was imprisoned seemed to demonstrate the government's concern for maintaining just rule—though some feel Umemura was simply being made a scapegoat for the failure of the government's early policies (see Ema 1985b; Ōtsu and Kobayashi 1990).

There were no more cases of open rebellion in the Furukawa area, with the exception of an isolated tenant uprising in nearby Sugisaki in 1870 (Furukawa-chō 1986:346–349). Policies enacted by the central government, however, continued to have a dramatic impact at the local level. In 1871, Hida was lumped in with neighboring Shinshū province to the east to form Chikuma Prefecture. From this time forward the Hida region ceased to function as a distinct political unit. In 1876 the prefectural boundaries were revised once again; this time Hida was merged with former Minō Province to the south to form Gifu Prefecture. The new prefectural capital was established at Gifu City, located on the Minō plains just north of Nagoya. This meant that the people of Hida now had to take their orders from an administrative capital located well outside the boundaries of their own territory.[13] The sense of isolation from the capital was particularly acute for communities like Furukawa which lay beyond the drainage divide separating Hida into its northern and southern halves.

The new prefectural assembly was convened in Gifu City for the first time in 1879 and consisted of about fifty representatives. From the beginning there were disagreements over the apportionment of funding for public works. The members were split into two major factions: one representing the lowlands (Gifu and Ōgaki plains) and the other the mountain belt (Hida and Tōnō). The lowlands representatives wanted funding for navigation and flood control projects along the Kiso, Nagara, and Ibi Rivers, while the mountain belt faction favored the construction of roads and bridges in the north. The lowlands contingent held a distinct majority, and persistently channeled funding into their home territories. They were supported in their efforts by prefectural governor Ozaki Rijun, himself a lowlands native. Massive improvement projects were initiated along the three rivers, and the lowland plains of southern Gifu Prefecture developed into a major rice-producing area (Gifu-ken Kōtō Gakkō Kyōiku Kenkyūkai 1988:9). The Hida region, on the other hand, lagged far behind in terms of economic development for many years to come.

Compulsory education was instituted in 1872. Seven new schools were established in and around Furukawa, replacing the old Buddhist temple schools (terakoya) that had been in use prior to the Restoration. The educational system was to become a major force for creating national uniformity. Schools all over the country were placed under the authority of the newly established Ministry of Education. Course schedules and textbooks were standardized so that all children in Japan would receive basically the same instruction, administered by teachers appointed from outside the local area.

The school system played a particularly important role in the propagation of a nationalist ideology known as the "family state" (kazoku kokka). The Confucian tenet of filial piety, which stressed that children must be loyal to and honor their parents, was metaphorically extended to the emperor as the ultimate father figure, with the Japanese people placed in the role of his respectful and obedient offspring. The state, therefore, was perceived as a kind of huge extended family, with its people bound to the emperor through filial obligations.

The basic principles of this ideology were set forth in an influential document known as the Imperial Rescript on Education (Kyōiku Chokugo), issued by the government in 1890. It encouraged the people to "advance public good and promote common interests; always respect the Constitution and observe the laws; should emergency arise, offer yourselves courageously to the State; and thus guard and maintain the prosperity of Our Imperial Throne coeval with heaven and earth" (Tsunoda et al. 1958:140). Through the Rescript, the Meiji leadership "sought to imbue the Emperor and his government with the sanctity and legitimacy that would suppress political opposition and dissent" (Pyle 1978:99–100). It was prominently displayed along with a portrait of the emperor in every public school building, and recited by students in unison on ceremonial occasions.

The elite samurai class had been officially dissolved following the Meiji Restoration. However, since most of the new leadership were products of this class, they tended to impose its values on the rest of the population in implementing their reforms. In Ueno's (1987: S78–S79) estimation, Meiji dissolution of the Tokugawa-period class system "meant not the 'commoner-ization' of the samurai class but the 'samurai-zation' of the commoners." Samurai values were embodied in the Meiji Civil Code of 1897, which among other things instituted the practice of male primogeniture and the household registration system (Bachnik 1983; Ueno 1987:S79; Kondo 1990: 169–172).

Important structural changes facilitated propagation of the new ideology. Scattered settlements were amalgamated into villages and towns, "thus augmenting the fiscal base of local government and improving its administrative efficiency" (Fukutake 1980:146). These new units were linked through the prefectural administration to the central government, creating a channel whereby the latter could more effectively impose its authority into local affairs.

In a parallel arrangement, local Shinto shrines were merged to form larger units, one in each of the new administrative municipalities. Political and religious boundaries were thus made to coincide, each appearing to acknowledge the validity of the other. Prior to the Meiji period, local shrines were largely free to conduct rites in their own manner according to the needs of their parishioners. This changed radically after the Restoration, however:

In the Meiji period a national calendar of rites centering on the nation and the imperial house was introduced that dramatically altered the character of ritual life. While the emperor had always had a sacerdotal role, the people previously had been little aware of it. Now his rites were to be their rites. The new calendar of rites gave him a high-profile, center-stage role as head priest of the nation. (Hardacre 1989:101)

The government also prescribed a liturgical format *(keishiki)* for use by each individual community during its annual shrine festival. The standardized liturgy was part of a systematic effort to redirect the focus of people's religious identity away from the local community and toward the newly created nation-state, whose legitimacy was symbolized by the Grand Shrine at Ise (located along the Pacific coast in Mie Prefecture, roughly one hundred kilometers southwest of Kyoto):

> Through these various rites, the emperor's religious authority was based on the unity of his person with Amaterasu, the apical ancestress of the imperial house. The idea that all other deities were putatively descended from her had a parallel in the notion that all the Japanese people were ultimately descended from the imperial house. Similarly, all deities being ultimately linked to Amaterasu, all shrines were ultimately subordinate to Ise. Thus Ise was the apex of a pyramidal hierarchy of shrines; their rites should conform to imperial rites conducted both at Ise and in the palace. In the person of the emperor was bound up the unity of the nation and its people and myriad deities. This unity was symbolized in local society by shrines and shrine rites. (Hardacre 1989:103)

Thus the local Shinto shrine festival was destined to become an expression of nationalist religious ideology whose essential purpose was to acknowledge the authority of the central government. Hardacre suggests, however, that most people failed to recognize the significance of such ideological manipulation of their religious symbols:

> Where people were aware of change, however, they were generally pleased to have the gods they worshiped locally recognized by the new government. For one thing, they were encouraged to incorporate deities having some patriotic significance into their pantheon, and if that change were successfully accomplished, their shrine could assume the title of *jinja*. ... To most people, the new title for the local shrine sounded like a promotion, suggesting an elevation of the status of the area and its people. That the incorporation of new deities could fundamentally change the character of shrine life was not immediately apparent. (Hardacre 1989:84)

In 1871, by order of the Meiji government, Furukawa's guardian deity Sugimoto Myōjin was officially replaced with Ōkuninushi no Kami ("Great Land-ruling Deity"), a member of the Shinto pantheon as recorded in the ancient myth-histories. This can be seen as part of the government's effort to purge Shinto of the Buddhist influence, since local deities were often associated with syncretic folk beliefs (Kuwahara et al. 1991:10). Installation of an officially recognized guardian deity automatically linked Furukawa into the political symbolism of the state. At the same time, the name of the shrine was changed to "Ketawakamiya." As mentioned in Chapter 3, this name had appeared in a ninth-century imperial history, and thus implied greater legitimacy. Use of the name "Ketawakamiya" (literally "junior Keta shrine") also created a nominal association with the grand Keta Shrine in Ishikawa Prefecture.[14]

Furukawa's tutelary shrine had in effect become a symbol of imperial authority, and its annual *matsuri* an instrument of nationalist ideology. The ornate neighborhood festival wagons continued as before to pass in review before visiting officials from Takayama, but these officials now represented the regional administrative headquarters of the new Meiji government. The purpose of their visit was to oversee the proceedings, mediate disputes, and ensure against deviations from the prescribed order.

Appropriation of local religious symbolism is even more obvious in the case of the grand *taisai,* performed every few years at one of Hida's major shrines. The *taisai* drew the tutelary shrine of every Hida town and village into a single religio-political alliance, transforming the *matsuri* from a purely local affair into an instrument of the National Learning movement and Restoration politics.

Increasing centralization is also apparent in such fundamental aspects as the reckoning of time. In 1873, Japan officially adopted the Western (Gregorian) calendar, replacing the old lunar–solar calendar that had traditionally been used. The date of the Furukawa *matsuri* was now fixed for September 20 by the new calendar, placing it at roughly the same time of year as before.[15]

In 1875 the surrounding villages of Koreshige, Kamikita, Shimokita, and Numamachi were amalgamated with the neighborhoods of old Furukawa *(Furukawa machikata mura)* to form a new administrative unit known as "Furukawa-*machi*" ("Furukawa Town"). Settlements which had long acted independently were now obliged to conduct themselves as a single body whose political affairs were dominated by the wealthy landlords and merchants of Ninomachi. Kiriyama Genbei, the first mayor of the new amalgamation, was a Ninomachi resident, as were the vast majority of subsequent mayors through the end of the Second World War.[16]

Around 1878 the old neighborhoods in Ichinomachi and Ninomachi were slightly realigned. In both streets, block one was now designated the "upper" *("kami")* neighborhood, and block four the "lower" *("shimo"*—the terms "upper" and "lower" relate to physical elevation, the "lower" areas being further downstream). At the same time, blocks two and three were combined to form the "middle" *("naka")* neighborhoods. This caused no major difficulty in performing the *matsuri*, however, as the two middle sectors in both streets were already sharing a single *yatai*. Mukaimachi had been incorporated into the town several years earlier. In 1882 it gave up its old *yatai* and assumed the role of performing the *kagura*, obtaining a used Kaguradai from Takayama.

Sociopolitical Change

Chapters 1 and 2 alluded to Scott's concept of a "hidden transcript," and the possibility that it might be revealed during performances like the *matsuri*. Yet the applicability of Scott's work to the present study goes beyond the use of the carnival-like atmosphere as a means of airing discontent. In particular, his observations on the political economy of colonial Southeast Asia offer interesting parallels to the Japanese experience. Scott (1976) has asserted that Southeast Asian peasants traditionally recognized a "moral economy" geared not toward maximizing profit but rather toward the assurance of subsistence security in the event of crop failure, flood, or other calamity. This is important in understanding the relationship between wealthy landlords and their less prosperous tenant cultivators. The tenants were willing to accept subservient positions and yield a considerable portion of each year's harvest as rent, but in return they expected rent reductions and material assistance from the landlord in times of need. Distinctions in wealth and social status were thus acceptable to the extent that landlords fulfilled their role as local benefactors, using their surplus wealth to assist the less fortunate.

Conditions changed drastically, however, with the advent of Western colonial intervention. In order to ensure a reliable flow of revenue to finance their expanding bureaucracies, colonial governments instituted fixed head and land taxes, payable only in hard currency, with no allowance for fluctuations in yield. The peasants were now obliged to convert to growing cash crops or to seek employment in the wage labor market. They were thus drawn into an economic system that lay well beyond their limited sphere of influence. Of perhaps even greater significance was the impact on landlord–tenant relations. The wealthy patron landlords were increasingly attracted to new social and economic opportunities available to them in the burgeoning towns and cities. This led them to neglect their traditional obligations to the local community, though they continued to extract the same amount of rent as before. From the point of view of the tenants the relationship had become inherently more exploitative, thereby endowing them with the moral justification to rebel. Indeed, Scott links the incidence of peasant rebellion in Southeast Asia to the larger historical forces that destroyed the traditional social order and the subsistence economy that supported it, namely "the development of capitalism, the commercialization of agrarian relations, and the growth of a centralizing state" (1976:189).

This pattern may not appear immediately relevant to the Japanese situation due to the fact that Japan has never been colonized by a Western power. Yet there are striking parallels between rural Japan during the Meiji period and the colonial Southeast Asian societies Scott was addressing. These include (1) the establishment of a strong centralized bureaucracy capable of extending its authority into even the most remote areas, (2) institution of a fixed land tax to replace the more flexible payment-in-kind arrangement, (3) loss of rights to common lands, (4) commercialization of agriculture and absorption of rural villages into a market economy, and (5) subsequent breakdown of traditional exchange relationships. In fact it may be argued that the Meiji government essentially colonialized its own peasantry in order to feed its industrial expansion, thereby approximating the Southeast Asian experience.

Prior to the Meiji period the Hida peasantry had been largely self-sufficient, obtaining what few goods they could not produce themselves through barter or payment-in-kind arrangements. The new economic policies adopted by the Meiji government in directing Japan's modernization drew the rural areas more deeply into the market economy. In 1874 the Meiji government instituted a land tax revision *(chiso kaisei)* which ended the practice of payment in kind as a percentage of the harvest *(nengu)*. The tax was now fixed at an annual cash payment equal to three percent of the assessed land value. Landholders were made directly responsible for payment of the tax and in return granted title to their lands.

The tax revision was intended to both modernize the landholding system and provide a stable source of revenue for the central government, which desperately needed capital to invest in its huge industrialization project. The government had adopted a policy of taking as little as possible from commerce and industry under the assumption that these sectors would then reinvest their profits toward further expansion. The peasants, on the other hand, were taxed as heavily as possible; since they were still largely engaged in subsistence agriculture this was seen as the only way of extracting their wealth. Thus Japan's industrialization was to proceed by imposing the heaviest burden on those with least to gain—the rural peasantry.

Unlike the traditional system, the fixed payment made no allowance for fluctuations in yield or commodity prices. In the event of a poor harvest small farmers operating close to the margin of profit or loss had little alternative but to borrow from moneylenders in order to come up with the necessary cash payment. Inability to repay such a loan resulted in foreclosure, with the moneylender acquiring title to the land. In most cases, the former owner was then allowed to remain on the land as a tenant cultivator.[17]

Rent on tenanted land continued to be paid to the owner in kind as a percentage of the rice harvest. The owner then sold the rice on the open market, using the profits to pay the land tax. While the tax had been fixed by the government, however, rent on tenanted land was solely determined by the landlords themselves, and sometimes rose to exceedingly high levels. To ensure that its revenues would continue unimpeded, the government actively promoted the landlords' ability to collect their rent and consistently favored landlords over tenants in dispute settlements.

The Meiji land settlement, then, upset the previous distribution of power between landlords and tenants. Their property rights almost totally unrestricted, landlords were permitted by law to deal with tenants in any way they chose. Unprotected and to a great extent ignored by the government, tenants were more vulnerable to exploitation than ever before. (Waswo 1977:21)

In sum, tax policies imposed by the central government led to the erosion of traditional sociopolitical relations in rural areas:

[T]he Meiji land tax eliminated the village as a fiscal unit; land-holding was fully privatized, and the payment of taxes was made an individual responsibility. Under these conditions, the impending bankruptcy of small farmers unable to pay the land tax became a class issue and ceased to be a matter of collective village concern. (Vlastos 1989:430)

During the early 1880s, anti-inflationary tactics imposed by Finance Minister Matsukata Masayoshi triggered a nationwide economic depression. Prices of rice and other agricultural commodities fell, increasing the severity of the fixed-rate land tax. This created even greater hardships in the rural countryside, at times inciting the peasants to open rebellion (Irokawa 1985:155). Hane (1982: 103–104) explains that

the growing burden of taxation and the deflationary policy adopted by the government in the 1880s led to the steady impoverishment of most farmers, forcing them to give up their lands to pay their taxes and repay their debts. Their land, too, then passed into the hands of the wealthier landowners, moneylenders, and merchants.

The result was a trend toward higher rates of tenancy, with more land being acquired by a few privileged households. According to Waswo (1977:19), "the extent of tenanted land rose from 36 percent of all arable land in 1883 to 45 percent in 1908."

Furukawa was no exception to these nationwide patterns. There are no exact figures on the amount of tenanted land in Furukawa, but older residents estimate that as many as eighty percent of the local farmers were cultivating land owned by other households. Through rapid land acquisition during the period of so-called "Matsukata deflation," many of Furukawa's wealthy landlords rose to even greater prominence. The Sugishita household amassed huge amounts of land and at their peak were taking in about 4000 bales (240,000 kilograms) of rice per year as rent from their tenants. They held land not only in Furukawa but in surrounding villages as well.

The Satō household, with an annual income of about 1400 bales (84,000 kilograms), operated at a significantly smaller scale, but nevertheless employed as many as 150 tenant cultivators. Rent on tenanted land varied between fifty and sixty percent of the harvest and constituted roughly ninety percent of the household income, a condition which Nakamura et al. (1972:8) describe as "parasitic."

Merchant households, too, were able to capitalize on the new economic conditions, using their profits to purchase land or foreclosing on small owners to whom they had lent money. The Nakamura, for example, were able to acquire extensive paddy land in and around the hamlets on the opposite side of the Miya River, and in 1876 relocated to Koreshige. Most of the emerging merchant landlords, however, remained in Ichinomachi and Ninomachi. The more outlying neighborhoods continued to be occupied primarily by small owner and tenant cultivators.

As previously mentioned, there were several lines of Tajika in the Furukawa area. Tajika Rokusaburō, heir to the lumber merchant-*cum*-cloth dying and *sake*-brewing household in Ninomachi, used the profits from his businesses to acquire vast land holdings. Around 1892, Rokusaburō changed his family name from "Tajika" to "Honda," the new name intended as a contraction of "Hon-Tajika" ("main/principal Tajika").[18] The Hondas eventually transformed themselves into exclusively agricultural landlords, reaching a scale of ownership comparable to that of Satō and Okamura. At one time the Hondas were taking in around 1600 bales (96,000 kilograms) of rice as rent from their tenant cultivators, who are said to have numbered over 600. The Honda household also employed as many as twenty-two *deiri* servants. The Watanabe household in Ichinomachi also began brewing *sake* and acquiring land with the profits. Most of this land was concentrated in the vicinity of Kamikita between Tonomachi and the Ketawakamiya Shrine. At one time the household was taking in about 800 bales (48,000 kilograms) of rice from its tenant cultivators.

With the capital acquired from selling rice, prominent landholding households were well positioned to take advantage of new investment opportunities. The *sake* brewers, of course, had already established their own industries, but now could expand them. Fuse built the first mechanized silk thread-making factory in Furukawa. Satō, too, diversified into silk weaving, and together with Sugishita founded Furukawa Ginkō, the area's first bank. Honda, Nakamura, and Kumazaki were also involved in the financial services industry. In fact wealthy landlords virtually monopolized the local banking business, as they alone could assume the risks involved.

Economic advantages were accompanied by greater political influence, as local administrative offices were dominated by the same socioeconomic stratum. Again, the new constitution guaranteed voting privileges only to those who paid at least twenty-five yen in property taxes to the central government. This restricted direct participation in the political process to members of the wealthy landholding elite, which in rural areas such as Furukawa amounted to only a small minority of the total population. A voter registry compiled in 1889 lists only fifty-six eligible voters in Furukawa out of a total population of around six thousand.[19] Fukutake (1980: 154–155) notes that, with their exclusive voting privileges, members of this rural elite routinely elected their peers into public office, where they could ensure policies which favored their own interests:

> When elections were held, hamlet leaders generally controlled the votes by dividing up the hamlet and instructing the residents of each division to vote for a particular candidate. . . . The candidate for village-town council representative was almost without exception a powerful local landlord, and frequently he stayed in office for a long time. . . . The positions of mayor and deputy mayor, who were selected by the council members, usually went to the most powerful landlords, or to lesser landlords who would follow their lead.

This is supported by the Furukawa data. A list of individuals elected to the office of mayor shows the overwhelming majority to have been local landlords, most of whom resided in Ninomachi. Gotō Shigehide ("Nishi Gotō") and Watanabe Akira were elected to the first Gifu prefectural assembly 1879–1881. Watanabe served an additional term 1882–1884. Both men later became mayor of Furukawa, Watanabe in 1887 and Gotō in 1892. Honda Rokusaburō was a member of the Gifu prefectural assembly 1895–1899. He also served two terms as mayor of Furukawa, 1897–1898 and 1904–1906. At the national level, Nakamura Nobuo stood for the first election to the House of Representatives (Kokkai Giin) in 1890 and won by 155 votes. He later served as mayor of Furukawa 1898–1904. Likewise, Sugishita Tarōyuemon served two terms in the House of Representatives 1898–1902 and a term in the House of Peers (Kizokuin) 1907–1911. Though technically not a resident of Ninomachi, Sugishita nevertheless maintained a huge warehouse in that neighborhood for storing the rice he extracted from his tenant farmers.

In light of the Meiji emphasis on the unity of political and religious ideology, it is not surprising that the rural elite were dominating local shrine offices as well. Prior to the Meiji Restoration, overall supervision of the *matsuri* was assumed by two officials from the magistrate's office in Takayama. After the Restoration this role was taken over by the mayor, the Meiji counterpart to the feudal "headman." In 1889, the same year the new system of local government was instituted, supervision was transferred from the mayor to the *"shinji torishimari"* ("supervisor[s] of sacred rites"). As may be recalled from Chapter 4, this term is used at present in referring to the head of the shrine parishioners. At the time it was applied to three high ranking shrine officers who may be considered forerunners of today's parish elders. These men were given absolute authority over all *matsuri* proceedings, and were immediately superior to the director. A notebook on the *matsuri* kept by the Honda household includes a list of individuals who served in this capacity between the years 1889 and 1900. It reveals that they were almost without exception town-dwelling landlords who were included in the aforementioned voter registry. Three names in particular dominate the list: Honda, Tajika, and Watanabe. Other prominent households such as Nakamura and Fuse appear as well.

Admittedly, mere wealth alone was insufficient to garner such prestigious positions; aspiring candidates also had to command the respect and confidence of the townspeople at large. It must be recognized, however, that fostering this type of image on one's own behalf generally requires a substantial economic investment, thereby excluding all but the wealthy from active participation.

In addition to symbolically legitimating the existing social order, religious affiliations were being employed by the local elite to extend their sphere of influence. "Local projects to build a shrine or raise an existing shrine's rank provided a powerful vehicle for increasing the prestige and prominence of provincial elites. . . . Paying money to public administrators for a shrine could give provincials valuable contacts useful, no doubt, in a variety of contexts outside the original shrine-centered negotiation" (Hardacre 1989:108). Political ambition thus went hand in hand with active support for the Shinto ideology being propagated by the state, the latter helping to establish influential contacts through which the former could be pursued.

Recognition of class distinctions within the local community was inhibited, however, by efforts of elite members to stress their common interests as fellow residents and downplay obvious sociopolitical and economic inequities. In this sense the *matsuri* served as a convenient opportunity to curry favor through generous contributions of food and *sake.* Building or refurbishing *yatai* were cooperative efforts that united neighborhood residents. Maintaining the shrine building served a similar function on the level of the entire town. It is not surprising, then, that prominent households took an active interest in shrine affairs.

A similar pattern was unfolding at the national level. The imperialist attitudes and expansionism which eventually led Japan into the Second World War were already beginning to assert themselves at this time. Tremendous economic and industrial growth was accompanied by impressive military victories, against the Chinese in 1895 and against the Russians in 1905. These in turn provided the central government with the justification for continuing to exploit its own citizenry. "Competition for international markets and resources as well as political advantages in Asia exerted a profound influence on Japanese leaders, whose perception of the Western powers as potential threats provided an excuse to demand of the Japanese people their continued personal sacrifice for the good of the nation" (Hane 1982:10).

Religion was an important force in generating popular support for these efforts. Prior to this time the new ritual calendar and religious symbolism imposed by the central government had met with some resistance, but the government was now able to capitalize on the perceived threat from a common enemy in attempting to draw the people into a more cohesive polity:

While the outline of a new national ritual calendar was established in the 1870s, it was not until much later that it really began to be observed. Diaries of the 1880s indicate that the police had to force people to fly the national flag on the new holidays, and that for the most part the populace continued to be attuned to the old customs. . . . Like so many aspects of State

Shinto, things really began to change after the wars with China and Russia. These rites began to be incorporated in the schools as of the first decade of this century, and it was also about this time that local authorities began to promote the new holidays in many areas. (Hardacre 1989:102)

As the Meiji period progressed, industrialization, the transition to a money economy, and absorption into the world market widened the socioeconomic distinction between rural and urban Japan. While the urban–industrial centers were expanding economically, the rural areas remained virtually untouched by the purported benefits of modernization. This strained traditional patterns of social organization, particularly the relationship between landlord and tenant.

Waswo (1977:66) notes three trends which characterized Japanese landlords at the turn of the century: (1) a steady decline in the number directly engaged in cultivation themselves, (2) growing involvement in more lucrative economic opportunities and social attractions available to them in the industrializing urban areas, and (3) gradual increase in absentee ownership. Landlords thus grew more parasitic and less attentive to their traditional obligations as local benefactors:

By abandoning farming, investing or working in industrial and commercial enterprises, and departing for the towns and cities of Japan, landlords were, in one sense, responding positively to the new opportunities and new national goals of the post-Restoration era. But at the same time, by dissociating themselves from rural life, they were giving up the remaining bases of their elite status in the countryside. Whether absentee landlords in a geographical or a functional sense, they were no longer able to behave as their tenants expected or to perform their time-honored role in village life. (1977:137)

In sum, policies enacted by the Meiji government greatly enhanced the exploitative power of the rural elite:

The Meiji Restoration of 1868 and the land settlement which followed it brought about important changes in the status of landlords, providing them with hitherto unparalleled opportunities to profit from leasing land and enhancing their authority in both tenancy relations and village life. For the next half century or so they functioned as the dominant elite of the countryside and exerted considerable influence in national affairs as well. (1977:3)

This is an important link in my argument in that it integrates the landlord class and the central government into a single administrative hierarchy. Therefore, a ritual event such as the *okoshi daiko,* explained as an expression of opposition toward both (1) the local elite and (2) the imposition of authority by the central government, may actually be seen as a reaction toward a single exploitative system. That the people of Furukawa themselves recognized the connection is clear in their targeting local landlord and wealthy merchant households for attack during the Umemura Rebellion.

The new Meiji government had effectively asserted its control within a few years after the Restoration, but still faced pockets of resistance in some of the outlying areas. The Satsuma Rebellion led by Saigō Takamori in 1877 was the last major threat to centralized authority. Scattered opposition to government policies remained, however, especially among the rural peasantry. One of the most notable examples was the Chichibu incident of 1884–1885. This was basically a peasant uprising against usurious moneylending and debt foreclosure, both in turn related to the inflexible Meiji land tax. An army of peasants from the Chichibu district in what is now Saitama Prefecture took over the district office in Omiya and battled in vain with government troops sent to crush the rebellion. The incident marked a turning point in the means employed by peasants to express their opposition. As Hane (1982:27) observes, "[t]he suppression of the Chichibu Uprising signaled the end of any attempt on the part of the poor people's parties to rely on force to protect their interests. Although minor protest movements did occur afterward, they were readily squelched by the government."

Outright rebellion had thus been rendered futile. But less violent forms of political expression were equally limited. In fact the entire Meiji period was characterized by a steady process of restricting local autonomy and asserting the authority of the central government through administrative institutions, education, manipulation of religious ideology, and coercion by the police and military. Vlastos (1989:372) notes that:

the centralization of authority made it more difficult for the villagers to influence the very policies that most affected them. With respect to the land tax, the most frequent cause of conflict, the Meiji state was infinitely better prepared to resist than was the *bakufu* or daimyo [domain lord]. Not infrequently, the peasants' protests in the Tokugawa period had succeeded in wringing concessions from lords, even though the leaders might be severely punished. However, the creation of an efficient national bureaucracy and modern police and army drastically undercut the efficacy of traditional forms of protest.

Thus, as Scott (1985) reminds us, the absence of open hostilities does not necessarily imply widespread satisfaction with existing conditions; it could just as easily derive from an acute awareness of the risks involved in speaking out. Even so, rebellious sentiments may continue to find expression through a variety of more subtle devices, including the symbolism inherent in large communal rituals.

Ritualized Response

It is unclear from the historical record alone to what extent the people of Furukawa continued their opposition to the changes imposed upon them following the Umemura Rebellion. There is, however, compelling evidence in the form of civil and shrine regulations that the authorities were growing increasingly concerned about the direction the *matsuri* was taking, and began trying to control its more unruly elements from precisely this time. These regulations suggest that suppressed hostilities were assuming the form of a ritualized display.

In 1877, the head priest and other high ranking officials of the newly renamed Ketawakamiya Shrine issued their first official set of festival regulations *(sairei kisokusho)*. It begins with the following preamble:

The foundation of the yearly clan-god festival is primarily to pay homage to the deity, and thereby inspire the people. Heretofore in this town, the *yatai* of all the component neighborhoods have been brought out on the day of the festival and pulled along as an honor guard in front of the *mikoshi*. In

recent years, however, on the day of the festival various grievances have come to be expressed. This is disrespectful conduct
toward the deity and highly improper. Therefore, the evil conduct of the past shall be washed away and festival regulations
established. Thirteen copies shall be signed, and one copy each
shall be posted in the district office, town hall, and every neighborhood. These must be resolutely observed from now on.
(Furukawa-chō 1986:401–405)

The provisions in the document establish a detailed procedure for
settling disputes. The mayor and his assistants *(seifuku kochō)* are
designated the "supervisors of sacred rites," responsible for the overall performance of the festival. The *yatai* director (by this time
called *"shuji"* rather than *"gyōji"*) is now to be selected by drawing
lots, rather than following an established rotation as in previous
years. The drawing is to be held every year on September 10—ten
days prior to the *matsuri.* It is to be conducted by the mayor, not the
Shinto priest. The director then becomes responsible for leading all
yatai affairs during the festival. In the event of mishap or damage to
one of the *yatai,* the director is to inspect the situation and decide
what to do. If there is only a slight problem the proceedings should
pause so that it can be fixed. In the event of serious damage, however, the vehicle will be removed. Misconduct by any *taigumi* should
be reported to the director. If an argument or grievance emerges, the
antagonists should present their case before the director, who then
has four hours in which to settle the matter. If it cannot be settled
within the time allotted, it will be taken before the supervisor of
sacred rites (i.e., the mayor), who then has up to three hours to render a decision. If no decision has been reached at the end of this
time, the matter will be postponed until the following day so as not
to interfere with the conduct of the festival.

The regulations also state that damages to the *yatai,* worn paint,
or tarnished finishings are unclean and therefore offensive to the
deity; they must be repaired. If a *yatai* is damaged by fire or in some
other manner, this should be reported to the town hall as well as all
the other *taigumi.* A meeting will then be convened to decide the
length of time to be allowed for repairs. Repair of damages will ordinarily be limited to three years, and complete reconstruction to ten.
The document is dated "Ninth Month." In the absence of a more

specific date, it is unclear whether the regulations were instituted before or after that year's *matsuri*. It is signed by the leaders and two other representatives from every component *taigumi*, as well as the mayor (at that time referred to as *"kochō"*) and three assistant mayors *("fuku-kochō")*.

Amendments to the document issued the following year (appearing in full in Kuwatani 1969:3–6) made procedures even more explicit. Now the lottery ceremony was to be conducted by the head priest "in the presence of the *kami"* at Ketawakamiya Shrine. As mentioned in Chapter 5, conducting the ceremony as a sacred rite implies not just a lottery, but an act of divination. Selecting the director was now being left to an unimpeachable authority—the guardian deity itself.

Given the nature of Meiji political ideology, the deity was clearly becoming a symbol for the authority of the state. This is indicated in the words of high praise and reverence extended to the deity, as seen in the preamble to the 1877 document. These were not a prominent feature in the folk religion of the past. In a sense, the troubles now emerging during the conduct of the *matsuri* were not just disruptions of social harmony; they were challenges to the political order established by the state.

The suppression of animosities in one aspect of the *matsuri*, however, led to their reemergence in another. It is highly instructive that the police also in 1878 ordered that the name *okoshi daiko* (rousing drum) be changed to *"mezamashi daiko"* (eye-opening, or wakening, drum). This was the condition they set in return for granting permission to continue performing the event (Ōno 1974a:7, Kuwahara et al. 1991:17). It must be noted here that the word *"okoshi"* can be interpreted in various ways, including "rousing" people to rebel.[20] *"Mezamashi,"* on the other hand, holds no such connotations—it is simply a device for waking one from slumber (and is currently used in referring to alarm clocks). Thus by ordering the name change the police were trying to steer the ritual away from the subversive turn it was taking and restore it to its original purpose. This seems to have had little impact, as most people continued informally to refer to the ritual by its original name (Kuwahara et al. 1991:17).

Also in 1878 the term *"tsuke daiko,"* referring to the other neighborhood drums, appeared in print for the first time in a document entitled *Yatai Kishiki* ("Festival Wagon Standards"). Ōno (1973b:4) suggests that these drums were considerably larger than the *tsuke daiko* of today. At that time their object appears to have been simply to "attach" *(tsukeru)* themselves to the director's drum by lining up behind it on its course through town.

In 1884 the *tsuke daiko* were specifically prohibited in a revision of the festival regulations. Exactly what they were doing to warrant their restriction is not clear, but as in previous decades only a single drum—that of the directing *taigumi*—was authorized to pass through town. The following year, however, the townspeople found a clever way around the prohibition by simply referring to their drums as *"suke daiko"* (helping drum) rather than *"tsuke daiko"* and proceeding more or less as before, thereby obeying the letter, if not the intent, of the provision.[21] This too was banned the following year in a document referred to as the *"Naiyakusho"* (private treaty) (Ōno 1973b).

The *matsuri* was at the same time undergoing a series of time changes, ultimately resulting in its transposition from autumn to spring. In 1886 the grand *taisai* drawing together the tutelary deities from all over the Hida region was held in Furukawa during the month of April. Later that same year the regular *matsuri* had to be postponed due to a cholera epidemic, and was performed instead on November 5–7. Cholera epidemics had been sweeping the country for several years,[22] but due to its relative isolation Furukawa had until this time remained largely unexposed. Curiously, the following year the *matsuri* was resurrected as a spring observance, timed to coincide with the emerging cherry blossoms. The main event was now to be held on April 17.

In 1889 the *matsuri* was fixed at its present calendrical position of April 19–20. This final change was made to avoid conflicting with the spring festival in Takayama, which began on April 15 (Ōno 1974a). The festival in Furukawa now proceeded according to the following schedule: On April 17 the banners were erected at *chōnai* boundaries to welcome the deity. On April 18 the *yatai* were made ready for the next day's performance. On the morning of April 19 the deity was escorted down from the shrine via the *mikoshi* and temporarily housed in the *tabisho*. Early on the morning of April 20 the *okoshi daiko* was performed, and at daybreak the *yatai* assembled at the *tabisho* to officially welcome the deity. Then, with the *yatai* leading the way before it, the deity set out on a grand procession through town, which continued the entire day and on into the evening. On the morning of April 21 the deity was returned to the shrine and the banners were taken down. Later that afternoon the townspeople loaded up all their leftover food and drink and headed up into the mountains for the *atofuki* celebration.

The switch from autumn to spring seems rather drastic in light of the importance attached to *matsuri* tradition. Ōno (1974a) suggests that through the experience of the *taisai* the townspeople simply found a spring celebration more to their liking. I am not entirely satisfied with this explanation, and am more inclined toward another possibility. As described in Chapter 3, spring *matsuri* were held just before rice transplanting to request the deity's favor in protecting the community and ensuring them a successful growing season, while autumn *matsuri* were intended as expressions of gratitude for a bountiful harvest. However, an expression of gratitude would hardly have seemed appropriate to the people of Furukawa at that time considering the disastrous cholera epidemic that had afflicted them the previous year. Requesting the deity's favor, on the other hand, would have been in keeping with the desire to avoid a recurrence. The switch to spring could possibly have been an effort to regain the deity's benevolence and protection.

The spread of contagious diseases was more prevalent in the spring, as people began to renew contact with one another after a period of isolation imposed by the long winter. As a result, epidemics often coincided with the emerging cherry blossoms. In some parts of Japan, the two events came to be associated in the popular imagination: the opening blossoms were thought to release evil spirits into the air, thereby causing diseases. Rituals called *"hanashizume"* ("appeasing the blossoms") were performed to counteract the evil (Rotermund 1991). In Furukawa the blossoms begin to open from around mid-April. It is possible that "appeasing" them may have been part of the motivation for changing the Furukawa *matsuri* to precisely this time, though no direct evidence for this has as yet been forthcoming.[23]

In any case, the *matsuri* now followed immediately after a long period of isolation and confinement due to heavy snow and ice, offering the townspeople an opportunity to release their pent-up energies in boisterous communal activity. This in part explains why the *okoshi daiko* became increasingly unruly as the Meiji period progressed. The main motivational factors, however, were sociopolitical. Again, spring *matsuri* were intended for petitioning the deity or making a request, while autumn *matsuri* were primarily expressions of gratitude for a successful harvest. Airing grievances or petitioning the administrative authorities is much closer to the former motivation. Additionally, the religio-political concept of world renewal has far greater symbolic affinity with spring than autumn. Therefore a spring *matsuri* seems a more appropriate occasion for engaging in political activism. This is borne out in more recent decades by the "annual struggle" staged by organized labor, which customarily takes place in early May. The transformation of the *matsuri* from autumn to spring may thus be seen as both a product of political activism and a stimulus to its continued expression. Coincidentally, the Umemura Rebellion broke out in early spring, culminating in the young governor's being intercepted and shot on the Tenth Day of the Third Month. Converting to the Gregorian calendar places the rebellion at around the same time of year as the present *matsuri.*

The *tsuke daiko* had been prohibited since 1884. Around the turn of the century they staged a dramatic return. Once again they attached themselves to the director's drum and reportedly moved through town in a lively procession. The revival of the *tsuke daiko* was officially acknowledged in a subsequent revision to the festival regulations *(Ketawakamiya Jinja Reisai Kisoku)* enacted in 1901 (Ōno 1973b, 1976a:3).

It was reportedly from about this same time that the director's drum was placed atop a wooden framework to be paraded through the streets (Ōno 1973b). Thus the drum came to be handled in much the same manner as the *mikoshi* during its own procession later in the day.[24] The supporting framework was a rather simple affair constructed of rice-drying poles (called *"hasa"*) borrowed from resident farming households.[25] Each year, the neighborhood chosen to serve as director would assume responsibility for assembling the framework and attaching the drum, as well as furnishing the requisite number of people to carry it on their shoulders.

With its base at shoulder height the drum could no longer be struck from ground level, so the drumbeater began to ride upon the framework himself. It was presumably shortly thereafter that two drumbeaters came to be employed, one positioned on either side of the drum. Initially, however, they did not sit atop the drum as they do in today's event. Ōno (1973b:4) speculates that the drum in use at that time was merely a shallow disk-shaped object. It was probably positioned with the drum heads facing perpendicular to the direction of movement. The drumbeaters may have originally assumed a seated position atop the framework facing inward toward the drum, much as they do on the Kaguradai to this day. This would have allowed each of them to wield two sticks in producing a more complex rhythm than is presently employed. A few years later two additional men were positioned upon the framework, one in front of the drum and the other to the rear, each holding a lantern. A *sakaki* branch was placed at the front of the framework, marking the drum as a sacred object (Kuwatani 1969:31, Ōno:1973b).

The whole nature of the ritual began to change. With the *tsuke daiko* teams now competing against one another to be first in line behind the director, it became advantageous for them to carry smaller drums, the actual sound the drums emitted being less important (Ōno 1973b). Prior to this time the drums in use dangled loosely from a short beam shouldered by two men. Now they were lashed securely to long poles which could be held by several men at once. This new configuration made the instruments more wieldy and afforded greater leverage. It is apparent, then, that the neighborhood drums were undergoing a functional transformation. No longer simple percussion instruments, they were now becoming visible symbols of neighborhood identity, suitable for engaging others in physical confrontation.

The supporting structure of the main drum continued to change as well, gradually approximating its present appearance. The director now employed a special drum, larger and of oblong shape to produce a deeper, more resonant sound. None of the neighborhood *taigumi* possessed such a drum of their own, and purchasing a new one would have been too expensive. Instead, they borrowed the drum from Enkō-ji, one of the three major Buddhist temples in Furukawa, where it was commonly employed for ritual purposes. The barrel-shaped drum was positioned lengthwise with the heads facing fore and aft. The drumbeaters stood one at either end of the drum with long wooden sticks. These were swung at the drum in a horizontal arc, producing a slow cadence of alternating beats. The wooden framework subsequently grew larger and heavier, and the number of lantern-wielding riders increased. Morphological change in both the main drum structure and the *tsuke daiko* must thus be seen as related processes, as both were linked to the new symbolic meaning the ritual was beginning to assume.

Again, the neighborhood which had been chosen director each

year was responsible for providing all the manpower necessary to shoulder the drum on its passage through town. This was becoming increasingly difficult due to the drum structure's expanding bulk. Some neighborhoods contained only around thirty households and could by no means muster a sufficient number of able-bodied men from among their own constituents. Extra bearers had to be recruited from outside, and resident landlord households began enlisting the aid of their tenant farmers from neighboring villages, compensating them with food and drink and sometimes money as well. Thus participation was not limited to residents of Furukawa. Note, however, that the role of the outsiders was confined to shouldering the heavy framework—a rather servile position; they did not join the *tsuke daiko* teams or perform any of the other more important functions.

At some time around the turn of the century, the *tsuke daiko* began to lie in ambush for the drum structure and attack it as it passed through their respective neighborhoods. Ōno (1975b:3, 1976a:3; confirmed during a personal interview on September 14, 1990), based on accounts provided by his own informants nearly twenty years before the present study, reports that *tsuke daiko* team members tried to "crush the director" *(shuji o tsubusu),* by hooking their poles in through the crossbeams of the supporting framework and using them as levers to topple it over. In Sannomachi the drum had to enter a section where the street ran briefly along the Araki River with no houses lining either side. It was here that the director was particularly vulnerable, because without the protective cover of the houses its flank was left open to attack. Indeed, the *tsuke daiko* used this as an opportunity to press in upon the structure from the side, threatening to shove it into the river.[26] The director, in other words, was now being treated as an intrusive presence.

But such subversive tendencies were not restricted to ritual symbolism alone. The *okoshi daiko* began to exhibit a distinct tendency toward politically motivated violence. This relates in part to the use of the *matsuri* as an institutionalized opportunity for seeking vengeance or delivering a social sanction. During that night malicious acts could be carried out with little fear of punishment, especially prior to the advent of electric lighting.

This tendency toward seeking vengeance during the *okoshi daiko* can be seen early on in the murder of the peasant Zenkichi. One of

Ōno's (1972b) informants recalls that Zenkichi's assailants used the noise and boisterousness of the drum ritual to disguise their activities:

The place Zenkichi visited was the "Jizōba Teahouse" in Nikken Chaya [part of Lower Ninomachi]. The Fifth Day of the Eighth Month happened to be the pre-festival day [*shigaku-sai*] of the Furukawa *matsuri*, so, under the cover of the rousing drum [*okoshi daiko ni magire*], a group of about ten men, dressed in black and led by a certain *"oni,"* broke into the shop.[27] Zenkichi ran to the home of Ushimaru Chūsa next door, but there he was apprehended.

Ushimaru's own grandson provides further details:

On the eve of the Furukawa *matsuri* [Zenkichi] got chased in here and we hid him in a closet. But then more than ten men with towels wrapped over their heads [*hōkamuri o shita jūsū-nin no otoko*] came in. Pinching their noses to disguise their voices, they said "Give him up or we'll kill you too!" So we had him slip out the back toward a teahouse (named "Chūku Zakura"). Zenkichi, being cornered, crossed over the pontoon bridge and was killed along the river on the other side.

My grandfather said "The people involved are still living, so let's have no more of this tiresome talk." And that's all I ever heard of it. (Ōno 1972b)

Of course, the *okoshi daiko* of that time was a rather innocuous affair by today's standards. Even so, the night before the "main event" undoubtedly entailed drinking and revelry, and the *matsuri* as a whole had already developed as an opportunity for airing grievances. The cover of darkness and clamorous drum beating no doubt fed the inclination. It is not inconceivable, in fact, that the Zenkichi incident set a precedent for seeking vengeance during the *okoshi daiko*.

Subversive tendencies were further stimulated by the continuing impact of national and international political developments on the local area. Japan entered the war with Russia in 1904, and the peasants were compelled to tighten their belts again in support of the war effort. In keeping with the seriousness of the national emergency, the more festive aspects of the Furukawa *matsuri*—including the *okoshi daiko*—were temporarily suspended, though the prayers of supplication at the shrine continued as usual.

On August 25 of that same year, a great fire reduced most of Furukawa to ashes. All that remained for most households were the thick clay-walled storehouses called *kura* and the valuables contained inside. Enkō-ji was miraculously spared, but Honkō and Shinshū Temples were both burned to the ground. Most of the townspeople were left without homes. Many took refuge either in Enkō-ji or the small sheds set up amid the rice paddies for storing drying poles and other equipment. The damages were estimated at over 500,000 yen, for which Furukawa received a total of 1000 yen in compensation from the Japanese government. The money was offered as a gesture of sympathy from the imperial family. The hardships already incurred by the fire were no doubt magnified when the government raised the land tax that same year to help finance the war effort (Waswo 1977:117).

By 1906, despite the war's conclusion the previous year, the *okoshi daiko* had not yet been reinstated by the local leadership. On the night when it would ordinarily have been performed, however, an unusual incident occurred. No director had been chosen that year, so an officially designated "rousing drum" did not emerge. Nevertheless, the young men belonging to the various neighborhoods decided to bring out their *tsuke daiko* despite the absence of a lead drum, and with spirits high made their way through town in a lively procession. As they were passing in front of the police station the scene suddenly turned violent. The young men broke into the station building and began to lay waste to its contents, overturning furniture and scattering written documents about the room. A crowd of onlookers outside then began to pelt the station building with rocks. The local newspaper reported forty-nine window panes broken. Laborers sent to clean up the next day are said to have found enough rocks lying around to fill four big oil drums. Honda Rokusaburō, the mayor of Furukawa at the time, met later with the police chief to negotiate a settlement, and the matter was eventually concluded out of court (Ōno 1973b, 1976a; Kuwatani 1969:27; Furukawa-chō Kankō Kyōkai 1984:82–83).

This incident is particularly interesting in that suppression of the people's symbolic medium of opposition appears to have resulted in an actual attack on the authorities. The police were appointed by the prefectural government, and thus represented the imposition of authority from outside the local area. The incident can thus be interpreted as a local reaction to the growing power of the central government, understandable in light of the sacrifices the people had been obliged to make in supporting the government's war effort. According to some accounts, soldiers returning from the war were told of the abuses the townspeople had been subjected to in their absence at the hands of the police, and it was these returning soldiers who led the assault, though the actual perpetrators were never identified. One of Kuwatani's (1969:27) informants claims the trouble started because the police were intruding upon the ritual performance itself. In any case, the *okoshi daiko* was officially reinstated the following year, possibly in recognition that a ritual form of opposition was preferable to the real thing.[28]

In 1911, electric lights and telephone were introduced into Furukawa, and the following year a road was opened to automobile traffic between Furukawa and Takayama. Improvements in communications and transportation were making the town more accessible to the outside. Friends and relatives in surrounding villages were invited to the *matsuri* to join the festivities, one of the principle attractions being the drum ritual. As alluded to earlier, Okamura Rihei's 1911 travelogue *Hida Sansen* refers to the *okoshi daiko* as a "strange custom" which was gaining notoriety. His use of this term also indicates that the original name for the ritual was still in common use, even though it had been officially replaced by the less provocative *"mezamashi daiko."*

The emperor died of natural causes in 1912, bringing the long and eventful Meiji period to a close and ushering in the Taishō period (1912–1926). For the next two years the *okoshi daiko* was canceled in keeping with a nationally imposed official mourning period. The *mikoshi* procession was performed as usual, but without its grand complement of *yatai.*

The *okoshi daiko* was resumed in 1915. The two-year lull apparently had little effect on its level of exuberance. That year while attacking the big drum, the *tsuke daiko* team from Tonomachi got their pole hooked inextricably through the crossbeams of the supporting framework. The pole (with the neighborhood drum attached) was snatched away by the directing *taigumi,* who refused to give it back. A fight ensued. Significantly, the director that year was Ryūteki-*gumi* of Lower Ninomachi. The fight thus pitted a neighborhood composed largely of tenant cultivators (Tonomachi) against the home territory of the biggest landlord in Furukawa at the time—the Honda household.[29] Ōno (1973b:4, 1976a:2) reports that from this time forward *chōnai* leaders were obliged to ride upon the wooden drum framework. This, of course, was the origin of the "main guard." It is uncertain whether the original intent was to discourage unruliness by the other teams or control the aggressive tendencies of their own subordinates. There can be no question, however, that their presence upon the elevated platform constituted a highly visible representation of their sociopolitical ascendancy. Riding upon a conveyance borne by others is almost universally recognized as an indication of high status, as seen in the use of palanquin, sedan chair, and *mikoshi*.

The *tsuke daiko* teams now attacked with such enthusiasm that their poles sometimes struck the big drum itself, and since it was being borrowed from Enkō-ji the townspeople grew concerned that it might be damaged in the melee. In 1917, local landlord Hasegawa donated a number of short wooden beams of the type used in the mine shafts of Kamioka. These were placed in crosswise pairs, overlapping at the ends, to form a four-sided turret at the center of the framework. The drum was then positioned atop the turret, whose height is thought to have been about half that of the one in present use (Kuwatani 1969:31, Ōno 1973b). The higher elevation kept the drum up out of range of the *tsuke daiko*. Of greater significance, however, is the change it effected in the symbolic nature of the ritual.

The physical form of the drum structure now came to replicate the sociopolitical hierarchy. Again, riding upon the platform was reserved for neighborhood leaders; as Comaroff and Comaroff (1992:77) have noted, authority is commonly expressed through physical elevation. Moreover, the Japanese word for the turret is *"yagura,"* coincidentally the same word used in referring to the main tower or donjon of a fortified castle. This image is further enhanced by the terms used for the director's personnel—*"hon'ei"* ("main guard") in the case of those surrounding the drum on the platform itself, and *"kōei"* ("rear guard") for those positioned behind the platform at ground level to keep its challengers at bay. Considering the competitive nature of the event, such attributes undoubtedly encouraged the masses to attack the structure and possibly bring it down. In 1919, the shrine regulations warn against any reckless or foolhardy behavior on the part of the *tsuke daiko*.[30] This is apparently aimed at their inclination to "crush the director," as the regulations add that the *tsuke daiko* are to maintain a distance of at least fifteen *shaku* (around 4.5 meters) between themselves and the main drum (Ōno 1973b).

The sense of verticality would have been greatly enhanced with the addition of the two "top strikers," riding back-to-back atop the drum itself, their sticks raised high in the air as they are in today's event. It is not known exactly when this practice began, but both Ōno (1973b) and Kuwatani (1969), place its origin well into the twentieth century.[31] One of Kuwatani's (1969:30–31) informants maintains that it developed around the time of the Emperor Shōwa's official enthronement in 1929. The earliest known photograph of the *okoshi daiko*, however, allegedly dating from the first few years of the Taishō (1912–1926) period, shows that the young men had already assumed their positions atop the drum by that time.[32] The uncertainty may derive from the fact that each neighborhood performed the role of manning and bearing the lead drum according to

Figure 18. The *okoshi daiko* during the early Taishō (1912–1926) period. The drum is heading toward the camera. Photograph courtesy of Torii Mamoru.

its own proclivities. The dimensions of the drum structure, as well as the number of riders it bore, varied from year to year depending on the size and strength of the directing neighborhood. This was a time of transition, when both the drum and the ritual were assuming new forms. Thus it is quite possible that some innovative neighborhood took the initiative when its turn came round by placing the drum beaters *on top of* the drum. Other neighborhoods may then have resisted, reverting during their own turns to the former pattern, but eventually everyone followed suit.

In any case, the two men riding the drum in this earliest photograph appear to be clad in dark *momohiki*—close-fitting cotton trousers generally worn under work clothing—and are naked from the waist up. They are joined together by a band of cloth wrapped around both their waists. There are no foot rests or end pads to keep the riders from sliding off the drum as there are today. Instead the riders' feet are placed in stirrups of looped cloth, precisely as if they were riding a horse. The photograph shows the supporting framework to be somewhat smaller than it is now, and the wooden turret does indeed appear to be about half the height of the present one.

The smaller structure afforded less room to stand, so there are fewer riders. One man stands at the front of the structure holding a lantern in one hand and facing forward. Another man is similarly positioned at the rear facing back. Both are attired in the same fashion as the drumbeaters, naked from the waist up. Four other men stand directly beside the turret, two on either side. Each clings to the drum with one hand while holding a lantern in the other. Unlike the drumbeaters, however, they are fully clothed. These, presumably, are the leading members of the directing neighborhood, obliged to serve as the "main guard." The number of men riding upon the drum structure at that time thus totalled eight, as compared with today's twelve. It is uncertain when the two side drumbeaters were added at either end of the drum, but they do not appear in this early Taishō-period photograph.

One other point perhaps deserves mention. The men in the foreground leading the way before the drum structure all appear to be wearing towels wrapped over their heads and tied under the chin in a style known as *"hōkamuri"* ("cheek hooding"). This was obviously a way to keep the head warm, but also functioned as a form of concealment. It may be recalled that Zenkichi's assailants were disguised in this manner.

Another photograph taken in 1925 shows the drum structure sitting on the ground in Sannomachi the day before the *okoshi daiko* was scheduled to begin. In fact Lower Sannomachi was the chosen director that year (Ōno 1976b:2–3), so the big drum presumably had been assembled there in the home territory in preparation for the evening's festivities. Two young men in street clothes pose for the photograph. They stand on the framework and look toward the camera, holding sticks as if demonstrating for the photographer how to

Figure 19. The drum structure resting on the ground in Sannomachi the day before the *okoshi daiko,* 1925. Photograph courtesy of Furukawa Town Hall.

strike the drum. Visible in the background is the Byakkodai, Lower Sannomachi's *yatai,* with some schoolboys sitting in its upper level. It is apparent from this photograph that the drum framework at that time consisted of only three long beams as opposed to the present four. Also, the turret was made of only four overlapping layers of short crossbeams whereas today there are eight. The drum itself bore no identifying symbol, having been borrowed from one of the Buddhist temples. Likewise, no Shinto-based religious paraphernalia were placed on or around the drum structure as would be done today. These were later innovations ushered in with the Shōwa (1926–1989) period.

Symbolic Opposition

The *matsuri* as a whole had by this time come to represent the clash of two opposing ideologies within the context of a single public forum. The shrine ceremonies and *mikoshi* procession were associated with the local elite, acknowledging their prominence and linking them into the religio-political ideology being propagated by the central government. The *okoshi daiko,* on the other hand, emerged as a folk response to the officially-sanctioned liturgy—a ritual expression of opposition issuing from the ranks of the common people. At that time the *okoshi daiko* had no particular link with the Shinto religion—certainly not the nationalist variety devised in support of the emperor system. The drum itself, in fact, was borrowed from Enkō-ji, the Buddhist temple whose priests defied the government during both the Ōhara and Umemura disturbances. The oppositional symbolism is made even more explicit in that Furukawa's major Buddhist temples were located directly within the community. The shrine, on the other hand, was positioned outside (as well as above) the community—a fitting allusion to the centralized authority of the Meiji government.

It would perhaps be stretching the limits of credibility to envision the ritual as a physical reenactment of the Umemura Rebellion. Yet, while I have uncovered no direct written evidence to confirm such a possibility, the Umemura Rebellion is commonly cited as having led to the origin of the term "Furukawa *yancha,*" and several of my informants insist that the *"yancha"* spirit has been kept alive through the annual performance of the *okoshi daiko.* One thing is certain in any case: the Rousing Drum ritual evolved during the Meiji period as a collective public challenge to higher authority. This is inherent in the mere presence of the *tsuke daiko,* since all but the "official" drum had been specifically prohibited by both the shrine administration and the police. The *tsuke daiko* were obviously an important symbol of resistance, for, as Ōno (1976a:3) notes, "no matter how many times they were suppressed or prohibited, [the townspeople] always brought them back, rekindling their tenacious spirit."

It requires but a short incremental leap from defying the prohibition to challenging the director's drum—the symbol of authorized leadership. As previously mentioned, the *tsuke daiko* teams had begun the practice of harassing the drum as it passed through the darkened streets. When this symbolic object was removed (in 1906) they redirected their aggression toward an actual locus of political authority—the police headquarters.

Such instances demonstrate the lack of a clear distinction between the ritual and practical realms of human activity. Further evidence of such ambiguity is provided by the use of the *okoshi daiko* as an opportunity for settling scores. Ritual functioned here not merely as a form of symbolic expression; it also afforded an instrumental means of accomplishing a desired end—retribution for perceived injustices. In using it as such, the townspeople were capitalizing on one of the few opportunities immediately available to them for airing their grievances.

This ritual expression of animosity coincides with the various socioeconomic and political trends previously described: the imposition of authority by the central government and its appropriation of local religious symbolism; absorption into a market economy that lay well beyond the community's limited sphere of influence; and the emergence of a resident elite who sometimes failed to live up to their role as local benefactors. The ritual became a means for negotiating these changes at the local level, in the absence of more formal institutions. This will be examined more closely in the next chapter.

Chapter 8

FROM SYMBOLISM
TO INSTRUMENTALITY

Social unrest continued in Japan through the early decades of the twentieth century. Rapid economic expansion triggered by the First World War engendered a class of urban *nouveaux riches*. Their indiscriminate buying led to rapid inflation, making even the most basic commodities too expensive for the less affluent to obtain. Rice riots broke out all over the country, but were particularly intense in the area around Toki City in the extreme south-central portion of Gifu Prefecture. On the night of August 13, 1918, a mob of over two hundred angry peasants attacked the homes of prosperous *sake* brewers, rice merchants, and retailers in Oroshi Village, smashing their buildings with rocks and timbers. On the following night in the town of Dachi, residents cut power lines to throw the town into darkness, then proceeded to vandalize local rice merchants and loot their grain supplies; police called in the military to help quell the disturbance. That same evening in Tsumaki Village a mob of over one hundred residents cut the street lighting and started a riot, then marched on the village administrative headquarters demanding lower prices. Likewise in Toki Village on the night of the fifteenth the lighting was cut and merchant homes wrecked. A rice merchant's home and storehouses were burned in Kasahara Village. In the town of Tokizu a mob led by the local fire brigade attacked a prominent merchant household and threw its goods into the street (Gifu-ken Shakai Undōshi Hensan Iinkai 1971:609).

While these incidents did not directly involve the Hida region, they nevertheless reveal widespread animosity toward certain elements; namely, prosperous landlord, merchant, and *sake*-brewing households. They also set local residents in opposition to the police, whose role in maintaining order meant in this case defending the interests of the upper socioeconomic strata. Finally, such incidents illustrate the tactics employed by the peasantry in expressing their anger: nighttime mob-inspired violence, cutting of street lights to ensure anonymity, and smashing buildings with rocks and other objects. Similar animosities may be seen from time to time within the ritualized format of the *okoshi daiko*. Turning the problem around, Michael Lewis (1990:96) offers the following description of massive urban riots in Nagoya during August that same year: "Observers among the protesters and the public noted that rather than being somber, funereal gatherings of the grim-faced poor, the gatherings were festive, and as in the traditional *matsuri* (festival), rioting included processions, chanting, dancing, and drinking." *Matsuri* and political protest, in other words, began to overlap.

The recession that followed shortly after the First World War, combined with the effects of the devastating Kantō earthquake in 1923, had serious repercussions nationwide. The impact on agriculture, supported largely by rice and silk production, was particularly heavy. The silk industry was an important source of supplementary income for farm households, especially in mountainous regions like Hida which had always been somewhat marginal rice producers. Most of the farm households in Hida were involved in the silk industry to some extent, both in the production of raw silk at home as a cottage industry and in sending their daughters to labor in the silk factories in neighboring Nagano Prefecture. Thus the collapse of the silk market overseas during the Great Depression threw the regional economy into chaos and forced a number of local bank failures.

Amendments to the constitution extended voting privileges to successively larger numbers of people, lowering the minimum tax payment required to ten yen in 1900, five yen in 1919, and finally eliminating the requirement altogether in 1925.[1] Such reforms did little to alter the sociopolitical order in rural areas, however, as local landlords were still able to capitalize upon informal social mechanisms—namely, status differences and recognized ties of pseudo-filial obligation—in telling their subordinates how to vote. At the national level, rapid development of industrial capitalism and the market economy greatly enhanced the political strength of urban-oriented entrepreneurs. "The relative importance of the landlords in national politics waned rapidly during the early decades of [the twentieth] century, but their position of political leadership in the villages was sustained, though gradually weakening, until the [post-Second World War] land reform" (Fukutake 1980:185).

The Taishō emperor passed away in 1926, and the coronation ceremony for the new Emperor Shōwa (known outside Japan as Hirohito) was held in 1928. In Japan, the death of an emperor is often equated with the passing of an era.[2] In Taishō's case, the era was characterized by a brief experiment with liberal democratic principles. Unfortunately, this was accompanied by the increasingly corruptive influence of private industry in bureaucratic affairs. Widespread dissatisfaction with the political system partly explains why the reins of power were seized once again by the military establishment.

Formative and Semantic Transformations

In spite of developmental changes in the Japanese economy, the Furukawa *matsuri* continued to be closely associated with irrigated rice cultivation. The underlying purpose of the *matsuri* was to petition the deity for a successful harvest, and rice symbolism was pervasive in the conduct of shrine rituals. During the *mikoshi* procession, offerings to the deity were presented in the form of rice—or of *sake,* a product of rice. The framework used in bearing the drum during the *okoshi daiko* was originally constructed of rice-drying poles (known locally as *hasa*), as were the single beams to which the *tsuke daiko* were attached. The great drum itself was wrapped in a sheath of rice straw, lending it the appearance of a massive *tawara,* or bale of rice.

On a more practical level, local farmers used to perform *"tanimaki"*—sowing their rice seeds in nursery beds for later transplantation—on the morning of April 19. With this task accomplished, they were free to attend or participate in the *okoshi daiko* and other festivities. This was true for residents not only of Furukawa, but of surrounding villages as well. It is possible that invitations to feast during the *matsuri* were used to establish or maintain cooperative work relationships (though my informants were uncertain on this issue). Such relationships would have been vital for the important task of transplanting the rice seedlings a few weeks later.

During the late 1920s the townspeople received permission to obtain cedar wood from nearby mountain land (by this time held privately by resident landlord households) to put together a permanent set of poles and crossbeams for the big drum framework (Ōno 1973b). With a standard set of components, the framework no longer varied in size from year to year. Prior to the great fire of 1904, the streets of Furukawa had been very narrow. Indeed, this is one of the reasons the fire spread so quickly from house to house. When the town was rebuilt, however, the houses were set back a bit from their former positions so that the streets could be made wider. As a result, the streets of Furukawa were now able to accommodate a bigger structure, and the new drum framework was enlarged accordingly (Kuwatani 1969:30).

This larger, heavier structure required a considerable number of laborers to help shoulder it through the streets—more than two hundred by some estimates (Kuwatani 1969:30). Again, mustering the requisite manpower was one of the responsibilities of the directing neighborhood. Though the assignment came round only about once every eight years, it nevertheless represented a considerable burden for some of the interior neighborhoods.[3] These neighborhoods consisted of only thirty or forty households, and could by no means supply the necessary manpower by drawing solely from their own constituents. The only solution was to enlist the aid of outsiders.

Each constituent household was made responsible for providing a certain number of drum bearers, the number varying with the household's wealth and status. Ordinary households were assigned a quota of perhaps four or five individuals, relying mostly on relatives and friends from neighboring villages. Farmers were preferred because they were physically strong and accustomed to heavy labor. The enlistees were compensated with food and *sake* and sometimes paid a nominal fee as well. The larger landlords were expected to supply considerably more bearers than other households, drawing from the ranks of their *deiri* servants and tenant farmers.[4] The tenants were also compensated with food and drink, but they were no doubt motivated primarily by a sense of obligation toward the landlord. The current head of one prominent lineage boasts that his household alone provided as many as fifty of its tenants to shoulder the drum structure. Another recalls mustering thirty to forty. The usual quota for the large land-holding households of Ichinomachi and Ninomachi, however, appears to have been around thirty individuals (see Kuwahara et al. 1991:20).

Not all the additional drum bearers had to be recruited from other villages. For example, since Mukaimachi was not itself qualified to serve as director (allegedly due to its role in sponsoring the Kagura vehicle), its residents could be called upon to assist those neighborhoods that were. Again, this often involved landlord–tenant relations, as Mukaimachi at that time consisted mostly of tenant farmers. Also, reciprocal relationships developed between households belonging to different neighborhoods, each supplying additional manpower when the other's turn arrived. These labor exchange relationships were often based on affinal kinship ties—between a bride's adoptive household and her natal home, for example.

Tonomachi consisted mostly of small-owner and tenant cultivators; it had no major landlords to furnish extra bearers. What it lacked in wealth, however, it made up for in strength of numbers—Tonomachi was big enough to perform the task without enlisting outside aid. This was an important factor not only in bearing and defending the drum structure, a responsibility which came round only once every several years, but also in assembling a formidable *tsuke daiko* team. The same was true for Mukaimachi, which was even then expanding on the other side of the river. Though prohibited from serving as director, it did field a team to challenge the main drum. In early photographs of the Rousing Drum, the *tsuke daiko* of Tonomachi and Mukaimachi are nearly always at the fore, pressing in on the drum structure.

Lower Ninomachi, which was expanding along the main road in the downstream direction, could also provide a sufficient number of bearers with no outside assistance. The interior neighborhoods of Middle and Lower Ichinomachi, Upper and Middle Ninomachi, and Upper and Lower Sannomachi, on the other hand, were locked in by their surroundings. The only way to compete was by drawing on their social and economic relationships.

By the early 1920s the *okoshi daiko* had come to approximate its present appearance. The big drum together with its supporting framework was becoming too large—and perhaps too valuable—to subject to the kind of treatment it had been receiving. Now the effort to "crush the director" was aimed primarily at bringing about the structure's collapse. This was achieved by placing the *tsuke daiko* up onto the rear of the framework and forcing it down, causing the bearers to buckle under the extra weight. The intent was to dishonor the directing neighborhood by impeding its mission. The *okoshi daiko* had to cease at daybreak, and failure to complete the entire course would be viewed with great disdain, especially by the neglected neighborhoods.[5] Team members also used their poles as levers to shake or jostle the structure as if to topple its passengers, perhaps serving to remind the elite of their tenuous position.

The directing neighborhood was not merely a passive recipient of this treatment, however. It also mustered a gang of burly guardsmen positioned at ground level directly behind the drum platform, their function being to keep the *tsuke daiko* teams at bay. In addition, the entire structure could at any time suddenly reverse direction, pressing backward to menace its would-be attackers. Such defensive tactics served to raise the overall level of animosity. The defenders fought back to avoid disgracing their own neighborhood. Half-hearted resistance would be taken as a sign of weakness. The highest shame would result from allowing the platform to be brought down.

The *okoshi daiko* began around 2:00 a.m. and continued on until just before the break of dawn, eventually completing a circuit of the entire town. The drum had to return to its point of origin in the director's home territory before the other festivities could begin, and it would have been considered a great loss of face for the director not to complete the entire circuit. This, however, was no easy task. For the men laboring underneath, the huge drum structure seemed to grow increasingly heavy as the night wore on, especially with the *tsuke daiko* pressing in on them relentlessly. The smaller *chōnai* were at a serious disadvantage in this respect, as the outsiders they enlisted to help carry the load had less personal investment in the director's reputation. Some of them would sneak away during the course of the evening, creating an even greater burden on the remaining bearers. As a result, the whole structure would sink progressively lower, and by dawn the men were sometimes reduced to cradling the beams of the framework in the crooks of their arms.[6] One of Kuwatani's (1969:32) informants admitted that "[o]n the night of the *okoshi daiko* we had our drinking guests disrobe and we would take their clothes before sending them out to help shoulder the drum.[7] If you didn't take their clothes they would just go home." This suggests that, for this household at least, guests invited to the feast were expected to reciprocate by serving as drum bearers. It also indicates that bearing the drum was not a particularly enjoyable task, and that some amount of coercion was necessary to ensure its execution.

While serving as drum bearer was a low-status occupation open to practically anyone, riding upon the elevated platform as a member of the main guard was a prestigious position reserved for only a select number. Again, the directing neighborhood was responsible for supplying the *okoshi daiko* personnel, and, not surprisingly, the most prestigious positions were assumed by its own leadership. This included holders of special religious or political offices such as parish elder *(ujiko sōdai)*, block chief *(kuchō)*, counselor *(sōdanyaku)*, or advisor *(komon)*. In the case of the interior neighborhoods of Ichinomachi and Ninomachi, these roles were invariably occupied by prominent landowners. It would have been deemed highly inappropriate for such individuals to join with the masses in shouldering the drum or involve themselves in the frenzied charges of the *tsuke daiko*. Riding atop the drum structure, on the other hand, constituted a physical expression of their elevated social status.

The most coveted position of all was atop the drum itself, riding high above the others at the very center of the spectacle. In those days the *okoshi daiko* continued for two or three hours, but the drum personnel changed only once or twice. Pounding the drum for an hour or more required special strength and stamina and was therefore assigned to the younger men. Beyond age, opinions vary on the specific attributes an aspiring drum beater was required to possess. The discrepancies derive from the fact that each neighborhood employed its own selection criteria and that these criteria sometimes had to be relaxed out of practical necessity.

The most commonly mentioned attributes were that the young man be: (1) the eldest son *(chōnan)* in his household, also implying that he was destined to succeed as its head, (2) as yet unmarried, (3) from a household of prominent standing in the community, and (4) recognized as having good character. Of course the candidate had to be physically strong enough to perform the required task. An impressive physical appearance was also mentioned as a desirable quality. Some informants insist that only the sons of the elite were eligible to ride upon the drum. At *matsuri* time, they say, the young man's household was expected to contribute one barrel of *sake* to the neighborhood—the cost being prohibitive to all but the affluent.

During the Taishō (1912–1926) and early Shōwa (1926–1989) periods, however, the sons of the wealthy landowners began drifting away toward higher education and employment opportunities in the cities. The eldest sons may have eventually returned to take over as heads of their respective households, but by that time they were already at or approaching middle age. In addition, the middle class began to expand at about this same time, absorbing some of both rich and poor alike, so the pool of eligible young men among the wealthy landlord class grew increasingly small. The larger neighborhoods were able to maintain their rigid selection criteria, such as being the eldest son or not yet married. The smaller ones, on the other hand, were eventually obliged to relax their standards due to a shortage of qualified men, and physical strength became the most important attribute. However, even though participation was being opened to a wider socioeconomic spectrum in the smaller neighborhoods, the sons of households having greater power and influence in the community continued to receive preferential treatment in the selection process (Yamada 1938:173).

Thus far I have discussed the local leaders and the drum bearers who supported them from below. The attacking *tsuke daiko* constitute the third major element in this ritual scenario. Each neighborhood *taigumi* sponsored its own team, with team members drawn from its young men's association *(seinendan)*.[8] Unlike those who shouldered the big drum, therefore, the *tsuke daiko* personnel consisted entirely of *chōnai* residents. During the *okoshi daiko* they would wait in ambush for the big drum to pass through their respective territories, then rush out from a side street and advance upon it from the rear.

The structure was well protected both front and rear, but dangerously vulnerable from the sides. This was usually not a problem since the narrow streets were lined with buildings, ruling out the possibility of a broadside attack. As mentioned previously, however, at certain points along the customary route the big drum had to pass along the riverbank or cross over bridge abutments, momentarily exposing one or both of its flanks. At these points the *tsuke daiko* would sometimes press in from the side, threatening to topple the drum structure into the river. Older informants cannot recall that the threat was ever carried out, adding that the drum and rectangular framework were considered too valuable to be treated with such disregard. Rather, the object appears to have been to demonstrate that through combined effort such action was possible.[9]

One informant related a tale about an attack on the drum structure from above. In those days the roofs of houses were made of wooden shingles, with boards laid across them and rocks placed on the boards to hold the shingles in place against strong winds. Some men supposedly climbed up on the roofs and lay hidden, ready to ambush the *okoshi daiko* by tossing some of the rocks down upon it. But residents of the directing neighborhood found out about the plan. They started a fire in a boat house across the Miya River, then shouted an alarm to create a diversion. While the would-be assailants were preoccupied with the blaze, the big drum passed by uninhibited.[10] Another version of the same story holds that the assailants were actually planning to push the drum structure into the river and were lying in wait when the fire distracted them. Again the big drum was allowed to pass by unimpeded. These stories sound a bit dubious, and have perhaps been embellished over the years. Even as folktales, however, they demonstrate that the prevailing attitude toward the director was antagonistic.

There is again another dimension to this ritualized struggle— that which pitted *chōnai* against *chōnai* as they vied for position in advancing upon the main drum. In time the primary objective for the *tsuke daiko* teams became outmaneuvering the other neighborhoods to occupy the esteemed position immediately behind the director, then proudly displaying their drum insignia for everyone to see. This is sometimes referred to as *"chikara kurabe"*—a comparative test of strength. The victors enjoyed boasting rights when the action was later recounted.

The two dimensions of ritual conflict—neighborhood against neighborhood and common townspeople united against the director —often resulted in actual fighting. Informants recall that in the old days the *okoshi daiko* was a true "fighting festival" *(kenka matsuri)*, and that conflict was an ever-present element. There seems to have been an informal proscription against admitting to personal injuries incurred during the *okoshi daiko*. Those requiring medical attention would travel surreptitiously to a bonesetter in a neighboring county so that no one in the local area would know (Kuwatani 1969:32, Kaba 1984:35–36).[11]

Aggression was not confined to the ritual participants alone. During the prewar period *taigumi* members sometimes fought with operators of the small food and amusement stands that lined the major thoroughfares during festival time. In addition to being outsiders, these operators often had organized crime *(yakuza)* connections and thus were not well received by the townspeople. There were also fights with *yakuza* members from nearby Takayama who had come to observe the action and perhaps take part in the drinking and revelry.

Symbolic Expression and Practical Impact

The ritual scenario thus far described presents several interesting interpretive possibilities. Douglas (1966:128) has suggested that "rituals enact the form of social relations and in giving these relations visible expression they enable people to know their own society. The rituals work upon the body politic through the symbolic medium of the physical body." Similarly, Comaroff and Comaroff (1992:71) note that cultural meanings take root in the body and are acted out through its postures and movements: "Physically framed experience, then, seems to resonate with the forms of 'objective' reality."

These ideas may inform our understanding of the *okoshi daiko*. The elite occupied a highly visible position atop the main drum platform. They were borne literally upon the shoulders of the masses, many of whom were actually tied to the elite through landlord-tenant relations. The drum structure thus embodied the symbolism inherent in any palanquin-like vehicle—a physical affirmation of the riders' elevated status. This is reinforced by use of the term *"ninsoku"* (literally "human legs," but more closely approximating the word "coolie") in referring to the bearers.[12]

But such internalization of the social order does not preclude the possibility of introducing change. "The crucial role of the body . . . derives from its position as a mediator between the self and the world. The human frame encodes the categories and processes that shape social systems and the subjects they presuppose, and it re-presents them as a tangible means for collective action" (Comaroff and Comaroff 1992:90). Despite their subordinate status, the bearers held the structure aloft, and their collective efforts determined its speed and direction of movement. This served as a graphic reminder to the elite from whence their privileged position ultimately derived. More significantly, the common townspeople, represented by teams of young men, attacked the structure and threatened its collapse. The ritual thus carried with it an implicit warning—that being a member of the elite is a precarious position, which persists only through the consent of the common people. In attacking the drum structure, the *tsuke daiko* were demonstrating that if necessary the masses could unite in overthrowing their oppressors, just as they had during the Umemura Rebellion. This aspect was not present in the original form of the ritual; it emerged later in conjunction with sociopolitical and economic changes triggered by modernization.

The ritualized expression of rebellious sentiments, however, extends well beyond the purely symbolic level. Of equal import is the temporary license and anonymity the *matsuri* afforded, allowing the *okoshi daiko* to escalate into genuine acts of destructive violence. The ritual was performed in the early predawn hours—an unusual time for people to be out running about in the streets. This sense of transgressing the bounds of normal behavior, combined with the mass assembly of rambunctious celebrants and obligatory *sake*-drinking, created an atmosphere conducive to deviant behavior. Again, the *matsuri* was an opportunity for settling old scores—for airing what the local people refer to as "habitual resentment" *(higoro no urami)*. Aggressive attitudes could later be blamed on the effects of the alcohol, and random acts of vandalism would likely go undetected in the general confusion:

A usurious old man was dumped into a canal. A nit-picky young policeman was thrown off Daikan Bridge into the river several meters below. Likewise, another policeman in the habit of calling out and fining people for trivial matters had his lodgings wrecked. . . . During the *okoshi daiko* everything becomes indistinguishable in the noise and confusion, so the perpetrators remain unknown. (Kaba 1984:36)

In some cases the drum structure itself became the very instrument of retribution. It would on occasion "mysteriously" lurch to one side, crashing into the home of a pompous landlord or stingy merchant. Though far too heavy for any individual alone to affect its direction, a concerted effort, welling up from the depths of shared conviction, could easily send the massive structure careening into a predetermined target. Here was an opportunity to seek revenge with no fear of punishment—in a sense the perfect crime. The bearers, increasingly fatigued and intoxicated as the night wore on, were not always in complete control of their movements, so any mishaps would appear accidental. And even if suspicions were aroused, no specific individuals could be singled out for blame. In fact, considering that the *matsuri* was a religious event and the drum structure itself a sacred object, any damages incurred could conceivably be interpreted as expressions of supernatural disfavor. The drum structure in effect became like the pointer on a ouija board, divining the "truth" through its seemingly erratic movements.

In addition, the *tsuke daiko* teams, charging recklessly toward their goal, sometimes ran wide of the mark and ended up ramming their poles through an adjacent wall or store front. This holds perhaps even greater significance in terms of intra-communal tensions. In the case of the main drum structure, many of the bearers had to be drawn from other parts of town as well as nearby villages (though, significantly, this was not the case when Tonomachi served as director). Each *tsuke daiko*, on the other hand, was wielded exclusively by members of the same neighborhood, and could therefore be used against its own specific rivals. One of my informants recalls "if there was some hated, despicable merchant, the *tsuke daiko* would go crashing through his front door. . . . At times like that the police would stay hands-off. It was a custom among the townspeople, so [the police] looked the other way."

The commotion generated by the ritual provided an almost irrefutable alibi; it would have been very difficult under the circumstances to prove whether any damages had been premeditated. There is another deterrent to singling out the perpetrators, however—it draws attention to oneself as the target. Others might conclude that there had been some reason to warrant such treatment.[13] This, in turn, would foster the impression that the targeted parties were indeed greedy, mean-spirited, arrogant—whatever accusations had been directed their way. As a result, no official complaints were registered, no damages reported. Here also is a better explanation for stealing away to another county to have one's wounds attended—not to maintain an image of stoic resilience but to avoid the stigma of having been victimized.

It is important to note that the seriousness or extent of the damages was immaterial—what mattered most was subjecting the target to public exposure. This follows a precedent established in earlier incidents of outright rebellion. "Smashing" of houses *(uchikowashi)* during the Umemura Rebellion often entailed no more than hacking away at the front of the building, or its central interior pillars, with hatchets, hoes, and sickles. The object was to mark the target for others to see—not to completely destroy it. Similarly during the *okoshi daiko,* the drum had merely to smash through a window or knock down a fence to get the point across.

A similar mechanism applied to the contributions *(kifu)* given the *chōnai* by its residents. The appropriate amount was graduated based on relative income, and prominent households were expected to give more. The name of the donors and amounts they had given were posted on a board at the central meeting place. Those who gave too little relative to their wealth and position ran the risk of being vandalized or having their house fronts bashed by the drum.

The yearly ritual thus promoted a visible, if somewhat artificial, concern for others. In particular it appears to have been directed against the prospering merchant landlord households of the interior sectors. These households were well positioned to take advantage of the new opportunities available to them in the emerging market economy, and were amassing wealth at others' expense. Social decorum ordinarily prohibited any outward display of animosity toward them. On the night of the *okoshi daiko,* however, their homes lay vulnerable to surreptitious vandalism.

Opposition to the Police

The best-documented use of the drum to deliver a social sanction, however, involves yet another attack on the police headquarters, this one occurring in 1929. The incident is recounted with great enthusiasm and, one senses, a certain air of proud defiance. Beyond its importance in the local tradition, it illustrates the friction that existed between police and townspeople in prewar Japan, and the way this friction was expressed during the annual *matsuri.* More to the point, it provides a detailed example of many of the themes thus far presented.

Various explanations are offered as to why the incident occurred, but it appears to have been the culmination of a number of intersecting variables. The police in prewar Japan were strict and intimidating—the most immediate agents of a militarist central government imposing its authority into local affairs. They maintained a rather superior attitude toward the villagers and insisted on rigid enforcement of seemingly trivial rules. In Furukawa some of the police were facetiously referred to as *"shōben junsa"* ("pee police") because they were inclined to arrest people for such trivial matters as urinating out of doors. During routine hygiene inspections of private homes, one officer reportedly used to make the residents get down on the floor and lick the straw bedding to prove it was clean (Kuwatani 1969:29). Also, farm households used to dry their azuki beans and wild mountain vegetables by laying them out on straw mats along the street, and while the authorities had traditionally turned a blind eye, the police now prohibited the custom as an impediment to traffic.

Such fastidiousness led to widespread disgruntlement among the townspeople, but since the police were so powerful there was little to be done in the way of opposition. The deviant atmosphere surrounding the *okoshi daiko*, however, afforded them some degree of anonymity and criminal license. Older informants insist that only on that night were the police not to be feared; on that night alone the townspeople had the courage to defy them.

One of the most detested figures was a young police officer known as the "caramel cop" *(kyarameru junsa),* so named because of his inclination to entice young women with offers of caramel (which was difficult for ordinary people to obtain in those days). One year during the *okoshi daiko* as the big drum was passing along the street in front of his lodgings, four or five men climbed up onto the drum structure and in through a second-floor window to his room. The police officer, sensing danger, had fled the premises just moments before. Finding the room vacant, the intruders proceeded to lay waste to its contents. This incident is thought to have occurred around 1925.

Ill feelings toward the police had thus been prevalent in Furukawa for quite some time already, but in 1929 they intensified. During the New Year observances earlier that year the police had raided a gambling party, and many of those they arrested turned out to be members of the local fire brigade.[14] In those days it was possible for influential third parties to intervene on behalf of the accused to gain their release, but in this particular instance the police held their ground, and the gamblers were obliged to spend several days in confinement.[15] Rumors were flying that there would be big trouble during the *okoshi daiko* (Furukawa-chō Kankō Kyōkai 1984:84, Furukawa-chō Kyōiku Iinkai 1987:474).

The directing neighborhood had been borrowing its drum from Enkō-ji, one of the local Buddhist temples. But that year, to commemorate the recent coronation of the Shōwa emperor, a new drum was dedicated specifically for use during the *okoshi daiko*.[16] In honor of its inaugural employment, Lower Ichinomachi, the chosen neighborhood, decided to have a Shinto priest ride upon the drum, waving a *haraigushi,* or purification wand over homes and onlookers as the procession made its way through town (Ōno 1976b:3, Furukawa-chō Kyōiku Iinkai 1987:475).[17] According to some informants, the priest merely rode upon the platform; he was not seated atop the drum itself. This priest had no particular relation to Ketawakamiya Shrine, but was merely a resident of the directing neighborhood. The other *chōnai* were upset since there was no precedent for such an unusual innovation; this added to the tension already surrounding the ritual.

Traditionally, the fire brigade had been responsible for providing security during the *okoshi daiko;* they routinely patrolled the event to keep the action from getting out of hand. That year, however, due to ill feelings toward the police stemming from the gambling incident, the fire brigade refused to perform its customary duties, and the event went largely uncontrolled.

One of the police officers—reportedly the man who had led the raid on the gamblers and who had been most adamant in refusing to release them—had taken up residence in Mukaimachi. As the *okoshi daiko* passed by, the huge wooden framework crashed into his house (Furukawa-chō Kyōiku Iinkai 1987:475). Some informants add that the officer was hiding inside but escaped out a back entrance into the paddy fields.

The *okoshi daiko* then proceeded on to a scheduled rest stop just before crossing from Mukaimachi over Kasumi Bridge back into the main part of town. On the other side of the bridge stood the police headquarters.[18] When the rest period ended, the mass of bearers once again hoisted the massive drum structure onto their shoulders and proceeded across the bridge. As they were rounding the corner in front of the police station to head down Ninomachi, however, the trailing end of the structure suddenly swung wide and tore down the boarded fence lining the station building. For a time the structure continued on down the street, but then abruptly reversed itself and moved back toward the station. At this point a crowd of bystanders began pelting the station with rocks, smashing the windows facing the street. Some informants report that the drum structure crashed into the station building in the manner of a battering ram and broke through the front door; others claim the *tsuke daiko* joined in the assault, using their poles to break into the interior of the building.[19]

The sudden outburst was precipitated in part by the sight of a group of policemen's wives and consorts looking down upon the spectacle from the second floor windows of the station building. The presence of the Shinto priest, riding the drum and waving a purification wand, had transformed the *okoshi daiko* into a sacred event. It was therefore considered taboo to look upon it from above.[20] According to some witnesses, the fact that the onlookers were women was particularly galling, as females in that era were often barred from participating in Shinto rites. Also, looking down from above suggested an air of superiority, reinforcing the image of arrogance already associated with the police. A contributing factor may have been that the town administration had failed to provide sufficient funds for the electric street lighting that year, so the streets were shrouded in darkness. There were lights on in the station building, however, making the group of wives and consorts appear all the more conspicuous.

One of the eyewitnesses—in fact the man who was sitting upon the drum at the time as the rear-facing drum beater—recalls noticing about twenty new bearers slip in under the back of the drum structure as it set out from Mukaimachi to cross the bridge. He claims these newcomers were responsible for swinging the structure through the fence, and that most of the other bearers were innocent. He also denies that the *okoshi daiko* participants had anything to do with the rock barrage (Furukawa-chō Kyōiku Iinkai 1987:476–477). One of my own informants, also an eyewitness, concurs that most of the rocks were thrown by the crowd of onlookers. He claims that earlier in the day a pile of coarse gravel had been placed at the corner opposite the police station by a road maintenance crew, purportedly for filling potholes in the earthen streets. This pile conveniently provided much of the ammunition used during the attack (this is corroborated by another eyewitness in Furukawa-chō Kyōiku Iinkai 1987:479).

Hostilities that night did not end with the attack on the police station. The *okoshi daiko* continued on down Ninomachi, made the turn at the end, then headed up through Sannomachi along the bank of the Araki River. At this point the team from Tonomachi succeeded in hooking their pole through the crossbeams of the drum platform and were threatening to tumble the entire structure into the river. A little farther along the route another team pressed in from the side with a ladder held horizontally, forcing the drum structure dangerously close to the edge of the embankment. The director managed to make its way back to Ichinomachi, only to find that someone had built a bonfire there in the middle of the street, bringing the entire procession to an abrupt halt (Furukawa-chō Kyōiku Iinkai 1987:476).

At this point the director had had enough and refused to continue on into Tonomachi in accordance with the prescribed route. The block chief *(kuchō)* and other representatives from Tonomachi soon arrived to protest the delay, and a heated argument ensued. Ōno (1976a:3) reports that a fight broke out between Tonomachi and Lower Ninomachi, though the cause is not given. Finally at daybreak the *tsuke daiko* dispersed and the director's group was left to carry on alone. They passed through Tonomachi without incident before finally returning to their home neighborhood—an anticlimactic finish to a rather bizarre affair (Furukawa-chō Kyōiku Iinkai 1987:476–477, Ōno 1973b).

Later in the day most of the men who had participated in the *okoshi daiko* were rounded up by the police in an investigation of the rock-throwing incident. Additional police were summoned from Takayama and Kamioka to assist in the interrogation. The police were under the impression that the attack on the station building had been premeditated—that the instigators had capitalized upon the absence of street lighting to ensure their anonymity. Most of the police investigators were from other towns and were unfamiliar with the particulars of the *okoshi daiko*. They accused the directing neighborhood of initiating the rock barrage. The suspects countered that they were all wearing the close-fitting *momohiki* trousers, which had no pockets for concealing rocks, and in any case had their hands full bearing the drum structure. At this point the interrogation turned from the rock barrage to the flattened fence.

Needless to say, the investigation cast a pall over the rest of the *matsuri.* Over two hundred men were held for questioning. The police station was not nearly big enough to accommodate them all, so the majority were temporarily housed next door in Honkō-ji or in the county office located just across the river. The night of April 20 was very cold, and it began to snow. Families brought food and bedding for the men being held, but were denied access to their place of confinement. The questioning was reportedly very severe, and some of the suspects were beaten. One of my informants recalls being warned during the interrogation that the power of the police was second only to that of the imperial family.

The police investigation continued for several days and was widely reported by the local media (see *Hida Mainichi Shimbun* 1929:3). Honda Akinori (Rokusaburō's son), at the time serving as both mayor of Furukawa and representative to the prefectural assembly, intervened on behalf of the townspeople and eventually secured the release of most of the suspects. According to one of Kuwatani's (1969:28) informants, however, seven of the men were still being held in mid-May, just prior to the "Twenty-Five Rite" *(Nijūgo Matsuri)* on May 15. This was another annual observance, involving a hike up Mt. Anbō. The purported aim was to worship briefly at each of the twenty-five stone buddha statues placed at intervals along the path, though as with other events of this nature the participants drank *sake*. On the evening before, one of the town council members asked the chief of police, "Is it right to detain some-one that long? Tomorrow is the Twenty-Five Rite and there will be *sake*-drinking. Under the influence the fire brigade might attack the police." The remaining prisoners were released that same evening.

In the end, three men were sentenced for their role in the inci-dent. It is significant that informants refer to these men as *"giseisha"* (scapegoats), the very term used for those given up for punishment during the peasant rebellions. Use of this term suggests an attitude of moral conviction and solidarity in defying the authorities.

The police were perhaps unusually wary at the time due to events that had occurred earlier in the year. Government plans for improve-ment projects along the Saikawa River in southern Gifu Prefecture were threatening the livelihood of the peasants downstream. In Jan-uary, about seven thousand farmers in the villages of Sunomata and Musubu had risen in opposition. The rebellion was suppressed and the projects were eventually carried out as planned (Gifu-ken Kōtō Gakkō Kyōiku Kenkyūkai Shakaika Bukai 1988:10), but the inci-dent was fresh in the minds of the regional authorities and may have led them to be especially vigilant against further outbreaks of sub-versive activity.

Like the Umemura Rebellion, the 1929 attack on the police station has become one of the best-known and most frequently recounted episodes in Furukawa's history, and yet another testimony to the spirit of *yancha*. It is variously known as the *"keisatsu shūgeki jiken"* (attack-on-the-police incident), the *"tōseki jiken"* (rock-throwing incident), and the *"sōjō jiken"* (riot incident). Several informants observed (in comments unsolicited by me) that the incident resembled a peasant rebellion in that it involved the people rising up against oppression. At that time, they say, the police were abusing their authority, and the attack was an open expression of the people's defiance. To this day, they continue, the police avoid getting too near the *okoshi daiko,* preferring instead to observe from a safe distance.[21] As in the old days, it is the local fire brigade that patrols the event.

Scott (1990:65–66) explains why power holders find mass assemblages of ordinarily disaggregated subordinates so threatening:

First, there is the visual impact of collective power that a vast assembly of subordinates conveys both to its own number and to its adversaries. Second, such an assembly provides each participant with a measure of anonymity or disguise, thereby lowering the risk of being identified personally for any action or word that comes from the group. Finally, if something is said or done that is the open expression of a shared hidden transcript, the collective exhilaration of finally declaring oneself in the face of power will compound the drama of the moment. There is power in numbers, and it is far more significant than the now long-discredited sociology that treated crowds under the rubric of mere hysteria and mass psychopathology.

Likewise, the *okoshi daiko* contains the implicit suggestion that the masses, normally divided by intra-communal rivalries, are capable of uniting against an oppressive authority. This too has historical resonances. The police in the prewar period were attempting to implement national policy with little regard for local customs or preferences. In this they were repeating the errors of Umemura Hayami almost sixty years earlier.[22]

The 1929 police station incident is compelling theoretically in that it blurs two basic categorical distinctions. First, like the earlier incident in 1906, it marks a situation in which ritualized conflict transcended the bounds of the purely symbolic and entered the realm of genuinely destructive violence. Second, the rock barrage in this case involved not just the ritual participants but the spectators as well. Taken together, these factors suggest that ritual has the power to incite participants and observers alike toward direct, politically motivated action.

This also raises the question of how participation in ritual should be defined. Simple observation may be seen as a kind of participation, given ritual's affective impact. Again, however, the nature of the impact varies with the individual. The *okoshi daiko* may instill feelings of pride, envy, resentment, or fear, depending on the observer's perspective. In this sense the elite did not have to be directly involved in the rousing drum to get its point: the symbolic challenge to their authority was being acted out on their very doorsteps as they watched from their windows above.

Further Changes

Changes were instituted in the conduct of the *matsuri* in response to the problems that had occurred. A 1930 revision to the festival regulations includes the warning that "for no reason whatsoever will the directing group's drum reverse its direction" (Ōno 1973b). The drum structure was thus prohibited from going back along its route as it had during the attack on the police station the year before.

Two photographs of the *okoshi daiko* shed some light on its condition at the time. Both were taken in 1929—the year of the attack on the police station. The first shows the big drum passing through Middle Ninomachi, and thus had to have been taken just after the attack. The drum structure is proceeding away from the camera, and Tonomachi's *tsuke daiko* has attached itself to the rear. A young man sits atop the main drum holding a stick above his head, poised to strike a beat. Though not clearly visible, the individual behind him (facing away from the camera) is wearing what appear to be ceremonial robes; this presumably is the Shinto priest. The white blur above his head probably represents the paper streamers of a purification wand. In other respects, the ritual appears to have been conducted much as it is today, though on a somewhat smaller scale. Auxiliary drumbeaters have been added, and the main guards now stand away from the drum. Most of the riders are naked from the waist up, clad only in dark *momohiki* trousers. Members of the *tsuke daiko* team may also be shirtless since their arms are exposed. The bearers underneath the drum structure, however, are fully clothed. One interesting difference from today's event is that the main guard appears to be composed of younger men. Considering the traditional emphasis on seniority in Japan, this seems to contradict my informants' insistence that only the most influential members of the community were qualified to ride upon the drum.

The second photograph affords a rare view of the front of the drum structure, and thereby clears up the confusion caused by the first. The man standing at the helm is obviously somewhat older, and exudes a very authoritative attitude in his long festival jacket. He is flanked by two equally mature-looking men, one of whom has chosen to strip to the waist. These three men are undoubtedly neighborhood leaders, and it is significant that they are positioned at the head of the drum structure, well away from the struggle taking place at the rear. The trailing end is guarded by the younger men, who are better able to fend off the sudden intrusion of an errant pole.

Two points deserve mention. The first is that the varied ages of the drum guardians are entirely consistent with the population profile of that time. Even in a prominent neighborhood like Middle Ninomachi, the senior heads of influential households could not have numbered more than a few individuals, and during the *okoshi daiko* these had to be distributed among two or three different shifts. Local leaders *did* ride upon the drum platform, but they rode at its head in keeping with their stature. The second point is that elite status is not a function of age, but of membership in a prominent household. In this respect either a father or a son would serve as an acceptable representative.

In the second photograph, the Shinto priest no longer sits atop the drum. Looking closely at the right side of the platform, however, one can recognize a figure dressed in ceremonial robes facing inward toward the drum, with the purification wand now resting on his shoulder—the priest has changed position. This explains the contradictions I noted among my informants, some of whom described the priest riding atop the drum while others insisted that he stood down upon the platform.

The bearers of the drum structure are much more visible in this second photograph. Most of them wear the standard laborer's costume of trousers, shirt, and short jacket. Many also wear towels wrapped over their heads in the *hōkamuri* style. Thus while the *okoshi daiko* is presently touted as one of Japan's traditional "naked festivals" *(hadaka matsuri),* this is in reality only a fairly recent development, at least as far as the bearers are concerned. Older residents recall that clothing was necessary to protect their shoulders from chafing under the heavy beams of the drum structure.[23]

An article appearing in the September 1931 issue of the journal *Minzoku Geijitsu* (Folk Arts) contains a description of the rousing drum written by Mizuma Yoshio, a Furukawa native who was born

Figure 20. The *okoshi daiko* in 1929, the year of the attack on the police station. The drum is headed away from the camera. Photograph courtesy of Furukawa Town Hall.

Figure 21. A view of the *okoshi daiko* from the front, taken the same year. Prominent members of the directing neighborhood customarily took positions at the head of the drum structure. Photograph courtesy of Fuse Shirō.

in Ninomachi but moved to Tokyo at the age of nineteen to work for a newspaper. He mentions that preparations for the *matsuri* begin when the director is determined by lottery on April 3. The *okoshi daiko* commences just after midnight on April 20 and continues for four hours. The drum structure is shouldered by around 150 "half-naked men." In the past, he adds, the drumbeaters went completely naked, "but since this was deemed improper from the view of morality they have taken to wearing *momohiki*" (Mizuma 1931:387–388). He also alludes to the young men being "bathed in *sake*" *("abiru hodo sake o nonda wakamono")*.

As for the ritual itself, Mizuma describes the *tsuke daiko* waiting in ambush for the main drum as if it were an enemy. His description of the ensuing clash proceeds as follows:

"Now!"—a team of *tsuke daiko* bearers comes flying out and throws itself toward the rear of the drum structure in order to make contact. The people of that same neighborhood rise up in support. But the director's side gets in their way so as not to be struck, and a struggle ensues; even so, the defenders eventually get broken through, and everyone crowds in after the drum.

They continue on to the next intersection, where another *tsuke daiko* bursts forth. But the team that connected previously gets in its way so that it cannot make contact; likewise the men of the director's side try to block it from coming near, and a three-faceted struggle begins. In this way they progress from street to street, taking around four hours to cover the entire town. It is said that during the course of its circuit the drum structure occasionally used to deliver a punishment [*seisai o kuwaeru to iu koto ga ō-ō atta*] to those who were disliked, but this doesn't happen anymore. (1931:388–389)

This last statement is interesting, as it was written just two years after the infamous attack on the police station. Mizuma, the author, was a Furukawa native. He *had* to have been aware of the incident in light of all the commotion it generated. He may have chosen to ignore the issue due to its sensitive political nature, or to avoid bringing indignity on his home town. Perhaps he was being subjected to police censorship. The nation as a whole was heading into a period of militant expansionism, and symbolic challenges to authority would not have been kindly received by the central government.

Another article, written by Hida ethnographer Yamada Hakuba (1938), appeared a few years later in the journal of Hida folklore *Hidabito* (People of Hida), though it was based on observations made a few years earlier. Yamada offers a much more detailed account, and includes an interesting passage relating to the *okoshi daiko*:

> [D]uring the course of the ritual performance, the gang at the core of the *okoshi daiko* will sometimes dare to trample and crush some despicable fellow or raid some house of bad reputation, beginning with the door lattice and on to destroy the house, pillars, even the foundation, trampling them to pieces in a wild rampage. After all, it is said, they are spirit-possessed. (1938:175)

This is followed by the inevitable disclaimer: "Recently, this doesn't happen very often, but it used to be practiced quite liberally" (1938: 175). The entire passage is noteworthy because it fails to mention direct use of the drum structure itself. In fact it fosters the image of an angry mob of vigilantes, going around town bearing lanterns and banging on a drum, looking to roust out suspicious characters and inflict upon them a crude form of justice. Yamada himself describes the phenomenon using the term "spirit-possessed sanction" *(kami-gakari no seisai).*

In fact one of my informants, who was born in 1925 and raised in Upper Ichinomachi, described the prewar *okoshi daiko* using the English loanword "lynch" *("rinchi").*[24] He went on to explain that the performance was used as a means of delivering a punishment or sanction *("seisai o kuwaeru"),* and that much of the animosity was directed against merchant households *(shōten).* He claimed this tendency remained until around the beginning of the Shōwa period, but thereafter became increasingly ritualized *(gishiki ni natta).*

From the perspective of ritual symbolism, this conforms to the use of the drum as an instrument of purification. The drum goes around town expelling evil influences and preparing the way for the deity to pass. At the same time, however, the evil elements are being singled out and punished, in a sense purging the community of their negative influence. Thus purification and expiation are conceptually related.

A sequence of three photographs offers a glimpse of the *okoshi daiko* in 1933. By this time the drumbeaters and main guard had donned the short pants and white *sarashi* waist wrapping used in the present day. Their headbands too are white, and tied with the knot in front. Their *tabi* footwear, on the other hand, appear to be dark. The bearers underneath the drum structure are still fully clothed.

The first two photographs show the big drum passing through Ichinomachi in front of the Kaba and Watanabe houses. A *chōchin* procession leads the way, and a banner bearing the characters *"shu-ji"* immediately precedes the drum. The street is packed with a throng of spectators, and people can be seen leaning out of their second-floor windows to get a better look. Two *tsuke daiko* teams close in from behind—those of Tonomachi and Mukaimachi. Their members also wear headbands, but these are tied behind the head in the ordinary manner.

These photographs reveal some curious features. For one, there appear to be several extra men riding the drum platform. Though stripped to the waist and holding lanterns like members of the main guard, they are clearly distinguishable in that they wear dark trousers and their headbands are tied in back. Furthermore, above the masses congregated directly behind the drum structure in the first photograph there is a young man sitting upon the horizontally-held pole of Tonomachi's *tsuke daiko*. He is clothed in the same manner as the extra riders on the platform—naked from the waist up, regular trousers, and a headband tied in back. By the second photograph he has disappeared, presumably having slid off the pole into the crowd below. Informant opinions vary as to what this man is doing. Some think he is helping to guard the main drum and has climbed up onto Tonomachi's pole in an effort to force it down away from the platform. Others suggest he is a resident of Tonomachi himself, and is celebrating the fact that their team is in the lead. Whatever the case, in my opinion it would have been very difficult for him to scramble up onto the pole from ground level with another team pressing in from behind. I think it is more likely that he was on the drum platform himself before the picture was taken and had merely climbed down onto the pole from above. This is supported by the fact that he is dressed in a manner similar to the extra riders.

The second photograph shows the drum a little further down the street. One of the extra riders now appears to have squeezed in between two regular members of the main guard, where he stands

Figure 22. The *okoshi daiko* passing through Ichinomachi, 1933. The drum structure is headed away from the camera, and additional riders occupy its trailing end. Photograph courtesy of Tsuchibora Akio, who appears atop the big drum facing the camera. (His father Zengorō stands to the left at the head of the drum structure.)

smiling broadly and waving with both hands at the crowd. A third *tsuke daiko* pole can be seen driving in from the left, though its drum and insignia are obscured. The throng of spectators presses in from behind, almost as if they were joining the charge.

In the third photograph, the scene switches to Upper Ninomachi, which happened to be the directing neighborhood that year. The back of the drum structure is passing by at close range, and two of the extra riders remain furthest to the rear alongside one of the main guards. A *tsuke daiko* team has succeeded in attaching itself to the platform; it appears to be that of Middle Ichinomachi. One other notable feature is that the faces of the bearers supporting the structure from below all appear darkened by exposure to the sun. These are people accustomed to working outdoors—farmers, carpenters, and sawyers.

Upper Ninomachi has always been one of the smallest neighborhoods in terms of numbers of households. Where then did all the bearers come from? A woman who had married into Upper Nino-

Figure 23. Same scene, moments later. The drum structure continues down Ichinomachi, with the crowd closing in behind. Photograph courtesy of Furukawa Town Hall.

Figure 24. The scene switches to Upper Ninomachi. Again the drum structure is headed away from the camera, and a *tsuke daiko* has attached itself to the rear. Photograph courtesy of Tsuzuku Shigezo.

machi offers part of the answer. She recalls that in 1933, the same year the photographs were taken, her household had been assigned to provide nineteen bearers, and were perplexed about how to fill the quota. (This would have been the first time her neighborhood served as director after the drum structure was enlarged.) The woman's natal household was just across the river in Mukaimachi, so she asked her relatives there to help enlist the needed bodies from among their own neighbors. The enlistees were each given a bottle of *sake* and treated to a feast. The woman recalls that this was a major expense—more than they had paid for the annual house cleaning prior to the new year holiday. Other households in Upper Ninomachi apparently resorted to similar means. The feast was held upstairs in the neighborhood meeting hall, and the number of invited bearers was sufficient to fill two large *tatami*-matted rooms totalling abourt forty-five square meters (Kuwahara et al. 1991:20).

But if Upper Ninomachi was so short-handed, what explains the presence of several extra men upon the drum platform, as seen in the photographs? Are they invited guests or unwanted intruders? Perhaps the camera has captured an insurrection—an attempt by one or more of the other neighborhoods to take over the drum. Since none of my informants can recall the details, I will suggest one possible explanation. Mukaimachi had by that time emerged as a growing population of farmers and laborers. Even so, it was still ineligible to serve as director, allegedly due to its role in performing the *kagura*. Thus its residents could help other neighborhoods shoulder the drum structure but were denied the opportunity to ride it themselves. It is possible, then, that Upper Ninomachi offered to let some of them ride the structure as part of their incentive for toting the drum. It is also worth noting that they were positioned at the back end, not at the front.

Meaning and Perspective

Why would resident landlord households continue to offer their patronage despite the subversive messages the *okoshi daiko* had come to embody? It is possible they recognized the need for a cathartic release of pent-up energy through ritualized rebellion, which Gluckman (1954), Norbeck (1963), and Turner (1969:166–203) suggest staves off the development of more serious opposition. A more plausible explanation, however, is that while the neighborhood leaders were submitted to a bit of jostling, their very presence atop the drum platform served nonetheless to reaffirm their elevated social positions. The *okoshi daiko* thus represented different things to different people, its meaning varying with the participant's role.

In any case, the most parasitic members of the local elite—the large agricultural landlords—lived not within the town of Furukawa itself but in neighboring villages located just upstream. These absentee landlords belonged to other shrine precincts and thus had no control over the *matsuri* of Ketawakamiya Shrine. Herein lies the suggestion that the town-dwelling landlords were capitalizing upon their position within the community, as well as their patronage of the local *matsuri,* to strengthen their economic and political standing relative to the large absentee landlord households. By going along with the momentary ordeal they were able to present themselves as "good sports," still cognizant of the interests of the community at large. This is an arena in which the large agricultural landlords could not compete; being located outside the area protected by the shrine, they were not eligible to participate in its annual *matsuri.*

Also, while the *okoshi daiko* expressed a message of generalized opposition toward the local elite, socioeconomic disparities within a particular neighborhood went largely unchallenged. The director confined itself to providing the requisite number of people to carry, ride upon, and guard the main drum platform; it did not field a *tsuke daiko* team to advance upon the structure from behind.[25] Consequently the members of any particular neighborhood were never brought into direct confrontation with their own resident elite, but only with those of other neighborhoods. Socioeconomic differences were overridden by a sense of communal identity, which was greatly enhanced through competition with outside groups.

The ritual could in fact be seen in terms of simple inter-neighborhood rivalry. The *tsuke daiko* teams were competing with one another for position while advancing upon the director, and the director's drum itself was the responsibility of one particular *chōnai.* As mentioned previously, however, place of residence is embedded in other socioeconomic and political categories. Most of the prominent landlord and merchant households were clustered together in the interior sectors of Ichinomachi and Ninomachi. In fact Ninomachi alone was home to most of Furukawa's major landholders. These included Honda, Nakamura (until 1876), Tajika, Hasegawa, Kumazaki, Ushimaru, and three rival lines of Gotō, not to mention the huge rice warehouse owned by Sugishita, the giant Hida land baron.

It is important to recognize, however, that while these major landowners resided in a specific neighborhood, their land holdings were scattered throughout the surrounding basin. Outer neighborhoods like Tonomachi and Mukaimachi were predominantly composed of small-owner and tenant cultivators, many of whom were working land owned by wealthy interior households through rather unfavorable sharecropping arrangements. Neighborhood affiliation thus automatically invoked basic socioeconomic and political disparities. Inter-neighborhood rivalry was inextricably meshed with tensions between different social strata.

The meaning of the rousing drum ritual varied, therefore, not only with the social identity of the actor, but with that of the neighborhood as well. To the interior *chōnai*, serving as director was considered a great burden, as all the work had to be shared by a relatively small number of households. By this time over 300 men were required to ride, bear, and defend the massive drum structure. A neighborhood consisting of thirty-five households could at best provide only about fifty or sixty able-bodied adult males; the rest had to be recruited from the outside. Wealthy landlords could enlist the aid of their tenant farmers, but the less prosperous households had to draw on their connections, cajoling friends, relatives, or work-related acquaintances into taking on what was considered a rather unpleasant task. The enlistees had to be compensated with food, drink, and money, or perhaps the promise of a favor in return (Kaba 1983, Kuwahara 1991:19–20). Furthermore, to prominent members of these neighborhoods the opportunity to lead the proceedings was no special reward, as they were accustomed to making decisions and issuing orders as part of their everyday activities.

In the case of Tonomachi, however, serving as director was a rare opportunity to "lord it" (so to speak) over the other *chōnai.* During the *matsuri,* even the most prominent landlords had to bow to the director. The rousing drum was above all a demonstration of strength, and in this respect Tonomachi enjoyed a distinct advantage. It could provide a sufficient number of bearers from among its own residents, and most of these residents were farmers who were well-accustomed to shouldering heavy loads. With their own neighborhood's reputation at stake they could be counted on to put forth their best effort, staying right through to the ritual's completion.

Tonomachi could also assemble a formidable rear guard to ensure that the drum structure never was "crushed." Its leaders thus rode confidently atop the platform, revelling in their brief moment of ascendancy.

Likewise, during ordinary years Tonomachi could muster an impressive gang of strong young men to wield its *tsuke daiko*. Though the number of participants was somewhat limited by the length of the stout pole they carried, Tonomachi could select from a wider pool the strongest and most aggressive candidates, thereby ensuring that its own team would break through. Membership in a neighborhood's *tsuke daiko* team was limited to its own residents; the other neighborhoods could not draw on their connections to help them in this regard.

The subversive nature of the rousing drum is perhaps most significant in the case of Mukaimachi, which was denied the opportunity to serve as director. It did, however, field a *tsuke daiko* team to charge against the main drum. The interior *chōnai* were locked in by other neighborhoods, but Mukaimachi was free to expand. In time it grew to rival Tonomachi in simple strength of numbers. Again, old photographs consistently show Tonomachi and Mukaimachi at the fore, challenging the authority of the directing neighborhood.

It is this competitive show of strength that best explains why the *okoshi daiko* was tolerated by the elite, and why the drum structure grew larger and heavier over the years. Tonomachi had issued a challenge to match its strength; failing to answer the challenge would have discredited the other neighborhoods. This is what led residents of the interior *chōnai* to draw on their contacts, doing anything in their power to muster more bearers. Here, in fact, was another activity the landlords could share with their less prominent neighbors in the interests of communal solidarity.

The rivalry between Tonomachi and Lower Ninomachi is particularly enlightening, as they were fairly well matched in terms of size but quite different socioeconomically. Tonomachi was composed primarily of small-owner and tenant cultivators, while Lower Nino-machi was overwhelmingly populated by merchants. The merchants had to remain on good terms with their fellow residents to ensure their success in business, but the cultivators could afford to be more independent. In a sense Tonomachi was comparable to the insular farm village so often described in the anthropological literature. Ninomachi, on the other hand, more closely resembled the old *"shi-*

tamachi," or "downtown," areas of larger towns and cities. To exacerbate matters, Lower Ninomachi was home to the Honda household—Furukawa's largest town-dwelling landlord and for several decades the dominant force in local politics. A Honda served as Furukawa's mayor 1897–1898, 1904–1906, and 1927–1946, as well as the area's representative to the prefectural assembly 1895–1899 and 1917–1935. Challenging Lower Ninomachi was not only a demonstration against the growing power of wealthy merchants and landowners; it was also akin to writing an angry letter to one's elected representative. This would have been particularly significant prior to the extension of voting privileges.[26]

To the other residents of Lower Ninomachi, Honda obviously belonged to a higher socioeconomic realm; but he was also a neighbor and benefactor. Again, focusing on a common challenge from the outside helped divert attention from socioeconomic disparities among fellow *chōnai* residents; in this sense the *matsuri* tied them all together. Furthermore, as merchants they were not subjected to the kind of exploitation inherent in the landlord–tenant relationship.

On the level of the entire town, Honda was an intermediary between the local people and higher realms of administrative authority. As a major landlord and politician he was directly linked into the increasingly centralized administrative and economic systems, as well as being a beneficiary of the changes those systems engendered. As a fellow resident of Furukawa, however, he could be counted on to represent local interests (especially when they coincided with his own). This is demonstrated by his efforts to intervene on behalf of the townspeople in their conflicts with the authorities. Landlords as a whole constituted a rather ambiguous category. While enriching themselves largely at the expense of their fellow residents, they nevertheless had to assume great burdens of social responsibility: listening to their neighbors' complaints, arbitrating disputes, and drawing upon their influence to cope with local difficulties.

Relations with the police, on the other hand, entailed no such ambiguities. As agents of the central government, they were seen as complete outsiders. With no direct socioeconomic ties nor any prior tradition of paternalistic benevolence, there was nothing to justify their abuse of authority in the minds of the townspeople. This explains why the police were attacked with such vehemence. It also explains unwillingness by the police themselves to acquiesce to such treatment.

Use of the *matsuri* as an opportunity to lash out at the police is by no means unique to Furukawa. Writing in 1919, Yanagita Kunio cites an interesting case from northeastern Japan. The *mikoshi* procession in a rural village there had become rather violent and every year crashed into three or four houses. The police were inclined to look the other way, such things being in the nature of a *matsuri*. This particular year, however, the *mikoshi* had crashed into their station building. Yanagita uses the incident to challenge another scholar's explanation—that carrying a heavy object creates instability, and thus the *mikoshi* is quite naturally inclined to hit a building now and then. The other scholar had coined the phrase "physics of faith" *(shinkō butsurigaku)* in describing the tendency to interpret such occurrences as expressions of the divine will. Yanagita counters that the damages incurred are not always accidental, and that the "belief" that the deity is directing the *mikoshi* should not necessarily be taken literally.

Yanagita (1962b:399–400) explains this and other instances of conflict with the police during *matsuri* as an understandable reaction by the local people to the sociopolitical changes being foisted upon them with the advent of a new era. In the past rural villagers had been accustomed to policing themselves, typically through the agency of the local fire brigade. Following the Meiji Restoration, however, they were increasingly drawn under the legal authority of the central government, the police being the principle exponents. The police earnestly set about enforcing the new standards, while ignoring or reviling the ways of the past. Their seeming arrogance and fastidiousness initially created a great deal of resentment. This, too, suggests a parallel with the Umemura Rebellion. The changes may have been well-advised, and motivated by good intentions; the problem was that they were being implemented too quickly.

Wartime Austerities

In time the people came to accept the state's intrusive presence, bowing to the emperor's photograph and reciting the Imperial Rescripts. This attitude was greatly enhanced by the perception of a national emergency and unifying sense of purpose following Japan's military expansion into the Asian continent during the 1930s. Though far removed from events in the major power centers, rural Japan was by no means oblivious to the rising tide of war. "The village," Fukutake

(1980:158) observes, "became the last link in the chain of organization for the all-out war effort and lost all vestiges of autonomy under the pressures of national administration."

Perhaps the most effective control on the *okoshi daiko* was its gradual absorption into the symbolism and ideology of State Shinto. The drum originally had to be borrowed from a Buddhist temple, and was therefore associated with the realm of the profane (at least from the Shinto perspective). Over time, however, it came to be treated as a sacred object, which was ritually blessed and purified before being launched into the fray. The great drum itself became the exclusive property of Ketawakamiya Shrine, where it was housed when not in use. The transition is most dramatically indicated in the 1929 use of a Shinto priest riding upon the drum structure and performing a ritual of purification as it passed through the streets. Significantly, this was the year of the attack on the police station, as well as of several attempts to impede the drum's progress.

In December 1936, Watanabe Ichirō, head of one of Furukawa's major *sake*-brewing households, donated a new and bigger drum to commemorate the birth of his first grandson.[27] This is the same drum used in today's event, bearing the familiar hollyhock symbol of Ketawakamiya Shrine on its leather heads (Ōno 1973b). From that time on the drum was inextricably associated with the shrine and its ideological underpinnings.

During the 1930s many of the local men were called away to military service, so the townspeople resorted to enlisting the aid of Korean laborers brought from their homeland to work in the mines of nearby Kamioka. As might be expected, their participation in the ritual was limited to shouldering the drum structure. Here again is an example of how the politics of subordination were physically enacted through the ritual medium of the *okoshi daiko*. This particular instance, however, involves ethnic as well as economic subordination—Korea at that time having been under Japanese authority. One of my informants recalls that, in a gesture of gratitude, the Korean laborers were invited to attend the *atofuki* celebration on April 21.

With Shinto having been drawn into the ideology of the state, local shrine festivals all over the country became increasingly oriented toward the national goal of military victory. The prayers and ceremonies performed during the Furukawa *matsuri* were no exception. Significantly, however, the *okoshi daiko* was not viewed in quite the same manner. In keeping with the seriousness of the war situation, the parish elders and block chiefs together decided in 1938 to temporarily suspend the ritual, though the shrine ceremonies and *mikoshi* procession were conducted as usual. This decision was poorly received by the townspeople, however, and the *okoshi daiko* was resumed in 1940 (Ōno 1973b, 1976b).

The following year the ritual was performed for the first time in broad daylight, beginning at 2:00 p.m. (Ōno 1976b). The reason for this is unclear, but it most likely had something to do with the austerity measures adopted in support of the war effort. Since 1878 the event had been officially referred to as the *"mezamashi daiko."* That same year, 1941, the original name *"okoshi daiko"* was reinstated by an amendment to the earlier regulations (Ōno 1973b). The change was presumably made because the term *"mezamashi"* ("eye-opening" or "wake-up alarm") was no longer appropriate for an afternoon event. As mentioned earlier, the alternative term *"okoshi"* can be interpreted in various ways, and is not limited to a simple wake-up signal. The event was again performed during the afternoon in 1943. This time it began at 4:00 p.m., and made only a single pass through Ichinomachi (Ōno 1976b).

Due to the threat of allied air raids, the Japanese government imposed a nationwide blackout in 1944. This ruled out any nighttime outdoor activities, so the *matsuri* as a whole had to be greatly curtailed. The *mikoshi* procession, which normally lasted all day and on into the evening, was canceled outright. The neighborhood *yatai,* which ordinarily accompanied the *mikoshi,* merely lined up together briefly along Ōyoko-chō, the major side street. The *okoshi daiko* began that year at 2:00 p.m. (Ōno 1976b).

The ritual had largely become devoid of meaning with the transition to a daytime context and the spirit of austerity compelled by the war effort. By this time so many of the local men had been called away to military service that there were hardly enough able bodies remaining to shoulder the drum structure. In 1945 the *okoshi daiko* was abandoned altogether, along with the *mikoshi* procession, though the prayers of supplication continued to be performed at the shrine as usual.

From Symbolism to Instrumentality   **259**

CHAPTER 9

COMMODIFICATION

Postwar Reforms

The prevailing mood immediately following the war was one of disillusionment and shame—hardly conducive to the kind of festive atmosphere the *matsuri* occasioned. In any case, the event could no longer be properly celebrated due to serious shortages of food and other supplies—not the least of them *sake*. Nevertheless, in 1947 some of the young men who had returned from military service overseas led a movement to resurrect the *okoshi daiko*. The Tonomachi contingent voluntarily assumed the role of bearing the drum. Initially they were unable to gain the consent of either the parish elders or the town's elected officials, and for two years the ritual was performed without authorization. The young men made their own alcoholic beverage called *"doburoku"*—a type of crude *sake*. There were so few participants that the drum bearers reportedly had great difficulty keeping the structure at shoulder level and were reduced to cradling it in the crooks of their arms.

In response to pressure by the neighborhood young men's associations, the event was officially reinstated in 1949. Now, however, some changes were necessary. The land reform instituted under the auspices of the Allied occupation had effectively dissolved the prewar landlord class. In 1947 voting privileges were extended to all citizens, male and female, who were at least twenty years of age. As a result of these and other democratic reforms, former landlords no longer held the authority to enlist the additional labor necessary to carry the huge drum structure. The center of town consisted mostly of merchant households whose members were not physically as strong as those engaged in agriculture, and in any case the old interior neighborhoods were too small to draw sufficient labor power from among their residents alone. A decision was made to divide the town into four new territorial units called *"okoshi daiko gumi"* ("rousing drum groups"), each large enough to provide the requisite number of drum bearers from among its own constituents. Because of their size, Tonomachi and Mukaimachi were each made to constitute entire units—"Seiryū" and "Suzaku," respectively. Sakaemachi, Lower Ichinomachi, and Lower Ninomachi were combined to form "Genbu." The remaining neighborhoods—those lying in the interior—were all lumped together as "Byakko." Responsibility for conducting the rousing drum was to rotate among these four territorial groupings. The old *taigumi* divisions would remain intact, but their function would be limited to the *yatai* procession and internal neighborhood activities.

The new arrangement resulted in the rather complex chain of command described in Chapter 5. From this point on, two separate directors had to be chosen each year during the lottery ceremony—one to be responsible for the *yatai* escort and the other for the *okoshi daiko.* These two components of the *matsuri,* once performed in unified progression, would thus come to function as separate events. In the case of the *okoshi daiko,* the highest-ranking member of the directing group was now referred to as *"sōtsukasa"* (commander), and customarily rode at the front of the drum platform as the lead member of the main guard.

Reflecting the postwar emphasis on egalitarianism, the new fourfold *okoshi daiko* divisions placed Mukaimachi on an equal footing with the old established neighborhoods. Mukaimachi now for the first time became eligible to participate in the lottery ceremony and serve as director for the *okoshi daiko.* This initially led to a rather embarrassing episode. When Mukaimachi was first chosen director in 1952, one of its responsibilities was of course to assemble the drum structure. Its residents had never done this before, and mistakenly placed the drum so that the three-leafed hollyhock symbol of the shrine was upside down. The other neighborhoods found this highly amusing. Some Mukaimachi people claim they were purposely misled by the elders they consulted in the other neighborhoods.

With the institution of the larger divisions there was no longer any need for individual households to enlist the cooperation of friends, relatives, and work-related associates from outside the neighborhood. While easing the burden on households within the directing territory, however, the overall effect was to render participation more insular, as there was less need to maintain relationships with neighboring communities for the purpose of securing extra hands. This parallels the increasing independence and overall decline in reciprocal economic relationships among Japanese households in the postwar era.

The four *okoshi daiko* divisions remained in effect for over twenty years. Within that period, however, the "donut effect" *(dōnatsu-ka genshō)* created by households moving from the center to the outskirts of town caused a serious imbalance in the number of households per neighborhood. In 1973 it was decided that, rather than having the directorship rotate among the four divisions as had been the practice, the role would now be shared by the town as a whole. Each *taigumi* in Furukawa would every year provide one quarter the number of its *ujiko* membership to perform the director's duties. As a consequence, however, the *tsuke daiko* were made to charge not against a rival territory, but a generic cross-section of the entire population. This was hardly conducive to an enthusiastic attack. In 1977 the four *okoshi daiko* sectors were reinstated, with the directorship rotating among them as before. This time, however, Sakaemachi was taken out of "Genbu" and placed into "Byakko" with the smaller neighborhoods, thereby creating a more equitable distribution of households.[1]

The ambivalence has not been completely eliminated, however. Each of the four territorial sectors now contains a sufficient number of residents to simultaneously bear the drum structure, form the rear guard, *and* allow each of its component neighborhoods to field a *tsuke daiko* team. This unavoidably results in teams from the directing sector clashing with residents of their own neighborhoods serving in the rear guard. The problem is particularly evident in the case of two neighborhoods—Tonomachi and Mukaimachi—both of which comprise entire sectors in themselves. When either of these two serves as director, in other words, its *tsuke daiko* team as well as the people riding, bearing, and defending the lead drum all belong to the same neighborhood. As might be expected, resistance from the rear guard in such instances is half-hearted at best. In fact, when the main guard member positioned upon the framework at the rear of the structure sees that the *tsuke daiko* from his own neighborhood has successfully arrived at the fore, he will sometimes reach down and pound upon their drum in celebration. The *tsuke daiko* of the director's own territory is thus virtually assured of making a successful strike, the only major obstacle being competition from other teams.

This, it may be recognized, is a purely postwar phenomenon. Before the war, the directing neighborhood did not field a *tsuke daiko* team, so its residents were never pitted against one another. The lines were more clearly defined, and the opposition between the director and the rest of the town was more intense.

The young men's association *(seinendan)* had been idle during the war because so many of the young people had been called into military service. It was partially revived in 1948, but organized as a group encompassing the entire town. Membership was later opened to females (the characters used to write *"seinendan"* imply no inherent gender bias), and the members engaged mostly in recreational rather than service oriented activities. From the mid-1960s, young people were drawn toward other social and recreational opportunities, and the association gradually faded into oblivion. However, a parallel to the old prewar version can be seen in the various neighborhood young men's associations (Sōgakubu, *deku hozonkai,* etc.) currently employed during the *matsuri.*

Reforms instituted by the Allied occupation in large part dissolved the rigid authoritarian hierarchy that existed before the war. Fukutake (1980:101) observes that, following the introduction of Western democratic ideals, positions of authority within rural *matsuri* were no longer monopolized by a few prominent lineages:

> The *ujiko* group is now more egalitarian, and the elitism of the past is almost imperceptible. The families that once monopolized the lead roles in festivals and ceremonies can no longer handle the financial burden that these impose because of the lowering of their economic position since the land reform (1947–50). In addition, the influence of democracy on hamlet people is such that the kind of class distinctions which were once implicit on religious occasions will not be tolerated.

Furukawa may be seen as somewhat of an exception in that many of its resident landlord households were able to regain their privileged status after the land reform. Honda Akinori continued as mayor of Furukawa until 1946, then again from 1954 to 1956. His statue is prominently displayed in front of the town hall. His son Akihiro served as representative to the prefectural assembly for five straight terms from 1967 to 1987, part of which time he was chair of that body. Kaba Shigeo served as mayor from 1950 to 1954, and Fuse Magojirō from 1956 to 1966. The Kaba and Watanabe families, of course, continued to operate very prosperous *sake*-brewing establishments. The Tajika, too, remained a successful merchant household. All of these were principal supporters of the *matsuri* throughout the postwar era.

Even so, the nature of social relations had become far more democratic, and there was no longer any pressing need for ritualized expressions of opposition toward an exploitative elite. Riding upon the drum structure as a member of the main guard was still restricted to prominent members of the community. Prominence, however, came to be defined less by material wealth and political influence than by personal reputation and community service.

As for the *mikoshi* procession, until the end of the Second World War only men of wealth and status donned the *montsuki* and *kamishimo* costume to stroll along as members of the honor guard. Now the head of practically every participating household owns a set of the formal garments, and joins in the procession on a rotating basis as a representative of his home neighborhood (the role still being restricted to males). Due to the length of the procession's course, however, the role tends to be seen more as a burden than a privilege. With the exception of the shrine officers, the representatives are changed at half-day intervals, thereby spreading the burden among larger numbers.

The *tsuke daiko* continue to clash with the rear guard in advancing upon the main drum. Now when they reach the rear of the drum structure, however, it is deemed sufficient merely to hold their poles directly over the back of the wooden framework rather than placing them atop it and trying to pull it to the ground. The riders are jostled a bit as they are carried through the streets upon the elevated platform, but there is little danger of being pitched off or toppled.

Periodic occurrences of the drum structure crashing into houses continued well into the 1960s. The potential for mishaps is suggested in Matsui's (1965:6) description of the drum's movement: "The great structure slowly advances, pitching and swaying, now this way, now that way in the midst of the turmoil." During the postwar era, merchants began to enjoy the benefits of economic prosperity well before the rest of the population, and this understandably led to feelings of resentment. According to several local residents, many of the prominent merchant households resorted to lining their store fronts with boards on the night of the *okoshi daiko* to keep from being smashed. The boards, they say, were later replaced by sliding metal shutters.

A local resident and I were looking at some photographs of the *okoshi daiko* during the mid-1960s. One of them showed the drum passing through Ninomachi in front of a prominent merchant house. The photograph revealed that the occupants had indeed taken the precaution of erecting boards across the front of their building to protect it from damage. My friend immediately pointed to the boards and said "See? They put those there because they were getting hit all the time." It must be noted, however, that this particular shop is located on the corner of a major intersection, where it is especially vulnerable. Considering the noise and confusion which the *okoshi daiko* engenders, simple accident could easily explain the numerous instances of the shop being hit (or some of them at least). Rumors abound, however, about certain households being targeted for vandalism or pilfering, or how an incidental surge of the drum structure happened to crash into the home of an arrogant or contentious neighbor. And while sliding metal shutters have been installed on storefronts all over Japan for simple security reasons, the impetus for introducing them in Furukawa is attributed to the *okoshi daiko.*

It has been reported in the anthropological literature on other societies that accusations of witchcraft often derive from jealousy or resentment. Prosperous neighbors are likely targets, especially when their success seems otherwise inexplicable or undeserved (Lehmann and Myers 1997:189). In Japan, a related phenomenon has to do with the belief in "animal spirit holders," who are said to afflict their victims through possession by spirits of animals such as fox and dog. The ability to use such powers is thought to remain in certain family lines, whose members are therefore subjected to marriage discrimination, avoidance, and continual suspicions. Blacker (1975: 60–61) attributes this form of ostracism to resentment against the growing prosperity of the *nouveaux riches.*

Yoshida (1984:99) addresses another dimension, relating not to fear of being accused of employing evil powers, but of having them used against oneself:

Clearly, since it is believed that arousing the envy or resentment of animal-spirit holders can lead to being possessed by their spirits, most people try to conduct themselves in ways that do not provoke the envy, resentment, or anger of holders. Belief in spirit possession constrains social conflict, we must presume. To villagers it is wise to live in an inconspicuous manner, since the undue display of wealth or success is taken as a sign of greediness and punished by the spirits of envious spirit holders. Openly stepping above one's peers is a dangerous move.

The *okoshi daiko* likewise represents the use of a supernatural agent to chastise the arrogant and pretentious. It may thus be seen as a clever mechanism for enforcing humility—a kind of egalitizing presence. As with the shopworn phrase *"deru kugi wa utareru"* ("the nail that sticks up gets pounded back down"), people who feel themselves superior to others must be taught a lesson or put back in their places. The annual performance of the *okoshi daiko* is an institutionalized opportunity to do so.

This is particularly instructive when comparing Furukawa to Takayama. It is widely held by residents of both towns that Takayama is more hierarchically inclined. In fact, to many people, events like the *okoshi daiko* are almost inconceivable in Takayama due to its rigid social strictures.[2] Yet it is impossible to say which came first, the anti-elitist attitude or the mechanism that enforces it. If the ritual had emerged simply in response to social inequalities, then it would certainly have appeared in Takayama where the need for it is greater. This raises the question, why did the ritual develop as it did in Furukawa but not in Takayama?

Part of the reason undoubtedly has to do with Furukawa's position as "younger sibling" to the larger town, and the resentment engendered by being "number two." People in both towns note that Furukawa has a higher concentration of agricultural households, and that farmers tend to be more independently minded than merchants. Additionally, Takayama long functioned as the seat of Hida politics and was therefore more tightly under the control of the authorities. Furukawa was further removed from the locus of power and could afford to be less obsequious. There were no government representatives headquartered in Furukawa following the departure of the Kanamori and the subsequent takeover by the Tokugawa regime. From that point onward directives were issued from Takayama where the magistrate's headquarters were located. Takayama thus became associated with higher authority, toward which the *okoshi daiko* emerged as a symbolic challenge.

Tradition and Tourism

Prior to the Second World War, the Furukawa *matsuri* was conducted primarily by and for the local people. There were very few automobiles at the time and no railroad until 1934. Lack of easy access limited visitors from outside the basin area.

In those days there were few opportunities for diversion, and the annual *matsuri* was an anxiously awaited event. The coming of spring signified a yearly renewal, and the *matsuri* was a celebration of the renewal process. This relates to social as well as natural phenomena, as the *matsuri* provided an opportunity to reestablish contact after a long period of isolation due to the harsh winter. A resident of a nearby village recalls that on April 20 all the schools in the area would cancel classes so that children could attend the Furukawa *matsuri,* beginning with the *okoshi daiko* the night before. He claimed the crowds of spectators were nearly as big as they are today because *all* the people in the surrounding area turned out for the festivities.

As mentioned earlier, local farmers would sow their rice seeds in nursery beds on April 19, then ready themselves for the *okoshi daiko* later that evening. This applied not just to Furukawa, but to farmers throughout the basin area. Some of them were enlisted to help carry the drum structure; but most simply went to enjoy the festivities, perhaps at the invitation of resident households.

Even ordinary people who passed their lives in frugal simplicity used what they had managed to save to sponsor lavish feasts, inviting friends and relatives from other neighborhoods. The host household would in turn be invited to the feasts of its guests when their own local festivals were held. The whole *matsuri* system thus functioned as a means of maintaining a network of reciprocal exchange relationships. Therein lies the true significance of *yobihiki* (the "calling-pulling" of guests).

The postwar period was characterized by rapid economic growth, bringing widespread prosperity and further dissolution of socioeconomic distinctions. The most dramatic changes in the *matsuri* in recent decades have resulted from efforts to capitalize upon this new prosperity. The significance of the *okoshi daiko* as a symbolic expression of opposition has faded away along with the rigid authoritarian hierarchy toward which it was at one time directed. But the ritual itself has assumed a new function as an economic resource—one that can be packaged and marketed to the public.

In 1952, at the request of Furukawa's Chamber of Commerce and Industry, the starting time for the *okoshi daiko* was moved ahead a few hours, from 1:00 a.m. on April 20 to 10:00 p.m. on April 19, the purpose being to facilitate attendance by tourists from outside the local area. This further established the *okoshi daiko* as an independent event conducted on the evening before the regular festivities. Formerly the drum ritual had led directly into the *yatai* procession, with no break in between. Now after the conclusion of the *okoshi daiko* the townspeople went home to sleep a few hours before rising to participate in the other activities.

In 1956, as part of a nationwide program to consolidate towns and villages into larger political units *(chōson gappei)*, the town of Furukawa was combined with the nearby villages of Hosoe and Kotakari to form Furukawa Township (Furukawa-*chō*). This had no major impact on the development of the *matsuri*, however, since the boundaries of the Ketawakamiya shrine itself were unaffected. In fact the *matsuri* can be seen as a way of perpetuating Furukawa's identity as it existed prior to amalgamation. The other villages, too, maintain their own shrines and festivals.

That same year the *okoshi daiko* was chosen to be filmed by the American Disney company as part of a documentary on Japanese folk customs. On this occasion the ritual had to be performed during the daytime to ensure adequate lighting for the color film. As with the ill-fated daytime performances during the war years, however, participants and onlookers recall a rather half-hearted atmosphere. The documentary film, entitled "Japan: Customs and Traditions," was released by the Disney Corporation in 1964, perhaps timed to coincide with the interest generated by the Tokyo Olympics. The *okoshi daiko* footage was not incorporated in the final version.

The *okoshi daiko* went "on the road" in 1969 for the filming of a television program on Hida folk traditions by NHK (*Nippon Hōsō*

Kyōkai, the Japan Broadcasting Corporation). Various cultural attractions from all over the Hida region were assembled and performed before the cameras on the grounds of a high school in Takayama. In the wide-open area of the school grounds the *tsuke daiko* were able to attack not only from the rear but the sides as well. And since there was no equivalent to the rear guard along the sides, the *tsuke daiko* could make contact freely and even slide their poles over top and onto the framework. The result was a lapse into general confusion.

The daytime rendition and the school grounds fiasco together underscore the link between the form of a ritual and the environment in which it develops. The *okoshi daiko* evolved in the narrow streets of the town, with intersections to provide opportunities for the *tsuke daiko* to rush out and attack. The cover of night added an air of mystery and encouraged the venting of suppressed animosities. When temporarily removed from such a setting, the whole event lost its significance and appeal.

Additional changes were made to accommodate the tourists. The evening *yatai* procession, for example, traditionally marked the end of the festival as a communal celebration. Indeed, the *hikiwakare* (pulling away) at the procession's conclusion signified a farewell until the following year. During the late 1960s the evening procession was moved to April 19 so that tourists who had come to see the *okoshi daiko* could enjoy both events.

With increasing mobility and disposable income resulting from Japan's period of rapid economic growth during the 1960s, Japanese city-dwellers began travelling more frequently and further from home. As a result, the Furukawa *matsuri* began to attract attention from well beyond the immediate area. Many of the local people see 1965 as a major turning point in the *matsuri*'s developmental history. Up until that time tourists were few and the festival was conducted much as it had been before the war. But this was the year for Furukawa to host the grand Hida *taisai,* and people came from all over the region as well as outside to witness the spectacle.

In 1966 the *okoshi daiko* was designated one of Gifu Prefecture's "intangible cultural properties" *(mukei bunkazai).* In 1970 Furukawa's *yatai* were added to the list as "tangible cultural properties" *(yūkei bunkazai).* In January, 1980 the *okoshi daiko* and *yatai* procession were together raised to the status of "important intangible folk cultural properties" *(jūyō mukei minzoku bunkazai)* as officially recognized by the Japanese government.[3] This has given the Furukawa *matsuri* a certain degree of national exposure, though it is by no means as well known as the Takayama *matsuri* or some of the large urban festivals.

As mentioned in Chapter 3, Hida had always been considered rather isolated due to its distance from major urban areas, heavy snowfall, and rugged topography. But recent improvements in transportation facilities have made the region far more accessible from other areas. Perhaps the most significant event in Hida's modern history was the opening of the Takayama rail line in 1934. The line followed the narrow river valleys running north and south through Hida's center. It passed directly through Takayama and Furukawa, providing them for the first time with a convenient link to other cities—Toyama along the Sea of Japan and Gifu and Nagoya near the Pacific coast. The first scheduled stop of a steam locomotive at Furukawa Station was considered so important that all of Furukawa's *yatai* were rolled out to mark the occasion. The line has been steadily improved over the years, though it remains single-track for its entire length, and the locomotives are diesel rather than electric-powered. One recent development is the addition of several new limited express trains departing from either terminus at regular intervals.[4] When the line was first opened, the journey between Furukawa and Nagoya took two days. Now the same distance can be covered by limited express train in a little over two-and-a-half hours.

The Japan Railway (JR) companies have proven willing partners in promoting local festivals, as they stand to profit by shuttling tourists back and forth from other areas. The huge color posters made each year to advertise the Furukawa *matsuri* are produced by JR and hung in the stations of major cities as far away as Osaka. During the *matsuri* itself, special trains are added to the normal schedule to handle the increased flow of passengers.

Automobile traffic, too, has been greatly facilitated by road and highway improvement projects. Local roads were linked together and widened to form National Highway 41, which first opened in 1968. This is a two-lane highway that roughly parallels the rail line through the same narrow valleys, running from Nagoya through Gifu, Takayama, and Furukawa, then on to Toyama. National Highway 158 crosses east and west through Hida, linking Takayama with Matsumoto in neighboring Nagano Prefecture. The road to Matsumoto used to cross a high mountain pass which was closed for several months during the winter. In 1997, however, a new tunnel was completed through the Japan Alps to provide year-round access, just in time for the winter olympics held in Nagano the following year. A high-speed, four-lane highway is being built between Nagoya and Toyama. The planned route follows another valley to the west and does not pass through Furukawa. Even so, the new highway will render Furukawa and other parts of northern Hida even more accessible from the major cities lining the coast.

The tourist industry has been given further impetus by a government program referred to as *"furusato zukuri"* ("native place-making"). The program was designed to promote regional economic development by transforming local features into tourist attractions. The term *"furusato"* is often translated "native place," but is used to evoke not so much a specific geographical location as an emotion-laden image. Robertson (1991:16) attributes the cogency of this image to a "diffuse sense of homelessness" resulting from postwar urbanization—a pervasive longing for a simpler place and time. "The dominant representation of *furusato* is infused with nostalgia, a dissatisfaction with the present on the grounds of a remembered or imagined past plenitude" (Robertson 1991:14). The government's program is designed to capitalize on this nostalgic sense of longing by helping rural towns and villages develop (or perhaps in some cases invent) their own unique attractions. Furukawa's one big claim to fame is the *okoshi daiko,* and it is upon this ritual performance that much of the town's future development aspirations depend (Furukawa Machi-Zukuri Kenkyūkai 1993).

One obvious problem with developing the *matsuri* as an economic resource is that, as an annual event, it is capable of drawing tourists only two or three days of the year. The solution has been to create facilities that allow tourists to sample the *matsuri* all year round. In 1992, a spacious new museum was completed near the center of town, immediately adjacent to the plaza where the *okoshi daiko* now begins. Christened the "Hida–Furukawa Festival Hall" (Hida–Furukawa Matsuri Kaikan), it includes a special theater where a three-dimensional film of the *matsuri,* shot in 1991 by the Sony Corporation, is shown to visitors at regular intervals. The museum also features a display containing three of Furukawa's *yatai,* one of which turns slowly on a revolving platform. The *yatai* are changed every three months in fixed rotation so that all the neighborhoods are equally represented.

The *tabisho,* or temporary resting place for the deity, sits to one side of the museum. Together these buildings form an L enclosing two sides of the central plaza. The entire compound is referred to as the "Home of the Rousing Drum" (Okoshi Daiko no Sato). It is located across the street from the town hall and within convenient walking distance from the railroad station and various points of interest.

But this is only one component of a comprehensive plan to reorient the town toward the tourist industry. The plan was developed with the assistance of the Japan National Trust Foundation (Kankō Shigen Hogo Zaidan), using "native place-making" funds provided by the Ministry of Home Affairs (*Jichishō*—see Kankō Shigen Hogo Zaidan 1987; Furukawa Machi-Zukuri Kenkyūkai 1993). Beyond

Figure 25. The Hida–Furukawa Festival Hall *(Hida–Furukawa Matsuri Kaikan).*

the open corner of the plaza stands another museum called the "Artisans of Hida Culture Center" (Hida no Takumi Bunkakan), completed in 1989. It is intended to explain regional carpentry and woodworking techniques dating back to the time of the Hida *takumi*. Located further away on the other side of the railroad is a large facility known as the "Hida Mountain Wood-Cutting Hall" (Hida Sanshōkan). Completed in 1992, it is dedicated to the people who once made their living as lumberjacks and sawyers in the forested mountains of Hida. Included are an elaborate collection of traditional hand tools and wood products, along with displays explaining their use. Nearby on the same street is a smaller building called the "Furukawa Local Folk Craft Hall" (Furukawa-chō Kyōdo Mingei Kaikan). This houses a large exhibit of regional folk arts and their products, and was opened in 1986. A new pedestrian bridge has been built across the railroad to make both facilities more accessible. Incorporating the temples, castle remains, and other attractions, the entire town is emerging as an integrated tourist complex. The number of tourists visiting Furukawa in 1993 was estimated at 500,000 (Ōtsuka 1995:183).

Another tourism-related problem is overnight accommodation. The attractions in Furukawa can easily be seen in a few hours, so many visitors return home the same day. Others base themselves in Takayama and include Furukawa in their itineraries as a side excursion. Overnight lodgings are in great demand only during the *matsuri*, when it is more convenient—and also more exciting—to stay within the town itself. Furukawa contains a number of small, Japanese-style inns that cater to travelling business people, construction workers, and random groups of tourists, but they cannot begin to handle all the visitors who come to see the *matsuri*. As a result, many people have to stay in Takayama or other nearby towns and commute from there.

Even so, within only the past six years two Western-style hotels have been built in Furukawa along the main street leading from the train station. Though only five or six stories in height, they nevertheless tower over the surrounding buildings and have visibly altered the town's appearance. The hotels were built to provide additional accommodation for tourists and visitors to nearby ski facilities, which are accessible by bus from the station. They are said to be having difficulty filling their rooms during most of the year.

Form versus Substance

The rousing drum itself has undergone several substantive changes. Public attention has discouraged the more violent or unruly aspects, and steps have been taken to limit the danger, if not the hostility, the ritual entails. Attacks by the *tsuke daiko* have been prohibited while the drum structure is crossing bridges or passing along the river bank in Sannomachi. In recent years placing the pole directly onto the drum structure has also been discouraged, as it is seen as endangering those members of the main guard who stand toward the rear of the framework. Nevertheless, every year at the consultation meeting *(tsuke daiko uchiawasekai)* held several days prior to the *matsuri,* team captains have to be cautioned against such activity, as making direct contact is still considered the ideal. (Kuwahara et al. 1991:40).

Formerly the *tsuke daiko* could attack at random from any point along the course. Now the striking places are largely predetermined, and random attacks are rare. This policy was implemented only about twenty years ago, again in an attempt to limit injuries. Not only is the location predetermined, but who goes first as well, with team captains meeting beforehand to establish the order of attack. In a sense, the event is being staged for the benefit of the onlookers. Likewise, the rear guard have become less adamant in defending the drum. As mentioned in Chapter 4, there is an unwritten rule that a *tsuke daiko* team should be allowed to *"tsukeru"* on its own territory. Without this agreement, the smaller neighborhoods would never have a chance. Usually the rear guard comply, putting up a good fight but eventually allowing the home team to break through.

Even so, the *okoshi daiko* remains a rather wild and boisterous affair. Despite the order of attack, once the neighborhood teams have launched themselves toward the drum structure they are free to use whatever means necessary to fight their way to the fore. A large number of inebriated young men concentrated in one area, motivated by inter-group rivalries and a tradition of unruly behavior, sets the stage for violent outbreaks. Fighting is still prevalent, and injuries persist. One of the most common dangers is stumbling during the *tsuke daiko* charges and being trampled by the masses pressing in from behind. Around 1970 one of the participants was killed at the point where Ninomachi meets the side street that runs across Kasumi Bridge—approximately the same spot where the rock-throwing incident occurred in 1929. Apparently the man was drunk and fell into one of the open gutters, hitting his head on the concrete. When the crowd had passed he was found lying motionless in their wake.

While efforts are made to limit such injuries, it must be admitted that the peril explains some of the appeal, much like the famous running of the bulls in Pamplona. In fact neighborhood team members will sometimes invite friends visiting from other areas to don the white shorts and *sarashi* wrapping and join in the action. The special attire immediately invests participants with an aura of reckless bravery, and the young men are admired as local heroes by the spectators. The acrobatics performed atop the *tsuke daiko* are a fairly recent development, emerging only during the past fifteen years. This too has become a popular attraction for the tourists, and is often featured in promotional materials.

The procession of lantern-bearers preceding the drum has grown over the years so that it now includes more than a thousand people. This is only possible as a result of the fourfold territorial divisions introduced after the war, as few of the old neighborhoods could have mustered such numbers independently. Foot rests and other stabilizing features have been added to the drum so that the "top strikers" maintain a symmetrical upright posture. The long strip of white cloth wrapped around their waists to bind them together now also passes through a metal loop attached to the drum itself, acting much like a safety belt.

The most telling change, however, occurred in 1967, when a set of wheels—complete with inflated rubber tires—was installed beneath the huge grid-like platform that bears the drum. This is not readily apparent to onlookers during the *okoshi daiko,* as the undercarriage remains concealed within the mass of bearers. The two wheels are positioned at the middle of the platform so that it can still be rocked back and forth in the manner of a seesaw, but the structure itself is now virtually impossible to topple over or bring down. With most of the weight borne by this undercarriage, the endurance effort once required to heft the great drum through the streets is no longer necessary. Now the so-called "bearers" shuffle along underneath, pushing more than carrying the structure. Older informants note derisively that today's young people are not accustomed to physical labor and are too weak to shoulder the heavy load; this, they say, is the main reason the wheels had to be added.

In any case, the drum platform now remains at a constant height right through to the end of the performance, evoking no sense of imminent collapse. The wheels also keep the structure on a steady course and afford greater control when turning corners. The "ouija board phenomenon," in which the drum structure moved freely from side to side—seemingly animated by supernatural impulse—is now a thing of the past.[5] Earlier it was mentioned that members of the fire brigade run alongside the big drum to warn bystanders out of the way, but part of their job is to prevent the *tsuke daiko* from hitting adjacent buildings. As a result of these changes, there is no longer any significant danger (or, one might add, implied threat of vengeance) to households lining the way.

As described in Chapter 4, the *mikoshi,* too, now rides along on a set of four inflatable tires. The undercarriage is constructed so that the portable shrine itself remains at approximately shoulder height just as in the old days, though actual shoulders are no longer employed. While the wheels make the vehicle easier to convey, however, they also prevent the *mikoshi* from descending the long flight of steps leading down from the shrine to the road into town. Instead it has to be rolled out a side exit and down a back lane. Protocol, however, demands that the deity continue to be led through the main entrance as befits its high status. The solution has been to wheel the *mikoshi* around to the bottom of the steps where it waits for the deity to be carried down in a wooden box. As a result, "moving the deity" *(kamiutsushi)* must now be performed in two stages— one to place it in the box and another to move it from the box into the *mikoshi.*

In defense of these changes, it must be remembered that both the *mikoshi* procession and *okoshi daiko* have considerably more territory to cover now than in the past. In the case of the *mikoshi,* the wheels are partly intended to reduce wear on the conveyance itself. This also explains why banner bearers now take the place of the treasured *yatai* in leading the *mikoshi* procession. With the recent emphasis on tourism, the *yatai* constitute another important attraction, and their safety and preservation have become an overriding concern. Dragging them all over town was thought to cause excessive wear, so in 1961 banners bearing their names were substituted for the vehicles themselves.

Thus, while the *yatai* traditionally led the *mikoshi,* symbolizing the unity of shrine and neighborhood, in recent years the relationship between these two components has become increasingly vague.

The vehicles now make only short passes along predetermined routes. In former years, if it began to rain during the procession the *yatai* would simply be covered with tarps and continue on unless or until the director ordered them to stop. Now the *yatai* are returned to their storehouses *before* it starts to rain to protect them from water damage. The vehicles themselves appear to have become more important than the successful completion of their procession, and the religious significance they once held has all but disappeared.

This in fact is a general trend apparent in other aspects of the *matsuri*. Originally, inscriptions on the festival banners erected at neighborhood boundaries did not simply bear the name of the shrine as many do today; they were intended as messages to attract and welcome the deity on its visit into town. This is still the case with twelve out of the seventeen sets of banners in Furukawa. The problem is that the inscriptions are written in rather obscure Chinese-derived characters that very few people today are able to read. This problem was brought to light in the following incident. The banners are subjected to strong winds and other natural forces, and periodically need to be repaired or replaced. They are erected in pairs in which the inscription continues from one banner to the other, so that both must be read as a unit to make any sense. However, in ordering new banners to be made, one of the neighborhoods simply had the characters that appear on one side repeated verbatim on the other. Since no one could read the inscription, the significance of the error went unnoticed until the work had been completed.

Demographic Changes

Recently the *matsuri* has been facing the problem of residents moving out of the old neighborhoods. As previously mentioned, a large proportion of Furukawa's residents may still be characterized as half-agricultural, half-commercial. Thus even though they engage in merchant or other types of commercial activity they may also own rice paddies in the surrounding area. Many are converting these paddies into spacious new housing sites. They then sell their town properties to neighboring residents, shop owners, or small factories like the *sake* breweries who wish to enlarge their facilities, resulting in a net loss of households. The new highway bypass has been another major influence. Merchants are moving their businesses away from the center of town to be near the bypass where there is more traffic. All the new stores have spacious parking areas—impossible in the center of town. This makes them more accessible to people living farther away and complements a nationwide trend toward increasing use of automobiles.

Ninomachi in particular used to consist almost entirely of merchant households who lived upstairs or in back of their shops. Neighbors patronized each other's businesses through a series of mutual exchange relationships: one had only to cross the street or go a few doors over to obtain groceries, dry goods, and other supplies. Now the shops are fading away, unable to compete with the big supermarkets out along the new bypass highway that offer ample parking space and can capitalize on economies of scale. The small household shops can no longer generate a decent income, so members of the younger generation do not want to take over. As the parents grow too old to take care of business any longer, the shops disappear. One by one they are converted to ordinary residences or parking facilities.

This has an impact on the conduct of the *matsuri*. Movement from the old neighborhoods in the center of town to the outlying areas creates a drain of talented young people necessary for learning and passing on the traditions. As a result, "time-honored" traditions are in danger of fading away.

A similar trend has emerged on the national level. Even the organizers of the large urban festivals are having trouble generating sufficient participation. Ironically, the number of spectators continues to grow while the number of performers dwindles. The famous Gion *matsuri* in Kyoto, once primarily a local event, is now performed largely by outsiders. With companies and office buildings moving into the area and ordinary households moving out, there are no longer enough actual residents to perform all the roles. Many of the roles are now assumed by college students on summer vacation, for whom the Gion *matsuri* has become a form of part-time employment.

The problem is compounded by the fact that, while neighborhood boundaries have stayed the same, the *taigumi* attached to some of the outer neighborhoods—Seiryū (Tonomachi), Kirin (Lower Ichinomachi), Ryūteki (Lower Ninomachi), Kagura (Mukaimachi), and Tōkeiraku (Sakaemachi)—have been expanded to include new houses cropping up amidst the rice paddies. The *taigumi* attached to the inner neighborhoods, on the other hand—Sanbasō (Upper Ichinomachi), Hō-ō (Middle Ichinomachi), Sankō (Upper Ninomachi),

Kinki (Middle Ninomachi), Seiyō (Upper Sannomachi), and Byakko (Lower Sannomachi)—are entirely boxed in and unable to expand in any direction. As a result, membership in the outlying *taigumi* has grown considerably while that in the interior has steadily declined. This creates a shortage of young people to carry on the traditions in the interior neighborhoods. It also places a heavy financial burden on the remaining residents. Money for maintaining *yatai,* for example, comes from donations made by member households. The fewer the number of households, the greater the burden each must assume. This is the main reason Upper Ichinomachi's Sanbasō vehicle continues to "rest."

Population decrease among the inner *chōnai* has actually broadened participation in one sense; since there are no longer a sufficient number of boys to perform the festival music while riding the *yatai,* two of the neighborhoods have had to open participation to girls as well. Though girls were traditionally prohibited from riding the vehicles, these two *chōnai* have opted for greater flexibility over the complete demise of their erstwhile traditions.

Another potential threat is posed by current employment priorities. The *matsuri* was originally scheduled as a brief interlude in the agricultural calendar, preceding a time of particularly heavy labor. Most working adults are now employed outside the agricultural sector and have trouble taking time off from their jobs to devote themselves to the *matsuri.* Many have found jobs outside the town, particularly in Takayama, where managers are not inclined to grant leave for attending a local festival. As a result, participation in traditional gatherings like the *atofuki* celebration has been steadily declining over the past few decades. Though scattered groups of friends and relatives still go independently to the old location on Sakakigaoka for a picnic lunch, the custom of *atofuki* no longer exists as an organized event. This is particularly regrettable for the women, as it nullifies a well-deserved expression of gratitude for all their hard work.[6] The reason most often given for abandoning the custom is that people simply no longer have the time to spend a leisurely afternoon under the cherry blossoms—at least not on a workday. Contemporary employment patterns lead one to ponder: have the old patriarchs been allowed to retain their authority in directing the *matsuri* through respect for their age and experience, or simply because they have more free time than younger residents?

Recent demographic changes have also affected communal solidarity within neighborhoods. This has partly to do with movement away from the interior to the surrounding rice paddies where there is room to build. Again, the boundaries of the outer *taigumi,* particularly Seiryū (Tonomachi), Kirin (Lower Ichinomachi), and Ryū-teki (Lower Ninomachi) have been greatly expanded to include the scattered houses located out among the paddies. The new boundaries draw in different kinds of people in contrast with the old established households of the interior. Even without this influx of new members, however, increasing occupational diversity produces a similar effect. Tonomachi, for example, used to be heavily populated by agricultural households and in many ways exhibited the insular solidarity of a farm village. Now, however, several of its residents work as salaried employees outside the town. Different occupations foster different interests—differing points of view, making the neighborhood far less cohesive. It is said that during the postwar era Tonomachi could muster the votes necessary to elect two at-large town council members from within its own territory. Now it can manage only one at best.

Many of these demographic factors are reflected in the most recent changes in the *matsuri.* In Chapter 4, I described the *mikoshi* procession as requiring three days to complete and making over sixty stops on its circuit through town. In 1996, however, the number of stops was reduced to around twenty so that the same route could be covered in a day and a half. The procession begins on the afternoon of April 19, just as before, but now it is completed by 5:00 p.m. on April 20, and the deity is returned to the shrine that same afternoon. The entire *matsuri* has thus been condensed into two days, allowing the townspeople to return to their normal activities one day earlier. The effect on tourism is minimal, as most visitors depart following the *yatai* performances on the afternoon of April 20.

I chose not to amend the earlier description for two reasons. The first is that this condensed version of the *mikoshi* procession was presented to the people as a trial arrangement, leaving open the possibility of returning to the original agenda should the new one prove unsatisfactory. The second is to underscore the fact that ritual and tradition are ongoing processes—the *matsuri* continues to change even as this book goes to press. In any case, with less than one-third as many stopping points, the people must now bring their contributions to the nearest point the day before. Individual household contributions are consolidated, then dumped into the offering cart when the procession comes around.

The *okoshi daiko* has been subjected to scheduling changes of its own. In 1994 the drum structure's launch was moved ahead from 10:00 to 9:00 on the night of April 19. This caused a great deal of complaining among the townspeople, as it left too little time to get ready after the evening parade of *yatai.* The following year the launch was returned to 10:00 p.m., but in 1997 was scheduled for 9:30.

One other change has been the recent appearance of a new *tsuke daiko* team—that representing Miyamoto-*gumi* of the Kamikita neighborhood, located at the base of the shrine. As mentioned earlier, Miyamoto-*gumi* had never participated in the boisterous drum ritual; its role was confined to escorting the deity down from the shrine at the beginning of the *matsuri,* then back up again at the conclusion. With increasing emphasis on the *matsuri* as an economic resource, and the rousing drum as its principal attraction, sponsoring a *tsuke daiko* team affords Miyamoto-*gumi* a more prominent role. On a more practical level, with the town's population shifting out away from the center, Kamikita now has a sufficient number of young men to field a decent team.

Whose *Matsuri* Is It?

The emphasis on promoting tourism has created friction between administrative personnel, who advocate continued economic development, and the shrine officers, who insist on preserving the *matsuri* as a religious performance. In 1991, for example, some conflict arose during the making of the film for the new museum. The film crew had asked that certain accommodations be made to facilitate the project. Along part of the route they wanted to attach a small platform and camera to the rear of the drum structure to record the charge of the *tsuke daiko* and their clash with the rear guard. Some of the shrine officers objected that the *okoshi daiko* was a sacred rite *(shinji),* and that placing a camera anywhere on the drum structure would violate its integrity. They complained that the filming was taking first priority and that the religious essence of the event was being ignored. A compromise was finally reached when the town hall offered to build a mock-up of the rear portion of the framework, complete with its own set of wheels underneath. The camera could then be placed upon the mock-up and dragged along behind without threatening the sanctity of the actual framework.

I was participating as a member of my own neighborhood team that night as, with cameras rolling, the *tsuke daiko* advanced upon the mock-up in the first attack. The action was, if anything, more exuberant than usual. Participants were acutely aware that the moment was being captured on film for posterity—not to mention conspicuous display in the museum.

After this initial charge, the mock-up was disconnected and the drum structure allowed to proceed as usual—for the moment, that is. As previously mentioned, the high point of the *okoshi daiko* is when it passes through Ichinomachi, as the street is lined on both sides by well-preserved old buildings, including the two big *sake* brewing households of Kaba and Watanabe. It is also at this point that all the *tsuke daiko* teams converge upon the drum structure at once. This creates an ideal opportunity for taking pictures, and most of the photographs used to publicize the *okoshi daiko* are shot at this juncture. The Sony film makers therefore positioned themselves throughout Ichinomachi for what would perhaps be the most important scene. To ensure that the cameras were able to capture all the action, the film crew requested that the big drum pass twice through the same neighborhood—there were to be two takes, in other words. This resulted in an unprecedented occurrence—the entire procession backing up to the end of the street for a second pass. Participants and onlookers alike complained that the whole affair was being staged for the cameras.

Similar objections have been raised in relation to the ritual being launched from the central plaza adjacent to the new museum. Until only a few years ago the *okoshi daiko* began and ended in the directing neighborhood's territory, with the starting point rotating from one year to the next. Now, however, the drum was to be launched from the same place every year, lending a much more generic feel to the event. Tonomachi and Mukaimachi initially refused to go along with the decision, insisting on performing the launch from within their own territories. Notably, these are the two neighborhoods that are big enough to constitute entire *okoshi daiko* groups by themselves. With only one component leader they are able to present a unified front toward the other sectors—particularly the interior merchant and artisan-filled neighborhoods of Ichinomachi and Ninomachi.

Tonomachi eventually relented after some cajoling (and promises of certain concessions) from the town hall, and launched the *okoshi daiko* from the central plaza for the first time in 1996. Mukaimachi, on the other hand, has been more adamant. When its turn last came to serve as director in 1995, its leaders agreed to start off from the central plaza, but insisted on finishing back in their home territory in keeping with the former custom. This was not as crucial to the town hall, as few tourists were expected to remain to the very end at around 2:00 a.m.

The matter of starting and ending points may seem rather trivial. It must be noted, however, that Mukaimachi has always been somewhat marginalized due to its location across the river, so that keeping the festival activities in its own territory has greater symbolic importance. As for Tonomachi, its initial resistance is not unlike the expression of *kujō* (resentment) described in previous chapters. Here, again, the *matsuri* was being employed as a negotiating tool—an instrument of agency used by the actors in procuring certain advantages. A posture of stubborn resistance is a rational ploy to adopt, considering that favorable conditions can be demanded for ceasing to resist.

In recent years a new form of conflict has emerged—one pitting the actors against the tourists who have come in droves to witness the spectacle. The latter now constitute such a major presence that they often interfere with the *okoshi daiko*'s progress.[7] In the old days it was the police station or some unpopular merchant's house that periodically got smashed. Now the more likely targets are the automobiles of hapless tourists who park in the wrong alley or blunder into the midst of the action. The combination of alcohol and adrenalin, the sound of the drum, and the self-fulfilling legacy of Furukawa *yancha* create a volatile atmosphere in which hostilities "explode" when ignited by certain stimuli.

While participating in the *tsuke daiko* again in 1992 I had the opportunity to witness the effects of such stimuli. It was shortly after the ritual began, and our team, along with several others, lay in waiting at a darkened side street for the big drum to pass. Then we charged out, fighting our way to the fore and eventually reaching the back of the drum structure. We were able to remain there for what must have been a few hundred meters before yielding to pressure from behind and veering off into a narrow alley. Along one side of the alley was a row of parked cars. These obviously belonged to outsiders, as local people would have known better than to park in such a vulnerable location. Emotions were so high from the charge that some of the young men began smashing the row of empty vehicles with their fists, elbows, and feet before cooler heads intervened. As we ran off into the night toward the next point of ambush I looked back to see that the cars had their sides caved in and their windows shattered.

But the animosity directed toward tourists ultimately derives from a deeper form of conflict, in which the defenders of *matsuri* tradition struggle against efforts to package the event as a marketable commodity. Again, the issue is: who controls the *matsuri?* Many residents object to what they see as a tendency to give economic development first priority, while cultural tradition takes second place. They are frustrated with a scenario that increasingly places them in the role of entertainers for the tourists. Emphasis on economic development is obscuring the underlying religious significance of the *matsuri,* not to mention its social structural (and antistructural) aspects.

Town officials, however, should not be portrayed as simple profiteers. They are genuinely concerned about ensuring a vibrant future for the town, and that requires employment opportunities for its young people. Economic success has brought widespread prosperity to urban and rural Japanese alike. Even so, rural towns and villages still lag well behind the larger cities in terms of economic development, and young people continue their flight from the countryside, searching for opportunities in the more densely populated areas. Part of the rationale behind the government's "native place-making" program is that it will help reduce regional economic disparities, making the rural areas more attractive places to live and eventually resulting in a more equitable population distribution. Thus local attractions like the *matsuri* have become economic resources in the battle to stem the flow of young people to the cities.

Tourism is, of course, a service industry, and the supplier must cater to consumer preferences. During the 1970s, the national railways mounted a massive "Discover Japan" campaign to encourage domestic tourism and coincident use of the rail network. Its advertisements were aimed at the "Westernized" urban masses, urging them to rediscover their cultural heritage through travel by train. Following the assertions of renowned folklorist/ethnographer Yanagita Kunio, the campaign portrayed the Japanese rural landscape as the ancient repository of native tradition (Ōta 1993:392–394, Ivy 1995:29–65). One needed merely to board a train to be transported back in time to a simpler, more meaningful way of life.

Local *matsuri* were prime candidates for this kind of image production. With their communal ethos, dynamic folk performances, and worship of mysterious ancestral deities, they harked back to Japan's tribal roots, before the encroachment of "foreign" ideas. Attending *matsuri* thus became a kind of sentimental pilgrimage for the urban masses, seeking to reclaim the spiritual and emotional attachments they found lacking in their own lives (Robertson 1995: 92–93).

As is clear from the preceding pages, however, the assumption that *matsuri* represent static images of the past is mistaken. The irony is compounded by the fact that, as Kelly (1990:70) observes, the lives and attitudes of ruralites in contemporary Japan are "in many ways indistinguishable from those of the . . . tourists." Rural inhabitants seek to shed their yokel image by embracing the increasingly westernized values and preferences of the urban center. Urban dwellers, on the other hand, while disparaging the countryside as backward, nevertheless pine for the spirituality and communalism it is thought to embody.

This imaginative yearning on both sides for the aesthetic qualities of the other is illustrated by the following episode. During the late 1980s, a group of local music enthusiasts established the Hida–Furukawa International Music Festival (Hida Furukawa Kokusai Ongakusai) as an annual event, and managed to persuade several highly regarded musicians and composers to perform in Furukawa. In 1991, they offered an award of appreciation to contemporary composer Takemitsu Tōru and invited him to visit Furukawa. Takemitsu took a liking to the town and made several return visits, one of them during the *matsuri*. He later based an orchestral composition on the images evoked in him by the *okoshi daiko*. The composition was entitled "Spirit Garden" *(Seirei no Niwa)*, and was performed for the first time in July 1994 by the Tokyo Metropolitan Symphony Orchestra. Five busloads of Furukawa residents travelled to Tokyo to attend the premiere. A promotional leaflet for the performance bears the following quotation from Takemitsu, which echoes the nostalgic longing for tradition alluded to above:

In the town of Hida-Furukawa there is a spring festival held every year for three days on April 19, 20, and 21. In particular, it is famous for the name *"okoshi daiko."*

When I received the Hida-Furukawa Grand Music Award, I began visiting this town whenever I had the opportunity. From the first I was enchanted by this small Hida mountain town and the people who lived there. But above all, when I experienced its annual *matsuri* I became thoroughly captivated. The mixture of violence and refinement was highly unique, and the composed and sonorous booming of the great drum is something I will never forget.

That this kind of sacred space still exists upon the earth is something I feel to be priceless and irreplaceable. That is why this work, commissioned by the town of Furukawa, is entitled "Spirit Garden."

The composition was studio-recorded and appeared on compact disk the following year. The music itself is mysterious and wistful, hardly evoking the kind of raucous dynamism associated with the *okoshi daiko.* Nevertheless, the distinctive beat of the great drum is readily discernable at two places in the composition, rendered by orchestral timpani.

Kelly (1986:612) describes the way a local *matsuri* in northeastern Japan was "discovered" by the media and elevated to the status of a national treasure. This led to an incursion of outside spectators and a negative reaction by local residents. But there were also positive aspects in terms of raising the area's self-image. In particular, national exposure sparked a renewed interest among local youth in learning and passing on their traditions. Likewise, in Furukawa the throng of spectators gets in the way, but nevertheless serves as visible confirmation that the actors themselves are engaged in an important event. It conveys to the townspeople that their *matsuri,* and by extension their community as a whole, are somehow distinctive and worthy of all the attention. This is one way in which outsiders are drawn into the purposes of the local population—by confirming its sense of legitimacy and self-worth.

Several authors have challenged the notion that tourism destroys the "authenticity" of cultural phenomena. Kelly (1987:15) suggests that "[w]hat we should be looking for is not the authentic performance but arguments *about* what an authentic performance is." Ōta

(1993) likewise contends that authenticity is ascribed by the actors themselves, and should not be measured in terms of adherence to past patterns. He suggests that what the local people create in the present should be considered "as authentic as any other cultural elements documented in ethnographies" (1993:408). In addressing the condition of the "folk performing arts" *(minzoku geinō)* in Japan, Hashimoto (1996) adds that rigid adherence to past patterns limits the subjectivity and creativity of the performers. He views tourism as a positive influence for generating new forms and traditions, quoting one informant as saying that "[i]f we did [our ritual] the same as in the old days, it would gradually die out" (Hashimoto 1996:186).

Indeed, without the support of the tourist industry and the interest it engenders, many cultural links with the past would already have disappeared. Furukawa's "Three-Temple Pilgrimage" held in mid-January, for example, had been discontinued for several years during and after the Second World War. Through the impetus of promoting tourism, however, it was revived in 1977. As for the spring *matsuri,* the practice of adorning the *yatai* with paper lanterns for an evening pass through town was also abandoned during the Second World War. It was resurrected only in 1968.

The lanterns themselves are another example. Most paper lanterns in Japan are now mass-produced in factories. The hand-made variety are highly admired for their quality and durability, but are much more expensive to obtain. Virtually all of the paper lanterns employed during Furukawa's *matsuri* are hand-made by a single artisan located in Lower Ichinomachi. Each is adorned with custom lettering to identify the neighborhood and/or role of the bearer (see Chapter 4).

A related product is the so-called *"wa-rōsoku,"* or "Japanese-style candle," made by hand from wax extracted from the fruit of the *haze* tree *(Rhus succedanea).* Such candles are attributed with various qualities that supposedly make them superior to the "Western" (paraffin) version, and are highly prized as gifts and souvenirs. Most of the paper lanterns used during the Furukawa *matsuri* are illuminated from within by these hand-made candles, the only exceptions being those adorning the *yatai* (which are now illuminated by battery-powered light bulbs). The lanterns are equipped with clever swivelling holders inside to keep the candles in upright position even when the lanterns themselves are tilted. This is the type used by the "main guard" while riding upon the drum platform. Again, only one traditional candle-making household remains in Furukawa; it has been located in Upper Ichinomachi for many generations and, thanks to the tourist trade, will continue into the next generation as well.

Without events like the annual *matsuri* and Three-Temple Pilgrimage, these traditional industries could no longer survive. Nor would there be any incentive to continue practicing the *shishi* dance, flute and drum music, mechanical puppetry, and other artistic traditions the *matsuri* entails. The same might be said of the neighborhood *yatai,* with their intricate carvings and tapestries, elegant lacquerwork, and other embellishments. Every year maintenance costs for each vehicle range between 300,000 and 400,000 yen (2400–3200 dollars). It is not just the vehicles themselves, however, but the thick, clay-walled structures *(kura)* in which they are stored that cost so much to build and maintain. Part of the income from the tourist industry is now used to offset these costs, thereby relieving the burden on neighborhood residents.[8]

Many of Furukawa's citizens dislike the packaging and promotion of their festival as a marketable commodity, not to mention a similar process that threatens to transform the very streets of their town into a living folk museum. They see, however, that their economic situation has vastly improved as a result of these efforts, making objections more difficult to broach. As in the past, opinions are often divided along occupational categories. The merchants generally favor any effort to draw customers into the area, while the "farmers" (virtually all of whom now combine agriculture with other sources of income) are more concerned with preserving traditions.

Looking back over the past sixty or seventy years, my informants consistently remark that while the basic structure of the *matsuri* has persisted, the old enthusiasm is missing from today's event. The prewar *matsuri,* they recall, was more highly animated by the unruliness of *"yancha."* The *tsuke daiko* were more aggressive, with team members determined to fight their way forward and place their own neighborhood drum upon the main platform. Though the ritual was simpler than today's grand spectacle, my informants recall that the overall effect was somehow more awe-inspiring.[9] There were fewer street lights at the time, so at night the town was almost completely dark, and although the *chōchin* procession leading the way before the drum was more modest than at present, the candlelight emanating from the paper lanterns created a mysterious and powerful effect. Now the brave *okoshi daiko,* they say, has become a mere spectacle performed largely for the benefit of the tourists.

While such a transformation is perhaps regrettable from the perspective of a previous generation of participants, it is in a larger sense only the most recent phase of an ongoing developmental process, whereby the ritual is adapted to the changing needs of its practitioners. The aggressiveness emerged during a time of political oppression and economic inequities. These have now been largely overcome. As a tourist attraction, the *okoshi daiko* is capable of drawing additional income into the community, which is much more in keeping with present concerns.

CHAPTER 10

RITUAL, CHANGE, AND AGENCY

It is apparent from the preceding chapters that the Furukawa *matsuri* has undergone many significant changes
throughout the course of its development. The *matsuri* has
been used at various times by its participants to commune with the
supernatural, establish or strengthen interpersonal relations, generate and preserve a sense of collective identity, garner prestige, further political ambitions, assert or reaffirm the authority of the local
elite and/or the state, challenge that authority, seek retribution for
perceived injustices, relieve tensions through cathartic expenditure
of energy, settle old scores, and stimulate economic development.
The *matsuri* remains a vital part of the community because it has
been flexible in responding to present needs. This brings to mind
Bestor's (1989:49) assessment of his Tokyo neighborhood, which
"continues to evolve and change in response to contemporary conditions; it is neither an ancient nor a static inheritance from the
past."

Yet it would be misleading to assume that the nature and direction of change is entirely independent of historical patterns. As
Smith (1989:722) has stated in assessing scholarly attempts to
understand the weight of cultural tradition on contemporary Japanese society:

We were wrong to think that culture is either immutable or
chimerical and that tradition is limited to beliefs and practices
of long standing. We were equally wrong to think that contemporary institutions are either legacies from the past or

innovative ruptures with it. Rather, they are the current moment through which past is linked to present, and present to future. How they are linked, and by what forces, are the central questions of cultural analysis.

Likewise, the changes in the *matsuri* did not occur as bold new introductions, fully formed, but as alterations—mutations, if you will—in a previously existing structure. The *okoshi daiko,* for example, began as an innocuous preliminary to the main festivities. Later it developed into an expression of opposition against certain sociopolitical and economic imperatives. Most recently it is being marketed as a tourist attraction—the linchpin in an effort to "revitalize" the community.

It is important to note, however, that the *matsuri* as a whole engages the participation of thousands of people representing a varied range of interests, and is beyond the power of any particular segment to monopolize completely. Bell (1992:186) observes that while ritual requires adherence to form, this does not necessarily imply a shared understanding of its symbols. Thus "ritualized practices afford a great diversity of interpretation in exchange for little more than consent to the form of the activities." This allows for what she calls "noncommittal participation" in which individual actors assign different meanings to a single pattern, based on their own interests and perceptions.

In Furukawa, however, it is not just the meaning, but the very form of the ritual that has been altered. Working within the framework of the *matsuri,* it is possible to direct either the performance or the symbols it contains toward certain ends. This is precisely the kind of interplay between structure and agency to which Giddens, Sahlins, Ortner, and others have alluded.

And this, I would argue, is where the true significance of the *matsuri* as a "cultural performance" resides—not in the static repetition of previously existing patterns, but in the strategic quest for influence and control. If the *matsuri* does indeed constitute a microcosm of the sociocultural system as the cultural performance concept suggests, then its annual enactment becomes a crucial period in the sociopolitical and economic lives of the local people—a time to maneuver for more advantageous position. As Bell (1992:195–196) contends, "ritual practices are themselves the very production and negotiation of power relations."

The Furukawa *matsuri* contains two major demonstrations of power—one authoritarian and the other subversive. The religious rituals performed at the shrine and the *mikoshi* procession through the streets of the town became associated with the upper levels of the social hierarchy, acknowledging their privileged positions and linking them into the religio-political ideology being propagated by the central government. The *okoshi daiko,* on the other hand, emerged as a folk response to the officially sanctioned liturgy—a ritual expression of opposition issuing from the ranks of the common people. The *matsuri* as a whole thus represents the clash of two opposing ideologies within the context of a single public forum. During the day the Shinto deity is led through town in a grand procession and treated with great deference by the townspeople, who present offerings of rice and money. At night, however, there is an entirely different kind of procession—the *okoshi daiko.* The drum, too, originates from the shrine and follows roughly the same path through town. Unlike the *mikoshi,* however, it is not welcomed, but rather attacked as if it were an intruder. The Furukawa *matsuri* thus presents contrasting themes of deference and opposition.

Yet to treat the *okoshi daiko* as a ritualized class struggle would be to seriously oversimplify the issue. During my fieldwork I remember being confused that what I saw as an obvious case of conflict between social strata was commonly described by my informants as inter-neighborhood rivalry. Gradually I came to recognize that socioeconomic distinctions are imbedded in territorial boundaries, as is most clearly illustrated by the contrast between Tonomachi and Ninomachi. Actual conflict is the product of both dimensions, inextricably woven together. Which is predominant depends on one's point of view. Just as I am led by my academic training to see social stratification and resistance, the people themselves are led to overlook such discrepancies by their own cultural preconceptions, which emphasize communality and egalitarianism.

To make matters even more complex, there is a distinct generational dimension to the conflict as well. The principle antagonists during the *okoshi daiko* are young men who have not yet entered the upper ranks in the established sociopolitical hierarchy and are thus denied access to greater channels of influence. They must resign themselves to waiting until the older members relinquish control; in fact the elders may be seen as impediments to upward mobility. Note that the main guard who ride upon the drum structure are distinguishable by their advancing years as well as their special status, and that the *tsuke daiko* that challenge them are wielded by younger men. It is these young men who are most likely to display rebellious tendencies, not merely as a manifestation of their youthful vigor but also because they have less invested in the status quo. It is significant in this regard that the impetus for resurrecting the *okoshi daiko* after the Second World War came from the young men of the town —older residents apparently being content to let the whole thing lapse into oblivion.[1]

At its core, however, the *okoshi daiko* is not simply a rebellion against the dominant elite, nor the jural authority of aging patriarchs, but the ideal of social harmony itself—that one must sublimate his or her personal desires and ambitions in conforming to the expectations of the community as a whole. On the surface Furukawa appears to be a peaceable, harmonious community, but competitive passions seethe underneath. This is demonstrated by the efforts of individual neighborhoods to outdo one another in *yatai* construction and the institution of the lottery and stamp-affixing ceremonies to ensure strict adherence to the prescribed order. The *okoshi daiko* is merely the most blatant expression of such animosities.

Thus, despite my emphasis on the transformation of the *okoshi daiko* following the Meiji Restoration, it would be misleading to assume that disturbances were absent from the *matsuri* prior to that time. Nor were the integrative and oppositional elements so neatly divided into day and night as they are in the modern version. Rebellious tendencies were present early on, as is evident in the expression of grievances during the premodern *yatai* procession. Later they were suppressed, only to reemerge at night in the form of the *okoshi daiko*. This ritualized expression of conflict then began to escalate, eventually overshadowing the main event. The preceding chapters have attempted to explain both the suppression and escalation by relating them to larger historical patterns.

Tradition and Agency

During my fieldwork in Furukawa a Shinto priest from a neighboring village mentioned to me one afternoon that, though the form of religious customs may be passed down faithfully from generation to generation, the meaning behind them is often forgotten, and most participants go through the motions largely unaware of their original significance. On the surface his comment echoes the standard view of ritual as repetitive behavior, in which people engage through simple force of habit. On further reflection, however, the comment suggests the means whereby ritual functions as an adaptive mechanism. When the original meaning is lost and only the pattern remains, the participants are free to interpret the movements in ways that are most relevant to their immediate circumstances. It is expedient, therefore, that the original meaning of a ritual is forgotten or obscured, as this lends the ritual greater adaptive potential.

Jennings (1982:117) describes ritual "as a way of coming to know, that is, as a way of searching for and discovering knowledge." By intently repeating an established pattern of movements, the actor "discovers" their inherent meaning. From Jennings' perspective, the performance of ritual does not necessarily depend upon preconceived knowledge; rather, it is through the performance itself that knowledge is gained. Ritual thus serves as a pedagogical device. Adopting Turner's (1974:13–14) idiom, it might be said that participants used the "liminal interim" of the *okoshi daiko* as an opportunity for discovery, revealing not only the conditions of their existence, but the means whereby these conditions might be transformed.

The *okoshi daiko* conforms to a model proposed by Dirks (1988: 856) for explaining the development of annual rituals of conflict, which he defines as "rites or periods of celebration that call for one segment of a community to speak or act antagonistically toward another." This definition accurately reflects the confrontational nature of the *okoshi daiko,* as neighborhood teams vie against one another as well as the director in attacking the drum structure. Rituals of conflict generally manifest themselves as annual events; Dirks examines their incidence worldwide in order "to elaborate a theory of annual rituals of conflict that both explains and predicts their occurrence" (1988:856).

Statistical analysis of cross-cultural data leads Dirks to two basic conclusions. First, "groups prone to imposing conformity across the widest spectrum of action are those in which rituals of conflict are most likely to be found" (1988:858). This is particularly relevant to the present study in that emphasis on cooperative behavior and subordinating one's individual concerns to the interests of the group are widely considered important distinguishing features of Japanese society. Furthermore, pressures to conform were particularly heavy during the early to mid-Meiji period, when a new political ideology was being imposed upon the people with all the pressures the central government could bring to bear in ensuring its propagation.

Dirks' second conclusion links rituals of conflict with seasonal food shortages: "Peoples whose annual cycles include periods of food scarcity and starvation are more likely than others to celebrate yearly rites containing some sort of agonistic expression" (1988: 861). Lack of food is no longer a problem in the Hida region. It was, however, an ever-present concern throughout the Tokugawa era (when grievances first came to be expressed during the *matsuri*) and on into the early Meiji period (when the *okoshi daiko* developed as a challenge to authority). In any case, Dirks (1988:866) concedes that not all rituals of conflict occur in areas prone to seasonal food shortages and allows the possibility that other stress-producing factors might be involved. The crises that periodically afflicted Furukawa: devastating fires, epidemics—even oppressive administrative policies—could easily be placed in this category.

Perhaps most significantly, Dirks acknowledges "the propensity for rituals, as they evolve toward more polished and specialized communication devices, to drift free of their original stimuli and assume new functions" (1988:866). This correlates with the use of ritual as an instrument of human agency. The elite, for example, employed the *matsuri* to demonstrate their generosity and acknowledge their privileged positions. The "common people," likewise, expressed their opposition by escalating what was once a rather insignificant feature of the same *matsuri* into a wild and rebellious demonstration of their collective power. In the present day the townspeople are responding to the need for economic development —again through the ritual medium of the *matsuri*.

This kind of mutability has significant methodological implications for the historical ethnographer. Scott's (1990) concept of a "hidden transcript" warns of the dangers of placing too much faith in official versions of what happened. Yet relying solely on informant accounts or local interpretations can be equally misleading. This has little to do with simple ignorance or deceptiveness on the part of the local people; nor does it relate to the existence in ritual of "latent functions" of which the participants themselves are largely unaware. It derives more from the participants' immediate needs, and their use of tradition to fulfill them. Recovering the objective truth about a ritual's former condition and how it has changed over time is only a problem for the social scientist; it holds minimal interest for the actors themselves. They are more concerned with placing their ritual into some meaningful frame of reference in relation to their present circumstances. To this end their own folk explanations are usually quite sufficient, whether historically accurate or not.

There is an ironic trade-off here between change and continuity in the passing on of tradition. It is necessary for the people of Furukawa to maintain some sense of continuity with the past in order to preserve their own cultural identity, but it is equally necessary for them to remain adaptable in the face of changing conditions. Local traditions such as those contained in the *matsuri* lend the requisite sense of continuity; yet if they remain too rigid or specific they run the risk of becoming irrelevant. The solution has been to tailor tradition to present needs, then project the alterations back into the past, thereby lending them greater legitimacy and appeal.

This is illustrated by a number of well-known ink brush paintings by local artist Fuse Naoji (1891–1966). One of the paintings is displayed inside the meeting hall at Ketawakamiya Shrine; another hangs in the reception area of the Buddhist temple Juraku-*ji,* which is located in the nearby hamlet of Taie; a third adorns one of the guest rooms at a local inn (see Figure 26). The paintings themselves are nearly identical: they all show a mass of rather impish-looking characters participating in the *okoshi daiko.* The scene is quite familiar from a contemporary point of view: the main drum is surrounded by lantern-bearing guards; two men sit back-to-back astride the drum and beat it with sticks; *tsuke daiko* team members struggle enthusiastically toward the rear of the drum structure, and some of them appear to be trying to force it to the ground. Unlike today's event, however, the participants are barefoot and clad only in loin cloths. More significantly, they all wear their hair in the *"chonmage"* style—long, but with the crown of the head shaved and the remaining hair drawn back to form a topknot. This was the style worn by men during the Tokugawa period; the implication is that the ritual as such dates back to that time. As explained in Chapter 7, however, the drum beaters did not begin riding atop the drum until around the early Taishō (1912–1925) period, and the *okoshi daiko* did not exist as this kind of mass demonstration of rebelliousness prior to the Meiji Restoration.

This demonstrates how misplaced assumptions are transformed into "facts." They are printed up in the literature and passed on to future generations, becoming ever more firmly entrenched in the local tradition. After a time no one bothers to question them. They therefore constitute a kind of truth in the sense of representing widely shared opinion. Thus while "time-honored" traditions are commonly assumed to have been transmitted faithfully from past generations to the present day, they are in reality the products of continual change and reinterpretation. In fact, it is this adaptive potential that explains their longevity, for without it they would eventually be abandoned for lack of interest.

Here is another area of overlap between history and anthropology; indeed, "invented tradition" is a topic that has received significant attention in both disciplines (Hobsbawm and Ranger 1983; Vlastos 1998). The term itself is a bit misleading, however, in that it tends to equate invention with deception. It also implies that "invented" traditions exist in opposition to authentic or genuine ones. As various authors have suggested, *all* tradition is in some sense invented—not only invented, but routinely modified, reinterpreted, and transformed. This in no way detracts from its functional importance; rather, it lends tradition even greater significance in terms of social process. That tradition is mutable is altogether fitting and proper; how else could it continue serving a useful purpose in contemporary society? The maintenance of "tradition" is a matter neither of careful preservation nor of pure invention, but of tailoring the available cultural resources to present needs.

But what of the anthropologist interested in the use of ritual as an instrument of sociopolitical change? To this end the folk explanations appear to be of little value because they fail to describe actual

Figure 26. Ink painting of the *okoshi daiko,* by local artist Fuse Naoji. Photograph by Shirakawa Shūhei, courtesy of Yassan.

conditions and occurrences. The problem is usefully illustrated by the two competing explanations for the origin of the *okoshi daiko.* The "wild animal" version is dubious in light of certain biogeographical and historical cross-referents. It has nevertheless been embraced by the local people, making it difficult to dismiss as an ethnographic resource. Rather than focusing on whether the story is historically accurate, it might be instructive to consider why it became so popular. It apparently represents something its adherents feel to be inherently "true," if not strictly factual.

According to the story, the drum was intended to ward off wild beasts during a late-night procession through the forest to the shrine. It is obviously related to other examples of drums being used to guard against danger or expel evil influences, and is thus congruent with the larger theme of purification. The story also conveys an appealing sense of introducing civilization and culture into the darkness of the wilds, thereby establishing order out of chaos. It could further be seen as a metaphor for expelling unwelcome outside influences—the police, the military, the tourists.[2] Thus the story is "true" in the manner of myth or ritual—a metaphorical expression of existing realities.

In fact the folk tradition may itself be seen as an interesting exercise of human agency. For example, many of my informants alluded to the use of the massive drum structure as a means of delivering a social sanction. This undoubtedly occurred, particularly before the wheels were attached; but how often, when, and to whom, specifically? The answers to such questions are far less forthcoming.[3] In a sense, the oral tradition has become more effective than the actual occurrence. Either the drum structure or the *tsuke daiko* may occasionally strike a building purely by accident. It is in the interests of the community at large, however, to foster the impression that the contact was deliberate. This is particularly useful for the "havenots" in seeking to offset certain economic and political inequities. Whether the drum intentionally crashes into someone's house is immaterial—it is *said* that it does. The saying itself performs the "levelling" function, prompting the wealthy to share their good fortune, the arrogant or contentious to make amends. This is what leads my informants to look at old photographs of Ninomachi storefronts shrouded with boards and exclaim, "See? They put those there because they were getting hit all the time."

The power of oral tradition leads to the related issue of self-fulfilling prophecies. The young men of Furukawa behave aggressively during the *matsuri* because it is *expected* of them, in keeping with the tradition of Furukawa *yancha*. The aggression is partly why tourists are drawn to the *matsuri* in such numbers; and, ironically, it is now occasionally turned upon the tourists themselves. The *yancha* spirit, ritually instilled through the *okoshi daiko*, spills over into the conduct of everyday living. This is attested to by the reputation Furukawa has acquired in the eyes of its neighbors. Such a reputation may hold certain benefits in negotiating with other communities, as it conveys the impression that Furukawa is not to be taken lightly. This is perhaps why "Furukawa *yancha*" is so widely celebrated in the local folklore.

Similarly, did Umemura's given name "Hayami" oblige him to move too quickly in implementing his reforms? Was Tajika Rokusaburō able to gain political support for his household by changing their name to Honda, thereby presenting them as the legitimate heirs to a long and prestigious lineage? Was the drum ritual more intimidating as an *"okoshi daiko"* ("rousing drum") than as a *"mezamashi daiko"* ("wake-up drum")? As mentioned previously, describing a thing in terms of a certain condition helps bring that condition into being. This perhaps explains the ancient Japanese emphasis on *"kotodama"*—the magical efficacy attributed to the utterance of words (see Kitagawa 1987:121, 154; Ebersole 1989:19–22).

The propensity for inventing tradition could just as easily be applied to the ethnographer's own perceptions. In considering the *okoshi daiko,* for example, the form assumed by the two young men who position themselves back-to-back atop the drum seemed to me to be curiously reminiscent of the mythical Ryōmen Sukuna figure. As mentioned in Chapter 3, the *Nihon shoki* describes Ryōmen Sukuna as having ruled the Hida region before its subjugation by Emperor Nintoku. This image, I reasoned, could have been resurrected as a symbol of local identity in opposition to the growing authority of the central government. As an ethnographer seeking to decode the symbolism inherent in the ritual, I very much wanted this to be true. I began raising the possibility with my informants, hoping for a response to the effect that "Ah yes, I remember hearing from my grandfather that the two young men were originally placed back-to-back upon the drum to effect the image of Ryōmen Sukuna." Unfortunately, however, not one of my informants acknowledged anything more than an intriguing similarity. Neither is there any written evidence supporting a direct link.[4]

Even so, the symbolic relevance of the Ryōmen Sukuna image

cannot be ignored. He supposedly had two faces aligned in opposite directions, and could thus face both forward and backward at the same time. Multiple faces indicate uncommon wisdom and are a fairly standard image in Asian religious symbolism. Ryōmen Sukuna is also an appropriate caricature for the local elite, who both exploited the people and contributed to their welfare. The guardian deity itself is attributed with both a gentle *(nigimitama)* and a violent *(aramitama)* nature. The *okoshi daiko* can perhaps be seen in the same way, as enacted by the two young men who sit atop the drum. One faces forward toward the docile procession of lantern-bearing townspeople, the other to the rear where all the conflict occurs. Moreover, it may be recalled that Hida straddles the drainage divide between two major watersheds, one flowing south toward the Pacific Ocean and the other north toward the Japan Sea. In a sense, then, Hida "faces" in two directions, just as does the mythical character. Images such as Ryōmen Sukuna capture the imagination, not simply as tantalizing glimpses into the distant past but as epitomizing symbols of actual relationships and conditions.

Informant Perspectives

The social scientist and the subject people pursue different aims. It is not surprising that their explanations sometimes fail to coincide. It might therefore be interesting to consider how well my interpretations of the symbolism inherent in the *okoshi daiko* correspond with informant opinions. Of the scores of people I talked with during my field research, nearly all shared the opinion that the *matsuri* was a time for engaging in behavior that under ordinary circumstances would be considered inappropriate. Many noted that the *okoshi daiko* was an opportunity for settling old scores, and that fighting was an inevitable element. One senior woman who had lived all her life in Ninomachi recalled seeing many fights occur right outside her front door. She also noted that the house directly across the street was often bashed by the drum structure while her own was left undisturbed. Most informants observed that such violence was much less evident now, with the emphasis on attracting tourists.

When asked what motivated the development of the *okoshi daiko*, the most frequently given answers were (1) that it is an expression of the *yancha* attitude, and (2) that it is a means of relieving stress ("*sutoresu kaishō*"). The explanation generally ended there, with no further speculation on why the *yancha* attitude itself developed, or what generates the tensions that need periodic venting.

One of the parish elders—an enthusiastic participant in the Furu-kawa *matsuri* preservation association—offered the following explanation for the *okoshi daiko*. The townspeople are ordinarily obliged to exercise restraint, suppressing their emotions in the interests of maintaining harmonious social relations. As a result they are unable to express what they truly feel; the rest is kept hidden away inside them. But once a year at *matsuri* time their pent-up emotions are given free reign. The young men in particular emerge half-naked for an evening of drinking and wild revelry in the streets. The *okoshi daiko* involves abandoning the normal social order; on that evening abnormal behavior becomes the rule rather than the exception. The whole affair may thus be seen as a means of relieving tension, a safety valve for suppressed emotions.

This is highly evocative of Gluckman's structural-functionalist explanation for rituals of rebellion, and it is perhaps significant that the informant was himself a member of the local elite. But because this explanation is so similar to the functionalist perspective, it is also subject to similar objections: if the *okoshi daiko* ultimately supported the existing sociopolitical order, why were there so many attempts to suppress it? Why did the townspeople employ the ritual as an opportunity to settle old scores? Why was the violence so often directed toward politically relevant targets?

Few of the local people would characterize their *okoshi daiko* as a symbolic expression of political opposition toward the local elite. They were unanimous, however, in noting that it would have been inconceivable for any member of the old prewar landlord class to help shoulder the drum structure or participate in the *tsuke daiko* forays, and equally inconceivable for ordinary people to ride upon the platform as members of the main guard.[5] Many noted that one had to be among the politically influential *(yūryokusha)* or wealthy *(okanemochi)* to assume the latter role. Senior residents assured me that the inclination to "crush the director" was indeed expressed through various attempts to bring down the drum structure or impede its progress.

Explanations also varied with neighborhood affiliation. Residents of the interior sectors, Ichinomachi and Ninomachi, generally ascribed conflict during the *matsuri* to inter-neighborhood rivalry or personal grudges. Residents of Tonomachi and Mukaimachi, on the other hand, routinely cited resentment toward the wealthy landlords and merchants of the inner neighborhoods as the motivating factor. As previously mentioned, Tonomachi and Mukaimachi were populated by small-owner and tenant farmers.

A senior resident of Mukaimachi recalled that everyone looked forward to the *matsuri* because it was the only time they got to see the big landlords humble themselves. When I asked him to elaborate, he noted that during the *mikoshi* procession the director issued orders and everyone else had to comply. The director controlled everything, so the *yatai* could not move without his permission. When it began to rain, each neighborhood had to seek the director's consent in order to put tarps over their precious *yatai* or get them back into their storehouses. The director might purposely deny permission to a certain neighborhood; then its most prominent citizen would have to go to the director, bowing and grovelling until permission was granted. This was a rare opportunity for some of the less affluent neighborhoods. The informant referred to landlords collectively as the *"sakushu kaikyū"*—"exploitative class."

Regardless of which neighborhood they belonged to, however, my informants consistently used the term "habitual resentment" *(higoro no urami)* to explain the violence expressed during the *okoshi daiko.* "Habitual" resentment refers to that which continually lurks beneath the surface but seldom finds overt expression—except during occasions like the *matsuri.* It can be seen as deriving from ever-present conditions of structural opposition—neighborhood versus neighborhood, poor versus wealthy, younger generation versus established elders, common citizens versus the authorities.

One elderly informant asserted that the *okoshi daiko* developed as a demonstration of power by the people of Furukawa toward the administrative authorities in Takayama. This man had been born and raised in Tonomachi, but later moved to Takayama in pursuing his teaching career; he was thus familiar with attitudes in both localities. The owner of a tavern in Ichinomachi offered a similar explanation, though he claimed the subversive message was originally directed toward the Tokugawa *bakufu.* There was apparently some confusion here, as the *okoshi daiko* did not assume a prominent role in the *matsuri* until after the Meiji Restoration. In any case, both these informants interpreted the ritual as an expression of opposition toward an outside authority.

As mentioned in Chapter 8, I interviewed several of the men involved in the attack on the police station in 1929. A few of them had been arrested and interrogated by the police. I was struck by the enthusiasm with which they recalled the incident—how their eyes lit up and their movements became more animated. There was no mistaking that this to them was a proud moment. Beyond their evident distaste for the prewar police, however, there was little in the way of political commentary. Most saw the incident as an isolated occurrence, with no motivation other than simple revenge.

However, one informant, an elderly man who had worked for the prefectural government in Gifu City for several years but had returned home to Furukawa upon retirement, suggested that the police station incident was motivated by a growing awareness of political oppression. He described the people of Hida prior to the 1900s as simple peasant folk with little experience of the outside world. With the coming of the Taishō (1912–1926) period and the spread of democratic principles, new ideas gradually began to filter in. This is attributable in part to the spread of popular literature: magazines such as *Chūōkōron* (Central Issues), *Kaizō* (Reconstruction), and *Akahata* (Red Banner), as well as the so-called *"enpon"*— reprints of Japanese and world literature sold in serial form for one yen per issue. He noted that this was also a time when many of the young people were engaging in migrant labor *(dekasegi)* in other regions, bringing back new ideas when they returned. The neighboring Shinshū region (now Nagano Prefecture) was, in contrast to Hida, fairly progressive. Its educational system was well-developed, and several notable literary figures emerged from there. He then raised the possibility that the silk factory girls (described earlier), sent to work in Nagano Prefecture, were a major source of new ideas filtering into the Hida region. If so, they might have been partly responsible for growing animosity toward the authorities, which eventually resulted in the 1929 attack.[6]

It is doubtful, however, that the participants themselves were thinking in terms of political insurrection. They were merely reacting to tensions imposed upon them during a period of rapid sociopolitical change. Many of my informants described the people of Furukawa as being kind-hearted and gentle, but said that when pushed too far they had a tendency to "explode" in violent outbursts. This tendency was cited in explaining such phenomena as the Ōhara and Umemura rebellions, attacks on the police station, and the origin of

Furukawa *yancha*. The following are examples of how these various themes are woven together, drawn from independent writers' contributions to local newspapers:

When did the term "Furukawa *yancha*" first originate? . . . If I am correct in my thinking, it can only have been the time of the Umemura Rebellion. . . . In order to understand the Umemura Rebellion, one must first consider the Ōhara Rebellion of one hundred years earlier. Beaten during the Ōhara Rebellion, always hungry—ever hungry, working all year just to grow the tribute rice and having nothing to eat, the resentment and bitterness passed down from generation to generation until it had seeped into one's bones—this is what led to the Umemura Rebellion. It was motivated by the strategic wisdom of the Tenmei [phase of the Ōhara] Rebellion, whereby the peasants, uniting behind reasonable demands, were able to effect the punishment of a bunch of officials under Ōhara Kamegorō. With this Ōhara Rebellion as the groundwork, there was an explosion during the Umemura Rebellion like lighting fire to an oil tank. (Sugata 1975)

Some say Furukawa *yancha* is all about censuring some targeted person during the performance of the *okoshi daiko,* or raising a grievance during the *yatai* procession, but I do not think so. To me it represents the kind of moral courage displayed by the men of Kumamoto;[7] it is like magma in the earth's crust, concealing the potential to sometimes explode. That is what led to the aforementioned attack on the police station, even expanding into rebellions such as the Ōhara and Umemura incidents. (Kaba 1983:10)

The 1929 police station rock-throwing incident is still talked about as an explosion of the resisting temperament among the people of this town. This was indeed a heroic act, and it is possible to discover here the true height of Furukawa *yancha.* The magnificent *yatai* aim at the cultured intellectual, while the brave *okoshi daiko* reveals a healthy sportive spirit.

In other words, Furukawa *yancha* does not refer simply to rough men; it speaks to the determined spirit of the townspeople which, through a combination of originality and craft, aims for something higher than the level of the self. It is the proud heart of a "number two,"[8] a mixture of bitterness and resistance to constantly being placed subordinate to Takayama, even while having dominated the center of Hida culture from ancient times and prospering as a castle and merchant town following the arrival of the Kanamori.[9] (Morishita 1991:6)

Note that all three of these excerpts employ the image of an explosion. The magma metaphor in the second excerpt is particularly revealing. It symbolizes the effort to restrain one's emotions during the course of everyday social interaction in the interests of preserving harmony; it also suggests the possible outcome of such habitual restraint. Many Japanese are reluctant to openly air their grievances due to respect for authority or social pressure to conform. It is not surprising, then, that such grievances periodically "explode." This book has provided evidence that the explosions are not entirely spontaneous—that occasions such as the *matsuri* are intentionally employed in a kind of grass-roots political activism.

Community and Conflict

As mentioned earlier, the use of a drum to announce the advent of the *matsuri* was a fairly common practice in and around the Hida area, but only in Furukawa did it escalate into a full-fledged ritual of conflict. One question that remains to be addressed is why such rebellious sentiments came to be so clearly manifested in Furukawa and not in other communities. Some possible answers have been suggested already. Furukawa possessed the critical mass of residents necessary to perform such events as the *okoshi daiko,* while surrounding villages did not. As both a commercial and agricultural center, it brought people of various occupational categories into frequent interaction; this led to use of the *matsuri* as a public forum for expressing different points of view. Furukawa was small enough, however, to maintain a kind of village intimacy, where even the elite remained accessible to the rest of the community. Within this context the *okoshi daiko* became an important levelling mechanism, admonishing imperious or uncaring attitudes.

The other side of internal cohesiveness, of course, is insularity and underlying resentment of outside intervention. This too is recognizable within the performative structure of the *okoshi daiko* in the challenge posed by the other neighborhoods to the director's intrusive presence. As alluded to in one of the passages above, Furukawa represents the rather unusual case of an established and fairly prosperous town relegated to the status of a "number two." The rousing drum's symbolism was directed not only inward toward the resident elite, but outward toward the locus of cultural and political ascendancy in Takayama.

But there remains yet another, more compelling possibility: that rebellious sentiments *were* being expressed in other forms in other communities but have simply gone unnoticed. The oversight may derive from the failure to apply a historical approach to the development of ritual and the emphasis on *matsuri* performances as means of social integration, augmented by the pervasiveness of the "harmony model." Furukawa is not a hotbed of rebelliousness amidst an otherwise placid rural landscape. Its people are generally cooperative and friendly, seldom displaying the defiant *yancha* attitude for which they are famous. If ritualized conflict has manifested itself in Furukawa, it has very likely done so in other places as well. As noted earlier, *matsuri* are widely recognized opportunities for exhibiting unusual or aggressive behavior, and the so-called *"kenka matsuri,"* or "fighting festival" is a fairly widespread phenomenon. So far, however, the wider sociopolitical implications of such performances have not been sufficiently examined.

Have I, on the other hand, exaggerated the subversive nature of the rousing drum as a ritualized expression of conflict and resistance? A few scholars have recently challenged what they perceive as an overemphasis on resistance as an analytic paradigm, and consequent neglect of other aspects of social interaction like cooperation and harmony. Michael F. Brown (1996), in particular, objects to the moral fervor with which ordinary acts are interpreted as resistance to hegemony. "If there is any hegemony today," he asserts, "it is the theoretical hegemony of resistance" (1996:730).

To overreact by abandoning the resistance approach entirely, however, would be equally ill-advised. This is particularly true in the case of Japan, where the significance of the approach has yet to be fully realized. Furthermore, I suggest that resistance itself entails the creation and maintenance of communal identity, which in turn elicits other patterns like harmony and cooperation.

A sense of common bond does not emerge simply through the existence of inherent similarities, but through the purposeful manipulation of symbolic resources. People must be conditioned to see themselves as a community by focusing on the attributes they share while ignoring those that set them apart from one another. Their unity may be usefully celebrated (and further ingrained) through a symbolic expression of these shared attributes. This may take the form of a legendary figure such as Ryōmen Sukuna; a historical incident such as the Umemura Rebellion; a character trait thought to represent the collective personality such as "Furukawa *yancha;*" or a totemic representation of group unity such as the guardian deity, neighborhood *yatai,* or *tsuke daiko.*

The mere assertion of common interests or affinities, however, is insufficient; communal identity depends on the members emphasizing not simply what they are, but also what they are not. They require an outside referent—a contrasting category against which to assert their own distinctiveness; and the greater that distinction can be made to appear, the more closely related the members will perceive themselves to be.

Such manipulations are particularly effective in the face of a common challenge, typically involving the outside referent itself. This explains why conflict is essential to the maintenance of group identity. Faced with a common challenge from the outside, members are led to focus on their affinities and recognize their dependence on one another. In the examples introduced in previous chapters, the challenge often presented itself as an imposition of authority from the outside, as in the case of the young governor Umemura. But it could just as easily appear in the form of competition among relative equals, as in rivalry between neighborhoods during the *okoshi daiko.* Resistance, in other words, is simply another form of inter-group conflict. If the outside challenge does not exist, it may be imagined or created, explicitly for the purpose of generating greater internal cohesiveness.[10] That is one reason why occasions like the *matsuri* are so important. Its rituals have been coopted by the common people, local elite, and central government, each in pursuit of its own interests.

Ortner (1995:176–177) asserts that resistance studies adopt a simplistic, one-sided viewpoint by focusing almost exclusively on the relationship between the dominant and the dominated:

If we are to recognize that resistors are doing more than simply opposing domination, more than simply producing a virtually mechanical *re*-action, then we must go the whole way.

They have their *own* politics—not just between chiefs and commoners or landlords and peasants but within all the local categories of friction and tension: men and women, parents and children, seniors and juniors; inheritance conflicts among brothers; struggles of succession and wars of conquest between chiefs; struggles for primacy between religious sects; and on and on.

"Going the whole way" presumably entails a return to what anthropologists have traditionally done best—holistic, integrative analysis informed by intensive ethnographic field research. This is a suggestion that I wholeheartedly support.

It might be appropriate to conclude with the following anecdote from my field experiences. Toward the end of my initial stay in Furukawa in 1991, I was invited by the town hall to deliver a lecture to the townspeople on the results of my research. I welcomed the opportunity, as it would allow me to explain what I had been doing there all that time, asking so many questions and making so many requests. I also felt I should be as open and frank with the audience as possible, so I included a brief summary of the theoretical background that had informed my research. One of the ideas I mentioned was Scott's (1985) "weapons of the weak." I explained that the term referred to strategies employed by the common people in dealing with the more powerful forces that impinge upon them, noting that the *okoshi daiko* could perhaps be seen as one such device. At the end of my presentation, one wizened old gentleman stood up in the back and said "These ideas are all well and good, but I would like to remind the *sensei*"[11] (did I detect a note of sarcasm in his use of the term?) "that the people of Furukawa *are not weak.*"

I have often thought about that comment and what it implies. As Ortner (1989) has argued, the so-called "small people" may be at a disadvantage in terms of access to wealth and resources, but they are not hapless victims with little alternative but to be buffeted about by the winds of change. They have the ability to form alliances, negotiate deals, prevail upon their influential neighbors for representation and support, and eventually carve out niches for themselves in the newly established order. Their periodic "explosions" convey a simple warning: "Don't push us too far; don't push us too fast." That is the message reverberating in the beat of the rousing drum.

Notes

Chapter 1. Ethnological and Historical Perspectives

1. Notable attempts to bridge the gap include proponents of the so-called "new history" (Stone 1981:21–23), as represented by the works of Natalie Davis (1975), Emmanuel Le Roy Ladurie (1979), and Robert Darnton (1984). On the anthropology side, Marshall Sahlins (1985), Jean Comaroff (1985), and Maurice Bloch (1986) have all made extensive use of historical materials in their ethnological inquiries. It is significant in terms of the present study that all these works focus at least to some extent on the use of ritual in expressing opposition or negotiating change. Eric Wolf (1982), of course, has been a major advocate for placing local societies within the context of wider political and economic relations.

2. Lukes (1975) foreshadows Bell in describing public ritual as a negotiating process in which individuals or component groups compete with one another in pursuit of their own interests. He suggests that "political rituals can be analysed as part of what has been called the 'mobilization of bias'— [quoting Bachrach and Baratz 1970] that 'set of predominant values, beliefs, rituals and constitutional procedures ("rules of the game") that operate systematically and consistently to the benefit of certain persons and groups at the expense of others.'" Leach (1954:278) had expressed a similar opinion years earlier:

Myth and ritual is a language of signs in terms of which claims to rights and status are expressed, but it is a language of argument, not a chorus of harmony. If ritual is sometimes a mechanism of integration, one could as well argue that it is often a mechanism of disintegration. A proper assimilation of this point of view requires, I would maintain, a fundamental change in the current anthropological concept of social structure.

Turner (1967, 1969, 1974) was able to effect such a change through his delineation of *communitas,* which he conceived as another dimension of social interaction in addition to the purely structural.

3. Indeed, this is an important factor in my own analysis of the Rousing Drum ritual in Furukawa, as will be explained more fully in later chapters.

Chapter 2. *Matsuri* as Communal Ritual

1. Bestor (1989:225) notes that the themes which suffuse social life in his Tokyo neighborhood field site are most clearly revealed in the local Shinto shrine festival, and Robertson (1991:39) describes *matsuri* as "a particularly cogent symbol of and condition for an 'authentic' community." Likewise, Nelson (1996:134) describes the annual shrine festival as epitomizing the local character.

2. I use the term "ideology" not strictly in the critical Marxist sense of coercive dogma or "false consciousness," but in its broader application as a system of belief employed by its proponents to unite, organize, and/or motivate themselves as well as those who fall within their sphere of influence. Geertz (1973:220) notes that "[w]hatever else ideologies may be—projections of unacknowledged fears, disguises for ulterior motives, phatic expressions of group solidarity—they are, most distinctively, maps of problematic social reality and matrices for the creation of collective conscience." He further suggests that "[w]here science is the diagnostic, the critical, dimension of culture, ideology is the justificatory, the apologetic one—it refers [quoting Fallers 1961:677–678] 'to that part of culture which is actively concerned with the establishment and defense of patterns of belief and value'" (1973:231). This by no means limits the use of ideology to an exploitative elite. In a footnote Geertz adds that "[t]he patterns of belief and value defended may be . . . those of a socially subordinate group, as well as those of a socially dominant one, and the 'apology' therefore for reform or revolution" (1973:231).

3. The act of "binding" is referred to as *"musubi,"* which Grapard (1982: 197–198) describes as

trapping the power of the divinity within the sacred space. When the priest invokes a divinity, he first purifies his own body and practices a number of austerities before entering the sacred area to summon down the divinity. He expresses the gratitude and requests of the community and then sends the divinity back. This ritual pattern has changed very little through the centuries.

4. The term *"wasshoi"* has no lexical meaning but is often used during lively activities of this nature and is usually translated "heave-ho!"

The Japanese verb for becoming intoxicated, *"yo-u,"* can also be used in referring to feelings of elation or enchantment, which do not necessarily require the consumption of alcohol.

5. Despite Sonoda's use of the term "stark naked," participants in the *okoshi daiko* do, in fact, wear a modicum of clothing. This will be made apparent in my own description of the event in Chapter 4.

6. In fact Sonoda's distinction between the dignified formality of the shrine rituals and the boisterous revelry of the *okoshi daiko* might best be characterized not as "ritual" versus "festival" but rather as "ceremony" versus "carnival."

7. Readers familiar with Japanese culture may note interesting affinities between Scott's public-transcript-versus-hidden-transcript model and the Japanese distinction between *tatemae* ("facade," referring to one's public or outer demeanor) and *honne* (true or inner feelings, generally kept to oneself or revealed only in the presence of trusted cohorts).

8. Drums are commonly used in rituals intended to drive away evil spirits or pestilence (Yokoyama 1993).

Chapter 3. Territorial and Collective Identities

1. *"Gun"* is a suffix indicating "district" or "county."

2. Such associations are fairly common in Japanese cities, but are usually organized on the basis of prefectural, rather than regional, boundaries.

3. Average annual snowfall in Furukawa is 389 centimeters, though during the past few years total accumulation has been as high as 837 centimeters (Furukawa-chō 1990:4). Snowfall is, of course, much heavier at higher elevations where some of the mountain hamlets are located.

4. Since most of the arable lowlands were devoted to irrigated rice cultivation, the terms "forest" and "mountain" are largely synonymous.

5. Geertz (1963:29–31) and Lansing and Kremer (1993:100) have discussed the importance of dissolved nutrients in irrigation water as a major source of nourishment for rice plants in "wet rice" cultivation.

6. The mountain deity *(yama no kami)* is considered locally to be female.

7. The general term for this arrangement is *"iriai."* The word consists of two characters: *"iri,"* meaning to enter into, and *"ai,"* referring to a meeting or association. Thus the two together imply joint access. The local term for common land, however, is *"nakama no yama"* ("comrades' mountain"), referring to a mountain held collectively.

8. The term *"sukuna"* (literally "embodiment of evil") possibly derives from a biased rendering of *"sukune,"* a title of honor which in ancient times was awarded to influential clan leaders. Thus in retrospect the name switch would help justify the imperial government's actions.

9. The *Man'yōshū* is the earliest extant collection of Japanese poetry, compiled by imperial order during the eighth century.

10. In the last line of the poem, the pronunciation of *"hito,"* meaning "one" or "single," is the same as that for the word meaning "person," implying that the poet has a loved one in mind.

11. The *emishi* are often mentioned in the ancient documents. They are the aboriginal people whom the Yamato displaced in asserting themselves in central Japan. They are considered by some to represent the forerunners of the Ainu.

12. This type of riotous vandalism against houses, shops, and storage facilities is called *"uchikowashi,"* literally "knocking to pieces." It was commonly employed against merchants and usurers during popular uprisings of the Tokugawa period. Extreme cases might involve completely burning down *("yakiharai")* a building, but this was seldom used in towns and cities due to the danger of the fire spreading.

13. Written with the characters for "water" and "void," the more formal reading of the name "Suimu" is "Minashi." The name is presumably an allusion to the shrine's topographical position. Being situated precisely at the divide between two drainage systems, it is figuratively a place "without water." The shrine is also referred to as "Hida Ichinomiya," referring to its status as the highest-ranked shrine in old Hida Province. It is located near a town also bearing the name "Ichinomiya."

14. See, for example, the educational comic book *Nōmin Ikki,* an account of the Ōhara Disturbances designed for elementary school children. It closes with the following passage (Kodama and Yokoyama 1987:136): "The course of history is never short-lived. The pleas of the masses will one day certainly be answered. But persistent effort and sometimes great sacrifices were also involved. Overcoming such obstacles—is this not the duty of people living today?"

15. Called *"kurofune"* ("black ships") because of their black exteriors, these were military gunboats, some of which were powered by steam. This was Japan's first exposure to steam locomotion.

16. I am using the term "patron" here in the sense of a wealthy landowner who uses his power and prestige for the benefit or protection of his less prominent fellow residents. The Japanese word *"danna"* is usually rendered in English as "lord" or "master." In this instance it is roughly equivalent to the term "landlord," though *"danna"* implies a certain level of cultural refinement and a moral obligation to assist less fortunate members of the community.

17. This nostalgic search for *"furusato"* (literally "the old village"), an idealized evocation of the traditional rural community and the values it embodied, has been a major driving force behind the domestic Japanese tourist industry for the past several decades. Further details will be provided in Chapter 9.

18. Takayama's castle was also dismantled following Hida's takeover by the *bakufu* in 1692.

19. The two were a peasant named Mansuke from Ōmura—the collective label for Kamino, Nakano, and Shimono, the three hamlets lying across from Furukawa on the other side of the Miya River—and another named Katō Iemon of Kamikita, just north of Tonomachi. The latter had simply been asked to write the petition *(gansho)* because of his skilled calligraphy, but was held responsible because he refused to reveal the names of the actual authors. (In those days petitions were signed in the so-called "umbrella" style *(kasa jōren banjō)*, with the names written as if radiating out from the center. All the signatures thus together formed a circle with no beginning or end, thereby concealing the identities of the ringleaders.) These two men are referred to as *"giseisha,"* a word that is often translated "scapegoat" but whose actual meaning indicates sacrifice for the benefit of others. Iemon's grave is prominently displayed on the grounds of the Shinshū Temple in Sannomachi. Manzuke's is located across the Miya River in Shimono.

20. There are three other Buddhist temples in the immediate area. Fukuzen-ji (Blessing All Temple) derives from the Tendai sect and is located directly behind Enkō-ji. Seigan-ji (Sacred Entreaty Temple), further downstream directly adjacent to the town hall, belongs to the Ōtani Pure Land sect. Rinshō-ji (Forest Brightness Temple) is of the Zen sect and is located beyond the elementary school grounds on the other side of town.

21. *"Ujigami"* is now virtually synonymous with the terms *chinju no kami* (tutelary deity) and *ubusunagami* (deity of one's native place). These various concepts, in other words, have merged into one. See Robertson (1991:113) for a succinct explanation of the three concepts.

22. This is not to be confused with the administrative unit known as Furukawa-chō (Furukawa Township), which encompasses a much larger area.

23. The annual festival is formally referred to as *"reisai."* The term is written with the characters *"rei,"* meaning custom or precedent, and *"sai,"* the Chinese-derived pronunciation of the character used to write *matsuri.* The shrine is the locus of periodic rituals, generally aimed at ensuring the welfare and prosperity of the townspeople. A *tsukinamisai,* or "monthly rite," is held on the first and fifteenth of every month. The ritual begins at 9:00 a.m. and is conducted by the head priest regardless of whether anyone else shows up or not. A few of the townspeople, most of them elderly women, stop by individually to offer a brief prayer, but attendance is generally very sparse. Beyond these monthly observances, the remainder of the rituals conducted at Ketawakamiya Shrine are annual events, having some association with the seasonal round of irrigated rice cultivation, changing seasons, or stages in the life cycle. The ritual calendar as a whole is similar to that described by Ashkenazi (1993) and Nelson (1996).

24. *Tono* is an honorific title roughly comparable to the English "lord," and was used in addressing or referring to members of the feudal warrior

class. "Tonomachi" thus meant "lords' district"—that section of town where the warriors resided.

Ichi, ni, and *san* correspond to the numbers one, two, and three, respectively. *No* is a particle which generally denotes association or possession, but in this case acts to ordinalize the numbers. *Machi,* as noted, refers to a district or section within the larger town, generally constituted by the aggregation of houses lining both sides of a major street. The names of these three residential areas thus mean "First Street," "Second Street," and "Third Street," the number increasing with distance from the castle site.

25. The *dōzoku* pattern, a hierarchical arrangement of households consisting of a main line of descent and its subordinate branch lines, is not a prominent feature in Furukawa. This pattern has been thoroughly researched and documented in other parts of Japan, particularly the northeast. The founder household typically allocates some of its land in establishing a branch, then continues to provide economic support as the need arises. In return for such patronage, the branch household provides labor assistance as well as certain ritualized expressions of deference to the main household (see, for example, Norbeck 1961; Befu 1963; Cornell 1964; Brown 1966; Nakane 1967).

Though there are several cases in Furukawa of households that share the same family name and whose members consider themselves to have descended from a common ancestor, they are not economically interdependent—in fact, some have become rivals in the same enterprise. The absence of the *dōzoku* pattern may derive from the fact that arable land is so limited: a single household cannot afford to parcel off its holdings in establishing a branch. As a consequence, siblings of the designated heir are generally adopted into other households or move away in search of employment.

26. This is the local designation for such neighborhoods. In other areas they are referred to as *chōnaikai* or *chōkai.*

27. Nelson (1996:139) reports similarly competitive sponsorship of vehicles in his description of the Okunchi festival at Suwa Shrine in Nagasaki.

Chapter 4. Furukawa *Matsuri:* Performance

1. *Bon* (also referred to as *"Obon"* using the honorific prefix) is a Buddhist observance honoring the spirits of the deceased ancestors. In the Hida region it is celebrated from August 13–15.

2. The main shrine building (or *honden*) is situated directly atop a burial mound *(kofun)* dating from around the sixth or seventh century. This appears a rather odd juxtaposition of opposites given Shinto's alleged aversion to death and decay. The identity of the individual interred within it is unknown, though archaeological excavations have uncovered several personal artifacts including pottery, ear ornaments, and a sword.

3. The term *sōdai* is usually translated "representative" or "delegate." I have chosen to use the word "elder" to reflect the authority and air of dignity and respect associated with the position.

4. Again, *yatai* is the local term for the large wooden festival wagons employed in many parts of central Japan. The word *taigumi* consists of two characters: *"tai,"* meaning "stand" or "pedestal" and drawn from the word *"yatai,"* and *"kumi"* (there is a phonetic change from the initial "k" to "g" when combined with another character), referring to a group or band of people. *Taigumi,* then, alludes to a group of residents that owns and maintains its own *yatai* vehicle.

5. *Miyamoto* means "at the base of the shrine." In the case of Miyamoto-*gumi* the term refers not only to their geographical position but also to their special role as shrine guardians.

6. The head priest during an interview actually described the parish elder as a "big man," using the English loan word.

7. The name is customarily pronounced with a phonetic change of *"tai"* to *"dai,"* perhaps because of the double consonant which precedes the final vowel in *"byakko."*

8. This music is popularly known as *"kankakokan"*—an onomatopoeic description of its sound.

9. The term itself is written with two characters: *"shu,"* meaning "chief" or "master," and *"ji,"* meaning "matter" or "affair." The combination *shuji* is usually translated as "director," "manager," or "superintendent," though the actual meaning is closer to "master of ceremonies."

10. The term is composed of two characters: *"bun,"* meaning "portion" or "division," and *"rei,"* meaning "spirit."

11. While handling the *bunrei,* both the priest and *gohei* bearer wear white gloves and a paper mask covering nose and mouth. This is the standard covering used by the Japanese to prevent spreading infectious germs to others when they have a cold. Use of this mask is customary when handling the *kami* to avoid polluting it with human breath.

12. The name *"montsuki,"* literally meaning "mark-attached," refers to the fact that the wearer's household mark or crest *("kamon")* is affixed to both sides of the chest area.

13. These represent a kind of first-fruits offering, and rice is the central component. Rice, I was told, is considered the most important "because [Japan is] the land blessed with an abundance of rice" *("mizuho no kuni da kara"),* my informant citing a line taken from the *Nihon shoki.*

14. The eighth member is the *sōdanyaku,* or "consultant."

15. I have used the gender-neutral term "chairperson" here to reflect the original Japanese term, which is also gender-neutral. However, this should not obscure the fact that women are largely denied access to the higher administrative positions.

16. As before, the entity actually being moved is referred to as *"bunrei,"* indicating that only a portion of the deity is being taken from its normal place of enshrinement.

17. See note 11.

18. These men are the "dangerous year" attendants *(yakudoshi hōshiin),* so-called because they are forty-two years of age. This will be further described in the next chapter.

19. The fact that offerings consist of either rice or *sake* rather than simple monetary contributions implies a deeper symbolic meaning. Rice was the form in which contributions were traditionally made; indeed, it was the standard currency used in any form of payment. Yet I was consistently told by informants that households that grow rice offer rice to the deity, while those that do not grow rice give money instead. Offering rice is therefore akin to returning some of the fruits of the harvest.

20. The term is written with two characters which together mean "travel place."

21. The lanterns were traditionally illuminated with candles, but in recent years these have been replaced by battery-powered electric light bulbs.

22. The wooden platform is carried shoulder-high, and the turret raises the drum well above the platform, placing the heads of these young men at an elevation of about four meters.

23. *"Medeta"* refers to auspiciousness. The chorus of the song advises the listeners not to be overly concerned about material things—that even without money or food the people will get along by helping each other (Furukawa-chō Kankō Kyōkai 1984:25).

24. Fortunately a bit of padding has been added to the end of the pole in the form of wrapped cloth.

25. This is perhaps why *jikatabi* are worn on the feet, as they provide sure footing but are made of canvas with thin rubber soles and are less likely to inflict injury.

26. The drum itself may perhaps be seen as the female counterpart, though this requires a bit more imagination. Mortar and pestle, however, are widely recognized symbols for female and male, employed in various rites of fertility and fecundity. Since a mortar was used for grinding cereal grains and pounding the glutinous rice cakes called *mochi,* it was also associated with an abundant harvest. The drum and stick could easily be placed in the same structural relationship. In fact Yamada (1938:210–212), a folklorist observing the ritual during the prewar period, drew this very parallel, though he stopped short of addressing the sexual connotation.

27. Robertson (1991:54) notes that "[a]lthough the 'male:public::female: private' equation has been roundly critiqued and dismantled by feminist theorists, it nevertheless informs the dominant representation in Japan of men's and women's social spaces."

Chapter 5. Furukawa *Matsuri:* Mobilization

1. The custom is also referred to as the *mikuji shiki,* or "divination ceremony."

2. According to folk tradition, a man's forty-second year is considered a "dangerous" one—a time when he is particularly susceptible to serious illness or misfortune. Men of this age can volunteer to help pull the *mikoshi* on its procession through town, thereby gaining some protection against the danger. The equivalent age for women is thirty-five.

3. The office of *kumichō* is normally assumed by a woman, but for the purposes of planning and executing the *matsuri* it is her husband who assumes responsibility. This will be described more fully later in the chapter.

4. Again, it is apparent in both cases that the institutions of civil administration are being drawn into a hierarchy of authority deriving from the shrine. The block chief—an elected public official—is made subordinate to the *shuji* leader, who is essentially an ecclesiastical representative. Strictly speaking, this violates the separation of government and religion, as mandated by the new democratically oriented constitution promulgated in 1946.

5. This leadership role is comparable to the role of the senior member *(senpai)* in the *senpai-kōhai* relationships so often described by social scientists working in various Japanese social contexts (see for example Nakane 1970; Rohlen 1974).

6. Two basic tunes are employed, with each neighborhood using its own particular version. The first, called *"Michiyuki"* ("advancing down the road"), is generally used while the *yatai* are in motion; the second, known as *"Hikiwakare"* ("pulling away"), is played at the end of the festivities when the *yatai* break up and return to their home neighborhoods. The tunes have reportedly been passed down unchanged from long ago, and constitute part of what gives each neighborhood its own distinctive identity.

7. This will be described more fully in Chapters 6 and 7.

8. This technique is generally referred to in Japan as *nemawashi,* or "root binding." The term alludes to the practice of digging around a tree to sever its roots prior to transplanting, making the actual transfer much easier to accomplish.

9. In fact the Chinese character used for writing the word "gateway" is a pictographic representation of a pair of these banners.

10. Many scholars have raised doubts about describing Japanese society in terms of "rules" such as patrilocality and patrilineality (see, for example, Befu 1963; Kitaoji 1971; Shimizu 1987; Bachnik 1983; Ueno 1987). The basic argument is that such "rules" should be seen merely as expressing the favored choice among a range of alternative succession arrangements, and even then perhaps applying to the majority of the population only after pro-

mulgation of the Meiji Civil Code in 1897. Nevertheless, succession by the eldest son *(chōnan sōzoku)* and patrilocal residence are considered the preferred patterns for established households in Furukawa.

11. Following my own participation in the *matsuri* I was told by several of the local people that I had now become a full-fledged resident of Furukawa. While such comments were no doubt meant to make me feel at home and should not necessarily be taken at face value, they nevertheless serve to underline the fact that participation in the *matsuri* defines membership in the community. Participation may thus be seen as an annual affirmation of that membership.

12. Rohlen (1974:105–107) characterized these two contrasting principles in terms of (1) a "formal pyramid" essential to the everyday functioning of the business office and (2) an "informal circle" symbolizing group unity and most clearly expressed during recreational activities. Bestor (1989:164–165) made a similar distinction, noting that neighborhood activities were planned and executed through "elaborately structured hierarchies" despite a pervasive "ethos of communal egalitarianism" evoked largely through oppositional interaction with outside agencies.

13. The sound of the drum is ingrained in Furukawa youth from infancy. It is not unusual for students away at college to have their mothers telephone from home when the *okoshi daiko* is passing by. The mother then holds the receiver out through a window or door so that her child (typically a son) can hear the drum.

Chapter 6. Origins and Development

1. Miyahara Taisuke is also referred to as Miyahara Tsumoru, the latter being the name he was assigned at birth. Later, as an adult, he changed his given name to Taisuke.

2. Masamura was born a Kaba, the younger son of the famous *sake* brewer in Ichinomachi. He later married into the Hasegawa household as an "adopted son-in-law" *(muko yōshi),* whereupon he took their family name. However, his elder brother, who had been designated to succeed to the headship of the Kaba household, died unexpectedly at an early age. Masamura returned to his natal household to succeed as its head and thereby prevent the line from dying out. Known in later years as Kaba Tokurō, he became an accomplished literary figure. Throughout his life he was fascinated by local history and culture. His description of the Furukawa *matsuri* is considered highly reliable.

The term *"kakiage,"* which appears in the work's title, is rendered using characters meaning "to write" and "to offer up," implying that the account was being humbly presented to the (higher-ranked) officials who had commissioned it.

3. At this time dates were reckoned by the old lunar–solar calendar, so the months were not strictly comparable to those employed by the western system. For this reason I have chosen to designate the months using direct translation from the Japanese—"First Month," "Second Month," "Third Month," for example, instead of "January," "February," and "March," respectively.

4. These are place names. "Ryokan" refers to the vicinity of the old castle site. "Naka no Tame" means "medial sink," possibly referring to an irrigation reservoir. This area was located beyond the Miya River on the downstream end of town; it is now know as "Miyagimachi." "Machiura" means "behind the town" and referred to the open area mortheast of Ichinomachi, again in the downstream direction. "Shimomachi" is the former name of Mukaimachi.

5. Wada was located on the eastern edge of Kamikita. The preceding section was added later by Tomita. Kaba's description begins here.

6. Kaba adds that the *okoshi daiko* "sets out from the neighborhood of that year's acting referee (*nengyōji*, a term equivalent to the present '*shuji*')" (Furukawa-chō 1984:655).

7. Kaba adds that the *mikoshi* "customarily sets out from the shrine on the Fifth Day, but the location of the *tabisho* is not fixed so the specific route varies with the year" (Furukawa-chō 1984:655).

8. Kaba adds: "The *yatai* immediately following Sanbasō goes to last position the following year. Pulling them through town also follows an established order which changes annually."

9. This is a hill leading into the mountains where Ketawakamiya Shrine is located. It is now called Sakakigaoka, or "Hill of Sakaki [Trees]."

10. A short jacket made of thick cotton cloth worn over work clothes.

11. This final portion was added by Tomita to Kaba's description. The term originally used for "block" was "*chōme*." In the case of Furukawa, *chōme* was essentially the same as today's *ku*.

12. In other words, the order rotated forward one position each year, and when a *yatai* reached the position directly behind Sanbasō it returned to the rear of the lineup and became the acting referee.

13. As mentioned in Chapter 3, autumn *matsuri* are intended as expressions of gratitude for a successful harvest. It may seem odd, then, that such an expression would be given *prior* to the harvest itself. This, however, was a fairly common practice referred to as "*yoshuku*." The term is written with characters meaning "prior" and "celebration"—a celebration before the fact, in other words. It relates to the belief in the magical power of utterances—that ritually proclaiming a condition helps bring that condition into being. By celebrating beforehand, the people of Furukawa were attempting through ritual to effect a good harvest.

14. In fact the northeast is sometimes referred to as the "*kimon*," written with two characters meaning "demon gate."

15. Some historians speculate that the Araki River had originally entered the Miya further upstream, later shifting its course to the present location. The original Furukawa developed in the old riverbed, hence its name meaning "old river" (Tokoro 1989:1000).

16. The Koreshige area is also known as "Kanmachi," employing the Chinese characters for "deity" and "town." "Sugimoto" means literally "base of the cedar." "Myōjin" is a common appellation for the names of Shinto deities.

Yamada (1938) speculates that the name "Sugimoto" originated from a legend regarding a giant cedar *(sugi)* tree, which allegedly stood in the Koreshige area. A shrine to the spirits was erected at the base *(moto)* of the tree, and came to be known as "Sugimoto." Eventually the great tree fell over. It was so tall that its topmost portion *(saki)* reached as far as Sugisaki hamlet, which explains how the latter got its name. Yamada does not mention a source for this idea. The story is obviously apocryphal, as the distance between the Sugimoto site and Sugisaki hamlet is nearly three kilometers. The part about a shrine being located at the base of a large cedar tree is quite plausible, however. Large trees and other awe-inspiring natural phenomena were considered *yorishiro*—places to which the spirits were drawn.

17. Zen was widely associated with the warrior elite, while True Pure Land Buddhism, with its message of hope and compassion, appealed more readily to the masses. In fact True Pure Land Buddhism was closely associated with a form of religiously inspired peasant rebellion known as *"ikkō ikki" ("ikki"* means "rebellion;" *"ikkō"* is written with characters meaning "one side" or "one direction," but was commonly used as an alternative way of referring to the True Pure Land sect (Gotō 1994:7–8; Ikegami 1981).

18. A third castle gate is said to have been moved to Jōtoku-ji in the village of Nakano (across the Miya River from Furukawa), but there is no reliable evidence for this.

19. This was an official census conducted in Furukawa by *bakufu* administrators upon assuming control of Hida. The full title of the document is *Genroku Hachi-nen Furukawa-machikata Yahō Go-kenchi Suichō*—"1695 Census of Merchant Establishments in Furukawa Town-type Village").

20. Tonomachi was colloquially referred to as *"baba dōri"*—"horse place street."

21. See Note 16, Chapter 3.

22. "Household" is the gloss I am using for the Japanese *"ie,"* which is also translated as "stem family." The nature of the *ie* has been extensively dealt with by previous scholars. For an excellent overview of the *ie* concept see Kondo (1990:121–136).

23. That these merchant lineages originated in other villages is clearly recognizable in their *"yago,"* or "house names." Prior to the Meiji Restora-

tion in 1868, only the elite samurai and a few privileged landowners had surnames. But the house name often functioned as a surname for members of the merchant class. In the 1695 census, for example, merchants are identified by their *yago,* followed by their given names. Most of these merchant households adopted as their *yago* the names of the towns and villages where they originated (though a few used the name of the product or commodity they purveyed). The *yago* in the census indicate that the new arrivals came from all over Hida and even beyond. In a few cases the same name appears two or three times, showing that a single household operated more than one establishment. The old *yago* are still used informally among Furukawa residents.

24. The confusion about which was the main line arose in the following manner. In 1715, the head of Sugisaki-Gotō, the main household, left his eldest son in charge of the house and moved with a younger son to a new location, still in Ninomachi but further upstream. This effectively created a new branch. The younger son took over as head of this new household when his father retired. In so doing he retained the appellation "Sugisaki-Gotō," inherited from his father. However, since the eldest son had been left to take over the original household, his descendents later claimed that *he* had been heir to the main line. The eldest son's household ("Hon-Gotō") is also known by its *yago* "Kagaya."

25. Not all Kaba in Furukawa are closely related, however. Kaba Ikumi, author of various books and articles on Hida and Furukawa, is not of this lineage.

26. Only genuine landowners were allowed to fill political offices such as village elder. This coincides with Befu's (1965:22) assertion that "[i]n most villages only the propertied peasants were the full-fledged members of the group, tenants and their families being usually included in the family of their landlord."

27. The practice of displaying *matsuri* contributions on a signboard for public inspection has continued to the present day, as noted in Chapter 5.

28. Since the vehicles are customarily pulled by hand using stout ropes, they are also known as *"hikiyama"* ("pulling mountains"). In the Kantō area around present day Tokyo such wagons are called *"dashi."* The term is written with two characters meaning "mountain" and "vehicle." These, however, are used for their ideographic rather that phonetic value. The pronunciation of the term derives from the verb *"dasu,"* "to put out" or "to stick out," in this case referring to a vertical protrusion used to attract the *kami.*

29. They are listed by their given names of Bunzaburō, Hikobei, and Yosoyueimon, respectively. This was not a one-time contribution, but a pledge to donate the same amount every year.

30. The current predilection for antiques was hardly in evidence during the Tokugawa period. The skills and materials were still available at that

time to produce new objects which were of equal quality to those they were replacing. Old, dilapidated *yatai* in particular were seen as an affront to the *kami*, who were believed to be attracted by the fresh and new. Takayama neighborhoods used their *yatai* only about fifty years, then replaced them with new ones.

31. Rinkō is also known as "Hayashi Takamura," based on an alternative reading of the characters used in his name.

32. Yamamoto (1986) has suggested that in Takayama the wealthy *danna* households sponsored *yatai* construction as a way of quelling resentment toward the privileges they enjoyed. Suda (1990) adds that Takayama *yatai* were offered as prayers for a bountiful harvest, noting that their construction or reconstruction coincided with periods of famine. In Furukawa, the building of a new Kinkitai by Middle Ninomachi in 1776 predates the Tenmei famine of the 1780s. It does, however, coincide with the early phases of the Ōhara rebellions. The rebuilding of the Kinkitai in 1840 seems more in line with Suda's hypothesis, as it coincides with the Tenpō famine of the 1830s and 1840s.

33. The document does not mention the specific year; it reads simply "Year of the Rabbit, Eighth Month." It was originally discovered, however, inside a bundle of letters which date from the beginning of the Tenpō era. Tenpō 2 (1831) was the nearest Year of the Rabbit, so the document presumably dates from that year (Ōno, personal communication, June 18, 1997).

34. This bridge is now known as "Kasumibashi" (Bridge of Mist). See Map 4 on page 67.

Chapter 7. Authority, Resistance, and Ritualization

1. Drums are widely attributed with the power to dispel evil. In some parts of Japan, specifically the Kansai area around Kyoto and Nara, drum rituals are performed in the rice paddies every spring to rid them of evil spirits and pray for a bountiful harvest. A summer version of the same basic ritual conducted from early to mid-July is called *"mushi-okuri"* ("expelling bugs"), and is attributed with the more instrumental function of chasing away noxious insects.

2. In fact the Japanese word for "palanquin" is *"koshi,"* though it is written with yet another character.

3. Having belonged to the *tenryō* is a source of considerable pride. This too is celebrated in a brand of local *sake* called "Tenryō," which is bottled in Takayama.

4. A similar offer was made in other parts of Japan at about the same time. The purpose was to gain the peasants' cooperation in accepting the authority of the new regime.

5. In fact the ideological underpinnings of the so-called "Mito School" of National Learning were used as a model for the new Meiji government in administering the entire country. See Ketelaar 1990:46–54.

6. Ōno (1971a) reports that fifteen of these statues were confiscated from Furukawa shrines alone. They were placed in a storehouse in Takayama. Elsewhere the peasants reportedly hid the statues away to avoid confiscation (Ema 1985b:36).

7. Traditional Japanese farmhouses consisted of a framework of wooden beams, mud-and-wattle for the outside walls, and a roof of thatch or wooden shingles. The interior was essentially one huge room divided into smaller cubicles by sliding doors made of heavy paper. The family living and sleeping quarters were generally confined to a single floor. Due to the transmissability of sound, sexual partners had to be very discreet to avoid being overheard. Therefore, if a young woman objected to a young man's advances, she had merely to call out to her parents or other family members in the adjoining rooms.

Some have speculated that the custom of *yobai* derives from the Heian era (794–1185) practice of duolocal residence, in which the husband continued to visit his wife in her parents' house even after their marriage. This custom was prevalent among the court nobility, and is thought to have later filtered down to the commoners as well (see Koyama 1960:1545).

8. A Tonomachi resident notes that the burden of compulsory service fell mostly on the poor. Wealthy families often arranged for a younger son to be adopted into another household as its *chōnan,* or "eldest son."

9. Scheiner (1973:580) notes that in Japan "[m]ost forms of peasant violence were aimed against the propertied classes, the juridically and socially superior, however unexpected and unpredictable the form of violence might be."

The rebels did not set fire to any of the buildings within the town itself, as the flames would have quickly spread to other buildings. The Satō house, however, was located outside the town and surrounded by rice paddies. Riots of this type usually involved looting, but during the Umemura Rebellion nothing was stolen from the buildings that were attacked. Rebel leaders were adamant that the violence remain purely political. Local residents recall the story of a fishmonger's house being vandalized, whereupon one of the participants took the opportunity to avail himself of a single salmon. He was forced to return the fish and soundly punished by the other rebels. Nor did the violence run amok; it focused only on specific targets.

10. In the case of the Umemura Rebellion, the lines were not so clearly drawn as the term "class struggle" suggests. Some prominent local households actually sided with the peasantry in opposing Umemura's reforms.

11. The man was named Shōhachi. He was a resident of Tonomachi and only eighteen years old at the time of his death. His grave is at Shinshū Temple.

12. There were rumors that the government had him killed to avoid the embarrassment of a public trial. Three of Umemura's closest aides also died in prison of mysterious causes at about the same time (Ema 1985b:402).

13. At that time, Takayama's population of 14,461 outnumbered that of Gifu City at 13,716 (Taga 1982:83).

14. As mentioned in Chapter 2, Furukawa is historically connected with the Toyama region via the drainage system, as the Miya River flows into the Jintsu, which continues on to Toyama. Ōkuninushi no Kami is described in the ancient myths as having dominion over the Izumo region. This further emphasizes the symbolic association of Furukawa with the Sea of Japan and, by extension, the Asian mainland.

15. As mentioned earlier, the traditional lunar–solar calendar year began several weeks later than the Western one, so the Sixth Day of the Eighth Month by the former corresponded roughly to September 20 by the latter.

16. Disputes over the apportionment of town expenses raged for years, and in 1888 Ōno, Kanmachi, Koreshige, Kamikita, Shimokita, and Numa-machi petitioned to separate from Furukawa. Koreshige, which held eighty percent of the town's taxable land area, was particularly resistant to amal-gamation. The town government was unable to negotiate a settlement, and in 1890 Ōno, Kanmachi, and Koreshige declared themselves independent. Furukawa-*chō* was now redefined as consisting of Mukaimachi, Tonoma-chi, Ichinomachi, Ninomachi, Sannomachi, Kawaharamachi (a short street near the Miya River—actually part of Sannomachi), Kamikita, Shimokita, and Numamachi.

17. Local residents describe the situation of poor tenant farmers using the phrase *"ikasazu, korosazu"* ("being neither allowed to live nor killed"), referring to the fact that the landlords would keep the tenants' heads just above water so that they could continue working the land, but never allow them a margin of profit sufficient to become independent.

18. "Tajika" is written with two characters, the first *(ta)* meaning "paddy field" and the second *(chika)* meaning "close" or "near." Rokusa-burō retained the initial character *(ta)* but attached as a prefix the charac-ter *"hon"* meaning "main" or "principal" to form the new name "Honda." Rokusaburō was thereby representing his own household as the main line and all the other Tajikas as subordinate branches.

19. This is an unpublished document entitled *"Shūgiin giin senkyo jin-meibo"* (Voting Register for the Election of Members to the [National] House of Representatives). It was compiled in 1889 and is limited to Yoshi-ki-*gun,* the northernmost county in Gifu Prefecture, wherein the town of Furukawa lies. The total population figure is a rough approximation based on a population of 4876 in 1880 and 5066 in 1883, as reported by Taga (1982:83).

20. The verb form *"okosu"* is used in the phrase *"sōdō o okosu,"* meaning to "create a disturbance" or "rise in rebellion." The character used in writ-

ing *"okoshi"* is also pronounced *"ki,"* using the Chinese-derived reading. It is the second character in the compound *"hōki,"* meaning "uprising" or "revolt." Drums themselves evoked images of rebellion, as they were commonly used to sound the alarm when trouble occurred.

21. The term *"suke daiko"* was in use for several decades thereafter, and appears in an official document as late as 1919. See note 30 below.

22. Epidemics of cholera, dysentery, typhoid fever, and smallpox swept the entire country during the mid-1880s, adding to the already considerable economic woes. The government, however, did little in response to the health crisis, and this became yet another source of popular dissatisfaction.

23. One of my senior informants did, however, describe the *okoshi daiko* as a "ceremony to guard against misfortune" *("yakuyoke no gyōji"),* adding that the naked condition was appropriate in such a situation. Another source associated the time change with the Zenkichi incident. He said since the murder of peasant Zenkichi had occurred on the night of the *okoshi daiko* it had cast a shadow over the ensuing festivities. The townspeople therefore decided to move the *matsuri* from autumn to spring in an attempt to avoid the negative connotations. This seems a rather dubious possibility, however, since the rescheduling occurred a full twenty years after the murder incident.

24. It is possible, in fact, that the original intent was to mock the *mikoshi* procession.

25. Some informants claim that both the size of the *yagura* and the number of people who rode upon it varied from year to year with the size of the directing neighborhood, as the smaller neighborhoods were unable to provide the requisite number of individuals to carry an excessively large burden.

26. There were other dangerous sections as well. Around 1918 some of the men shouldering the drum structure reportedly fell into the Araki River as they were crossing Kasumi Bridge (Kuwatani 1969:32).

27. The term used here is *"oni-nanigashi."* *Oni* literally refers to a fiend, demon, or ogre. It is sometimes used euphemistically in referring to a person who is physically big and strong, or who harasses others. People in Furukawa avoid using this individual's real name, so in the article he is simply referred to as "a certain *oni.*" His actual identity is fairly common knowledge among older residents.

28. The rock-throwing incident may have been seen as a local manifestation of a nationwide trend—growing dissatisfaction with the imperialist policies of the central government. Socialists were active in opposing military expansion and capitalist imperialism throughout the early years of the twentieth century. Government suppression eventually drove them to adopt radical measures, and in 1911 twelve individuals were hanged for treason in Tokyo for plotting to assassinate Emperor Meiji.

29. One of my informants recalled that the offending team had to go to the director's headquarters the next day with a peace offering of *sake* and make a formal apology before they were able to get their drum back.

30. They are still being referred to in this document as *"suke daiko."*

31. My own informants' conviction that the custom is much older demonstrates both the tendency to endow ritual with a long and venerable past and the speed with which such endowment can be achieved. In this case a recent development was successfully established as a time-honored tradition within the space of a single generation.

Today's participants note that, due to the nature of the motion required, the big drum can be struck more forcefully from the side than from above, thereby creating a more powerful percussive sound. However, the two young men who sit back-to-back atop the drum with their sticks held in vertical position high above their heads create a more striking visual impression. It would appear, then, that the two original drumbeaters were placed atop the drum primarily for dramatic effect, and that the two auxiliary drumbeaters were later added to amplify the sound.

32. Kuwatani's informant may have been confusing the coronation with another special event—Furukawa's turn to host the grand Hida *taisai* in 1923. Like the coronation, hosting the *taisai* usually entails some special effort on the part of the host community to mark the occasion. When Furukawa hosted the event in 1986, for example, a huge new *torii* (symbolic entrance gate) was erected at the foot of the stone steps leading up to the shrine compound.

Chapter 8. From Symbolism to Instrumentality

1. Voting privileges continued to be restricted to males of at least twenty-five years of age, however.

2. The *okoshi daiko* was canceled in 1927 in honor of the Taishō emperor's passing the previous year. The *mikoshi* procession made its circuit through town, again without the accompanying *yatai*.

3. Upper Ichinomachi, the smallest of these interior neighborhoods, consisted of only about twenty households. It was, however, exempt from serving as director, allegedly due to its fixed position at the head of the *yatai* procession.

4. Tenant farmers at that time still recognized certain filial obligations toward their patron landlord households. In Furukawa, one such obligation was helping to shoulder the drum when the landlord's neighborhood served as director.

5. Kaba (1985b) relates an incident she heard from older residents, which supposedly took place during the mid-Meiji period (around 1900). One year the *okoshi daiko* had taken a longer than usual time to perform,

and dawn began to break before the drum could pass through Upper San-nomachi. Nevertheless, the director issued the order to stop so that the participants could get ready for the day's activities. Since the *okoshi daiko* was allegedly intended as a wake-up signal, Upper Sannomachi's block leader sent word around to every member household to keep their doors locked and stay in bed. Soon the director's representative arrived to find out what was the matter, but was unable to rouse the block leader or anyone else in the neighborhood. Finally realizing what had happened, the director was obliged to reassemble the drum bearers for a single pass through Upper San-nomachi. At this point the block leader sent word around that dawn had finally arrived and it looked to be a fine *matsuri.*

6. Older informants recall that at times the main guard riding above would shout encouragement and raise their lanterns in an upward sweeping motion, urging the bearers below to hoist the structure back up to its proper level.

7. The exact phrase used here is *"ninsoku ni dete moratta"*—"had them go out as bearers."

8. The *seinendan* (young men's association) was very active in Furu-kawa prior to the Second World War. It was organized by neighborhood following *taigumi* boundaries. Young men joined their neighborhood chapter soon after completing their compulsory education, normally around the age of fifteen. Entry was not open to everyone: a candidate's family would request his admission, and the current members would meet to decide. The main purpose of such groups was public service: maintaining roads and bridges, chopping wood for the winter, performing emergency rescue and relief operations, directing *matsuri* activities. The age of retirement was around twenty-five, but varied from neighborhood to neighborhood— sometimes being thirty years or more. After leaving the *seinendan,* members often graduated to another level, called *"wakashakai"* (youth society). This group provided the leadership for the *seinendan* and held more authority. *Tsuke daiko* participants were drawn from both levels.

9. Lateral attacks were prohibited altogether shortly after the Second World War.

10. This story is also recorded in Kuwatani 1969:32.

11. This was a story repeated to me several times during my fieldwork. The bonesetter was located in the village of Higashi Ueda, just north of Gero in Mashita-*gun,* the next county to the south.

12. The term continues to be used in the present day.

13. In Japanese this concept is known as *"jigō jitoku"* ("self-induced consequences"). It implies that the victims bring misfortune on themselves through their previous behavior. Thus some people are ashamed to admit injury out of fear that others will assume they have done something to deserve it.

14. The fire brigade, consisting exclusively of local residents, and the police, mandatorially assigned from outside the local area, have traditionally been at odds in rural Japan.

15. Sonoda (1988:53–54) reports having been told of a similar incident during his own field investigations:

At the time of the previous year's *Bon* dance, a number of men became carried away by the atmosphere and participated in the dancing, dressed in women's clothing. The two police officers who were monitoring the occasion caught the men and started to lead them away. The watching crowd was incensed at the actions of the police officers and knocked them into a nearby ditch.

16. Though the emperor succeeded to the throne in 1926, his official coronation was not held until 1929 (Shōwa 4 by the Japanese chronology). Note that the gift symbolically associates the drum with imperial authority.

17. "*Haraigushi*" refers to a stick with a mass of white paper streamers attached to one end. It is used by a Shinto priest to ritually remove pollution or dispel evil similar to the use of the *sakaki* branch as described in Chapter 4.

18. The old police station was located on what is now the small parking lot on the bank of the Araki River in front of Honkō-ji, and stood there until the late 1970s. Prior to its demolition it was being used as a community meeting hall.

19. One of my informants, a lifelong resident of Ninomachi who was seventeen years old at the time, recalls that his *tsuke daiko* team had attached itself to the drum platform just prior to the impact. When the platform swung wide he and his teammates were thrown toward the building and crashed with their pole through the front window. There they lay in a heap with stones and broken glass raining down from above. He claims the rocks were thrown not just by the spectators but by members of the other *tsuke daiko* teams as well.

20. It is still considered taboo, for example, to look down upon the *mikoshi* procession conducted during the daytime. When the *mikoshi* passes, local residents come out of their homes and stand along the street to acknowledge the deity; they do not watch from their second-floor windows as they do in the case of the *okoshi daiko*.

21. At the conclusion of the *okoshi daiko* in 1991, one of the *tsuke daiko* teams was observed advancing upon a police car that had been slowed down by the crowd. The team was approaching the car from the rear, their pole held horizontally with the drum in upright position in a humorous attempt to "attach" *(tsukeru)* to the patrol car just as they would the drum structure.

22. There is an interesting coincidence here involving location. As men-

tioned earlier, Umemura commandeered Honkō-ji as one of his administrative facilities; that is why it was attacked and vandalized during the rebellion. Ironically, the police station was later built in roughly the same spot—immediately adjacent to the temple grounds. After the station was attacked during the *okoshi daiko* in 1929, the police themselves commandeered Honkō-ji to house the men detained for questioning.

23. In speculating upon how the practice of stripping to the waist began, some informants suggested that the participants simply became too warm during the vigorous activity. This seems unlikely due to the cold nighttime temperatures which lasted well into early spring. Others noted, however, that the naked condition was appropriate to a rite of purification *(misogi)*, so perhaps the original motive was of a more spiritual nature.

24. In Japanese this term has come to be used in referring to group bullying, and is less ominous than the English original.

25. This was a holdover from earlier times before a special drum had been designated for use during the *okoshi daiko*. As previously mentioned, in those days each neighborhood used a drum of its own, taking turns at performing the lead role while the other neighborhoods followed along behind. This carried over even after the creation of a special drum, with the directing neighborhood confining itself to manning the drum structure.

26. Kaba (1985b) relates a humorous episode from around the mid-Meiji (1868–1912) period. She begins by describing two men of Tonomachi who were known for their contentiousness. In those days the *yatai* had to have permission from the director before initiating any action. This included attaching tarps to the vehicles in case of rain. The *mikoshi* procession was passing along a side street between Sannomachi and Ninomachi when it suddenly began to rain. One of the men pulling Lower Ninomachi's Ryūte-kitai called out to the men of Tonomachi's Seiryūtai: "Its okay if your *yatai* gets wet, but ours is new—that's why we were allowed to attach our rain gear first!" To this one of the contentious men of Tonomachi replied "Are you saying our *yatai* is old? Well, if that's the case it doesn't matter if it gets wet, does it? We'll just sit right here and wait it out!" And there they sat in the middle of the street, preventing all the other *yatai* behind them from moving further. Finally Mayor Honda was called to intervene. "You're holding up the entire procession," he said. "Now stop this foolishness and get your *yatai* moving!" The leader from Tonomachi, in response, reached out and delivered two sharp raps to the great man's head, then became even further entrenched. Finally someone ran in from another direction. "Come quickly! There's a fight over at the *tabisho!*" At this point the contenders from Tonomachi ran off to see what was happening. In their absence the *yatai* set out again. The rain stopped and the procession went on as usual. Kaba adds that there had actually been no fight at the *tabisho.*

27. This grandson is the present head of the Watanabe household.

Chapter 9. Commodification

1. The four *okoshi daiko* divisions have since taken on a life of their own, and are invoked for purposes other than performing the rousing drum. During the 1960s, for example, the town's young people, male and female alike, competed annually in a recreational sports event known as the *"chō-min undōkai"* ("townspeople's athletic meet"). The competitors were divided into teams representing the four territories of Seiryū, Suzaku, Byakko, and Genbu. As a result, the townspeople have come to recognize these territories as legitimate intra-communal divisions, in some ways eclipsing the old neighborhood boundaries.

2. One of my informants claimed that this is what Takayama people mean when they refer to Furukawa as being characterized by *"yancha"*—they feel that Furukawa people do not show the proper respect for vertical relations.

3. See Thornbury (1994) for an explanation of the national government's designation of certain folk performances as "important intangible folk cultural properties."

4. The cars are equipped with specially widened windows that afford spectacular views of the narrow mountain valleys and river gorges. These trains are appropriately labeled "Wide-View Hida," employing the English loanwords.

5. The wheels have greatly increased the speed of the great drum. The drum structure used to be a bit of a sitting duck for the *tsuke daiko,* progressing slowly and ambling from side to side. Now it can virtually outrun its challengers should the need arise.

6. An elderly woman of Ninomachi recalls the occasion with great fondness:

> You know, long ago we used to have this thing called "Sugimoto *matsuri.*" It was on the twenty-first [of April] when the deity was returned. At that point everyone would take the leftovers from the *matsuri* feast, and just as the cherry trees were blossoming we would spread a tarp out under the cherry trees, and there we would drink *sake,* sing songs—it was like an appreciation party. We used to do such things, but not anymore. We used to go without fail—to that so-called "Sugimoto *matsuri.*" We went without fail. Then all the women would go together to drink and talk. That was, you know . . . that's all there was of the *matsuri* for women.

7. Entry to the Furukawa *matsuri* is open to all. There are no admission tickets to purchase and no security checkpoints to pass through on the way. Therefore it is difficult to determine the precise number of visitors who attend every year. According to official estimates, however, the number of

visitors at the *matsuri* has averaged around 55,000 for the past several years (Furukawa-chō Kikaku Shōkō Kankōka 1998:42). This is well over three times the population for all of Furukawa Township. Attendance is likely to be much higher for years when the *okoshi daiko* falls on a Saturday.

8. Lower Sannomachi's Byakkodai provides a shining example. The vehicle was originally equipped with a stage jutting out from the second level for performing an abbreviated kabuki drama, but this was discontinued sometime during the late 1800s. By 1930 the vehicle had become too decrepit to participate in the usual events. It was retired altogether in 1943. The neighborhood planned to build a new *yatai* and had begun collecting the funds to do so. The plans were never realized, however, due to wartime austerity measures and postwar inflation. Thereafter a debate went on for many years about whether to build an entirely new vehicle or simply refurbish the old one. It was finally decided to undertake an extensive restoration project, which was begun in 1981 and completed in 1986. At this time the stage was reattached and the kabuki performance resurrected after a hiatus of over one hundred years.

9. They describe the prewar *matsuri* using the term *"soboku,"* which can be translated as "plain," "rough," or "crude" but also has the favorable connotations of "pure" and "simple."

Chapter 10. Ritual, Change, and Agency

1. Takahashi (1985) addresses the role of young men's associations *(wakamono gumi)* in leading the peasant rebellions of the Tokugawa period.

2. It is interesting that Ōno places the story's emergence in the early 1930s—the height of government militarism and only a few years after the infamous attack on the police station.

3. Part of the problem relates to the code of silence surrounding the *okoshi daiko.* People are reluctant to relate specific acts of vandalism because they are embarrassing—not the sort of thing one would be inclined to recount, especially to an outsider.

4. I might add, however, that on at least two occasions the similarity was pointed out to me in passing without my having broached the subject. Also, Yamada (1938:214) mentions that upon first seeing the *okoshi daiko* as a child, his immediate impression was that they were bearing Ryōmen Sukuna. It is clear from his article that Yamada suspected more than a coincidence. He suggests, in fact, that the two young men were recreating the form of Ryōmen Sukuna as a representative image of the ancestral deities. No documentation is cited in support of this idea, so presumably it is based on his own conjecture. In any case, if the similarity was clearly recognizable by Yamada and at least two of my informants, there remains a possibility that it was intentional.

This does not seem congruent, however, with the symbolism thus far described. It was mentioned in Chapter 3 that Ryōmen Sukuna was locally considered a symbol of Hida's autonomy. Why then would its image be placed high upon a pedestal for other neighborhoods to attack? In addressing this question, it is important to consider the ritual's symbolic meaning *from the perspective of the directing neighborhood.* It was the director, after all, who decided how the drum riders would position themselves, at least during the *okoshi daiko*'s prewar, formative stages. By placing the two young men back-to-back atop the drum, the director could portray itself not as an oppressive outside authority, but as the cherished Sukuna, thereby relegating the other neighborhoods to the role of the (evil) imperial forces.

The differing perspectives have implications for interpreting the very nature of the ritual. Tonomachi, for example, with its population of small farmers, had little political influence in everyday affairs. In ordinary years, attacking the director's drum thus served as a ritual of rebellion. When Tonomachi itself became director, on the other hand, occupying the most esteemed positions atop the drum structure functioned more as a ritual of reversal.

5. As an anthropologist conducting research on the *okoshi daiko,* I of course felt it vital to participate in the ritual myself. My aim was to join the young men of my neighborhood in wielding the *tsuke daiko.* When I first approached the neighborhood elders for permission to participate, they were somewhat resistant to the idea. Part of their concern had to do with my safety, but they were also hesitant about my status as a "foreigner," and the fact that there was no precedent for such a request. However, since I had taken up residence in the neighborhood and had participated in its other activities, I was finally granted permission. "After all," one of them noted, "he isn't asking to ride on the drum platform."

6. These few examples demonstrate how interpretation of the *matsuri* varies with individual background and experience, even among the local people themselves. In general, members of former landlord households tended to dismiss the *okoshi daiko* as a mere spectacle or "show" (often using the English loanword). The true essence of the *matsuri,* they claimed, was embodied in the solemn rituals conducted at the shrine and the elaborate *mikoshi* procession through the streets during the daytime. They also emphasized the importance of *yatai* in preserving native traditions, including woodcrafting, lacquerwork, and various artistic and musical performances. Ordinary people, on the other hand, tended to focus on the drum ritual, motivated by the tenacious spirit of Furukawa *yancha.* It was these people who most lamented the ritual's becoming stylized and contrived.

7. The term employed here is "Kumamoto *mokkosu,*" referring to the alleged virility of the men of Kumamoto in northern Kyushu.

8. The English loanword *"nambaa tsū"* is used here.

9. The author goes on to describe how Furukawa *yancha* has been demonstrated by competitors in a recent folk singing contest.

10. This is one of the theories commonly offered to explain witchcraft accusations. The "witch" becomes the antithesis of accepted social behavior. By joining together in ostracizing such a figure, the members of a community reinforce their own sense of self-righteous solidarity. Allison (1994) describes how groups of contemporary Japanese businessmen engage in suggestive conversation with a bar hostess, at times bordering on sexual harassment. This, she suggests, is aimed not primarily at demeaning the hostess, but at strengthening the bonds of male camaraderie. Mihashi (1987) offers a similar argument in explaining the bullying problem in Japanese schools and discrimination directed against minorities such as Koreans and *burakumin*.

11. *"Sensei"* is a title of respect given to a teacher, professor, or recognized authority on a particular subject.

Biblioqraphy

Abrahams, Roger D., and Richard Bauman. 1978. Ranges of Festival Behavior. In *The Reversible World: Symbolic Inversion in Art and Society* (Barbara A. Babcock, ed.), pp. 193–208. Ithaca, New York: Cornell University Press.

Akagi Sei. 1935. *Tokugawa Jidai ni okeru Hida Jinkō* (Population of Hida during the Tokugawa Period). *Hidabito* 3(1):28–32.

Akimichi Tomoya. 1981. Riverine Fisheries in Nineteenth Century Hida. In *Affluent Foragers: Pacific Coasts East and West* (Shuzo Koyama and David Hurst Thomas, eds.). Senri Ethnological Studies No. 9, pp. 141–156. Osaka: National Museum of Ethnology.

Allison, Anne. 1994. *Nightwork: Sexuality, Pleasure, and Corporate Masculinity in a Tokyo Hostess Club.* Chicago: University of Chicago Press.

Anderson, Benedict. 1991. *Imagined Communities: Reflections on the Origin and Spread of Nationalism* (revised edition). London: Verso.

Ashkenazi, Michael. 1988. The Varieties of Paraded Objects in Japanese Festivals. *Ethnology* 27:45–55.

———. 1993. *Matsuri: Festivals of a Japanese Town.* Honolulu: University of Hawai'i Press.

Aston, W. B., trans. 1886. *Nihongi: Chronicles of Japan from the Earliest Times to A.D. 697.* London: Kegon Paul, French, Trubrer & Co.

Atsumi Reiko. 1979. *Tsukiai*—Obligatory Personal Relationships of Japanese White-Collar Company Employees. *Human Organization* 38(1): 63–70.

Bachnik, Jane. 1983. Recruitment Strategies for Household Succession: Rethinking Japanese Household Organization. *Man* (N.S.) 18:160–182.

Bachrach, Peter and Morton S. Baratz. 1970. *Power and Poverty; Theory and Practice.* New York: Oxford University Press.

Bailey, Jackson H. 1991. *Ordinary People, Extraordinary Lives: Political and Economic Change in a Tōhoku Village.* Honolulu: University of Hawai'i Press.

Bakhtin, Mikhail. 1984. *Rabelais and His World.* Bloomington, Indiana: Indiana University Press.

Beardsley, Richard K., John W. Hall, and Robert E. Ward. 1959. *Village Japan.* Chicago: University of Chicago Press.

Befu, Harumi. 1963. Patrilineal Descent and Personal Kindred in Japan. *American Anthropologist* 65:1328–1341.

———. 1965. Village Autonomy and Articulation with the State: The Case of Tokugawa Japan. *Journal of Asian Studies* 25:19–32.

Bell, Catherine. 1992. *Ritual Theory, Ritual Practice.* New York: Oxford University Press.

Bellah, Robert N. 1968. Civil Religion in America. In *Religion in America* (William G. McLoughlin and Robert N. Bellah, eds.), pp. 3–23. Boston: Beacon Press.

Ben-Ari, Eyal. 1991. Transformation in Ritual, Transformation of Ritual: Audiences and Rites in a Japanese Commuter Village. *Ethnology* 30: 135–147.

Bestor, Theodore C. 1985. Tradition and Japanese Social Organization: Institutional Development in a Tokyo Neighborhood. *Ethnology* 24: 121–135.

———. 1989. *Neighborhood Tokyo.* Stanford: Stanford University Press.

———. 1992. Conflict, Legitimacy, and Tradition in a Tokyo Neighborhood. In *Japanese Social Organization.* (Takie Sugiyama Lebra, ed.), pp. 23–47. Honolulu: University of Hawai'i Press.

Blacker, Carmen. 1975. *The Catalpa Bow: A Study of Shamanistic Practices in Japan.* London: George Allen & Unwin.

Bloch, Maurice. 1986. *From Blessing to Violence: History and Ideology in the Circumcision Ritual of the Merina of Madagascar.* Cambridge: Cambridge University Press.

Brow, James. 1990. Notes on Community, Hegemony, and Uses of the Past. *Anthropological Quarterly* 68:1–5.

Brown, L. Keith. 1966. *Dōzoku* and the Ideology of Descent in Rural Japan. *American Anthropologist* 68:1129–1151.

———. 1968. The Content of Dozoku Relationships in Japan. *Ethnology* 7:113–138.

Brown, Michael F. 1996. On Resisting Resistance. *American Anthropologist* 98:729–749.

Cohn, Bernard S. 1980. History and Anthropology: The State of Play. *Comparative Studies in Society and History* 22:198–221.

———. 1987. Anthropology and History in the 1980s: Towards a Rapprochement. Chap. 3 in *An Anthropologist among Historians and Other Essays.* Pp. 50–77. Delhi: Oxford University Press.

Comaroff, Jean. 1985. *Body of Power, Spirit of Resistance: The Culture and History of a South African People.* Chicago: University of Chicago Press.

Comaroff, John, and Jean Comaroff. 1992. *Ethnography and the Historical Imagination.* Boulder, Colorado: Westview Press.

Cornell, John B. 1964. Dozoku: An Example of Evolution and Transition in Japanese Village Society. *Comparative Studies in Society and History* 6:449–480.

Coser, Lewis. 1956. *The Functions of Social Conflict.* New York: The Free Press.

Darnton, Robert. 1984. *The Great Cat Massacre and Other Episodes in French Cultural History.* New York: Basic Books.

Davis, Natalie. 1975. *Society and Culture in Early Modern France: Eight Essays.* Stanford: Stanford University Press.

Davis, Winston. 1980. *Dojo: Magic and Exorcism in Modern Japan.* Stanford: Stanford University Press.

Dirks, Robert. 1988. Annual Rituals of Conflict. *American Anthropologist* 90:856–870.

Dore, Ronald P. 1978. *Shinohata: A Portrait of a Japanese Village.* New York: Pantheon Books.

Douglas, Mary. 1966. *Purity and Danger: An Analysis of Concepts of Pollution and Taboo.* London: Routledge and Kegan Paul.

———. 1973. *Natural Symbols: Explorations in Cosmology.* 2nd. ed. London: Barrie and Jenkins.

Durkheim, Emile. 1915. *The Elementary Forms of the Religious Life.* New York: The Free Press.

Earhart, H. Byron. 1982. *Japanese Religion: Unity and Diversity.* 3rd ed. Belmont, California: Wadsworth Publishing.

Ebersole, Gary L. 1989. *Ritual Poetry and the Politics of Death in Early Japan.* Princeton: Princeton University Press.

Ema, Nakashi. 1985a. *Yama no tami* (The Mountain Folk), Vol. I. Tokyo: Shunjūsha.

———. 1985b. *Yama no tami* (The Mountain Folk), Vol. II. Tokyo: Shunjūsha.

Embree, John. 1939. *Suye Mura, a Japanese Village.* Chicago: University of Chicago Press.

Fallers, Lloyd A. 1961. Ideology and Culture in Uganda Nationalism. *American Anthropologist* 63:677–686.

Fukutake Tadashi. 1949. *Nihon Nōson no Shakaiteki Seikaku* (The Social Character of Japanese Villages). Tokyo: University of Tokyo Press.

———. 1980. *Rural Society in Japan.* Tokyo: University of Tokyo Press.

Furukawa-chō. 1982. *Furukawa-chōshi—Shiryō Hen* (History of Furukawa Township: Materials Compilation). Vol. 1. Furukawa, Gifu Prefecture: Murasaka Insatsu.

————. 1984. *Furukawa-chōshi—Shiryō Hen* (History of Furukawa Township: Materials Compilation). Vol. 2. Furukawa, Gifu Prefecture: Murasaka Insatsu.

————. 1986. *Furukawa-chōshi—Shiryō Hen* (History of Furukawa Township: Materials Compilation). Vol. 3. Furukawa, Gifu Prefecture: Murasaka Insatsu.

Furukawa-chō Kankō Kyōkai. 1984. *Furukawa Matsuri: Okoshi Daiko* (Festival at Furukawa: the Rousing Drum). Furukawa, Gifu Prefecture: Furukawa-chō Kankō Kyōkai.

Furukawa-chō Kikaku Shōkō Kankōka. 1990. *Sūji de Miru Furukawa: Heisei Gan-nen Han* (Furukawa as Seen Through Numbers: 1989 Edition). Furukawa, Gifu Prefecture: Furukawa-chō.

————. 1998. *Sūji de Miru Furukawa: Heisei Kyū-nen Han* (Furukawa as Seen Through Numbers: 1997 Edition). Furukawa, Gifu Prefecture: Furukawa-chō.

Furukawa-chō Kyōiku Iinkai. 1987. *Furukawa no Mukashi no Hanashi* (Old Tales of Furukawa). Furukawa, Gifu Prefecture: Furukawa-chō Kyōiku Iinkai.

————. 1990. *Kyōdo Furukawa* (Hometown Furukawa). Takayama, Gifu Prefecture: Ōshinsha.

Furukawa Machi-Zukuri Kenkyūkai. 1993. *Hida Furukawa Taun Toreiru: Machinami, Machiaruki* (Hida Furukawa Town Trail: Rows of Houses, Walkabout). Furukawa, Gifu Prefecture: Murasaka Insatsu.

Furukawa Sadao. 1986. *Mura no Asobihi: Kyūjitsu to Wakamonogumi no Shakaishi* (Village Holidays: A Social History of Young Men's Organizations and Festival Days). Tokyo: Heibonsha.

Geertz, Clifford. 1963. *Agricultural Involution: The Processes of Ecological Change in Indonesia.* Berkeley: University of California Press.

————. 1973. *The Interpretation of Cultures.* New York: Basic Books.

Gerholm, Tomas. 1988. On Ritual: A Postmodernist View. *Ethnos* 53: 190–203.

Giddens, Anthony. 1979. *Central Problems in Social Theory: Action, Structure, and Contradiction in Social Analysis.* Berkeley: University of California Press.

————. 1984. *The Constitution of Society: Outline of the Theory of Structuration.* Cambridge: Polity Press.

Gifu-ken Kōtō Gakkō Kyōiku Kenkyūkai Shakaika Bukai. 1988. *Gifu-ken no Rekishi Sanpo* (A Walk Through Gifu Prefectural History). Tokyo: Yamagawa Shuppansha.

Gifu-ken Shakai Undōshi Hensan Iinkai. 1971. *Gifu-den Shakai Undōshi* (History of Social Movements in Gifu Prefecture). Tokyo: Gifu-ken Shakai Undōshi Hensan Iinkai.

Gilmore, David D. 1975. *Carnaval* in Fuenmayor: Class Conflict and Social Cohesion in an Andalusian Town. *Journal of Anthropological Research* 31(4):331–349.

————. 1987. *Aggression and Community: Paradoxes of Andalusian Culture.* New Haven: Yale University Press.

Gluckman, Max. 1954. *Rituals of Rebellion in South-East Africa.* Manchester: University of Manchester Press.

————. 1965. *Politics, Law and Ritual in Tribal Society.* Oxford, England: Basil Blackwell.

Goldenweiser, Alexander. 1979 [1917]. Religion in Human Life. In *Reader in Comparative Religion,* 2nd ed. (1979) (William A. Lessa and Evon Z. Vogt eds.), pp. 65–72. New York: Harper and Row.

Gotō Kichirō. 1994. *Kanamori-ke Rokudai Shō* (Summary of Six Generations of the Kanamori House). In *Hida Furukawa Kanamori Shi: Kanamori-ke no Ichizoku to Matsuei* (History of Hida Furukawa during the Kanamori Period: The Kanamori Family and Its Descendents) (Iwai Masao, et al., eds.), pp. 1–61. Furukawa, Gifu Prefecture: Furukawa-chō.

Gotō Shinzaburō. 1983. *Edo Jidai no Hidashi* (History of Hida During the Edo Period). Takayama, Gifu Prefecture: Takayama Insatsu.

Grapard, Allan G. 1982. Flying Mountains and Walkers of Emptiness: Toward a Definition of Sacred Space in Japanese Religions. *History of Religions* 21:195–221.

Guthrie, Stewart. 1988. *A Japanese New Religion: Rissho-Kai in a Mountain Hamlet.* Ann Arbor, Michigan: University of Michigan Press.

Hachino Chūjirō. 1979. *Hida: Ichinichi Ichiwa* (Hida: A Story Each Day). Takayama, Gifu Prefecture: Takayama Jin'ya.

Haga Noboru. 1991. *Yama no Tami no Minzoku to Bunka: Hida o Chūshin ni Mita Yamaguni no Henbō* (Mountain Folk Folklore and Culture: Transformation of Mountain Lands with Focus on Hida). Tokyo: Yūzankan Shuppan.

Hane Mikiso. 1982. *Peasants, Rebels, and Outcastes: The Underside of Modern Japan.* New York: Pantheon.

————. 1988. *Reflections on the Way to the Gallows: Rebel Women in Prewar Japan* (trans. and ed.). Berkeley: University of California Press.

Hardacre, Helen. 1989. *Shinto and the State, 1868–1988.* Princeton, New Jersey: Princeton University Press.

Hashimoto Hiroyuki. 1996. *Hozon to Kankō no Hazama de: Minzoku Geinō no Genzai* (Between Preservation and Tourism: The Present State of the Folk Performing Arts). In *Kankō Jinruigaku* (The Anthropology of Tourism) (Yamashita Shinji, ed.), pp. 178–188. Tokyo: Shinyōsha.

Havens, Norman. 1988. Translator's Postscript: Matsuri in Japanese Religious Life. In *Matsuri: Festival and Rite in Japanese Life* (Kenji Ueda,

Nobutaka Inoue, and Norman Havens, eds.), pp. 147–155. Kokugakuin University, Institute for Japanese Culture and Classics: Contemporary Papers on Japanese Religion No. 1. Tokyo: Kokugakuin University.

Hearn, Lafcadio. 1904. *Japan: An Attempt at Interpretation*. New York: Grosset and Dunlap.

Hida Mainichi Shimbun. 1929. *Furukawa Okoshi Daiko Jiken: Torishirabe Ichidanraku* (The Furukawa Rousing Drum Incident: A Pause in the Investigation). *Hida Mainichi Shimbun*, April 28, p. 3.

Hishimura Fumio. 1994. *Umemura Sōdō no Kenkyū* (Research into the Umemura Disturbance). Takayama, Gifu Prefecture: Takayama Insatsu.

Hishimura Masafumi. 1965. *Hida no Taisai* (The Hida Grand Festival). *Hida Shunshū* 10(97):2–7.

Hobsbawm, Eric, and Terence Ranger, eds. 1983. *The Invention of Tradition*. Cambridge: Cambridge University Press.

Honda Akinori. 1934. *Hida Furukawa*. Takayama, Gifu Prefecture: Hida Chūō Insatsu.

Hori, Ichiro. 1968. *Folk Religion in Japan: Continuity and Change*. (Joseph M. Kitagawa and Alan L. Miller, eds.) Chicago: University of Chicago Press.

Ikegami Hiroko. 1981. *Sengokki no Ikki* (Rebellions of the Warring States Period). In *Ikki* (Rebellion), Vol. 2: *Ikki no Rekishi* (History of Rebellions) (Aoki Michio, et al., eds.), pp. 91–136. Tokyo: University of Tokyo Press.

Inokuma Kaneshige. 1958. *Furukawa no Okoshi Daiko* (The Rousing Drum of Furukawa). In *Gifu-ken Shitei Bunkazai Chōsa Hokokusho* (Report on Officially Designated Cultural Properties in Gifu Prefecture), Vol. 2 (Gifu-ken Kyōiku Iinkai, eds.), pp. 54–55. Gifu: Gifu-ken Kyōiku Iinkai.

Irokawa Daikichi. 1985. *The Culture of the Meiji Period*. Princeton: Princeton University Press.

Ivy, Marilyn. 1995. *Discourses of the Vanishing: Modernity, Phantasm, Japan*. Chicago: University of Chicago Press.

Iwamizu Ryūhō. 1985. *Gifu-ken Yoshiki-gun Furukawa-chō Nobuka Chōsa Hōkoku: Shūkyō* (Report on an Investigation of Nobuka [Hamlet] in the Furukawa Township, Yoshiki County, Gifu Prefecture: Religion). *Gifu Joshi Daigaku Chiiki Bunka Kenkyūjō Hōkoku* No. 3. Gifu, Gifu Prefecture: Gifu-ken Joshi Daigaku Chiiki Bunka Kenkyūjō.

Izumi Seiichi and Gamo Masao. 1952. *Nihon Shakai no Chiikisei* (Regional Characteristics in Japanese Society). In *Nihon Chiri Shintaikei* (Revised Handbook of Japanese Geography), Vol. 2. Tokyo: Kawade Shobō.

Izumi Seiichi et al. 1984. Regional Types in Japanese Culture. In *Regional Differences in Japanese Rural Culture: Results of a Questionnaire* (N. Nagashima and H. Tomoeda, eds.) Senri Ethnological Studies No. 14, pp. 187–198. Osaka: National Museum of Ethnology.

Jannetta, Ann Bowman. 1987. *Epidemics and Mortality in Early Modern Japan.* Princeton: Princeton University Press.

Jennings, Theodore W. 1982. On Ritual Knowledge. *The Journal of Religion* 62(2):111–127.

Kaba Ikumi. 1984. *Hida Roman* (The Romance of Hida). Tokyo: Kōdansha.

———. 1985a. *Matsuri no Kujō* (Festival Grievances). *Hokuhi Nyūsu* No. 252, April 5, p. 2.

———. 1985b. *Matsuri no Kujō (2)* (Festival Grievances, Part II). *Hokuhi Nyūsu* No. 253, April 17, p. 6.

Kaba Masahiko. 1983. *Furukawa Matsuri, Mukashi to Ima* (The Furukawa Shrine Festival, Past and Present). *Hokuhi Nyūsu*, April 15, p. 10.

Kakar, Sudhir. 1982. *Shamans, Mystics and Doctors: A Psychological Inquiry into India and Its Healing Traditions.* New York: Alfred A. Knopf.

Kalland, Arne. 1995a. A Japanese Shintō Parade: Does It 'Say' Anything, and If So, What? In *Ceremony and Ritual in Japan: Religious Practices in an Industrial Society* (Jan van Bremen and D. P. Martinez, eds.), pp. 161–182. New York: Routledge.

———. 1995b. *Fishing Villages in Tokugawa Japan.* Honolulu: University of Hawai'i Press.

Kankō Shigen Hogo Zaidan. 1987. *Hida Furukawa no Machinami Machizukuri* (Layout and Construction of Houses in Hida Furukawa). Tokyo: Hoei Insatsu.

Kawakami Suenosuke. 1933. *Kyōdo Furukawa* (Hometown Furukawa). Takayama, Gifu Prefecture: Hida Chūō Insatsu.

Kelly, John D. and Martha Kaplan. 1990. History, Structure, and Ritual. *Annual Review of Anthropology* 19:119–150.

Kelly, William W. 1986. Rationalization and Nostalgia: Cultural Dynamics of New Middle Class Japan. *American Ethnologist* 13:603–618.

———. 1987. Rethinking Rural Festivals in Contemporary Japan. *Japan Foundation Newsletter* 15(2):12–15.

———. 1990. Japanese No-Noh: The Crosstalk of Public Culture in a Rural Festivity. *Public Culture* 2(2):65–81.

Kertzer, David I. 1988. *Ritual, Politics, and Power.* New Haven: Yale University Press.

Ketelaar, James Edward. 1990. *Of Heretics and Martyrs in Meiji Japan: Buddhism and Its Persecution.* Princeton, New Jersey: Princeton University Press.

Kitagawa, Joseph M. 1987. *On Understanding Japanese Religion.* Princeton: Princeton University Press.

Kitaoji Hironobu. 1971. The Structure of the Japanese Family. *American Anthropologist* 73:1036–1057.

Kodama Kōta and Yokoyama Toshio. 1987. *Nōmin Ikki* (Peasant Rebellion). Jinbutsu Nihon no Rekishi, Vol. 21. Tokyo: Shōgakkan.

Kondo, Dorinne K. 1990. *Crafting Selves: Power, Gender, and Discourses of Identity in a Japanese Workplace*. Chicago: University of Chicago Press.

Koyama Ryū. 1960. *Yobai* (Night Crawling). In *Nihon Shakai Minzoku Jiten* (Dictionary of Japanese Social Folklore) (Nihon Minzokugakkai Kyōkai, eds.), pp. 1545–1546. Tokyo: Seibundō Shinkōsha.

Koyama Shūzō. 1981. A Quantitative Study of Wild Food Resources: An Example from Hida. In *Affluent Foragers: Pacific Coasts East and West* (Shūzo Koyama and David Hurst Thomas, eds.). Senri Ethnological Studies No. 9, pp. 91–115. Osaka: National Museum of Ethnology.

Krauss, Ellis, Thomas P. Rohlen, and Patricia G. Steinhoff, eds. 1984. *Conflict in Japan*. Honolulu: University of Hawai'i Press.

Kuwahara Atsushi et al. 1991. *Heisei Gannen no Furukawa Matsuri* (The Furukawa Festival in 1989). Furukawa, Gifu Prefecture: Furukawa-chō Kyōiku Iinkai.

Kuwatani Masamichi. 1965. *Furukawa Matsuri* (The Furukawa Festival). *Hida Shunshū* 10(97):9–24.

———. 1969. *Furukawa Matsuri* (The Furukawa Festival). *Hida Shunshū* 14(141):1–33.

———. 1970. *Hida Rekishi to Fūdo* (History and Natural Features of Hida). Tokyo: Yūhō Shoten.

———. 1971. *Hida Keifu* (Genealogy of Hida). Tokyo: Nippon Hōsō Shuppan Kyōkai.

Lansing, J. Stephen, and James N. Kremer. 1993. Emergent Properties of Balinese Water Temple Networks: Coadaptation on a Rugged Fitness Landscape. *American Anthropologist* 95:97–114.

Leach, Edmund R. 1954. *Political Systems of Highland Burma: A Study of Kachin Social Structure*. Cambridge, Massachusetts: Harvard University Press.

———. 1961. *Pul Eliya, A Village in Ceylon: A Study of Land Tenure and Kinship*. Cambridge: Cambridge University Press.

Lehmann, Arthur C., and James E. Myers, eds. 1997. *Magic, Witchcraft, and Religion: An Anthropological Study of the Supernatural*. 4th ed. Mountain View, California: Mayfield.

Le Roy Ladurie, Emmanuel. 1979. *Carnival in Romans*. New York: Penguin Books.

Lewis, I. M. 1989. *Ecstatic Religion: A Study of Shamanism and Spirit Possession*. New York: Routledge.

Lewis, Michael. 1990. *Rioters and Citizens: Mass Protest in Imperial Japan*. Berkeley: University of California Press.

Lincoln, Bruce, ed. 1985. *Religion, Rebellion, Revolution: An Interdisciplinary and Cross-Cultural Collection of Essays*. London: The Macmillan Press.

Littleton, C. Scott. 1986. The Organization and Management of a Tokyo Shintō Shrine Festival. *Ethnology* 25:195–202.

Lukes, Steven. 1975. Political Ritual and Social Integration. *Sociology:* Journal of the British Sociological Association 9(2):289–308.

Mabuchi Kōsuke. 1990. *Yancha no Takumi ga Ude o Kisou Takayama no Kyōdai Toshi "Hida Furukawa"* (Takayama's Sibling City "Hida Furukawa," Where the Tenacious Woodcrafters Compete with Their Skill). *Sarai* 2(23):56–59.

Malinowski, Bronislaw. 1948. Magic, Science and Religion. In *Magic, Science and Religion and Other Essays*, pp. 1–71. Glencoe, Illinois: The Free Press.

Maraini, Fosco. 1962. *The Island of the Fisherwomen.* New York: Harcourt, Brace & World.

Matsubara Shōmei. 1987. *Gifu-Kenjin no Rūtsu: Sono Hokori Takaki Senjin no Ashiato* (The Roots of the People of Gifu Prefecture: The Proud Traces of Its Forebears). Gifu City, Gifu Prefecture: Chūnichi Shinbun.

Matsui Tokutarō. 1965. *Sanbyakugojū-nen no Dentō o Nokosu Okoshi Daiko* (The 350-Year Legacy of the Rousing Drum). Furukawa, Gifu Prefecture: Furukawa Matsuri Okoshi Daiko Dōkōkai.

Matsuyama Toshio. 1981. Nut Gathering and Processing Methods in Traditional Japanese Villages. In *Affluent Foragers: Pacific Coasts East and West* (Shuzo Koyama and David Hurst Thomas, eds.). Senri Ethnological Studies No. 9, pp. 117–139. Osaka: National Museum of Ethnology.

Mihashi Osamu. 1987. The Symbolism of Social Discrimination. *Current Anthropology* 28(4):S19–S29.

Mizuma Yoshio. 1931. *Hida Furukawa-Machi no Okoshi Daiko* (The Rousing Drum of Hida-Furukawa). *Minzoku Geijutsu* 4(5):387–391.

Moeran, Brian. 1984. One Over the Seven: 'Sake' Drinking in a Japanese Pottery Community. *Journal of the Anthropological Society of Oxford* 15(2):83–100.

Mogi Sakae. 1987. *Hida Furukawa Matsuri no Kōsei* (Structural Organization of the Shrine Festival at Hida Furukawa). In *Shashinbu: Hida Takayama, Furukawa Matsuri* (Photo Album: The Festivals at Hida-Takayama and Furukawa) (Katō Kenji, ed.) pp. 88–94. Tokyo: Sakurabonsha.

Moore, Sally F. and Barbara G. Myerhoff, eds. 1977. *Secular Ritual.* Amsterdam: Van Gorcum.

Morishita Sumio. 1991. *Moeru "Furukawa Yancha"—Kokoro no Kiseki* (Smoldering "Furukawa Unruliness"—Locus of the Heart). *Hokuhi Nyūsu,* April 17, p. 6.

———. 1994. *Moeru Furukawa Yancha: Takayama ni Chōsen Shita Sentōsha* (Smoldering Furukawa Unruliness: The Leaders Who Challenged Takayama). *Hokuhi Nyūsu,* April 17, p. 6.

Moriya Takeshi and Nakamaki Hirochika. 1991. *Nihon no Matsuri: Matsuri no Saundo Sukēpu* (Japanese Festivals: The Festival Soundscape). Tokyo: Maruzen.

Morris, Brian. 1987. *Anthropological Studies of Religion: An Introductory Text.* Cambridge: Cambridge University Press.

Myerhoff, Barbara G. 1970. The Deer–Maize–Peyote Symbol Complex Among the Huichol Indians of Mexico. *Anthropological Quarterly* 43: 64–68.

Nagakura Saburō. 1987. *Ketawakamiya Jinja* (Ketawakamiya Shrine). In *Nihon no Kamigami: Jinja to Seichi* (Japanese Deities: Shrines and Sacred Ground), Vol. 9 (Tanikawa Kenichi, ed.), pp. 104–107. Tokyo: Hakusuisha.

———. 1988. *Zokuzoku Takayama Matsuri Yatai Zakkō, San: Okoshi Daiko* (A Succession of Miscellaneous Thoughts on the Takayama Festival Wagons, Part 3: The Rousing Drum). *Hida Shunshū* 33(346):18–19.

Nagashima Nobuhiro. 1984. Regional Differences in Japanese Culture: A Statistical Study. In *Regional Differences in Japanese Rural Culture: Results of a Questionnaire* (N. Nagashima and H. Tomoeda, eds.). Senri Ethnological Studies No. 14, pp. 199–217. Osaka: National Museum of Ethnology.

Nakamura Masanori et al. 1972. *Hida, Jinushi Keiei no Kōzō* (Administrative Structure of Hida Landlords). *Herumesu* No. 23, pp. 1–28.

Nakane Chie. 1967. *Kinship and Economic Organization in Rural Japan.* London: Athlone Press.

———. 1970. *Japanese Society.* Berkeley: University of California Press.

Namihira Emiko. 1978. *Hare, Ke* and *Kegare:* The Structure of Japanese Folk Belief. PhD. dissertation, University of Texas at Austin.

Nelson, John K. 1996. *A Year in the Life of a Shinto Shrine.* Seattle: University of Washington Press.

Norbeck, Edward. 1961. Postwar Change and Continuity in Northeastern Japan. *American Anthropologist* 63:297–321.

———. 1963. African Rituals of Conflict. *American Anthropologist* 65: 1254–1279.

Okamura Rihei. 1911. *Hida Sansen* (Mountains and Rivers of Hida). Takayama, Gifu Prefecture: Jūi Shoten.

Ōno Masao. 1971a. *Furukawa Shidan: Umemura Sōdō* (Historical Account: The Umemura Rebellion), part 1. *Kōhō Furukawa* No. 141, April 15, p. 4.

———. 1971b. *Furukawa Shidan: Umemura Sōdō* (Historical Account: The Umemura Rebellion), part 5. *Kōhō Furukawa* No.145, Aug. 26, p. 4.

———. 1971c. *Furukawa Shidan: Umemura Sōdō* (Historical Account: The Umemura Rebellion), part 7. *Kōhō Furukawa* No. 147, Oct. 26, p. 4.

———. 1972a. *Furukawa Shidan: Umemura Sōdō* (Historical Account: The Umemura Rebellion), part 9. *Kōhō Furukawa* No. 150, January 13, p. 4.

———. 1972b. *Furukawa Shidan: Umemura Sōdō* (Historical Account: The Umemura Rebellion), part 11. *Kōhō Furukawa* No. 153, April 15, p. 4.

———. 1972c. *Furukawa Shidan: Gyōsei Kikō no Kaihen to Yakuba* (Historical Account: Change in the Administrative Apparatus and the Town Office). *Kōhō Furukawa* No. 159, October 27.

———. 1973a. *Furukawa Matsuri no Yatai* (Furukawa Festival Wagons). *Hokuhi Taimusu* No. 1087, April 15, pp. 2–3.

———. 1973b. *Furukawa Shidan: Okoshi Daiko no Konjaku* (Historical Account: The Rousing Drum Past and Present). *Kōhō Furukawa* No. 165, April 15, p. 4.

———. 1974a. *Furukawa Matsuri no Hensen* (Change in the Furukawa Festival). *Hokuhi Taimusu* No. 1133, April 14, pp. 6–7.

———. 1974b. *Yūkōsuru Kami: Furukawa Matsuri no Yatai to Nobori* (Moving Deities: Furukawa Festival Wagons and Banners). *Kōhō Furukawa* No. 177, April 17, p. 4.

———. 1974c. *Kaisetsu* (Commentary). In *Yūme Monogatari: Hishū Ōhara Sōdō Kaisōroku* (Tale of a Dream: Recollections of the Ōhara Disturbances in Hida Province). Watanabe Masatsura, pp. 1–6. Takayama, Gifu Prefecture: Hida Chūō Insatsu.

———. 1975a. *Furukawa Ninomachi Sanchōme* (Furukawa's Second Zone, Third District). *Hokuhi Taimusu* No. 1166, January 5, pp. 6–7.

———. 1975b. *Furukawa Matsuri no Jissō* (Factual Details of the Furukawa Festival). *Hokuhi Taimusu,* April 13, pp. 2–3.

———. 1975c. *Matsuri Yatai no Kenzō* (Construction of the Festival Wagons). *Kōhō Furukawa,* April 18, p. 4.

———. 1976a. *Furukawa Matsuri no Saiji* (Sacred Rites of the Furukawa Festival). *Hokuhi Taimusu* No. 1224, April 11, pp. 2–3; No. 1225, April 18, p. 6.

———. 1976b. *Matsuri Un'ei Hyakunen* (One Hundred Years of Festival Management). *Kōhō Furukawa* No. 202, April 15, pp. 2–3.

———. 1983. *Hida no Kuni Shōshi* (A Short History of Hida Province). In *Hidaji no Bunkaten* (Cultural Exhibit of the Hida Road) (Chūnichi Shinbun Honsha, eds.), pp. 108–110. Nagoya: Matsuzakaya Honten.

Ortner, Sherry B. 1984. Theory in Anthropology since the Sixties. *Comparative Studies in Society and History* 26:126–165.

———. 1989. *High Religion: A Cultural and Political History of Sherpa Buddhism.* Princeton, New Jersey: Princeton University Press.

———. 1995. Resistance and the Problem of Refusal. *Comparative Studies in Society and History* 37:173–193.

Ōta Yoshinobu. 1993. *Bunka no Kakutai-ka: Kankō o Tōshita Bunka to Aidentiti no Sōzō* (Objectification of Culture: The Creation of Culture and Identity in the Tourist World). *Minzokugaku Kenkyū* 57(4): 383–410.

Ōtsu Hikaru and Kobayashi Yoshitada. 1990. *Mito-Han Shi Umemura*

Hayami-Den (The Story of Umemura Hayami, Warrior of Mito Domain). Kashima, Ibaraki Prefecture: Ōgawa Insatsu.

Ōtsuka Kazuyoshi. 1995. *Hakubutsukan Gaku II* (Museum Studies II). Tokyo: Hōsō Daigaku Kyōiku Shinkōkai.

Paden, William E. 1988. *Religious Worlds: The Comparative Study of Religion.* Boston: Beacon Press.

Pharr, Susan J. 1990. *Losing Face: Status Politics in Japan.* Berkeley: University of California Press.

Pyle, Kenneth B. 1978. *The Making of Modern Japan.* Lexington, Massachusetts: D. C. Heath and Company.

Radcliffe-Brown, A. R. 1945. Religion and Society. *Journal of the Royal Anthropological Institute* 75:33–43.

Rappaport, Roy A. 1979. *Ecology, Meaning, and Religion.* New Haven: Yale University Press.

Reader, Ian. 1991. *Religion in Contemporary Japan.* Honolulu: University of Hawai'i Press.

Reischauer, Edwin O. 1988. *The Japanese Today: Change and Continuity.* Cambridge, Mass.: Belknap.

Robertson, Jennifer. 1991. *Native and Newcomer: Making and Remaking a Japanese City.* Berkeley: University of California Press.

———. 1995. Hegemonic Nostalgia, Tourism, and Nation-Making in Japan. In *Japanese Civilization in the Modern World* IX: Tourism (Tadao Umesao, Harumi Befu, and Shuzo Ishimori, eds.), pp. 89–103. Senri Ethnological Series no. 38. Osaka: National Museum of Ethnology.

Rohlen, Thomas P. 1974. *For Harmony and Strength: Japanese White-Collar Organization in Anthropological Perspective.* Berkeley: University of California Press.

Rotermund, Hartmut O. 1991. *Hōsōgami: Ou la Petite Vérole Aisément.* Paris: Maisonneuve & Larose.

Sadler, A. W. 1972. Carrying the Mikoshi: Further Field Notes on the Shrine Festival in Modern Tokyo. *Asian Folklore Studies* 31(1):89–114.

Sahlins, Marshall. 1985. *Islands of History.* Chicago: University of Chicago Press.

Scheiner, Irwin. 1973. The Mindful Peasant: Sketches for a Study of Rebellion. *Journal of Asian Studies* 32:579–591.

Schnell, Scott. n.d. Central Authority, Regional Opposition, and the "Fictionalized Ethnography" of Ema Shū. Forthcoming.

———. 1995. Ritual as an Instrument of Political Resistance in Rural Japan. *Journal of Anthropological Research* 51:301:328.

———. 1997. Sanctity and Sanction in Communal Ritual: A Reconsideration of Shinto Festival Processions. *Ethnology* 36:1–12.

Scott, James C. 1976. *The Moral Economy of the Peasant: Rebellion and Subsistence in Southeast Asia.* New Haven: Yale University Press.

———. 1985. *Weapons of the Weak: Everyday Forms of Peasant Resistance.* New Haven: Yale University Press.

———. 1990. *Domination and the Arts of Resistance: Hidden Transcripts.* New Haven: Yale University Press.

Shimizu Akitoshi. 1987. *Ie and Dōzoku:* Family and Descent in Japan. *Current Anthropology* 28(4):S85–S90.

Shimizu Sumi and Kamide Kayoko. 1993. *Shashin Kiroku: Hida no Joseishi* (Photographic Document: History of Hida Women). Gifu, Gifu Prefecture: Kyōdo Shuppansha.

Shin Kyōiku Kenkyūdan. 1949. *Hida Bunka wa Dōshite Hattatsushite Kita ka* (How Has Hida Culture Developed?). Tokyo: Shin Kyōiku Kenkyūdan.

Singer, Milton. 1955. The Cultural Pattern of Indian Civilization. *Far Eastern Quarterly* 15:23–26.

Smith, Robert J. 1961. The Japanese Rural Community: Norms, Sanctions, and Ostracism. *American Anthropologist* 63:522–533.

———. 1989. Something Old, Something New—Tradition and Culture in the Study of Japan. *The Journal of Asian Studies* 48:715–723.

Sōga Tetsuo, ed. 1967. *Dai-Nihon Hyakka Jitten* (Encyclopedia of Greater Japan). Vol. 14. Tokyo: Shōgakkan.

Sōmuchō Tōkeikyoku. 1996. *Heisei Shichi-nen Kokusei Chōsa Hōkoku* (1990 Population Census Report). Vol. 2, No. 2, Part 21 *Gifu-ken* (Gifu Prefecture). Tokyo: Nihon Tōkei Kyōkai.

Sonoda Minoru. 1975. *Shukusai to Seihan* (Festival and Sacred Transgression). *Shisō* No. 617, pp. 62–82.

———. 1984. *Matsuri: Genkūkan no Minzoku* (Festivals: The Folklore of Original Space). In *Koyomi to Saiji—Nihonjin no Kisetsu Kankaku* (Calendar and Sacred Rites—The Japanese Sensibility toward the Seasons), *Nihon Minzoku Bunka Taikei* (Outline of Japanese Folk Culture), Vol. 9 (Miyata Noboru, et al., eds.), pp. 283–356. Tokyo: Shōgakkan.

———. 1988. Festival and Sacred Transgression. In *Matsuri: Festival and Rite in Japanese Life* (Kenji Ueda, Nobutaka Inoue, and Norman Havens, eds.), pp. 33–77. Kokugakuin University, Institute for Japanese Culture and Classics: Contemporary Papers on Japanese Religion No. 1. Tokyo: Kokugakuin University.

———, and Uno Masato. 1979. *Hida Furukawa Matsuri no Dōin to Kōsei* (Mobilization and Structural Organization of the Festival at Hida Furukawa). *Kokugakuin Daigaku Nihon Bunka Kenkyūjō Kiyō* No. 44. pp. 141–203.

Steinhoff, Patricia G. 1989. Hijackers, Bombers, and Bank Robbers: Managerial Style in the Japanese Red Army. *Journal of Asian Studies* 48:724–740.

Steven, Rob. 1983. *Classes in Contemporary Japan*. Cambridge: Cambridge University Press.

Stone, Lawrence. 1981. *The Past and the Present*. Boston: Routledge & Kegan Paul.

Suda Keizō. 1990. *"Kikinji Saidai no Hisaisha wa Kaikyū Shakai de no dono Kaisō ka" ni tsuite no Rekishi Jinkogaku-teki Kenkyū* (Demographic Research about "Which Stratum in a Class Society were the Biggest Victims during Times of Famine"). *Hida Shigaku* 10/11:105–112.

Sugata Kazuei. 1975. *Furukawa Yancha Shi* (History of Furukawa *Yancha*). *Hokuhi Taimusu* No. 1167, January 12, p. 8.

Taga Akigoro. 1982. *Hida Furukawa-chō no Seiritsu Katei ni Tsuite* (History of the Administrative System in Hida-Furukawa Township). *Hida Shigaku* 3:83–85.

———. 1988. *Hidabito no Shūdan-teki Ishiki Kōzō no Keifu* (Genealogy of the Structure of the Hida People's Collective Consciousness). *Hida Shigaku* 9:3–13.

Tajika Bunzaburō, et al. 1990. *Ketawakamiya Jinja Yōkō* (A Synopsis of the Ketawakamiya Shrine). Furukawa, Gifu Prefecture: Murasaka Insatsu.

Takahashi Satoshi. 1985. *Minshū to Gōnō: Bakumatsu Meiji no Sonraku Shakai* (The People and the Wealthy Farmer: Village Society During the Late Edo and Meiji Periods). Tokyo: Miraisha.

Takayama-shi Kyōiku Iinkai. 1987. *Takayama-shi Shōgakkō Shakaika Bukai* (Takayama City Primary School Social Studies Meeting). Takayama: Ōshinsha.

Tanibana Hiroyuki. 1991. *Kanamori-shi no Shiro to Jōkamachi* (Kanamori's Castle and Castle Town). In *Hida Furukawa Kanamori Shi: Furukawa-chō no Rekishi to Jōka Machi* (History of Hida Furukawa during the Kanamori Period: Furukawa Township's History and Castle Town) (Iwai Masao et al. eds.), pp. 60–148. Furukawa, Gifu Prefecture: Furukawa-chō.

Tokoro Mitsuo, ed. 1989. *Nihon Rekishi Chimei Taikei* (An Outline of Japanese Historical Place Names), Vol. 21. Tokyo: Heibonsha.

Tomita Ayahiko. 1968. [1874]. *Hida Gofudoki* (A New Geographical Account of Hida). Tokyo: Yūzankaku.

Tsubouchi Shoji. 1981. *Kinsei Hida no Kuni Jinkōron* (Population Theory of Early Modern Hida Province).

Tsuchida Kichizaemon. 1962. *Hida no Shiwa to Densetsu* (Historical Stories and Legends of Hida). Takayama, Gifu Prefecture: Hokuhi Taimususha.

Tsunoda Ryusaku, et al. 1958. *Sources of Japanese Tradition: Volume II*. New York: Columbia University Press.

Tsurumi, Patricia E. 1990. *Factory Girls: Women in the Thread Mills of Meiji Japan*. Princeton: Princeton University Press.

Turner, Victor. 1957. *Schism and Continuity in an African Society*. Manchester, England: Manchester University Press.

———. 1967. *The Forest of Symbols: Aspects of Ndembu Ritual*. Ithaca, New York: Cornell University Press.

———. 1969. *The Ritual Process*. Chicago: Aldine.

———. 1974. *Dramas, Fields, and Metaphors: Symbolic Action in Human Society*. Ithaca, New York: Cornell University Press.

Ueda Kenji, Inoue Nobutaka, and Norman Havens, eds. 1988. Matsuri: Festival and Rite in Japanese Life. Kokugakuin University, Institute for Japanese Culture and Classics: Contemporary Papers on Japanese Religion No. 1. Tokyo: Kokugakuin University.

Ueno Chizuko. 1987. The Position of Japanese Women Reconsidered. *Current Anthropology* 28(4):S75–S84.

Uno Masato. 1987. *Furukawa Matsuri no Hensen* (Change in the Furukawa Festival). In *Shashinbu: Hida Takayama, Furukawa Matsuri* (Photo Album: The Festivals at Hida-Takayama and Furukawa) (Kato Kenji, ed.), pp. 96–106. Tokyo: Sakurabonsha.

Vlastos, Stephen. 1989. Opposition Movements in Early Meiji, 1868–1885. In *The Cambridge History of Japan*, Vol. 5: The Nineteenth Century (Marius B. Jansen, ed.), pp. 367–431. New York: Cambridge University Press.

———. (ed.). 1998. Mirror of Modernity: Invented Traditions of Modern Japan. Berkeley: University of California Press.

Waswo, Ann. 1977. *Japanese Landlords: The Decline of a Rural Elite*. Berkeley: University of California Press.

Weinstein, Stanley. 1983. Ujigami. Kodansha Encyclopedia of Japan 8:131.

Wilson, Monica. 1954. Nyakyusa Ritual and Symbolism. *American Anthropologist* 56:228–241.

Wolf, Eric R. 1982. *Europe and the People Without History*. Berkeley: University of California Press.

Wood, Raymond W. 1990. Ethnohistory and Historical Method. In *Archaeological Method and Theory*, Vol. 2 (Michael B. Schiffer, ed.), pp. 81–110. Tucson: University of Arizona Press.

Yamada Hakuba. 1938. *Soshin o Katsugu Okoshi Daiko* (The Crossover Drum which Bears the Ancestors). *Hidabito* 6(4):171–175, 6(5):210–215.

Yamamoto Shigemi. 1977. *Aa, Nomugi Tōge: Aru Seishi Kōjo Aishi* (Ah! Nomugi Pass: The Sad Story of the Silk Factory Girls). Tokyo: Tsunogawa Shoten.

———. 1986. *Hida Takayama Matsuri: Kenrantaru Minshū Aika* (The Hida Takayama Festival: Splendorous Elegy for the People). Tokyo: Asahi Shinbunsha.

Yamamoto Yoshiko. 1978. *The Namahage: A Festival in the Northeast of Japan.* Philadelphia: Institute for the Study of Human Issues.

Yamashita Shinji. 1996. *Kankō Jinruigaku* (The Anthropology of Tourism). Tokyo: Shinyōsha.

Yanagawa Keiichi. 1972. *Shinwa to Hankō no Matsuri* (Festivals of Affinity and Opposition). *Shisō* No. 582:66–77.

———. 1987. *Matsuri to Girei no Shūkyōgaku* (The Religious Study of Festival and Ritual). Tokyo: Chikuma Shobō.

———. 1988. The Sensation of Matsuri. In *Matsuri: Festival and Rite in Japanese Life* (Kenji Ueda, Nobutaka Inoue, and Norman Havens, eds.), pp. 3–19. Kokugakuin University, Institute for Japanese Culture and Classics: Contemporary Papers on Japanese Religion No. 1. Tokyo: Kokugakuin University.

Yanagita Kunio. 1962a. *Senzō no Hanashi* (About Our Ancestors). In *Teihon Yanagita Kunio Shū* (Collection of Yanagita Kunio's Original Texts), Vol. 10, pp. 1–152. Tokyo: Chikuma Shobō.

———. 1962b. *Sairei to Seken* (Festival and Society). In *Teihon Yanagita Kunio Shū* (Collection of Yanagita Kunio's Original Texts), Vol. 10, pp. 397–427. Tokyo: Chikuma Shobō.

Yokoyama Kenzō. 1993. *Miyako no Matsuri Saijiki* (An Almanac of Kyoto Festivals). Tokyo: Kōsei Shuppansha.

Yoshida Teigo. 1984. Spirit Possession and Village Conflict. In *Conflict in Japan* (Ellis Krauss, Thomas P. Rohlen, and Patricia G. Steinhoff, eds.), pp. 85–104. Honolulu: University of Hawai'i Press.

Index

Page numbers in *italic* refer to illustrations.

agency, 5–6, 16, 291, 298, 307–308
akatsuchi (red soil), 126
alcohol, consumption of, 18, 21, 23–24, 189, 242. See also *sake*
Allison, Anne, 21, 333n. 10
amalgamation: of shrines, 195; of villages, 195, 197, 268, 324n. 16
Amaterasu, 169, 170, 186
Anbō, Mt., 39, 63, 191, 242
Anegakōji clan, 48, 154. *See also* Anegakōji Ietsuna; Anegakōji Masatsuna
Anegakōji Ietsuna, 47, 56, 165
Anegakōji Masatsuna, 48
"animal spirit holders," 265–266
Araki River, 36, *39, 67,* 155
aramitama (violent spirit), 25, 27, 300
Ashikaga Takauji, 47
Ashkenazi, Michael, 112, 313n. 23
atofuki (mopping up afterwards), 112, 258, 279, 330n. 6; in 1870, 150

Bailey, Jackson H., 21
banners: neighborhood, 125–126, 211–212, 277, 317n. 9
Bell, Catherine, 8, 10–11, 291

Bestor, Theodore C., 29, 68, 112, 143, 290
Bloch, Maurice, 309n. 1
bon, 71, 314n. 1
Brown, Michael F., 306
Buddhism: *danka* system; in Furukawa 63, 65; in Hida, 61–62; in Japan, 61; and resistance, 65, 320n. 17; suppression of, 53, 189–190, 193; True Pure Land sect, 61–62, 65, 155, 320n. 17
bugyō (regional administrative officials), 150, 151, 173
bunrei (spirit portion), 83, 84
Byakkodai, 80, 107, 150, 170, 222–223; restoration of, 331n. 8
Byakko-*gumi, 115,* 116, 136, 261–262
bypass highway, *67,* effect of, 277–278

calendar: Gregorian, 197, 213; lunar-solar, 151, 197, 319n. 3
candle-making, 287–288
carnival. *See* festival
central government, opposition to, 45, 46, 53–54, 65, 325n. 28. *See also* Chichibu Uprising; Ōhara Rebellions; Umemura Rebellion
Chichibu Uprising, 207
Chikuma Prefecture, 193

chōinshiki. See stamp-affixing ceremony

cholera epidemics, 59, 211, 212

chōnai (neighborhood association). *See* neighborhoods

chōnin jinushi (town-dwelling landlords), 166

chōsen sai. See lottery ceremony

citizens' hall, 126, 167

collective identity, 70, 74, 268, 286; history and, 44, 307; resistance and, 306–307; ritual and, 60–61, 142–145; territory and, 33–34, 60, 141

Comaroff, Jean, 234, 309n. 1

Comaroff, John, 234

commander, 84, 96, 97, 98, 105, 116, 133, 134, 261

common lands, 40, 176, 311n. 7

communitas. *See* liminality

conflict. *See* harmony and conflict

Confucianism, 174, 194

"crush the director," 215, 229, 255, 301

cultural performance, 13, 30, 32, 139, 291

daikan (magistrate), 49, 172

Daikanbashi. *See* Kasumi Bridge

"dangerous" northeast, 154, 156, 319n. 14

danka. See Buddhism

danna shū (patron households), 55, 162–168, 312n. 16; competition among, 167; generosity, 166–168, 171; intermarriage, 167; leadership role, 167, 171; privileges, 173–174; sponsorship of *yatai,* 168, 170, 171, 322n. 32

Darnton, Robert, 309n. 1

Davis, Natalie, 301n. 1

deiri shū (part-time household employees), 163, 202, 228

deku hozonkai (puppet preservation association), 120, 263

director, 83–84, 117, *118,* 142, 209; aggression toward, 215, 219–220, 229, 233, 301, 305–306 (*see also* drum structure, aggressive treatment of); attitude toward assuming role of, 254–255; as bearer of lead drum, 180, 211, 213, 214–215; burden of role as, 139; division into two roles, 261; of rousing drum, 84, 109, 117–118, 123, 261; of *yatai,* 84, 93–94, 114–115, 123, 125, 261. *See also* referee

Dirks, Robert, 294–295

"Discover Japan" campaign, 284–285

Disney Corporation, filming by, 268

doburoku. See sake, home-made

"donut effect," 262

Douglas, Mary, 234

drum, as expiatory device, 31, 311n. 8, 322n. 1

drum bearers, 97, 99, 230, 250, 259, 260; apparel, 244, 245, 249; enlistment of, 214–215, 228–229, 230, 252, 254, 255, 260–262

drumbeaters, 97–98, 99, 109, 131, 275; apparel, 221, 244, 247, 249; first employment, 213–214; position atop the drum, 97, 98, 220–221, 299, 326n. 31, 331n. 4; qualifications, 134–136, 141, 231–232

drum platform. *See* drum structure

drum structure, *130, 132, 222;* aggressive treatment of, 181, 186, 215, 219, 229–230, 232–233 (*see also* director, aggression toward); assembly of, 128–131; reverential attitude toward, 95, 134, 301, 332n. 5; morphological changes, 214, 219, 221–223, 227–228, 244, 258, 275–276; origins and early form, 213–214

Durkheim, Emile, 16, 60–61

Ketawakamiya Shrine, 63, *64,* 71, 128, 156, 197, 258; head priest of, 71–72, 90, 96, 117, 153, 208; location of, 63, 223, 314n. 2; rituals conducted at, 313n. 23. *See also* Sugimoto
Kinkitai, 79, 150, 169–170, 171
Kirintai, 78–79, 107, 150, 170
Kiriyama Genbei, 197
Kiriyama household, 166. *See also* Kiriyama Genbei
kōei. See rear guard
Kofun period, 56
Kokugaku. See National Learning movement
kōminkan. See citizens' hall
Korean laborers, participation in Furukawa *matsuri,* 258
Koreshige, *39, 67,* 154, 172, 197, 202
Kotakari, 268
kotodama (spirit in words), 299
Krauss, Ellis, 17
Kremer, James N., 311n. 5
ku (block), 68, 73, 140; leader of, 118, 134, 141, 231, 241
kujō (grievance, resentment), 175, 283
Kumazaki household, 166, 202, 253
kumigashira. See village elders
Kusakabe household, 165
Kuwatani Masamichi, 147, 218, 220, 230, 242
Kyoto, *35,* 169

labor-exchange relationships, 227, 229
land concentration, 201–202
landlords, 55; absentee land ownership, 206, 253; animosity toward, 69, 191–192, 207, 225–226, 302; contributions by, during the *matsuri,* 166–168, 205, 228, 237, 258; dissolution of, as a class, 260, 263; domination of local shrine offices, 204–205; failure to fulfill

role as benefactors, 224; and financial services industry, 202–203; political influence of, 203–204, 206–207, 226–227, 256, 263; privileged role in *matsuri,* 173–174, 231, 252–253, 301. See also *danna shū*
landlord-tenant relations, 199, 206, 224, 228, 326n. 4
land ownership, 40, 41
land reform, 260
land tax, 49, 52, 160, 187–188; opposition to, 207; raising of, 217; revision, 199–201
Lansing, J. Stephen, 311n. 5
lanterns, votive, 95, 101, 125–126, 128, 150, 287
lead guard, 101
Lebra, Takie Sugiyama, 25
Le Roy Ladurie, Emmanuel, 143–144, 309n. 1
Lewis, Michael, 226
liminality, 17, 20, 143–144
local elite. *See* landlords
lottery ceremony, 114–117, 139, 247, 261, 293; as act of divination, 114, 210, 317n. 1; origins, 209
Lukes, Steven, 16, 309n. 2

main guard, 98–99, 131, 133; apparel, 98, 249; elevated status of, 134, 139–140, 231, 244–245, 292–293; number of, 221, 249–252; origins, 219; qualifications for, 141–142, 264, 301
Man'yōshū, 46, 311n. 9
market economy, transition to, 206, 224
mass assemblages, implicit threat of, 243
Masushima-*jō* (castle), 56–57, 154–155, 156
Matsukata Masayoshi: and "deflation," 201

181, 188, 215–219, 233, 248, 274–275, 283. See also *fure daiko*
Russo-Japanese War, 205, 216–217, 218
Ryōmen Sukuna, 44–45, 53–54, 299–300, 331n. 4
Ryūtekitai, 79–80, 150, 170

Sadler, A. W., 25, 28
"safety-valve theory," 10, 23, 252, 300–301
Sahlins, Marshall, 291, 309n. 1
Saigō Takamori, 207
sairei (communal celebration), 158. See also *matsuri*
sairei kisokusho (festival regulations), 208–209, 211
Saitama Prefecture, 207
Sakaemachi, *67,* 81, 108, 115, 120, 153
sake (rice wine): brewers in Furukawa, 43, 164–166, 178, 202; consumption during *matsuri,* 18, 94–95, 110, 175, 247; consumption following practices and preparations, 122, 131; as contribution, 231; home-made, 260; and local identity, 57; as offering to the deity, 91, 93, 97, *132,* 138–139; production, 43; and temporary license, 175, 242; use in tightening ropes, 131, 133; use in toast to conclude stamp-affixing ceremony, 125. See also alcohol, consumption of
samurai, 160
Sanbasō, 80, 115, 150, 151, 170
Sandera Mairi (Three-Temple Pilgrimage), 62, 287, 288
Sankōtai, 79, 150, 170
Sannomachi, 66, *67,* 155, 170, 178; composition, 177; Lower, 80, 150, 152, 222–223, 229; name, 314n. 24; structure, 75, 161; Upper, 80, 124, 150, 152, 229

Sannō *matsuri,* 169
sansai. See mountain vegetables, wild
Satō Hikozaemon, 191
Satō household, 163–164, 202, 323n. 9. See also Satō Hikozaemon
Satsuma Rebellion, 207
Scheiner, Irwin, 323n. 9
Scott, James C., 8–10, 22, 23–24, 143–144, 198–199, 295, 308
Second World War, 257–259
seinendan (young people's associations), 121, 133, 233, 260, 263, 327n. 8. See also *wakamono gumi*
Seiryū-*gumi, 115,* 116, 261
Seiryūtai, 74–75, *78,* 107, 150, 170
Seiyōtai, 80, 150
self-fulfilling prophecies, 298–299
sentō arasoi (battle at the fore), 103–104, *104,* 123–124
Setogawa (canal), 155, 166
shigaku (pre-festival), 149
shimariyaku (controlling officer), 171
shime daiko (bound drum), 121
Shimokita, *39, 67,* 197
Shinano Province, 174
shinji torishimari. See supervisor of sacred rites
Shinshū-ji. *See* Shinshū Temple
Shinshū Temple, 62, *67,* 155; destroyed by fire, 217
Shinto, 61; in Furukawa, 63; in Hida, 62–63. *See also* Shinto shrine festival; State Shinto
Shinto-Buddhist syncretism, 50, 61, 79
Shinto shrine festival, 2, 12. See also *matsuri*
shishi (mythical creature), 65–66
shishi daiko (*shishi* drum), 121–122
shishi dancing, 65–66; performance of, during *matsuri,* 83, 84, 85, 107, 108; practice of, 120–122; in 1870, 149
shishimai. See *shishi* dancing

About the Author

Scott Schnell, who received his doctorate from the Ohio State University, is an associate professor of anthropology at the University of Iowa. He has lived and conducted research in Japan for several years. Most recently he spent a year as a visiting scholar at the Japanese National Museum of Ethnology in Osaka.